Micha

R O P E

THE TWISTED LIFE AND CRIMES OF
HARVEY GLATMAN

POCKET BOOKS

New York   London   Toronto   Sydney   Tokyo   Singapore

An *Original* Publication of POCKET BOOKS

POCKET BOOKS, a division of Simon & Schuster Inc.
1230 Avenue of the Americas, New York, NY 10020

ISBN: 0-671-01747-0

First Pocket Books printing December 1998

10 9 8 7 6 5 4 3 2

POCKET and colophon are registered trademarks of
Simon & Schuster Inc.

Front cover photo courtesy of Corbis-Bettmann

Printed in the U.S.A.

For Mary Alice and Jim

The virtue of a camera is not the power it has to transform the photographer into an artist, but the impulse it gives him to keep on looking.

—Brooks Atkinson, *Once Around the Sun*

Contents

Preface

Harvey Glatman was a pioneer of sorts. Nine years before author John Brophy coined the term "serial murder," nearly two decades before FBI agent Robert Ressler dusted it off and made the tag a global household word, Glatman was already plying his trade in southern California. He blazed a trail that other, more ambitious ghouls would follow in Los Angeles: the "Hillside Strangler," the "Night Stalker," the "Trash Bag Killer," the "Skid Row Slasher," the "Freeway Killer," the "Sunset Slayer."

Glatman never had a catchy nickname, since he left few tracks and did his best to cover those. His victims disappeared without a trace; he left no bodies sprawled in alleyways, no bloody "Helter Skelter" messages inscribed on bedroom walls. Still, he was famous in his way: once he was dead and gone, his crimes—duly elaborated and romanticized, of course—provided fodder for a television movie and a best-selling mystery novel. He had become the stuff of urban myth, a quintessential bogeyman.

It was beyond what bashful, jug-eared Harvey ever

could have hoped for while he was alive, but fictional portrayals of the man do little to inform us why he killed, how monsters of his kind are bred in ever greater numbers—the majority of them American white males. For that, we have to seek the man himself, stripped bare of poetry and Hollywood clichés.

British author Colin Wilson writes that "[t]o understand Harvey Glatman is to understand the basic psychology of the serial killer." Unveiling Glatman, though, has been no simple task. In some four decades since his execution by the state of California, Harvey has been largely overlooked by journalists pursuing more flamboyant game. His case is briefly summarized in several crime anthologies, but careless research renders most of those accounts as worthless as they are abbreviated.

Searching out the truth about a forty-year-old string of crimes is challenging, to say the least. Glatman abducted victims from one county, killed them in two others, and was captured in a fourth. There were no FBI computer linkups in those days, no database of homicidal maniacs. His trial in San Diego called upon authorities from several other jurisdictions to divest themselves of crucial evidence; his execution, nine months later, naturally encouraged law enforcement agencies to purge their files and make room for the next ghoul . . . and the next. Much of the information that survived has disappeared with passing time, as transcripts, files, and court exhibits often do.

Against all odds, however, Glatman left a trail. I have been able to retrace it with assistance from the sort of men and women who make books like this one possible. Without their generous cooperation, *Rope* would not exist. Those who enabled me to follow Glatman, separating fact from fantasy along the way, include: the Honorable William T. Low, Glatman's prosecutor in 1958, later judge of the California Superior Court for San Diego County; Deanna Walker, deputy clerk of the San Diego County Superior Court; Gail Faukenthal, director of public relations for the San Diego County district attorney's office; the California State Archives; Robert Gillice, director of information services for the Boulder (Colorado) Police Department; members of the New York State Parole and Pardons Board; Kay Logan, at Denver High School; Bill Hoover, archivist for Time, Incorporated; Timothy Summerlee, at the Indio (California) Branch Library; Sgt. Bob Itzla, chief of public relations for the Yonkers Police Department; Detective William Rehm, with the Westchester County (New York) Sheriff's Office; Liz McDonough, with the Colorado Department of Corrections; Patricia Thorsen, local historian with the White Plains (New York) Public Library; Kay Wisnia and Eleanor Gehres, at the Denver Public Library; Barbara Petruska, with the Yonkers Public Library; Kath Pennavaria and the Kinsey Institute library staff at Indiana University, in Bloomington; Hayley Hyland in Los Angeles; and David Frasier, reference librarian at Indiana University, in Bloomington. My thanks to one and all for their unfailing courtesy, generosity, and apparent interest in my project. Any errors or interpretations of the facts which they so thoughtfully provided are, of course, my own. And finally, the work in hand would not exist without the efforts of my literary agent, Nancy Yost, at Lowenstein Associates, and the enthusiastic reception from Linda Marrow, my editor at Pocket Books.

Rope is the first attempt to survey Harvey Glatman's life in book-length format, but as previously mentioned, scattered details of his life and crimes are found in several secondary sources. Those of particular value include James Ellroy's *My Dark Places* and two books by British renaissance man Colin Wilson, *The Serial Killers* (coauthored with Donald Seaman) and *The Killers Among Us, Book II: Sex, Madness & Mass Murder* (coauthored with Damon Wilson). Material on the childhood development of serial killers is drawn from my own *Serial Slaughter*. Two outstanding reference works—*The Encyclopedia of American Crime* by Carl Sifakis and *The Encyclopedia of American Prisons* by Marilyn McShane and Frank Williams—provided useful information on the history of various lockups where Glatman spent much of his youth, while material on California's gas chamber was derived from Geoffrey Abbott's *The Book of Executions* and Denis Bryan's *Murderers Die*. Information on the aftermath of Glatman's case was obtained, in part, from Robert Ressler's *Whoever Fights Monsters* and *Who Killed Precious?* by H. Paul Jeffers. Newspapers consulted for details of Glatman's eighteen-year criminal career include the Albany (N.Y.) *Times-Union*, the Denver *Post*, the *Indio* (California) *News*, the *Los Angeles Times* and *Herald-Examiner*, the *New York Times*, the Riverside County (California) *Daily Enterprise*, the *Rocky Mountain News*, the *San Diego Union*, the *Santa Ana* (California) *Register*, and the Yonkers *Herald Statesman*.

I first heard of Harvey Glatman shortly after his arrest, in autumn 1958, when I was barely seven years of age. Another year or so would pass before I read my first pulp magazine account of Jack the Ripper and was hooked for life on the bizarre phenomenon (then unnamed) of serial murder. I didn't know a thing about such human monsters then, but Harvey captured my attention. As it happened, he had lived upstairs from a maternal aunt of mine, in a small Los Angeles apartment, and she was dumbstruck that the quiet, mousy "boy next door" had been engaged in killing women when he was not puttering about the business of his life, dispensing bashful smiles when they encountered one another in the parking lot or on the stairs.

Since then, we have become hauntingly familiar with a regiment of quiet, unassuming men whose secret lives left neighbors dazed and horrified: Dean Corll, John Gacy, Juan Corona, Jeffrey Dahmer, Bob Berdella, Gary Heidnik, Randy Kraft. None of them traipsed around the streets in blood-flecked hockey masks, and if their private histories provided any warning signs of murder waiting in the wings, they were the kind of clues that "normal" men and women managed to ignore, sometimes for years on end, while bodies piled up in the crawl space, in the spare bedroom, along the highways that connect our lives.

To that extent, at least, we must admit that Colin Wilson's diagnosis is correct. Glatman has paid for his atrocities, as much as any one man can, but there is something he can teach us yet. And in the teaching, possibly, he may save future lives.

1

Freeze Frame

THE CITY SWALLOWS STARS. AT SUNDOWN, WHEN THE neon comes alive, it washes out the sky in shades of orange, like the reflection from a distant forest fire. The highways teem with headlights, flowing like a swarm of white-hot embers from the larger conflagration, blown along by winds that hum with horsepower. The moon is visible above, of course, but otherwise a man can stand downtown all night, eyes on the sky, and see . . . precisely nothing.

Only when you leave the city lights behind you do the heavens come alive. The desert has a velvet darkness all its own, where ancient predators and prey enact a timeless drama every night, between the hours of dusk and dawn. Coyotes serenade the moon, out there, but otherwise the desert dwellers give no thought to the unearthly light show overhead. It takes a human eye and mind to pick out Ursa Major, Scorpio, the Lion—to appreciate the Milky Way.

The driver of the old black Dodge cares nothing for the stars tonight. His mind is on the four-lane blacktop bleached by headlights and the woman seated next to him. The woman most of all, in fact. He is peculiarly aware of her—her scent, her silence, and her body language. Huddled up against the door, almost beyond his reach, it would be no great trick for her to fling it open and spill out into the rushing darkness on the shoulder of the road. But she will not do that. He knows her secrets, knows the woman better than she knows herself.

She knows his secrets, too.

It is a problem he must deal with, soon.

The Dodge rolls south along the Santa Ana Freeway, clocking off a steady sixty-five. He watches the speedometer and rearview mirror, careful not to speed and thus invite a traffic stop. The woman might not break her silence if confronted with a badge and uniform, but he cannot afford to take that chance.

He has already raped her twice, the recent memory enough to stir him even now, when he should have his mind on other things. Considering his record, that means hard time if it goes to trial. He harbors no illusions about prison and has no intention of returning to a cage. He would prefer to die, but there is no good reason it should come to that.

Not if he plays his cards right by covering his tracks.

Of course, the woman has to die.

It troubles him, but there is no alternative. Her promises of silence if he lets her go are pitiful, transparent lies. He doesn't blame her for it given the circumstances. He has lied to her as well, from the beginning—and most recently, with his assurance that he means to let her live. She clings to that false promise, praying that he keeps his word. False hope, as much as any fear of broken bones, prevents her leaping from the car.

The freeway takes him south from L.A. proper to the suburbs: past Bell Gardens, slicing off a wedge of Downey, through the heart of Norwalk, La Mirada. Coming up on Buena Park and Disneyland, he has a choice to make. He can go east on Highway 91, across the desert toward Corona, Riverside, March Air Force Base, or he can keep on driving south through Anaheim and Santa Ana, Irvine, on toward San Diego. There is desert waiting for him that way, too, although the highway veers to hug the coast below Mission Viejo, servicing the coastal towns of San Clemente, Oceanside, Solana Beach, Del Mar, La Jolla.

Choices.

On a whim, he takes the eastern route and shortly leaves the city lights behind. Someday, in ten or twenty years, the desert may sprout tract homes and apartment houses, but tonight he has the wasteland to himself.

Almost.

"Where are you taking me?" She almost whispers it, as if afraid of startling him.

"I told you once, I have to drop you someplace safe and buy myself some time."

That much is true, at least.

"Why don't you let me out right here?"

He frowns, pretends to think about it, finally shakes his head. "Too close to town," he says. "You'd stop the first car passing by. I need more time."

His headlights bore a tunnel in the darkness; scavengers retreat from the high beams when he catches them at work on roadkill. There is nothing wasted in the desert, from a drop of water to a shred of flesh. The desert will accommodate him, help conceal his secret, as it has with others in the past.

His mind is racing, but the long drive helps relax him, fortifying his nerves. He has a sense of progress, moving *forward*, toward a destiny that has eluded him throughout his life. He has a chance to make up for his failures, put things right, claim the respect that every man deserves, but he must watch his step. One careless blunder, now that he has passed the point of no return, and it will all come crashing down around his ears.

The woman has that power, even now. She does not realize it, in her present state, but she can still destroy him.

If he lets her live.

He has already learned, the hard way, that it is a critical mistake to leave surviving witnesses.

He could have killed her back at the apartment, after raping her, but there were neighbors, friends, and family to consider. Even if he did not use the pistol in his pocket, if he kept it quiet, someone would have found her body in a day or two, and what would happen then? So many questions, the police involved. He had been careful with his fingerprints and used a phony name, but there were other ways.

Better to die than spend his life in prison.

Better still for *someone else* to die.

The desert highway seems to run forever, dark and lonely, but he needs more privacy for what he has in mind. The fact that he has met no traffic in a quarter-hour does not mean there won't be any in the next five minutes. All he needs, at this point, is a set of headlights bearing down upon him while he's dealing with the woman—maybe even a police car on patrol. Besides, it makes no sense to leave her body this close to the highway where it may be found so easily.

He needs a better hiding place, a little extra time.

An unmarked access road comes at him, on the left. He taps the brake, slowing enough to make the turn. Forget the signal; there is no one here to see it, anyway. It is a trivial offense; nothing compared to what he has already done, or what he has in mind.

The access road is gravel over dirt, no blacktop here. He holds the Dodge at fifteen miles per hour, listening to gravel crunch beneath his tires and rattle underneath the fenders, trailing dust behind him like a smokescreen. There is no point damaging the paint job. He is not in any hurry, now.

He has all night.

It makes no difference where the road may lead him, since he isn't going there. He keeps an eye on the odometer, marks off the better part of half a mile before deciding they have left the highway far enough behind. It would require a fluke—an act of God, no less—to save the woman now.

Too bad for her, since *he* is God tonight.

He stops the car, turns off the headlights, kills the engine. Sitting in the sudden darkness, he can hear the motor ticking as it slowly cools. He feels the woman next to him before he turns to face her and finds her staring out her window, as if there is something to be seen. She is afraid to face him, and that simple knowledge gives him strength. Somebody else's turn to eat the shit life dishes out to losers.

Sitting there and watching her, he feels the need again. It comes as no surprise. A part of him has known, throughout the drive, that he is not quite finished with her, yet.

Why waste a golden opportunity?

"Get in the back," he says.

The woman hesitates, but only for a moment. He is not required to show the gun this time. She has already seen it, felt the muzzle cold against her skin, and she believes that he will kill her if she makes things difficult. In fact, he would not shoot her in the car—too messy—but she follows orders, crawling awkwardly into the back seat of the Dodge. Another moment, and he joins her there.

"Take off your clothes."

This part is familiar to him from the first time, but he loves to watch it, anyway. Her flesh revealed to him in stages, bit by bit. He is rock-hard before she finishes, already fumbling with his trousers, and she offers no resistance as he shoves her backward, sprawled across the seat.

He has no style, no *savoir-faire.* They are not lovers, after all. He has a feeling of accomplishment just mounting her, his aching stiffness thrusting while she lies there, face averted, biting at her lower lip. He doesn't know or care what she is feeling as he pummels her. That mystery eludes him. He is vaguely conscious of her body, pale breasts jiggling beneath him, but the focus of sensation is himself, *his* needs, *his* hunger, building swiftly to the detonation point, until he spills inside her, gasping like a stranded fish. He is perspiring freely, horn-rimmed glasses slipping halfway down his nose.

He thinks the woman may be crying, but it does not matter. Straightening his clothes, he waits a moment for his pulse to stabilize, catching his breath. The woman does not move, all modesty discarded as superfluous.

"Get out."

She stirs, regards him dully, reaching for her dress.

"Leave it," he orders, and she does as she is told.

Outside, the night is cool. The southern California desert bakes by day, with temperatures frequently topping 100 degrees, but you wouldn't guess it after sundown. Local predators, who hide all day from the merciless sun, come out to do their killing after nightfall, under the sightless eyes of a bleak desert moon. The man is not afraid of them. If they are wise, the creeping things will stay out of his way.

He walks around behind the Dodge and opens up the trunk. The woman waits for him, no thought of running through the open desert barefoot, in her birthday suit. Where would she go? She can't outrun a bullet, and there may be worse things yet than death in store for her, if she attempts to flee and fails.

The trunk gives up a blanket and some precut lengths of rope. He puts the latter in his pocket, carrying the blanket as he joins the woman, takes her by one arm, and guides her to a piece of open ground just off the road. He spreads the blanket, orders her to sit, and kneels beside her.

"Put your hands behind your back."

There is a look of weary resignation on her face as she complies. The moonlight makes her look like something from a dream, all lines and shadows, pale flesh leached of color. She is ghostlike, hardly there at all, but he can smell her, touch her if he wants to, to remind himself that she is real.

"Stay here," he says, as if she had the will to run.

Another trip back to the Dodge, this time to fetch his camera and tripod from the trunk. He has already photographed the woman, both before and after raping her, in sundry stages of undress, but this is different. Better. She is absolutely at his mercy, and she knows it. He can see it in her eyes.

He needs to frame that knowledge in the camera's viewfinder and capture it on film. It will remind him of this moment, later, reassuring him that it was not another of his endless fantasies. Nothing seems real these days unless he captures it in black and white.

He leaves the trunk lid open, walks back to the woman on the blanket, with his gear. It is a simple moment's work to set the tripod up and mount the camera, checking out the flash attachment. Peering through the camera's eyepiece, he decides more light

is needed. Back again to switch the Dodge's headlights on, low beams for backlighting.

Perfect.

"Turn this way. Look at me."

She scoots around, the movement awkward since
she cannot use her hands. He frames the shot and
snaps one off to get the feel. The flashbulb makes
her wince, recoiling slightly.

Ruined.

"Keep your eyes open!" he snaps.

"I'm sorry."

Flash.

"Now arch your back."

Her breasts are small but firm, her nipples dark
and puckered from the chill. When he reviews the
photos later, he can always tell himself she was excited, posing for him naked like the little slut she is.
He half believes it now and will be totally convinced
by then, when he has gained some distance from the
actual event.

"Turn back a little to your left."

Flash.

"Now, this way."

Flash.

"Spread your legs." She whimpers but complies.
"Wider."

The camera is dispassionate, all-seeing.

Flash.

"Lie down on your left side."

She tries and topples over, grunting as she hits the
ground. The wool blanket is scratchy on her naked
flesh but offers little in the way of insulation from
the rocky hardpan underneath. No matter to the man
behind the camera. He will be finished with his shoot
before the bruises start to show.

"Now raise your right leg. Bend the knee. That's
it."

Flash.

He is hard again, amazed by his own stamina. It would be nice to take some action shots, the two of them together, but he has no remote-control cable for the camera. It may be just as well, though, since he isn't certain that he could perform on film. The women have it easy. All they have to do is spread their legs and lie there, while the man does all the work.

Do it!

He walks back to the Dodge and turns the head-lights off to save his battery. Moonlight is all he needs for what he has in mind. He kneels beside the woman, grimacing as gravel bites into his knees, and rolls her over on her stomach. Opening his fly to free himself, he moves between her splayed legs, reaching for her hips and lifting her into position. He penetrates her from behind, a different view and feeling, absolute submission as he thrusts against her, scuffing her face and unprotected breasts against the stony ground.

He finishes abruptly, separating from her, once more fastening his trousers. From a pocket, he extracts another piece of rope, some five feet long. He pulls her legs together, binds her ankles tight, and ties a slipknot in the free end, fashioning a noose.

"What are you doing?"

He ignores her, working swiftly, lowering the noose around her head.

"No, please!"

"Shut up!"

He yanks it tight to silence her, pleas stifled with a wheezing sound. He rises, planting one foot in the middle of her back, and hauls back on the rope with both hands, arching her spine as she fights for life. Desperation gives her strength, almost upsetting him, but he is stronger, leaning forward, pulling tighter on the rope.

It is no easy chore to strangle someone, not like in the movies where the victim rolls her eyes and dies in seconds flat. This woman wants to live, against all odds, but it is ultimately hopeless. Pressure from the rope around her neck cuts off the flow of blood through her carotid arteries and starves the brain of oxygen. By slow degrees, she loses consciousness, but that does not complete the process. Tremors rack the taut bow of her body, but he hangs on, sweating now, despite the cool night breeze. He cannot see her eyes bulge or the tongue protruding from between her lips. No sound escapes from her constricted throat, but he imagines screams that echo on the inside of his skull.

When it is finished, and the only motion of her body is produced by yanking on the rope, he kneels beside her once again and goes to work unfastening the knots. He will not leave the rope behind, a gift to the police.

Besides, it is his favorite.

Disposal of the body is a simple matter. He is counting on the desert to assist him. Gripping lifeless ankles in his hands, he drags the woman's body fifty feet or so across the sandy ground and wedges her halfheartedly beneath a thorny bush. Her flesh is pale and dusty from the dragging, the same color as the earth. No one will see her there from the roadway, and he will not invest the time or energy required to dig a grave. Let the coyotes, vultures, rats—whatever—fight among themselves to see who feeds. The ants will clean up what is left.

Fatigue kicks in as he begins to pack the car, stowing the blanket and his camera gear back in the trunk. He takes the woman's clothing from the floor behind the driver's seat and drops it in a rumpled heap beside her body.

All except the panties.

He will take those home with him, an extra souvenir.

When he is finished cleaning up the scene, he turns the headlights on again to double-check. Nothing remains that he does not intend to leave.

It is another job well done. And yet . . .

No sooner is he finished cleaning up, than he is stricken with remorse. The woman had to die, he knows that; it's a simple matter of security. And yet, he takes no pleasure in the killing. Raping her was one thing—*that* was perfect, better than he had imagined—and the photographs will tide him over, helping him relive their precious time together, fueling countless fantasies. The killing is a necessary evil, though. He knows the woman would have sold him out, betrayed him, if he had allowed her to survive.

Her death will spare him endless trouble, but the act of killing leaves him sickened and depressed. He feels like vomiting, but somehow keeps it down. It is a test of will.

This too, he knows, shall pass.

Tomorrow or the next day, he imagines, the distress he feels tonight will start to fade. A few weeks down the road he will remember nothing but the good parts, his remembrance aided by the photographs, the panties.

Time to go.

He twists the ignition key, feeling a stab of apprehension as the engine sputters, choking, before it turns over. *Jesus!* That would be the shits, to have the damned car die on him out here, with *her* so close.

Forget about it.

Agitated now, he shifts the Dodge into reverse and cranks the steering wheel hard right. The old car lurches backward as he steps on the accelerator, starting on the three-point turn that will allow him to reverse directions on the narrow, unpaved access

road. His left-rear tire is off the gravel now and
spewing sand as he shifts into drive, lurching forward. He feels another jolt of panic, shriveling his
scrotum, as the tires lose traction, spinning in place.

No, damnit!

And the sweet flush of relief as the Dodge leaps
forward, starting to fishtail. He eases back on the
accelerator, no rush now. The main thing is to watch
his step, draw no attention to himself. He needs to
put distance between himself and the corpse. Nothing else matters at the moment, except a smooth
getaway.

The perfect crime.

He does not think the woman will be found, but
what if he is wrong? A few days to denude her bones
of flesh, and the police will have a hard enough time
proving her identify, much less his own. He knows
that there are ways to match a name with bones—
the teeth; perhaps some other means, as well—but
none of that will lead investigators back to him.

He feels better already.

Moments later, he is back at Highway 91. A right-
hand turn, and he is westbound, rolling toward the
distant city lights. He switches on the radio and spins
the tuning knob to find a station, nothing much to
choose from out here in the wasteland. L.A.'s stations
come and go, aswarm with static, and he finally
gives up.

To hell with it.

The silence doesn't bother him tonight. He is accustomed to his solitude, and the thoughts that come to
him in darkness. He has come to terms with who
and what he is. The latest step is progress, taking
him to a new level of achievement.

He is on his way.

No turning back.

2

"A Healthy, Normal Child"

DECEMBER TENTH OF 1927 WAS A BUSY DAY. THERE WAS no end of news for residents of New York City to consider, marvel at, and worry over, as they went about their business on that frosty Saturday.

Mother Nature was flexing her muscles again, wreaking havoc with a major earthquake in Panama City, blanketing the American Midwest with an arctic storm that left thirty-six dead and sank three ships on the Great Lakes.

In Geneva, Switzerland, the League of Nations announced its settlement of a border war between Poland and Lithuania, while activist Jane Addams visited the White House, delivering a petition with 30,000 signatures that called upon President Calvin Coolidge to outlaw war entirely. "Silent Cal" agreed to take the notion under advisement.

Aviation was all the rage that weekend with "Lone Eagle" Charles Lindbergh receiving a standing ovation and a Congressional Medal of Honor from the U.S. House of Representatives. French pilot Pierre Corbu was not so lucky, plunging from an altitude

13

of 500 feet in a nosedive that claimed his life and that of his mechanic, at Le Bourget.

It was a day of leaders and has-beens. In China, General Chiang Kai-shek was appointed as an "omnipotent committee of one" to lead the ruling Kuomintang party, while a disgraced "Black Moses," Marcus Garvey, arrived in Jamaica, deported from the United States as an undesirable alien, after serving a brief prison term for fraud.

Prohibition, winding up its seventh year in "dry" America, was also much in the news. Mayor Jimmy Walker's wife declared the "Noble Experiment" a sad failure in New York, while the American Legion's national commander staunchly resisted any move toward repeal. And for bootleggers, it was business as usual, when hijacker Thomas Di Ploma was ambushed and riddled with bullets in the woods outside Paterson, New Jersey.

On the lighter side, in the Bronx, thousands lined the sidewalks of East 170th Street for a "baby parade," cheering wildly as 126 baffled infants competed for toys in a gimmicky contest arranged by the local merchants' association.

With so much going on, the birth of one more baby in the Bronx, that Saturday, passed without notice from anyone not directly involved in the proceedings. His parents were a Jewish couple, Albert and Ophelia Glatman, and they named their new son Harvey.

Given names are frequently significant—or meant to be. Most have a meaning or translation harking back to ancient times, and while new parents increasingly tend to name their offspring after sports heroes or movie stars, some still consider the inherent meaning of a name, hoping their child will grow into that name, in time reflecting its attributes.

Harvey is not a "Jewish" name, per se. It has no

special meaning in Hebrew or Yiddish. In the Teutonic languages, it translates as "soldier" or "warrior," but there is another meaning, too. In English, the name Harvey translates as *bitter*.

Life had often been bitter, indeed, for Harvey Glatman's coreligionists in the past 300 years. Historian Max Dimont alludes to exiled Spanish Jews reaching the New World as early as 1621, but the first officially recorded Jews in North America's colonies were twenty-three Portuguese travelers, who reached New Netherland from Brazil, in 1654. Governor Peter Stuyvesant, in New Amsterdam (now New York City), wanted to expel them from the colony, but he was overruled by his masters in the Dutch West India Company. The Jews remained, and they stayed on when the Duke of York captured New Amsterdam for England ten years later, renaming it New York.

It should not be supposed that they were always welcome, though. In 1737, the New York colonial assembly disqualified Jews from voting, and the ban remained in place for forty years, until a new state constitution was drafted during the American Revolution. Meanwhile, in 1740, an act of Parliament permitted Jews to become citizens of the British colonies after seven years' residence (a right, ironically, that was denied to Jews in England for another thirteen years). The Naturalization Act of 1740 encouraged migration of British Jews to the New World—indeed, that may have been the point—but there were still no more than a thousand altogether by 1776, out of a population pushing 2 million. Of that thousand, an estimated thirty to fifty families resided in New York City.

Establishment of the new American republic seems to have encouraged Jewish immigration, though the new arrivals still faced prejudice on every side. In

the half-century between 1789 and 1839, the United
States population more than doubled, from 3.9 million to 9.6 million souls, while the Jewish population
of America increased tenfold, from 1,350 in 1790 to
an estimated 15,000 in 1840. Six thousand of those
made their homes in New York.

As luck—or Fate—would have it, America was on
the verge of a great immigration wave, sparked by
revolutions and famine in Europe, which would
bring more than 4 million new arrivals to our shores
between 1840 and 1860. Jews were still a minority of
those who traveled to America, overshadowed in
those years by Germans and Irish, but their numbers
had increased dramatically. By 1845, there were an
estimated 40,000 Jews in the United States, increasing
to 150,000 on the eve of the Civil War. Despite their
growing numbers, and a reputation (spawned by
anti-Semites) for manipulating world events, most of
the Jewish immigrants found work as laborers or
peddlers. The professions were nearly off-limits: an
1838 survey of 2,000 Jews employed in New York
City, found only three doctors and three attorneys.

Max Dimont maintains that American anti-Semitism was "practically nonexistent" before 1880 and
then flourished only briefly, for ten years or so, in
certain depressed agricultural areas, but that claim is
clearly untenable. The latest immigration wave produced a countertide of "nativism" in the 1840s and
1850s, driven by such far-right groups as the Know-
Nothing movement and the American Protective Association. Catholics were a major target in the string
of bloody riots that resulted, but the bigots still had
ample venom left over for Jews and other "undesir-
ables." In New York City, during 1849, a mob of
German immigrants armed with guns and stones dis-
rupted Jewish funeral services at a local cemetery. A
year later, in September 1850, rumors of human sacri-

fice on the eve of Yom Kippur drove an Irish mob of 500, led by uniformed policemen, to ransack a New York synagogue, afterward beating and looting the residents of a nearby Jewish tenement.

If things were hard on Jews before the Civil War, they only got worse afterward. Between 1865 and 1900, America witnessed the rise of what historian Leonard Dinnerstein has called "a full-fledged anti-Semitic society." In 1866, following a series of fires in the Big Apple's garment district, seven major insurance companies agreed to strip Jewish businessmen of their fire insurance policies. Eleven years later, the New York Bar refused to admit an otherwise qualified candidate, Oscar Strauss, solely on the grounds that he was Jewish.

Discrimination aside, European immigrants were generally welcomed, after a fashion, by employers who craved cheap labor in the late 1860s and 1870s. All that began to change, though, in the 1880s, as the source of immigration shifted rapidly from northern and western Europe, to the south and east. Most of the 240,000 Jews who reached America between 1825 and 1880 came from Germany; the 2 million who followed, in the next four decades, were primarily from Russia, Poland, Romania, and Austria-Hungary. In Russia, Tsars Alexander III and Nicholas II drove Jews from their homes with a combination of orchestrated violence and deliberate starvation. Before the outbreak of World War I, an estimated one-third of all eastern European Jews had made their way to the United States.

They came in "steerage," crammed into the reeking holds of ocean liners, where the "better" paying passengers would not be forced to mingle with them. Most disembarked in New York, first at Castle Garden, later on Ellis Island, where one in five were set aside in cages, awaiting medical examinations for

disease. Their clothes bore coded marks in colored
chalk: *H* for heart disease, *K* for hernias, *Sc* for scalp
conditions, *X* for mental defects. Tuberculosis was so
common that observers branded it "the Jewish disease," while Jewish philanthropists rushed to con-
struct sanitariums in Colorado.

By the late 1880s, Jewish immigration had increased not only in raw numbers but also in propor-
tion to other groups, rising from less than 1 percent
of all European immigrants in 1881, to some 6.5 percent in 1887. It came as no surprise, therefore, when
Immigration Restriction Leagues began to organize
along the eastern seaboard, making their voices
heard in Congress. In 1891, federal legislation was
enacted, barring immigrants who carried any "loath-
some or dangerous contagious disease," along with
those whose passage had been paid by someone else,
unless the new arrival could demonstrate that he or
she would not become a public charge. Eight years
later, American immigration authorities began for the
first time to classify new arrivals by race, rather than
by country of nativity. In April 1892, the U.S. House
Committee on Foreign Affairs expressed concern
over the continuing violence in Russia, "as vast numbers of Jews driven from Russia are continually seeking refuge here." Despite their evident poverty, a
Baptist minister in New York archly warned that
"the Jew is the financial master of the world."

And still they came, one-quarter of them children
under age fourteen. Some Jews fanned out to other
cities, but the majority of new arrivals remained in
New York, most of those gravitating to the Lower
East Side of Manhattan, once a fashionable neighborhood in pre–Civil War days, now reduced to a teeming slum. By 1900, it was the most densely populated
section of New York City, with 700 residents per
acre. Leon Kobrin, a contemporary Yiddish writer,

described the Lower East Side as "a gray stone world of tall tenements, where even on the loveliest spring day there is not a blade of grass. The streets are enveloped in an undefinable atmosphere, which reflects the unique light, or shadow, of its Jewish inhabitants. The air itself seems to have absorbed the unique Jewish sorrow and pain, an emanation of its thousands of years of exile. The sun, gray and depressed; the men and women clustered around the pushcarts; the gray walls of the tenements—all looks sad."

One such tenement was the "Big Flat," an eyesore sprawling over six city blocks, from Mott to Elizabeth Street. The structure featured one water tap on each floor, its sink the sole receptacle for human waste. Three-room apartments had one window each, the interior rooms little more than dank caves, where tenants averaged 428 cubic feet apiece (versus the legal minimum of 600 cubic feet). Some of the apartments were actually sweatshops, with a dozen or more men and women hand-stitching garments by candle light. In the mid-1880s, tenants of the Big Flat died at a rate of forty-two per thousand, as compared to twenty-five per thousand in the city at large. Two-thirds of the dead were children below the age of five.

Nor was the Big Flat unique in those days. New York City had no Board of Health before 1868 and no street-cleaning department until the 1890s. At that, it would be 1898 before street sweepers made their way to the Lower East Side, described by director George Waring as "a region entirely neglected in previous years." That same year, the Tenth Ward counted 82,000 Jews living in half-a-square mile, plagued by poverty, suicide, and disease. The "white plague" of TB struck twelve in every thousand Jews, competing with sundry other ailments to increase the mortality rate.

As if all that were not enough, Jews also faced a daily threat of violence from their Irish, German, and Polish neighbors. As Alter Landesman, the historian of Brooklyn's Brownsville district, has observed, "No cause was required for hostilities to start. It was enough that a Jewish boy appeared on the street for gangs to set about him."

Nor was the mayhem strictly kid stuff. On July 30, 1905, Irish factory workers lobbed bricks and stones at a Jewish funeral procession along the East River. Furious mourners rushed the factory but were repelled by security guards. The procession was moving again, preparing to board a ferry, when New York police arrived, summoned by the factory's owner. Without provocation or warning, the cops drew their clubs and waded into the cortege, the inspector in charge flailing with his baton and shouting, "Kill those Sheenies! Club them left and right!"

Three years later, in October 1905, another Jewish procession was attacked by Irish and Italian workers in the same district, leaving several Jews hospitalized after they were struck down by flying objects. Most often on the receiving end of violence, New York Jews were stunned and furious in September 1908 when Police Commissioner Theodore Bingham declared that half of all the city's criminals were Jews. Demands for proof of the outrageous claim forced Bingham to recant and publicly apologize for his "mistake."

While New Yorkers debated the source of their criminal problem, a new wave of Jewish immigration from eastern Europe had begun in 1907, continuing until the outbreak of World War I in 1914. The census of 1910 found fewer than 4 million Jews in a nation of 92 million, but *McClure's Magazine* was still concerned enough to publish an exposé on "The Jewish Invasion of America" in January 1907. Author Burton

Hendrick saw Jewish plots everywhere, including the American garment trade. "Fifty years ago," he complained, "all our tailors were native-born Americans. Now they are Jews."

For once, there was some truth to the charge, although it hardly added up to any sinister conspiracy. Jews represented a higher percentage of skilled workers than other European immigrants, and some two-thirds of those—around forty percent of all Jewish immigrants employed—wound up in the garment industry between 1899 and 1914. In 1885, Jews owned 234 of New York City's 241 garment factories; five years later, on the Lower East Side, 12,000 out of 25,000 working Jews were somehow involved in the "rag trade." In 1900, New York easily led the country, producing $107 million worth of women's clothing, in a total market valued at $159 million. By 1914, the national garment industry was earning well over $1 billion per year.

It should not be supposed, however, that much of that wealth found its way to the workers laboring in factories and walk-up sweatshops. In 1890, Jewish garment workers took home an average of $7.97 per week, compared to $10.46 for meat packers and $15.39 for workers in iron and steel. Females in the trade earned even less, between three and six dollars a week in the mid-1880s. To earn that meager wage, they labored from sixty to eighty-four hours each week, under conditions that were cramped at best, deathtraps at worst. One hundred and forty-five employees, mostly young girls, were killed when flames raced through the "fireproof" Triangle Shirtwaist Factory, in March 1911. By that time, garment workers were risking their lives for a weekly wage of $10.32.

By the 1890s, Jewish settlement in New York City had expanded from the Lower East Side into Brooklyn, across the East River, first in Williamsburg then in more distant Brownsville. Fifty thousand Jews colonized Brownsville by 1905, while another wave flowed northward into the Bronx. Restrictive covenants barred them from settling in the exclusive Riverdale quarter, but thousands of Jews found homes in the eastern sector of the Bronx, along the Grand Concourse.

New York City's only mainland borough, the Bronx is named for Joseph Bronck, a Danish emigré who was among the first to settle beyond the Harlem River, in 1639. Early development surrounded the village of Morrisania, named for the prominent Morris family, which contributed signatories to both the Declaration of Independence and the U.S. Constitution. Part of Westchester County until 1868, when it was incorporated into New York City, the borough is today most famous for its zoo and Yankee Stadium, linked to Manhattan by twelve bridges and six subway tunnels. Many of its residents are still descendants of immigrants from central and eastern Europe, with more prosperous quarters to the north, while the depressed South Bronx presents scenes of poverty to rival those from any other part of the United States.

The problem was already shaping up in 1903, when one Yiddish journalist described the Bronx as "a beautiful area . . . a suburb that could have sun and air and cheaper rents. But the greedy landlords, knowing the workers will have to move uptown, are putting up Hester Street tenements. Go take a look— the Bronx is becoming our new ghetto." It was not entirely true, of course: while some working-class streets, like Simpson and Fox, were already as bad as the Lower East Side, better housing was available in the Bronx, thanks in equal part to unused space and new tenement laws that restrained the worst slumlords. Another observer in 1903, British novelist Arnold Bennett, found the Bronx harsh and materialistic, but with an "innocent prosperity," nearly devoid of the Jewish culture that flourished on Manhattan's East Side. "It is a place," he wrote, "for those who have learnt that physical righteousness has got to be the basis for all future progress. It is a place to which the fit will be attracted, and where the fit will survive."

Survival of the fittest was more difficult for Jews, though, during the Progressive era. Part of the trouble originated in far-off Georgia, where the lynching of accused child-killer Leo Frank, in August 1915, prompted a revival of the Ku Klux Klan two months later. The original KKK had been content to murder blacks and "radicals" below the Mason-Dixon Line; the new Klan would spread nationwide, expanding its enemies list to include Jews, Catholics, labor unions, and anyone else who was not "100 percent American." Inflamed by a post-war "Red Scare" that too often treated "Jew" and "Bolshevik" as synonyms, the Klan's recruiting officers—dubbed "kleagles"—managed to enlist an estimated four million members at ten dollars a head, rolling on to dominate politics in states as diverse as Alabama, Colorado, and Indiana.

The Klan invaded New York City in the summer of 1921, with King Kleagle C. Anderson Wright under strict orders to give Jews "the dickens." The official reception was generally hostile, but within a year, Klan literature was being handed out to worshipers at New York's largest Baptist church, while Wilson Bush, the "exalted cyclops" of Brooklyn, presided over Ku Klux Klan meetings in the city's traffic court. By early 1924, one out of seven residents in Suffolk County had signed on, and statewide membership was climbing toward its peak, around

200,000. That summer, the Democratic Party held its national convention at Madison Square Garden, foundering on the jagged rocks of Klan factionalism to ensure a Republican victory in November. On the rough-and-ready side, a Jewish druggist accused of child molesting was kidnapped by Klansmen and ordered to get out of town. Memorial Day parades in Queens and Manhattan dissolved into street brawls, as Klansmen squared off with police and civilian opponents. Official reaction to the violence was swift, embodied in an antimask law and a statute requiring public registration of Klansmen, but a dozen separate chapters hung on in New York City through the 1930s.

During the Twenties, Ku Klux kleagles got an unexpected boost from auto magnate Henry Ford. Himself a multimillionaire, Ford seems to have adopted anti-Semitism in 1915, unaccountably blaming Jews for the failure of his naive "Peace Ship" mission to Europe and later for the upset of his 1918 senate campaign. In 1920, Ford used his newspaper, the *Dearborn Independent*, to launch a four-year series of articles on "The International Jew," collected that November into a book of the same title. Freely plagiarizing the discredited *Protocols of the Learned Elders of Zion*, Ford attacked "the International Jew and his satellites" as "the conscious enemies of all that Anglo-Saxons mean by civilization." His attacks were vitriolic enough that they landed Ford in court by 1927, named as the defendant in a series of libel suits. Lacking the courage of his convictions, Ford issued a blanket apology for his tirades, while shifting most of the blame to employees "upon whom I relied implicitly." Staffers at the *Independent* were encouraged to corroborate the fiction that "Mr. Henry Ford did not participate personally in the publication of the articles and has no personal knowledge of what was said in them."

It hardly mattered, though. The damage had been done.

Albert H. Glatman was born in New York City, the son of Jewish immigrants; he migrated to the Bronx like countless others, and like countless others, he wound up working in the garment trade. By 1925, he was in ladies hats, more or less, employed as secretary for the Instructo Millinery Supply Company, residing at 33 Rochambeau Avenue. He met his soulmate on the job, sometime that year. Ophelia Gold was a Polish immigrant, born in Warsaw, in 1888. Already an "old maid" at thirty-seven, she was flattered, maybe even thrilled, when Albert asked her out. They hit it off; he popped the question, and she readily accepted.

Albert had saved some money. He was tired of hats, and with Ophelia at his side, he opened a small stationery store. It was a gamble, starting over on the brink of middle age, but Albert and Ophelia Glatman were determined to succeed, despite the handicap of Albert's diabetes. By early spring of 1927, when Ophelia confirmed her suspicions of pregnancy, they had a new incentive to succeed: a new life to support, their son.

Harvey Murray Glatman, in his mother's words, entered the world "apparently a healthy, normal child." Or, maybe not. Around age three or four, she noted "instances of strange behavior" on her son's part. How strange? As described in interviews three decades later, Harvey "tied a string around his penis, placed the loose end in a drawer, and then leaned back against the string." It was, indeed, bizarre behavior for a three- or four-year-old but not unusual enough to rate a consultation with professionals. Instead, Ophelia "passed it off."

The response was typical for Ophelia, whom Harvey would later describe as a "rather indulgent" mother. Father Albert, by contrast, "seemed interested" in his son but was always "quite strict." In that context, and knowing what we do today of Harvey's later life, it is instructive to compare his early years with FBI statistics on the childhood development of thirty-six convicted sex killers (including twenty-nine with multiple victims). More than half of the inmates studied (fifty-six percent) were eldest sons; sixty-six percent considered their mothers the dominant parent, while a whopping seventy-two percent had negative relationships with male caretaker figures. Almost three-quarters of the killers (seventy-three percent) had endured "sexually stressful events" in childhood, with significant results: eighty-two percent practiced compulsive masturbation prior to adolescence; seventy-nine percent indulged in unspecified autoerotic practices; seventy-two percent nurtured fetishes (that is, erotic fixation on some body part or object other than the genitals); and seventy-one percent enjoyed childhood voyeurism.

By age three or four, then, Harvey Glatman fit the early profile in all particulars except voyeurism, which would come to dominate his libido in later life. He was the only son of an indulgent mother and a strict, often disapproving father, and his early genital play appears to have gone far beyond the norm for his—or any other—age, including bondage verging on masochism. Indeed, as we shall see, the rope fetish would dog Glatman throughout his life and ultimately land him on Death Row.

What triggered such behavior in a three- or four-year-old? What, if any, "sexually stressful events" in those years propelled Harvey toward genital ligation and self-inflicted pain? Such potentially injurious "play" is fairly common among victims of early childhood sexual abuse, and we know that forty-three percent of the FBI's sex-killer sampling suffered such abuse, but Harvey Glatman never pointed fingers, even from the gas chamber. There were no siblings in the home, no playmates at that tender age to teach him kinky games. His mother was "indulgent," and his father "strict."

Years later, when it was too late, psychiatrists involved with Glatman's case made note of his "bizarre" childhood activity but asked no further questions on the subject. There is no one left alive today for us to ask what happened in the family home on Rochambeau Avenue. Perhaps young Harvey thought the sex games up all by himself.

Perhaps.

Whatever his burgeoning psychosexual problems, physically Harvey seemed no different than other boys his age in Depression-era New York. He was vaccinated for smallpox in childhood, and his mother would later describe him as catching "the usual childhood diseases, including whooping cough." His tonsils and adenoids were surgically removed when he was four years old, in 1932.

At age six, Harvey started school. Ophelia would remember him as "a very good student, never truant, [who] never gave anyone any trouble." Times had changed since the turn of the century, when most of New York's Jewish children were educated in their local synagogues. By 1918, barely one-quarter of the city's 275,000 Jewish students received any religious instruction at all, and nearly half of those received it after hours in their homes while spending their days in public school. The unfortunate remainder got their Torah straight, packed into sunless synagogue base-

ments which the city Health Department had described, by 1915, as "filthy fire traps."

There was never any question of Harvey Glatman
attending religious school. His parents had long since
abandoned any vestige of orthodoxy, devoting themselves to the stationery shop, in Ophelia's words,
"twelve hours a day, seven days a week." Sabbaths
went by the board, leaving Harvey ample time to
pursue his studies . . . or any other subject that
caught his fancy in those crucial years.

What Harvey Glatman saw, as he surveyed the city
of his birth, must have disturbed a school-age Jewish
child. Henry Ford's halfhearted apology of 1927, six
months before Glatman's birth, had no appreciable
impact on anti-Semites at home or abroad. It is true
that the executive board of the American Jewish
Committee, reporting in November 1930, heard few
complaints of overt anti-Semitic violence, but discrimination was rampant. In the professions, aside
from government jobs protected under civil service
statutes, Dr. I. M. Rubinow told the National Conference of the Jewish Social Service, that in major
branches of office and clerical work, "the door to the
Jew is absolutely closed."

That fact aside, Jewish successes in the garment
trade, in restaurants, and in wholesale and retail out-
lets still fueled paranoid delusions of a "Jewish plot"
to dominate America's economy. By 1930, there were
20 million Americans of German descent, many of
them sympathetic to Nazi claims that the heroic German army had been "sold out" and "betrayed" by
wealthy Jews in World War I. Karl Marx was Jewish,
and the men who seized upon his godless doctrine,
plunging Russia into communist dictatorship after
1917, read like a list of Zion's "learned elders." Jewish bankers were responsible for the stock market

crash and ensuing Great Depression. By 1933, when
Adolf Hitler seized power in Germany, President
"Franklin D. Rosenfeldt" was driving the United
States toward thinly disguised socialism with his
"Jew Deal" programs for economic recovery. Where
would it end?

For many German immigrants, one step toward a
solution was membership in the goose-stepping Teu-
tonia Society, reorganized as Friends of New Germany to honor the fledgling Nazi regime. Granted,
there were certain problems with the group. Leader
Heinz Spanknoebel was a fugitive from justice, indicted by the federal government in 1933 for failure
to register as a foreign agent, but his replacement
was even worse. Tough-talking *Bundesführer* Fritz
Kuhn had slipped into the States from Mexico in 1926
and quickly earned his reputation as a Jew baiter of
the first water. In 1937, with 6,500 members on his
rolls, he renamed the Friends of New Germany yet
again, christening it the German-American Bund. A
year later, the Nazi front group mustered 19,000 fans
for a rally at Madison Square Garden, chanting and
giving their stiff-armed salutes under banners reading "Smash Jewish Communism" and "Stop Jewish
Domination of Christian America."

Still, it is clearly oversimplifying things to say, as
Max Dimont does, that the 1930s rise in anti-Semitism was "a German import," blindly swallowed by
Teutonic immigrants and Dixie rednecks. If anything,
the reverse may be true, since Adolf Hitler later told
the press, "I regard Henry Ford as my inspiration,"
and a foreign branch of the Ku Klux Klan—the German Order of the Fiery Cross—was active in the Fa-
therland by 1925, while Hitler was sitting in jail, hard
at work on *Mein Kampf*. Back in the States, North
Carolina's William Dudley Pelley launched his Silver
Shirt Legion of America on New Year's Day 1933,

the day after Hitler assumed power in Germany, and he had ample competition in the field. George Death-erage defected from the Klan to lead his own Jew-hating American Nationalist Confederation, while "Kansas Führer" Gerald Winrod ran for president in 1936. Detroit's Father Charles Coughlin, with his national radio program, served as the spiritual fig-urehead for a Christian Front that called upon its members to "liquidate the Jews in America" by any means available. Charles Lindbergh visited Germany in 1938, accepting the Order of Merit from Reichs-marshal Hermann Göring and returned to sing Hit-ler's praises in America. A year later, while German-American Bundists flirted with the New Jersey Klan, congressional investigators compiled a list of fifty-four anti-Semitic groups in America, reporting that "not more than 25 per cent can be considered bona fide. The other 75 per cent are pure rackets or letter-head organizations created for the sole purpose of enriching their leaders."

In New York City, Father Coughlin's Christian Front was clearly part of the grim twenty-five per-cent. Its members closed ranks with black-shirted Bundists at Madison Square Garden in February 1939, and Christian Front rallies in New York were characterized by what one critic termed "plain, un-varnished incitements to murder." Joseph McWil-liams ran the Christian Front in New York City, telling his followers that he planned to lead "a revo-lution against the Jews first, then against democracy, then against the Democratic and Republican parties." His ideal leader was Adolf Hitler, billed by McWil-liams as "the greatest philosopher since the time of Christ." In case anyone missed the point, McWil-liams's sidekick, Joseph Hartery, told the faithful that "when we get in power, guys with my type of mind will go to work on them Jews with a vengeance. There won't be enough lamp posts to hang them on."

Nor was the Christian Front all talk. In August 1939, McWilliams joined Fritz Kuhn and George Deatherage for a rally in the Bronx, at Innisfail Park, before a shouting audience of 15,000 anti-Semites. Another Bronx rally that year, at the Tri-Boro Palace, featured pamphlets urging patriots to "Think Christian—Act Christian—Buy Christian." A list of "Christian" merchants was provided for convenience's sake, and brown-shirted pickets roamed the five boroughs, chanting venom outside Jewish-owned shops. The Christian Fronters stockpiled guns, under the guise of "sporting clubs," while roving goon squads harried and assaulted Jews at every opportunity.

It was a perfect time to leave.

Two decades later, looking back, Ophelia Glatman would describe the move as an attempt to boost the family's financial status. She and Albert had grown tired of ninety-hour weeks at the stationery shop, and the Great Depression showed no signs of letting up after ten years, no matter how much overtime they invested in the business. They needed a break, perhaps a change of scene. The city takes its toll. With relatives in Colorado, they decided that a move to Denver just might do the trick.

What did they have to lose?

3

"Girl-Shy"

DENVER WAS DIFFERENT, WHICH IS NEVER QUITE A SYN-
onym for better. There were those who said Jews
"had it good" in Colorado's Mile-High City, but it
all depended on *which* Jews you had in mind, and
what was meant by *good*.

The first Jews to arrive, like those back east, had
come from Germany. They found themselves at liberty to put down roots and prosper, just like anybody
else, as long as they recalled their "place." A multimillionaire like Simon Guggenheim might be elected
to the U.S. Senate, but he still could not join either
one of Denver's country clubs; that is, until the Jews
got wise and organized their own.

The eastern European Jews who made their way
to Denver after 1880 faced prejudice not only from
the Gentiles but from the older Jewish upper crust,
as well. The latter was not anti-Semitism, strictly
speaking, but rather a vague anxiety that poorer immigrants, including many victims of tuberculosis,
would somehow erode the station early Hebrew pio-
neers had managed to establish for themselves. There

was no Denver ghetto, though the Jewish TB sanitariums came close, but prejudice and ethnic slurs were
not to be avoided, even in the shadow of the Rockies.

The 1920s Klan had found a more receptive ear in
Colorado than in New York City. Organized in 1921
as members of the Denver Doers Club, the hooded
knights were confident enough to bring their sheets
out of the closet a year later, and Klansman Benjamin
Franklin Stapleton was elected as Denver's mayor a
year later. In 1924, Klan members Clarence Morley
and Rice Means were elected, respectively, to the
governor's mansion and the U.S. Senate. Dr. John
Galen Locke had been denied a Colorado medical
license, but he still qualified as the Klan's "grand
dragon," ruling his state—and, some said, the local
Republican party—with a fist of iron. He opposed
rampant terrorism in principle, although it didn't
stop Klansmen from twice bombing a black post-
man's home in 1921, and Locke himself ordered the
abduction of a nineteen-year-old Klansman, threatening the young man with castration if he failed to wed
a girl whom he had gotten in "the family way."

That was in January 1925. Three months later,
sweeping vice raids proved beyond a shadow of a
doubt that Denver's Klan-infested police force was
protecting brothels and speakeasies rather than shut-
ting them down. A dozen Klan cops were suspended,
and Dragon Locke got caught in the fallout and was
forced to resign his post in July. He swiftly organized
a rival Fascist group, the Minute Men of America,
but it was all downhill from there for Locke and the
Colorado Klan. By the time Governor Morley was
defeated in 1927, and subsequently jailed for stock
fraud, the KKK, as an effective force, had ceased to
exist in the Centennial State.

By that time, too, the residents of Colorado had
more pressing matters on their minds. A casual ob-

server might have thought the Wall Street crash of 1929 had no impact on Colorado, but in fact, the state's great agricultural and mining interests had been mired in a depression all their own since the conclusion of the First World War. Farming, mining and manufacturing had accounted for more than half of all Colorado jobs in 1920, a percentage that dropped to one-third by the end of the 1930s. Thirty-five thousand factory workers were unemployed by 1940, down thirty percent from two decades earlier, and Colorado's per capita income fell below the national average for the first time in history. Between 1930 and 1934, fifty-six of the state's 174 banks gave up the ghost and closed their doors.

Even the weather seemed malignant in those days, giving Denver a taste of what "Okies" and "Arkies" had already suffered at home. In early April 1935, Denver was smothered by a hellish dust storm: cattle by the thousands choked to death on sand, while three-foot drifts closed hospitals, blocked highways, and even brought the mighty railroads to a grinding halt. When it began to rain at last, on April twelfth—thin, muddy water dribbling from the beige sky overhead—some Denverites professed to see the hand of God at work.

Their real salvation, though, would come from Washington, D.C. Denver was still Republican and isolationist, opposed to Franklin Roosevelt and his insistence on preparedness for war with Hitler's Germany, but Coloradans were too wise to look a gift horse in the mouth. They welcomed federal dollars in the form of new construction projects: $1.5 million for a new federal prison, $1.2 million for luxury apartments at Ellsworth and Downing, more still for the Lincoln Park housing project, where apartments rented for $18.75 per month. Pearl Harbor would bring greater prosperity yet, a new economy fueled by blood and iron, but in 1939 that was still ahead, and a majority of Coloradans preferred to think that they had seen the last of war.

Ophelia Glatman later said the move to Denver was inspired primarily "by a desire for increased economic opportunity," but it didn't quite work out that way. They settled at 1133 Kearney Street, on Denver's east side, where Albert was reduced overnight from a self-employed merchant to a taxi driver, learning Denver's streets as he went, smiling and hoisting luggage for tips. His diabetes was controlled with insulin, but we can only speculate about his mood, the sense of failure that would follow giving up his shop after a dozen years to drive a cab. Ophelia helped out with the bills, taking a job at the Hollywood Hat Shop.

Harvey's relationship with Albert was not bettered by the move. He would describe his mother, in a later prison interview, as "soft" and "too maternal," while exhibiting "some bitterness" toward Albert.

Part of it, at least, was based on sex.

More than once, Harvey later remembered, he was caught masturbating at home by one or the other of his parents. He recalled unspecified punishment coupled with Albert's threat that he would sprout pimples if he continued abusing himself. Harvey would never stop, but he internalized the criticism, reporting "many ill feelings" over his solitary sex life, convinced that he was "queer" because he masturbated.

Conventional masturbation was never enough, though, to bring him relief. Around age twelve, within a year or so of moving from the Bronx, Harvey resumed his bondage games—that is, assuming he had ever stopped. His favorite method was to tie a rope around his neck, get in the bathtub, run the rope's free end around a crossbar in the drain, and pull it tight until he climaxed in a breathless rush.

For variation, he would sometimes climb into the attic and string himself up from the rafters.

One night, he took the game a bit too far. As Ophelia recalled the event, "We noticed one evening, when my husband and I got home, that Harvey's neck was all red and looked like rope marks. He said he went up in the attic, took a rope, tied it around his neck and tortured himself, and in that way he got satisfaction."

Harvey's sex game—variously known as autoerotic asphyxia, asphyxiaphilia, or hypoxyphilia—is not, strictly speaking, the same thing as masochism (or automasochism, the infliction of pain on one's self). Self-induced strangulation or suffocation during masturbation—the sex play of "gaspers"—is more common than most people realize, but since practitioners rarely seek therapy, they are typically exposed only when the play results in accidental death. Screen actor Albert Dekker is probably the most famous victim, but estimates of mortality range from 250 to 1,000 men in any given year.

"Gasping" appears to be an ancient practice. Professor Leopold Beitenecker, director of the Institute of Forensic Medicine at the University of Vienna, says "the technique had been practiced by Eskimos and by Asians before it was introduced to Europe by French Legionnaires returning from the war in Indo-China, where the technique was performed by prostitutes to increase the client's sensation of ejaculation." Asphyxiation itself creates excitement and eventual euphoria, even without genital stimulation, due to the adrenalin produced when the human body perceives a life-threatening situation. Play turns to inadvertent suicide when pressure on the carotid artery causes a "gasper" to black out and hang himself.

Author John Money, in his book *Lovemaps*, quotes

one asphyxiaphile who, like Harvey Glatman, assumed the practice in childhood.

And then the girl who I thought was my sweetheart hopeful drowned while swimming at the beach; and then my fascination of the word asphixia [sic] came into play. I used to sit and try to imagine her nude body drowning underwater, and I wondered what it was like to drown; and I started having dreams while sleeping about swimming underwater and drowning, and then swimming like a fish where I didn't need any kind of air tank. But I could swim and watch other people drown, mostly girls. Then I started to masturbate.

Two leading experts on the subject—Ray Blanchard and Stephen Hucker of Toronto's Clark Institute of Psychiatry—have collected a vast data bank from coroner's reports and other sources. They note a correlation of this and other paraphilias in their study of 117 men who died during autoerotic asphyxia.

This study investigated the relationships between: asphyxiator's ages; two paraphilias commonly accompanying autoerotic asphyxia, bondage and transvestism; and various other types of simultaneous sexual behavior. . . . Data concerning sexual paraphernalia at the scene of death or among the deceased's effects were extracted from coroner's files using standardized protocols. Anal self-stimulation with dildos, etc., and self-observation with mirrors or cameras were correlated with transvestism. Older asphyxiators were more likely to have been simultaneously engaged in bondage or transvestism, suggesting elaboration of the masturbatory ritual over time. The greatest degree of transvestism was associated with intermediate rather than high levels of bondage, suggesting that response competition from bondage may limit asphyxiators' involvement in a third paraphilia like transvestism.

This time around, the Glatmans were concerned enough to seek professional help. They took Harvey to their family doctor, who prescribed "some pills" and told the worried parents to keep their son busy.

"He'll outgrow it," the physician said.

But he was wrong.

Kinky pastimes aside, Harvey gave his parents no reason to worry where school was concerned. Enrolled at Sherman Elementary in September 1938, he graduated to Byers Junior High in January 1939 and transferred to Gove Middle School two months later. A 1939 bicycle accident, which fractured one of Harvey's ankles, apparently had no adverse effects on his attendance or performance in school. His cumulative record notes that both English and "Jewish" were spoken at home, suggesting an aptitude for languages that was reflected in his academic grades.

Standardized test results for junior high school rated Harvey as "very superior" in reading comprehension, arithmetic reasoning, and arithmetic comprehension, while his reading vocabulary and academic aptitude were scored as "excellent." Under academic achievement, he earned "high" marks (rating him in the upper 25 percent of his class) for Latin, math, and instrumental music, while all other subjects fell into the "medium" (fiftieth percentile) range. Evaluation of aptitudes found him to be "medium"—or average—in all categories. Under the heading "Evaluation of Adjustments," Harvey scored "high" for his response to authority and his ability to "face facts objectively"; all other scores were "medium," except for two. No rating was assigned to Harvey for attendance and punctuality or for his "mental" adjustment in school. As of grade nine, he planned on attending college, listing his vocational preferences as "aviation" or "mining engineer."

Personal notes in Glatman's file include three from "DML," with one listing Harvey's special activities and interests as athletics, the Boy Scouts, and photography. Another notes his Saturday employment as a delivery boy. Under the heading of "Resources that Can Be Capitalized," we find a notation that "Harvey is easily offended, but he willingly and readily accepts explanations." A final observation reads: "Has musical ability. Enjoys the band."

Harvey enrolled as a freshman at East Denver High School on February 1, 1942, in a transfer from Gove Junior High. Halfway around the world, American and native troops were doggedly resisting Japanese invaders in the Philippines, inflicting heavy losses on the army that had enjoyed a decade of unbroken triumph from Manchuria to Guam and Wake Island. At Berlin's Sports Palace, on January thirtieth, Adolf Hitler had pledged his dedication to "complete annihilation of the Jews," and special extermination camps were already under construction in Ophelia Glatman's native Poland, near the villages of Belzec, Sobibor, and Treblinka. In Libya, Rommel's Afrika Korps had captured Bengasi, driving shattered remnants of the Allied occupation force before him, toward Gazala and Tobruk. Closer to home, the French liner *Normandie* was gutted by fire at its berth in New York, with Axis sabotage suspected as the cause of the fire. Nine days later, President Roosevelt authorized summary internment of Japanese Americans in the western United States.

More than 60,000 Denver residents would serve in uniform before war's end, some 1,300 of them killed in action, but those who remained at home were determined to stay mobile, regardless of wartime rationing on cars, tires, and gasoline. The federal Office of Price Administration estimated that an average of fifty to seventy-five black-market cars were sold daily in Denver, at prices ranging from $300 to $400 above the legal limit. As for drivers—or cabbies—who wanted to stay on the road, it was simple to set up a "quickie," defined in those days as a home delivery of two or three gallons of gas, sold at exorbitant prices.

Harvey had no great concern over money. He was, by all accounts, an above-average student at East Denver High, earning straight A's in Latin, Spanish, and algebra, with a high B average in English, geometry, world history, and general science. His grades in gym were "satisfactory," and he maintained his musical interest, playing the cornet with sufficient skill to hold a B average in band and orchestra. In his final year at East Denver High, he added glee club to the repertoire and earned another A. When not at school or camping with the Boy Scouts, trying out for track, or working as an assistant in the chemistry lab, he played in a small music group. When gigs were scarce, he ushered at the Denver Auditorium and picked up other part-time jobs. Ophelia recalled her son as "thrifty and well-liked by everybody."

Except, of course, by girls.

There was a major problem with the opposite sex where Harvey was concerned. Ophelia sized him up as "girl-shy"—so much so, in fact, that he would "walk across the street to avoid females." Harvey, for his part, recalled that he never asked any girls for dates "because of fear of embarrassment should he be refused."

There were alternatives, of course.

The rope was one. Housebreaking was another.

Following his first conviction, Glatman admitted that he had begun "creeping" in December 1944. According to the notes of that interview, "[h]e states that he enjoyed it as he felt it was a game of cops and robbers and he did it mainly for the thrill." At first, he prowled apartments occupied by solitary females but avoided any contact with the tenants. He rarely stole money but did lift a .38-caliber revolver from one apartment.

The gun felt good in his hand. He was going to need it.

Sometime that fall or winter, Harvey underwent a drastic change in his attitude toward females. Instead of crossing the street to avoid them, he became frankly aggressive—to the point, in one observer's words, that he "would not even excuse himself after he had stepped on a woman's foot."

Discourtesy was the least of his problems, though. Emboldened by his break-ins and the pistol in his pocket, Harvey switched from prowling flats to stopping girls and women on the street. Ophelia Glatman had her own take on the situation, delivered to reporters years after the fact.

"Being so extremely girl-shy," she explained, "he accosted girls in the evening, maybe grabbed their purse, just for an approach, and then threw it back. On another occasion he entered an apartment where girls were alone and molested them in a similar way, [but he] never harmed anyone in a bodily way."

But mother love is often blind, and Harvey was involved in more than simply snatching purses from the girls he feared and lusted after, all at once. In fact, as he admitted more than once to jailers, "he committed a series of offenses in Denver in which he threatened females on the street with pistols. He would then take these women and tie them to a telephone pole and partially disrobe them. He mentions one particular instance in which he took a woman to her apartment and tied her up and took some of her clothing from her. He claims that he did not molest any of these women in any other way."

No rape, in other words. Not yet. Young Harvey drew the line at kidnapping and bondage, fumbling to undress his victims while they wept and pleaded to be left alone. He seldom took their money, and on those occasions was meticulous in separating what he stole from what he earned by working odd jobs, playing in the band.

He wasn't in the game for money. He was in it for the women. Dominating them and working up the nerve, at last, to touch them.

He was in it for the rope.

On May 8, 1945, Denver celebrated the collapse of Nazi Germany. It was a modest celebration, leaning more toward prayer meetings and church bells than toward orgiastic pub crawls. All might well be quiet on the western front, but there were still the Japanese to deal with, and each island stepping stone across the vast Pacific seemed to cost more lives, more blood, than the preceding battleground.

Ten days later, on a Friday night, Elma Hamum telephoned police to report an attempted burglary at her home on Vrain Street in west Denver. She had surprised the prowler and described him to a tee: late teens, big ears, a startled chipmunk face. The youth had fled without assaulting her. If they were quick enough, she thought, police might catch him in the neighborhood.

Denver authorities were working on a string of unsolved burglaries and robberies by then, women accosted in their homes or on the street. Eula Jo Hand had been one of the first, confronted near her home on Clarkson Street, within a mile or so of East Denver High, but most of the reports were clustered on the west side, well away from Harvey Glatman's home on Kearney Street. Detectives still didn't have a clue to their suspect's identity, but the crimes were unusual enough in those days, with their sexual overtones, that police were anxious to make an arrest.

Soon after Elma Hamum's call, Patrolmen V. L. Moore and K. I. Pizer found their suspect. He was waiting for an eastbound trolley, at the corner of 29th and Yates, two blocks west of the Hamum residence on Vrain. The trolley came, and the patrolmen followed him aboard. No sooner was the young man seated, than they saw him slip a bundle out from underneath his windbreaker and toss it underneath the seat in front of him. Upon examination, it revealed a length of clothesline, scissors, and a .25-caliber semiautomatic pistol registered to one of the recent burglary victims.

Harvey Glatman was arrested and transported to the station house where he was booked for investigation of burglary and aggravated robbery. A night in jail broke down his thin façade of resistance, and he spilled his guts on Saturday, relating details of various recent crimes. On Monday the twenty-first, he was formally charged with first-degree robbery in the case of Eula Hand. His parents promptly posted bail.

We have no way of knowing what was said at home about young Harvey's indiscretion. Based upon his later statements and Ophelia's comments to the press, we may assume that Albert may have had some harsh words for his son, while Harvey's mother minimized the beef and made excuses.

Their reactions carried no weight by this time, in any case.

Harvey was hooked on stolen thrills. His one concession to the recent bust would be to shift his hunting ground.

Meanwhile, he still had school to think about. Night prowling had a price tag, and his grades were slipping—from B's to C's in math and science, all the way to D's in general education, bottoming out with an "unsatisfactory" mark in gym class. He still scored well in music, though, and the grade-point average from his first two years was high enough that June 1945 saw him graduate in the top one-seventh of his high school class.

A month later, shortly after nine o'clock on Sunday night, July fifteenth, Glatman confronted Norene Laurel on a Boulder streetcorner. He showed her a pistol and told her to come along quietly, walking her back to his car. They drove up Sunshine Canyon, west of town, until he found a nice, dark place to park.

There, Glatman produced a length of rope and bound her hands. He gagged her with a strip of cloth to keep her quiet. What happened next was sketched in vague, official language, years after the fact: "They laid down together all night." Norene was not "attacked," according to police—no rape, again—and while Ophelia would insist until Harvey's dying day that "her son did not molest the victim," we may assume from Harvey's own admission that he fondled her, perhaps removing portions of her clothing. Sometime after 1 A.M., he let her go and gave her carfare to get home.

It was a critical mistake. He was identified almost immediately, from his *modus operandi* and the recent bust. Denver P.D. arrested him again and booked him as a fugitive, No. 27080, on a hold for Police Chief Worthing Masters from Boulder. By late afternoon, he was locked up in Boulder. His arrest card listed the offense as "molesting women," translated on his permanent rap sheet as "girl trouble."

A month later, on August 14, Denver celebrated the war's end in earnest. Japan lay in ruins, smoldering under mushroom clouds, and the world was finally safe for democracy, after a fashion. There were no sedate prayer meetings this time, as Denverites let themselves go. Sam Lusky, writing for the *Rocky Mountain News*, described the scene as "servicemen kissed their girls and they kissed somebody else's girl and pretty soon everybody was kissing everybody else, and nobody was complaining."

Albert and Ophelia Glatman, meanwhile, were more concerned about helping their son out of trouble. They consulted Dr. J. P. Hilton, who later summarized his findings for a court that was prepared to decide on Harvey's life or death.

Harvey Glatman first came to see me in August of 1945 at the age of seventeen [Hilton wrote].

At that time he had a history of having bruised his neck by tying a rope around it. He was sullen, morose and very disrespectful and for several years had felt that everyone was against him including his parents. He had been shy with girls prior to the past year when his attitude changed completely and he became aggressive with women.

His past physical history was negative except for a tonsillectomy. The family history was negative except that a cousin of his father had been institutionalized.

Dr. Hilton diagnosed Glatman as schizophrenic, a condition frequently misinterpreted by laymen as "split personality." In fact, the label is a blanket term for a group of psychiatric disorders, typically characterized by withdrawal from reality, illogical thought patterns, delusions and hallucinations, accompanied in varying degrees by other emotional, behavioral, or intellectual disturbances. Today, we know that schizophrenia is often linked to defects in the frontal lobe and/or an imbalance of dopamine, a neurotransmitter essential to normal functioning of the central nervous system. Low levels of dopamine are also associated with Parkinson's disease. Both ailments are believed to have genetic roots. In many cases, schizophrenia—like depression—can be chemically controlled.

In 1945, however, such medical breakthroughs were decades away. Schizophrenics were "crazy," potentially dangerous. In severe cases, they not only marched to a different drum but also heard voices directing the band. There was little Dr. Hilton could do for Glatman, except to recommend a defense of not guilty by reason of insanity.

Harvey's rap sheet shows another arrest by Denver P.D. on September 30, 1945, although no charge is listed. In the circumstances, it was probably a tardy revocation of bond, occasioned by the "girl trouble" in Boulder. The molesting charge would never go to trial, but it was still enough to take him off the street.

Harvey sat in jail until November 19, when he finally appeared in court on the first-degree robbery charge. Instead of trying the insanity defense, he pled guilty on advice of counsel and threw himself on the mercy of the court. Twelve days later, on December first, he drew a term of one to five years in prison.

Glatman was received at Colorado State Penitentiary, in Canon City, on December 5, 1945. He passed his eighteenth birthday in a cage, as inmate #23863, and soon thereafter was evaluated by the prison physician, whose anonymous report has survived in court files.

PHYSICAL EXAMINATION

Physical examination showed a well developed and well nourished male of 18: of athletic habitus [sic]. The hair is closely clipped. Features are Jewish, rather coarse. Teeth show good hygiene. Pharynx is negative. Heart and lungs normal. Blood pressure 115/75. Respiratory, gastrointestinal and genito-urinary systems negative. Neurological examination negative.

MENTAL EXAMINATION

He is a pleasant appearing, somewhat embarrassed and shy boy, who has been a model inmate in the Penitentiary and has been made a "trustee" [sic]. He is cooperative and attentive during examination. His reaction time is prompt. He is slightly retarded in his productivity. He is relevant and coherent. His thinking and his ideas progress in a logically associated manner. Emotionally he is complacent. The emotions are obviously resonant and he shows definite appropriate affective reaction to his situation, e.g., he shows embarrassment speaking of sex. He is not unduly depressed by his prison term, feels that he has not been done an injustice. Abnormal thought content cannot be determined. There is no history or obvious findings of any hallucinatory experiences and no delusional content can be elicited. The sensorium is entirely intact. His counting and calculation, general knowledge are consistent with his high school education. Rorschach examination shows a good contact with reality and ability to get along with other people. He is rigid in his concepts and his form perception is hyper-accurate. There is evidence of anxiety but emotions are well controlled. Practically no fantasy life is evident. There is color

shock and rejection of color cards which is consistent with a neurosis.

CONCLUSION: I feel this boy is probably a
Psychoneurosis-Compulsive or anxiety type without much depression. I can find no evidence of
schizophrenia and do not believe shock treatment is indicated.

Disagreement between physicians is common, particularly in assessing the mental state of criminal defendants: one analyst's psychotic is another's "antisocial
personality disorder." The problem is exacerbated by
disputes over what schizophrenia is—or whether it
even exists as a separate and distinct condition. The
most we can say, from comparing Dr. Hilton's diagnosis with the Colorado penitentiary report, is that
Glatman did not appear to be delusional: he wasn't
seeing Martians in his cell or having conversations
with the disembodied voice of God. As for the lack of
fantasies, we may assume, from prior and subsequent
events, that Harvey had devised himself a mask.

Under no circumstances should it be presumed
that he was "well."

Glatman served eight months of his minimum one-
year sentence on a prison labor gang, where he was
rated as an "average worker." His disciplinary record was "clear," and he won parole on July 27, 1946.
Ophelia later told the press that he was treated, upon
his release, by a private psychiatrist. If we can trust
her memory, the doctor prescribed a trip out of
state . . . and dancing lessons, to increase the young
man's confidence with girls.

It was a long shot, and there is no evidence that
Harvey ever took a dancing lesson in his life, but he
was all for ditching Colorado while he had the chance.

New York was calling.

He was going home.

4

Better Off Dead

OPHELIA GLATMAN TOOK HER SON TO NEW YORK CITY very shortly after his parole. They left Albert at home, in Denver, shuttling strangers here and there around the city in his cab. It was a doting mother's choice. Ophelia did not hesitate.

Whatever Harvey may have learned from eight months in the pen, if anything, was forgotten in a heartbeat once he hit the New York streets. There was no time to waste on burglaries. He bought a pocketknife and a plastic gun he thought would pass for real on cursory inspection, and he began to prowl the streets by night.

Late Saturday evening, on the seventeenth of August, Olga Metrick and Rose Gianzerra were walking home along Saw Mill River Road, in Yonkers, when a slender young man stepped out of the shadows. He drew a pistol and demanded silence. Rose unleashed a scream that brought a stranger running from the next street over. Their assailant heard the man approaching, calling out to them, inquiring what was wrong.

He turned and fled into the night.

A short time later, half-past midnight, he turned up on Worth Street, half a mile from the scene of his first bungled heist. Thomas Staro was out for a stroll with Doris Thorn, enjoying the night air, and they had reached a lonely stretch of road where anything could happen. Suddenly, they were confronted by a goofy-looking stranger with a pistol, insisting that the couple follow him into the shadows, further off the street.

Intimidated by the gun, they did as they were told. Staro did not resist when he was told to kneel with his hands clasped behind his back. The gunman relieved Staro of thirty dollars and some unspecified "personal papers," then bound his wrists and feet, immobilizing him, before he turned to Doris Thorn. He ordered her to stand against a nearby tree, tied her wrists behind her, and had begun to fumble with the buttons of her blouse when Staro strained against his bonds, infuriated—and his hands came free. Another moment, while the mugger was distracted by his prize, and Staro freed his legs.

Lurching erect, he charged the stranger, cursing and flailing with his fists. Instead of shooting Staro down, the gunman drew a folding knife and flicked it open, slashing wildly at his enemy. The blade went home—once, twice—and Staro staggered backward, grimacing in pain. He was not badly wounded, but the pause gave his opponent time to flee.

Yonkers police put out an all-points bulletin, but they were already too late. They had a fair description, but their man was gone.

By Monday morning he was on his way upstate to Albany.

We must assume that Harvey's mother had no knowledge of his latest crimes, and that she would have tried to put her foot down had she known. Still,

when the word got out, she did her best to sugarcoat
the Yonkers stabbing. In Ophelia's version of events,
Glatman had "lived a normal life for a while" in
New York. "Then, one night, he tried to molest a
girl, and her boyfriend put up a fight."

But he was gone now, fled beyond a mother's help.

He found a small apartment in Albany, on Colum-
bia Street, Number 55, and settled in. By Thursday
night, the twenty-second, he was back at work, mixing business with pleasure.

Florence Hayden, a young single woman, was on
her way home that night, when she became the first
victim of the man Albany police would dub their
"Phantom Bandit." As usual, she caught the bus at
State and Pearl streets, disembarking at Main for the
short walk back to her apartment on Lancaster Street.

"As I started toward my home," she later said,
"there was a nurse directly behind me, and for that
reason I didn't notice the man."

Or boy, as the case may be. It was eighteen-year-
old Harvey Glatman, zeroing in on the best-looking
woman he'd spotted so far. He had a plastic pistol
in his pocket and sufficient rope for all his needs.

The nurse turned off Main Avenue, after a block or
so, to enter Brady Maternity Hospital. Closing behind
Florence Hayden, Harvey saw his chance.

"The man came running at me," Florence said.
"He jammed a gun into my back and warned me to
keep quiet or he would shoot. I told him I would
not scream and that I would give up my money willingly if he would go away."

He relieved her of twenty-eight dollars, but the
cash was never first in Harvey's thoughts. Glancing
along the street in both directions, watching out for
witnesses, he ordered Florence into the darkness of
a nearby backyard.

"At that point I didn't know what to expect," she

recalled, "and I was terribly scared. He told me to turn around and started to bind my hands. I realized he was using both his hands and no longer held the gun, so I wheeled around, pushed him hard, and screamed—but loud!"

A muffled curse, and Glatman took off at a dead run, leaving Florence shaken but unharmed.

Another failure.

Friday night, the twenty-third, he tried again. Two women, this time, walking together down Hollywood Avenue. Beverly Goldstein and Evelyn Berger were startled when Harvey confronted them, pulling his "weapon" and demanding money. Details are scarce, but it appears that Glatman wasn't sure what to do with two women at once and settled for small change before he turned and fled. The women hiked directly to police headquarters and reported the assault.

Police Commissioner James Kirwin was outraged. Not that holdups were unknown in Albany, of course, and these were strictly small potatoes. Still, there was something in the Phantom's style that angered Kirwin. Perhaps it was the selection of female victims or the implication—at least in Flo Hayden's case—of intended rape. The man of mystery was clearly working up to something bigger, something worse.

Kirwin huddled with Night Chief William Mooney at Albany P.D. The man they wanted was a night-prowler who picked on female pedestrians, and they had no reason to think he would change his M.O. The word went out to Albany's detective bureau and every man on staff volunteered to work overtime for the duration. They fanned out after nightfall, covering the streets in what the *Albany Times-Union* would later describe as "the most intensive manhunt conducted" in recent memory.

It was hush-hush in the beginning, though, no tele-graphing the "invisible dragnet" to potential sus-pects. The detectives did their best to be everywhere at once, eyeballing suspicious men, shadowing young women with the look of easy prey about them.

Their vigilance paid off in the small hours of Sun-day morning, August twenty-fifth. Detectives James Hall and Anthony Manning were prowling Ontario Street, near Western Avenue, when they spotted a likely suspect. He was nearly six feet tall, around 140 pounds, with sandy hair, his big ears holding up a pair of horn-rimmed glasses. More to the point, he seemed to be hunting, moving closer by the moment to a woman who was cheerfully oblivious to the dan-ger approaching from behind.

Hall and Manning made their move, guns drawn, taking no chances with the Phantom. Turning out his pockets, they retrieved a plastic gun, a length of rope, and Harvey's wallet, with twenty-four dollars inside. A squad car was summoned and took him down-town, while officers descended on his apartment. A search of the flat turned up personal items taken from each of the Albany victims.

In custody, Glatman made no secret of his recent troubles with the law. He talked about his prison time in Colorado, and a phone call to Denver P.D. brought word that Mile-High authorities would gladly request the extradition of Harvey as a parole violator, if Albany chose not to prosecute. Glatman also described his forays in Yonkers, where warrants were sworn out on charges of robbery, attempted robbery, and assault.

Albany had no intention of letting the Phantom slip away, however. District Attorney Julian Erway was on hand Wednesday morning, the twenty-eighth of August, when Albany's grand jury indicted Glat-man for robbing Florence Hayden "by means of force and by placing her in fear of immediate injury." It made no difference that the gun was plastic, since *she* didn't know it. When Ophelia Glatman heard the news, she had her own take on the situation, telling herself—and anyone else who would listen—that Harvey had "molested two women along the usual pattern; never hurt anyone."

District Attorney Erway, meanwhile, took the opportunity to laud police for bringing Harvey in. "This defendant has been able to ply his trade of holdups in various cities," Erwin told Judge Francis Bergan's court, "until he came to Albany, where his crime career was cut short by our police. As he began operating here, the dragnet was spread so that every section of the city was covered by either a uniformed patrolman or detectives. He was unable to escape from that web purposely weaved to snare him. The police merit the thanks of every resident of Albany for a fine piece of work."

No charges were filed in the second case, but Glatman had trouble enough, as it was. He faced a second-degree robbery charge, and the Colorado conviction made him a two-time offender, liable to a stiffer sentence than someone arrested for the first time. Bond was denied, considering his history of flight and charges pending from two other jurisdictions, so he sat in jail, considering his options. In October, the D.A. accepted a plea bargain, reducing Harvey's charge to first-degree grand larceny in return for a guilty plea. Erway had studied Glatman and decided he could be reformed "with proper supervision and medical treatment."

On Friday, October eleventh, Glatman stood before Judge Earl Gallup for sentencing. He was handed a sentence of five to ten years, ordered to the reception center at Elmira Reformatory, where authorities would determine where he should serve the rest of his time.

Elmira Reformatory, named for the nearby seat of Chemung County in upstate New York, was one of America's first correctional facilities designed specifically for juvenile offenders. The first thirty inmates arrived in July 1876 to complete construction of the prison that was sometimes dubbed "the college on the hill." Its "students" were a rowdy lot, though, and Elmira's early years were tarnished by a series of escapes, along with the murder of Superintendent Zebulon Brockway's chief assistant.

In response to those disturbances, Brockway instituted a three-stage program which, in his terms, would convert the inmates into "Christian gentlemen." In step one, Brockway personally interviewed all new arrivals to compile detailed dossiers before they entered the second of three inmate "grades." Elmira was supposed to "treat" criminals rather than punish their crimes, and the main dose of "medicine" was contained in the second "grade," which included labor in the facility's iron foundry and factories, on its farm, or with the maintenance crew. Dinner was followed by formal education and occasional speeches by guest lecturers, while Sunday was reserved for mandatory worship. Inmates who earned three "marks" each for education, work, and good behavior every month for half a year were promoted to "first grade," while another six months of "nines" brought parole hearings before Superintendent Brockway and Elmira's five civilian managers. With indeterminate sentencing, model inmates might reach "third grade"—release to prearranged homes and jobs—within as little as a year. For those who broke the rules outside, it meant a trip back to Elmira and the "second grade" routine.

Zeb Brockway put the institution's best face forward at all times, rarely acknowledging a failure with his "students," but Elmira's public image was, in fact, the product of a shrewd public-relations campaign. Handpicked parolees were assigned as monitors, to keep an eye on "third grade" inmates, and Elmira's printing press spewed glowing annual reports together with an inmate newspaper, *The Summary*, which sketched a rosy picture of the warden and his men. A constant stream of visitors was treated to displays of inmate industry and discipline, including showy military drills. In 1888, when New York's legislature briefly outlawed prison industries, Elmira's cons were diverted into paramilitary companies, drilled long and hard by guards and inmate "officers." Their double-time maneuvers on the field were so admired by visiting administrators that Elmira's system was adopted, over time, by ten adult facilities.

Beneath the polished surface, though, Elmira hid a very different face. Rebellious inmates, brutal discipline, administrative scandals—these and more were showcased by investigations in the early 1890s. During 1893 and 1894, the New York State Board of Charities conducted extensive sworn interviews with Elmira's staff and inmates, including those paroled or transferred out to other prisons. The board's final report charged that Brockway himself frequently assaulted inmates, both during and after their initial interviews, while violence by guards was routine. Some inmates were shackled and hung from the bars of special "rest cure" cells, while the "mark" system had somehow turned into a system of pay-as-you-go, with inmates required to front money for various institutional services. Even so, Elmira's medical facilities were grossly inadequate, nepotism loaded the staff with corrupt or incompetent guards, and violence was rampant. Inmate "monitors" had used their trusted position at Elmira to brutalize selected inmates and extort sexual favors.

Brockway bitterly denied the charges, stepping up his own publicity campaign until the governor felt obliged to order a second investigation. The "official" findings exonerated Brockway, and he remained as Elmira's superintendent until 1900, when a new team of civilian managers forced his retirement, citing run-down facilities, staff corruption, widespread smuggling of contraband, and high recidivism rates.

Brockway's successors, including two physicians, shifted Elmira's focus from the old brand of "rehabilitation" to custody and treatment of youthful offenders. Newly developed psychological tests revealed that many of Elmira's inmates were mental defectives for whom there was little hope of reform. Dr. Frank Christian, serving as Elmira's superintendent from 1917 to 1939, was chief among those who regarded "defectives" as the prison's worst problem, both in terms of disruptive behavior and recidivism following parole. In 1945, the state established a reception center adjacent to the reformatory, designed to test and classify inmates ranging in age from sixteen to twenty-one years. It was here, rather than to the reformatory proper, that Harvey Glatman was sent on the first leg of his journey through the New York penal system.

Glatman was delivered to Elmira on October 24, 1946, as inmate #48337. There was no rush about evaluating him, since he had five years minimum to serve, and in fact, the process wound up taking nearly two years. A medical history was taken from Glatman upon his arrival at Elmira. It listed his occupation as "laborer," with a notation that Harvey could not remember his Social Security number. The examining physician found a deviated septum (with the nasal passage unimpaired) and a myopic left eye. Harvey was diagnosed with herpes zoster—i.e., "shingles"—on admission to Elmira, though a later copy of the same report would list his skin as "negative." Glatman admitted to "moderate" smoking, while denying any use of alcohol or drugs. His I.Q. tested at 126, characterizing Harvey as "endowed with superior intelligence." Brains aside, his evaluation closed on an ominous note.

PAROLE: SPECIAL NOTE: Because of his conforming attitude and high level of ability, he will probably have no difficulty in an institution and will do well in any program to which he is assigned in accordance with his ability. However, unless he receives intensive psychotherapy, it is not likely that a correctional institution will improve his deep-seated personality difficulties which make him potentially a dangerous individual to be at large.

Dr. Ralph Ryancale filed Glatman's psychiatric report at Elmira on January 3, 1947. It described him as follows:

A white male, 18 years of age, intellectually endowed with superior intelligence. Comes of an intact home, parents in good standing.

Inmate is a high school graduate; had visions for a time of going to college, primarily interested in mechanical engineering. In 1945, began to show peculiarities in behaviour, which was expressed through criminal activities.

It is difficult to state what his first motives were, but in his own mind he associated them with the impulse to become famous and do something unusual, and obtained a thrill burglarizing apartments. Broke into the apartment, he stated, and this gave him a thrill he is unable to explain. Admits peeping tendencies; finally he revealed his impulse to hold up women, tie them up and watch them; this afforded him sexual gratification, gave him a sense of stimulation, and finally was followed by feelings of remorse and repentance, so that the whole situation as it developed involved his going out periodically on one of these adventures when he felt the impulses become strong. The problem was getting more hazardous in that he was taking greater liberties and more aggressive [sic] and finally wound up with his incarceration.

A very adequate examinations [sic] by psychiatrists in Denver classified him as a schizophrenic type of personality. Following his release, however, [he] came to New York, became involved in similar issues but on a more reckless basis. He has never, however, assaulted any of his victims sexually. Never had any heterosexual experience, although admits masturbation in the course of which he gets an imagery of the crime that he commits. In his dream content, has similar fantasies. Has been largely an introverted personality with few friends.

The first impression that this inmate made to the examiner was that of a schizoid type of individual with sexually perverted series of impulses. There was no element of sadism uncovered, but, of course, this must always be kept in mind as a possibility. Sodium amytal was given to him intravenously under which inmate talked much more freely and indicated more

than ever his desire of becoming recognized and
famous, and uncovered that his crime act was
essentially a sexual one. Whenever he commits
these crimes, he feels that there is no need for
him to find sexual relief through masturbation.
A verbatim copy of the sodium amytal interview
has been made a part of this record.

Both the mother and the father have been seen
by the examiner. Are rather distraught over the
fast developing criminality of their son. The
mother is particularly disturbed, fearful in the
event he goes out he may become involved in
notorious crime *and wished him dead rather than
being faced with that kind of destiny.* Both parents
feel that the case is really a psychiatric one, and
are quite upset to find that the boy cannot receive adequate hospital attention. *In the interview
with the mother, she suggested to the examiner the
possibility of brain surgery, frontal lobotomy, in the
event that all other methods of psychiatric therapy
fail.* She is willing to give consent to this surgery
in the event that the psychiatric personnel of the
Correction Department feel that it might be a
recommended plan.

This boy should be further studied in the institution to which he is transferred. [Emphasis
added.]

Whether it was injury to others that Albert and
Ophelia feared or simply bad publicity, Dr. Ryancale's report doesn't say.

Glatman's final diagnosis at Elmira cut to the heart
of his problem. It read: "Psychopathic personality—
schizophrenic-type—sexually perverted impulses as
the basis for his criminality."

On September 8, 1948, Harvey was transferred
from Elmira to the state's maximum-security prison

at Sing Sing as inmate #107438. In convict parlance, he was going "up the river."

He would have to sink or swim.

Constructed in 1825–26, Sing Sing is the stony heart of New York's penal system. It stands on 130 acres once known as the Silver Mine Farm, owned by John Fleetwood Marsh. The site was chosen for easy access by boat, on the Hudson River, and for the large quantities of building stone nearby. With convict labor free of charge, it cost the state a mere $70,000 to build the original four-tiered, 482-by-44-foot building with individual cells for some 500 inmates. And cramped cells they were—seven feet deep, just over three feet wide, and six feet, seven inches tall—arranged back-to-back, in accordance with the prison's system of enforced perpetual silence.

From day one, Sing Sing was dominated by Warden Elam Lynds. A veteran of the War of 1812, Lynds left military service for a post as chief keeper at the new state prison near Auburn, New York. There, he took command, in effect, from an incompetent warden who gave Lynds a virtual free hand in matters of discipline, permitting brutal floggings for the least infraction (though he balked at Lynds's plan to give each guard a rawhide whip). In 1821, the warden died and Lynds succeeded him, swiftly earning Auburn a reputation as the harshest prison in America. That reputation, in its turn, marked Lynds for the assignment of constructing Sing Sing, four years later.

Officially, the prison was called Mount Pleasant until 1970, though the name hardly fit. The prison's nickname was derived from an adjacent village, Sing Sing, but the village elders heard so many grim reports about activities inside the prison walls that they changed the town's name, before the decade was out, to Ossining. It was the first of many indicators that the Lynds regime was fashioning a little hell on earth.

New York's state legislature ordered Lynds to pick 100 convicts from the Auburn lockup, "broken" men accustomed to his mode of discipline, and ship them to the site that would become their future home. They slept in tents and worked without surrounding walls or fences, cowed by Lynds and their sadistic guards. Those convicts were the first to wear striped uniforms—another hedge against escape—and worked all day, from dawn to dusk, beneath the gaze of guards empowered to whip them without consulting superior officers. By May of 1826, New York City's old Newgate Prison was emptied, its inmates transferred to Sing Sing, where work on the main building would continue through October 1828. (A century later, in 1928, another building was erected, containing a kitchen, hospital, and chapel.)

Sing Sing was run by the book, from the striped uniforms, lockstep marching, and eternal silence to a rule requiring that inmates pass each other with downcast eyes, to avoid confrontations. In the event of misbehavior, Lynds ordered his guards to "Punish! Punish! Whip 'em till they drop!"

"I don't believe in reformation for an adult criminal," Lynds once said, explaining his theory of penology. "He's a coward, a willful lawbreaker whose spirit must be broken by the lash. Why is it that one guard, armed with a whip, can control twenty convicts? They are afraid of him. I'll teach them to fear my guards—and all of them, guards included, to fear me. That is the only way to conduct a prison."

Nicknamed "The Whip of Sing Sing," Lynds set an example for his guards by meeting each group of new arrivals, selecting the worst of the lot from a review of the commitment papers, and delivering ten lashes on the spot, as an introduction to Mount Pleasant. In an average month, it was reported, as many as 3,000 lashes were dealt out at Sing Sing. Disruptive prisoners were also gagged, placed in straitjackets, and consigned to bread-and-water diets on a whim. Those who obeyed the rules were sent to quarry stone six days a week, from dawn to dusk, while Sunday was for rest, locked down in their unlit, unheated, and unsanitary cells.

Opinions varied on the end result. Rev. Louis Dwight, of Boston's Prison Discipline Society, gushed with praise for Sing Sing, writing that

> The whole establishment, from the gate to the sewer, is a specimen of neatness. The unremitted industry, the entire subordination and subdued feeling of the convicts, has probably no parallel among an equal number of criminals. In their solitary cells they spend the night, with no other book than the Bible, and at sunrise they proceed in military order, under the eye of the turnkeys, in solid columns, with the lock march to their workshops; thence in the same order, at the hour of breakfast, to the common jail, where they partake of their wholesome and frugal meal in silence. Not even a whisper is heard through the whole dining area. The convicts are seated in single file, at narrow tables, with their backs towards the center, so that there can be no interchange of signs. If one has more food than he wants, he raises his right hand, and the waiter changes it. When they have done eating, at the ringing of a little bell, of the softest sound, they rise from the table, form the solid columns, and return under the eye of their turnkeys to the work-shops.

At the close of the day, a little before sunset, the work is all laid aside at one [sic] and the convicts return in military order to the solitary cells; where they partake of the frugal meal, which they are permitted to take from the kitchen, where it was furnished for them, as they returned from the shops. After supper, they can, if they choose, read the Scriptures undisturbed, and then reflect in silence on the errors of their lives. They must not disturb their fellows by even a whisper. . . . The men attend to their business from the rising to the setting sun, and spend the night in solitude.

Sing Sing's inmates were not *entirely* alone after dark, however. French writer Alexis de Tocqueville visited the prison in 1833 and described it in his book entitled *On the Penitentiary System in the United States*. He described Warden Lynds prowling the silent galleries after lights-out, creeping on tiptoes, whip in hand, alert to any sound. An inmate talking in his sleep might have no warning as the cell door opened until Lynds was flailing at him in the dark. De Tocqueville's view of Sing Sing was dramatically opposed to Reverend Dwight's.

It was a tomb of living dead. . . . We could not realize that in this building were 950 human beings. We felt we were traversing catacombs. A faint glow from a lantern held by an inspector of the upper galleries moved slowly back and forth in the ghostly darkness. As it passed each narrow cell door we saw, in our imagination, the gateway to a sepulcher instead. . . . The watchman wore woolen moccasins over his shoes to deaden even the faint scrape of his shoes on the gallery floor. There was not a sound.

Three years before de Tocqueville's visit, in 1830, New York's commissioner of prisons, Samuel Hopkins, had already charged Lynds with brutality and administrative malfeasance, calling him an "absolute dictator" who showed no concern for the welfare of his charges. A select committee of the New York Senate formally exonerated Lynds, but he resigned in 1834, replaced by Robert Wiltse, who ran Sing Sing, in the words of one observer, as a "virtual slave camp." Wiltse in turn was replaced, in 1840, by reformer David Seymour. He relaxed the brutal discipline enjoyed by Lynds and Wiltse, only to be criticized for excess leniency and blamed for the unrest that rocked the prison throughout his four-year tenure.

Warden Lynds returned in 1844 and flogged the inmates back into docility. He got results, but there were still concerns about his honesty, including charges that he sold off "surplus" inmate rations as a means to supplement his $1,000 annual salary. Meat contractors, it was said, routinely billed the state for higher grades of meat than they delivered with Lynds kicking back half the difference and putting the rest in his pocket. Lynds also sold swill from the mess hall to local hog farmers, sometimes enriching it with food the convicts never saw. John Edmonds, New York's chief inspector of prisons, discovered that Lynds had also covered up several escapes, keeping absent inmates on the books in order to pocket the cash he received for their upkeep. Cons with extra cash could always purchase double rations on the sly, but most shared the experience of Colonel Levi Barr, an ex-army officer and attorney who served three years in Sing Sing, emerging to prove himself innocent. As Barr told the state legislature:

In my three years of confinement I ate no butter, cheese, milk, sugar, no turnips, beets, carrots, parsnips or vegetables of any kind save potatoes, no soups or strengthening drinks. I have gladly eaten the roots of shrubs and trees that I dug from the ground in which I labored. I saw no exception among the individuals around me. There were some who told me they ate the clay they worked in. At least it filled their stomachs.

Warden Lynds resigned under fire, in 1845, but criticism of Sing Sing continued, with reports of torture. "The trapeze," according to a *New York Times* report, "consists of two thin tarred ropes over a pulley. . . . The ends of these ropes are fastened to the thumbs of the convict who is to be punished. . . . The victim is lifted off his feet . . . and dangles in mid-air." Forty years later, a commissioner assigned to investigate Mount Pleasant reported that "stories of torture of prisoners in the Middle Ages sound like descriptions of luxuries in comparison with tales that have been told me of the lives some of the prisoners in Sing Sing live."

A year after that report was published, in 1914, reformer Thomas Mott Osborne became Sing Sing's warden. Two years later, Osborne brought the first psychiatrist to Sing Sing, Dr. Bernard Glueck, and inaugurated the era of "clinical criminology." In 1919, Osborne was succeeded by Lewis Edward Lawes, who ran Sing Sing for the next twenty-one years. Respected by guards and inmates alike, Lawes drastically reduced the incidence of corporal punishment. Before his retirement in 1941, he told the press, "Bit by bit, one reform at a time, the memory of Captain Lynds is being scrubbed out of the stones at Sing Sing."

It was still no country club, but it would have to do.

The first order of business for Glatman at Sing Sing was yet another psychiatric report. This one pegged his I.Q. at 130 and rated his intellectual capacity as "Very superior . . . High abstract and concrete learning capacity level enough for college education and highly skilled work." The examiner noted that Harvey was "[n]ot definitely mental defective or psychotic. Denies sex deviation but presents several schizoid states." And, once again, there was a warning. Under "Outlook," the new report described Harvey's prognosis as "Poor: should be psycho-educated and if still anti-social, should be segregated even if schizophrenia does not seem developed."

A report on Harvey's progress to the state parole board, dated August 10, 1949, pegged his I.Q. at 90— a decline of forty points in his eleven months at Sing Sing. The report itself, however, indicates that he was not exactly stagnating in stir. It reads:

He graduated from High School in Denver, Colorado, and rated in the high school levels on the achievement test. The psychologist reported average intelligence.

He was transferred here from Elmira in September of 1948 and he was enrolled in our radio shop class at that time. He had started a correspondence course in radio at Elmira with the National Schools but had no shop work while at the reformatory. He went on with the correspondence course here, completing it with excellent grades in December of 1948. At the same time he has been enrolled one-half day in our radio shop and has made average progress. He has a good grasp of radio principles but at the begin-

ning of shop work was rather sloppy because of
lack of experience. However, he has improved
considerably. He now has a good deal of shop
experience in set construction, tracing commercial receivers and diagnosing troubles. He has
built a large number of TRF circuits, super het-
erodyne circuits and amplifiers, including all
kinds of variations in the RF stage, oscillator and
output stages. He knows how to service a circuit,
using signal substitution, voltage analysis, and
has had a good deal of experience with the Meis-
sner signal tracer. It is my opinion that he is
much better qualified at this time than the average radio serviceman working at the trade for a
living, and that he could successfully discharge
his responsibility as a bench mechanic in a service shop. So far he has had very little experience
with FM and practically none with television
with the exception of theory.

He has worked here in the educational department the remaining half day in the library. At
the beginning he was not very much interested
and needed a good deal of prodding to carry on
his routine duties of racking books, etc. However
in recent months he has appeared to be more
interested and generally more cheerful. This man
was of course transferred here from Elmira Reformatory on the special project now being conducted in the hospital therefore he has some
basic personality problem that is not apparent in
his associations in the school; however, so far
as his general adjustment in this department is
concerned he has gotten along satisfactorily and
has given no outward evidence of being other
than a normal person.

Of thirty-three marks given for proficiency in radio
repair, Harvey rated five above average and twenty-

seven average grades; the two subjects in which he scored below average were "care and use of meters" and "vacuum tube voltmeters."

No detailed psychiatric records have survived from Sing Sing, but Ophelia once described that period in a single optimistic sentence. "We went to see him regularly," she told reporters, "and the doctors told us he was very cooperative and they were very pleased with the results."

We are within our rights to question how "regularly" Albert and Ophelia made the trip to New York, while residing in Denver, but author Colin Wilson agrees with Ophelia's general assessment of Harvey in jail. As Wilson puts it, citing unnamed sources, Glatman "proved a docile prisoner [and] seemed to respond to psychiatric treatment."

The key word, we understand now, would be *seemed*.

Sociopathic sex offenders learn to "play" the system early on, sometimes as children. After they have been arrested several times and spent some time in jail, as Harvey had, they know exactly what to say and how to act in any given situation, whether dealing with police, attorneys, or psychologists. Despite solemn assurances to the contrary, many sociopaths—particularly those with "very superior" intelligence—are fully capable of "beating" polygraphs, manipulating the results of psychological evaluation tests, and making therapists believe they have been "cured." One study from Washington state, published in the late 1980s, revealed that convicted rapists who graduated from a voluntary course of therapy had a *higher* recidivism rate than those who refused any treatment.

It is very possible, therefore—even predictable—that Harvey Glatman would become a "model" prisoner in Sing Sing. All we know for certain is that his parole was scheduled after two years and eight months "up the river." Good behavior had shaved six months off his minimum five-year sentence, although his supervision would continue through September 1956.

Harvey's coming out was scheduled for April 16, 1951.

It should have been a day for celebration, but the New York law was not entirely through with Glatman, yet.

5

A Frightening Environment

GLATMAN WAS NOT RELEASED FROM SING SING, IN THE normal sense, that Monday, the sixteenth of April. Officers from Yonkers were on hand and waiting for him with a warrant. He was wanted for the robbery of Thomas Staro, back in August 1946. They drove him back to Yonkers, fifteen miles due south, and lodged him in the city jail.

County Supervisor William Horan was appointed as Harvey's defense counsel. On Wednesday the eighteenth, he asked Judge Fiorillo for a brief continuance, and Glatman's hearing was postponed till Friday. Things looked bleak for Harvey, but his lawyer had an ace in the hole.

The Sixth Amendment to the U.S. Constitution guarantees a "speedy trial" to criminal defendants. It is designed, at least in theory, to prevent the innocent from languishing in jail for months or years on end without having a day in court before a jury of their peers. In practice, trials are frequently delayed at the request of the defense, while they pursue new evidence, consult experts, and so forth, but delays

71

occasioned by the state are often viewed as violations
of the "speedy trial" provision and, as such, may get
a case thrown out of court.

Attorney Horan knew that, and he used the rule to
good effect when Glatman stood before Judge Fiorillo
once again. Yonkers authorities had stalled for over
four years, when they could have prosecuted Glatman any time since August 1946. It was unconsciona-
ble and illegal. Speedy trial, indeed!

Under the law, Judge Fiorillo had no choice. The
charges were dismissed, and Harvey was a free man,
more or less. New York parole authorities approved
his plan to live in Denver, with his parents, on two
conditions. First, he would maintain the normal
check-in schedule with a Colorado parole officer.
And second, he would be referred to psychiatric
counseling on an outpatient basis.

Attorney Ira Quiat handled the arrangements in
Denver, setting up Harvey's first appointment with
Dr. Franklin Ebaugh. Glatman took various tests, results of which were described by the doctor as
follows:

ANALYSIS OF RORSCHACH:
   The Rorschach reveals an individual who is
likely to react immediately and concretely to the
circumstances he finds himself in, and can adjust
only when the environmental conditions are fa-
vorable to a good adjustment. He cannot tolerate
tensions within his personality, nor postpone immediate gratifications by organizing his efforts to
long range goals. Restless motoric activity, and
superficiality of affect and thinking characterize
this personality.
   There is a weakness in introspective activity.
He cannot visualize himself carrying out constructive activities in the reality situation, nor

does he intellectually inspect his own motives and wishes. Rather, he thinks in clichés and stereotypes, and thus avoids recognition of his own difficulties. Furthermore, there is a marked tendency to experience his difficulties as arising between the environment and himself, instead of within his own personality. He is very critical and somewhat hostile toward his environment.

The environment is also somewhat anxiety producing for him, and from the content we might hypothesize that in particular, authority figures are threatening to him. (On card 4, the father card, he sees "[a] couple of heavy feet there, looks like they might have heavy shoes on the feet.") Perhaps due to this fear of the authoritative aspect of society, he is extremely cautious and tends to withdraw from strong involvement in emotional relationships, and relates in a more passive, dependent way. He is disappointed in people, and unhappy in his relationships to them. While this attitude prevents his forming warm and satisfying personal relations, it may be an asset in this impulsive personality structure. That is, the cautious approach may be his one way of detering [sic] impulsive acting out. He will make some attempt to suppress his instinctual drives and immature moods in order to fit into his environment better.

Emotionally, he tends to put on a good front of conforming, adaptive feelings. But this has a forced quality to it and these effects intellectually derived from the context of the situation may not be appropriate to the situation. He does have some sensitivity to the feelings of others, but this may be an unpredictable trait, operent [sic] in unusual situations and not occuring [*sic*] when you expect it.

ANALYSIS OF THEMATIC APERCEPTION TEST AND
SENTENCE COMPLETION:

Family attitudes: The subject has mixed feelings toward his home and family. The home is seen as a fairly secure place which protects him from a frightening environment, and where he can be fairly [*sic*] certain that his immature needs will be immediately satisfied (story 19: "well, it is a nice little house and a nice happy little family living there. It's been snowing quite heavy but it's all drifted up around the windows and the roof. They're all stocked up with food so they'll just enjoy themselves"). However, there is a dependency-hostility conflict in the family situation. He may demand the attention and affection that he needs by getting into serious difficulty, and thus indirectly punishing the family (story 5: "she looks a little worried about something. Possibly her kid could be sick and she's looking in the door to see how he is. It's one of those— maybe pneumonia or something. It gives everybody a good scare and everybody is worried, but in the next few days, the peak of the thing is passed and he starts to get well again"). His anxiety about feelings of rejection lead[s] to a hostile need to demand attention and immediate satisfaction of his wishes to reassure himself that he was not rejected (as a child, my greatest fear was *being turned down*).

Of the parents, he is much more closely attached to the mother. He sees her as a kindly, solicitous individual who is supportive to him and concerned about his problems. (My mother is *very good and generous*). She may try to restrain him, but he recognizes this as ineffectual, and can openly express hostility about any restrictions she might place on his behavior (when he was punished by his mother, *he sulked*). The impression from the stories is that his mother is overly indulgent with him, and so needs to retain his affection that she has always had difficulty in setting limits for him (most mothers *are too possessive*). He tends to empathize with his mother and identify with her role, principally because she is most concerned about him (story 6: "there's a mother and their son. He has some kind of hard decision to make about some grave problem, and they're looking kind of worried about what the decision should be.")

There is considerable [*sic*] greater psychological distance between his father and him. He is much less accepting of his father's dominance than his mother's sympathetic empathy with his problems. He sees his father as a superior and somewhat punitive person who makes him feel inadequate at times (story 7: "well, that could be a father talking to his son, looks like he's giving him a piece of advice about something . . . so he probably will take the advice and find out that it was pretty good advice.") The father's inconsistency in role, sometimes punitive, sometimes indulgent, is all the more threatening to him since he can never be sure what to expect from a father figure (most fathers *are not very strict*; fathers *can be very strict sometimes*). He can't directly express his hostility toward his father, and relates to him in a passive way, seeking dependency on him and reassurance that he is not a threatening individual.

Attitude toward love, sex and marriage: Perhaps due to his difficulty in identifying with his father, and inability to attain reassurance that his father is not hostile to him, he is threatened by masculinity or possible loss of masculine status (story 2: "the son was killed".) He attempts to deny these fears, but does relate to men in a passive way, making dependency on them as a way [sic] of reducing his anxieties.

He feels inadequate in heterosexual situations, probably due to his more basic feelings of inadequacy as a male. He verbalizes this feelin[g] on card 13 as one of "helplessness and frustration". He is immature and self oriented in his heterosexual relationships. He primarily seeks self gratification and is unlikely to remain constant to one love object. He is hostile toward women, but this hostility does cause some guilt feelings.

Social attitudes: The principle motivation apparent in this area is a need for admiration from others. He is somewhat exhibitionistic (story 17: ["]He has probably broken some kind of record for getting up to the top and is feeling pretty good about things. Probably running through his mind is the acclaim that goes with success and he's anticipating it"). He tends to blame others for difficulties (I used to feel I was being held back by *other people.*[)] Authority figures are expected to be unpleasant, and while he recognizes social more[s], he tends to feel in conflict with them. He seems to identify with those people of marginal social status and can feel really comfortable only in this type of group.

Attitude toward work and planning: The subject desires high attainment, but he tends to give up active effort toward goals in favor of more satisfying fantasies about great success (story 1: "He probably isn't playing the violin too good. He's looking at it sort of wistful, daydreaming making plans how he's going to be a great violinist in the future.") He is essentially a pleasure oriented individual who is easily discouraged by any hard work involved in attaining a goal, and who lacks persistence in his motivation (If I think the job is too hard for me, *I quit*). Lack of success is rationalized as being due to the job or the boss rather than himself.

Techniques of adjustment: This is an immature individual who doesn't accept responsibilities or restrictions very easily. His primary motivation is to find a secure environment which will satisfy all his needs without placing any restraint on him (He often wished *he could do anything he wanted to*. I felt most dissatisfied when *I had to wait too long.*[)] A dependency-hostility conflict is seen. He cannot accept dependency relationships which would satisfy his needs for security and passive gratification because he becomes hostile when the person on whom he is dependent sets any kinds of limits. Emotions are superficial, easily and impulsively expressed, and short in duration. Some anxieties and minimal guilt feelings are seen, and may be an asset in detering [*sic*] immediate acting out.

He perceived himself as "in trouble" and "having things tough", but sees these difficulties as arising from the environment rather than himself. He tends to feel rejected by most of the people he encounters, and much of his acting out may be motivated by a need to gain the attention of others and proof of their affection. It is also motivated by a need to prove that he is an adequate individual.

Dr. Ebaugh diagnosed Glatman as a "secondary psychopath" and recommended that Harvey return "at regular monthly intervals." The suggestion was apparently ignored, since Ebaugh wondered, following Glatman's arrest for multiple murders in 1958, "if such tragedies could be prevented even with constant psychiatric supervision." By that time, Dr. Ebaugh had also apparently revised his opinion of Glatman, telling California probation officers, "I must say he was relatively free of all symptoms, although my diagnosis was clearly that of a character neurosis."

The environment that so threatened Harvey was the family home on Kearney Street, where he resided with his parents. Love it or hate it, he could never fully tear himself away, listing 1133 Kearney as his "home address" as late as his final arrest in California, when he had been living in Los Angeles for nearly two years.

Employment is typically a condition of parole, but Harvey was jobless for three and one-half years after his release from Sing Sing. Based on Dr. Ebaugh's findings, it seems probable that Glatman shied away from seeking work, but Ophelia predictably had a different take on the situation. As she explained it to probation officers, years later, Harvey "could not find employment because no bonding company would give him bond." Most jobs, of course, require no bond. It seems more likely, in the context of his personality, that Glatman was content to while away his days and let Ophelia care for him.

It should not be supposed that he was happy, though. Glatman would later tell probation officers that he "twice contemplated suicide" while he was on parole. The first time, he "considered" eating rat poison, "but gave up this idea because he couldn't stand the odor." Sometime later, he allegedly decided he should gas himself in the family garage. If we accept his version of events, he took the first step, sitting in his car, with the garage door closed and engine running, but he "lost his courage." As noted in the 1958 report, "He says simply that he does not have the 'guts for suicide.' " The interviewer blamed his suicide attempts on "outgrowths of despondency" that sprang from Harvey's failure to obtain a job.

There was a death on Kearney Street, in 1952, but it was Albert Glatman, finally done in by his long-running diabetes, on October seventeenth. Feldman Mortuary, at 17th and York, handled the send-off on Sunday the nineteenth, followed by interment at Mount Nebo cemetery. Harvey may have missed his father, on some level; at the very least, he knew enough to make the proper noises and to act bereaved. Ophelia was already working the millinery trade, and she soon opened a small hat shop of her own, to make ends meet, but that meant less time with her son.

At least while she was working, Harvey would be forced to take care of himself.

In October 1954, two years after Albert Glatman's death, Harvey found work as a butcher at Benny's Market, in the suburb of Aurora, east of Denver. The job paid sixty-five dollars a week, and Glatman stuck it out for ten months before leaving, for reasons unknown, in August 1955. Thereafter, he was jobless again until July 1956, when he went to work as a combination clerk and deliveryman at Rice's Market, for $1.25 an hour. The new job was closer to home, a mere eleven blocks north of the Glatman house on Kearney Street, but it still didn't please him, and Harvey was gone before Christmas.

No detailed record of Glatman's five years on
parole has survived, but his transition was briefly
described some years after the fact, in a summary transmitted from New York to authorities at
San Quentin Prison. The relevant passage reads as
follows:

When this subject was paroled from Sing Sing
and after disposition of the Yonkers warrant, he
returned to the home of his parents in Denver,
Colorado. He remained there until about October 1954 when he was permitted to change his
residence and obtain his own living quarters, as
he had been having some unidentified difficulty
with his mother. It was felt at the time that the
subject should be allowed more freedom, away
from his parents.

This was not a serious breach with the mother
as it is noted that later for about a month he
stayed with her while he was looking for other
living quarters closer to his employment. It is
further reported that he frequently visited his
mother and had meals with the family.

A review of his parole history shows that the
parolee's employment adjustment was quite er-
ratic. Most of his work was with various radio
and T.V. concerns and he took a course in the
Adult Education System in Denver along this
line, although we do not have a statement that
he completed this course. He also worked as a
mattress filler, a butcher, a truck driver and ship-
ping clerk. He apparently had difficulty in ad-
justing with some of his employers. One report
state[s] that he was fired for insubordination and
arrogant behavior.

Job troubles and lack of psychiatric treatment aside, Glatman was discharged from parole, free and clear, on September 7, 1956. As far as New York authorities were concerned, his debt to society had been paid in full. Colorado police, meanwhile, had managed to forget the niggling matter of his 1946 parole violation, which could have sent him back to prison for another four years on the Denver conviction.

For the first time in over a decade, Harvey was free. He could go where he wanted and do what he chose, without answering to courts or parole officers.

Where should go? What should he do? In January 1957, Glatman had a brainstorm. He was moving to Los Angeles.

6

Psycho Paths

By the time Harvey Glatman arrived, in January 1957, Los Angeles was well on its way to becoming America's third largest city—or, some might have said, the world's largest parking lot. It often seemed that *everyone* in L.A. was on wheels, from toddlers to the hopelessly decrepit, shiny chrome gas-guzzlers jamming streets and highways, turning the very sky beige with a mixture of vehicle exhaust and factory waste that some local wag had labeled "smog."

Los Angelenos had, in fact, been debating the state of their air for over a decade, since the end of World War II, and another year would pass before city fathers admitted the smog was claiming lives. Still, they insisted that L.A. had a handle on the problem. Air pollution watchdogs were confident that they would reach "the turning point in the war on smog" by mid-summer, while the new freeway system, sprawling like a giant octopus across the L.A. basin and beyond, was meant to channel traffic more efficiently and clear the city streets. (Unknown to Angelenos in those days, one of the freeway construction

workers, brooding Mack Edwards, was also a homicidal pedophile. By 1956, he had already planted
three victims, aged eight to thirteen, in the founda-
tions of L.A.'s freeway system, returning by day to
pave over their graves.)

Harvey Glatman, for his part, was more than content to get lost in the crowd. Living on his own for
the first time, without parents or jailers to make his
decisions for him, it helped to have cover. A social
faux pas meant less than nothing in L.A. If Harvey
embarrassed himself before strangers, the chances
were good that he would never see them again.
Groping his way toward a semblance of maturity, at
age twenty-nine, he needed all the help he could get.

And he needed a job.

To that end, Glatman enrolled at the National
Technical School in L.A., studying television repair.
It was a logical extension of his studies at Elmira and
Sing Sing, in the field of radio repair. TV was the
wave of the future, and Harvey meant to keep up
with the times, learning everything he could about
the device some critics were already calling the
"boob tube."

Television, more than any other trademark of the
era, was the growth industry of the 1950s. The first
crude sets had been invented, more or less simultaneously, by American researcher Vladimir Zworykin
and British counterpart J. L. Baird, back in 1923. Another American, C. F. Jenkins, produced the first
practical TV set four years later, and General Electric
aired its first experimental program in 1928, broad-
casting three days a week over station WGY-TV in
Schenectady, New York. RCA's first TV sets went on
sale in 1939, $625 for a twelve-inch screen, while NBC
produced the first televised sportscast that same year.
In 1941, the first TV commercial advertised a Bulova
watch, its manufacturers paying nine dollars for

twenty seconds of air time. Howdy Doody, roller derby, and professional wrestling hit the airwaves in 1947, Groucho Marx and Superman three years later. In 1951, NBC and CBS both broadcast the Kefauver Committee hearings on organized crime. A year later, Jack Webb began demanding "just the facts," in *Dragnet*, while Adlai Stevenson caught hell for pre-empting *I Love Lucy* for a presidential campaign speech. The rest was history: Army-McCarthy hearings and the first Oscar broadcast in 1954; Lawrence Welk, *Gunsmoke*, and the Mickey Mouse Club in 1955; Elvis Presley gyrating on Ed Sullivan's show in 1956.

Television was booming, and no anxious criticism could turn the tide. In 1946, only 8,000 American homes boasted TV sets; ten years later, there were 35 million, ten percent of those in Los Angeles. So many Americans were sitting home at night, watching old movies and sitcoms on TV, that national theater attendance was slashed nearly in half, plummeting from 90 million to 46 million per week.

Harvey had found himself a trade where he could grow in concert with the industry. And television suited him in other ways, as well.

It was, above all else, a *visual* experience.

And Harvey liked to watch.

Elvis, Howdy Doody, and Captain Kangaroo were all very nice, but much of the news conveyed by television in those days—as now—was grim in the extreme. On the last day of June 1956, a United Airlines DC-7 collided with one of TWA's Super Constellations over the Grand Canyon, plunging 128 passengers and crew to a screaming death. Less than a month later, the Italian luxury liner *Andrea Doria* was rammed by a Swedish steamer off Nantucket, carrying fifty-two souls to the bottom. Thirteen days later, on August seventh, a convoy of trucks loaded with dynamite exploded in the heart of Cali, Colombia, leveling eight city blocks and killing some 1,200 people. The echoes from that blast were still reverberating when an anti-Communist revolt broke out in Hungary, bringing Soviet tanks and artillery into the streets. Thousands were dead when the smoke cleared, but the Russians got a dose of their own medicine the following year, when a nuclear weapons plant blew up near Sverdlovsk, in the Ural Mountains, contaminating an area the size of Rhode Island with 50 million curies of radiation. In Warrenton, Missouri, more than 150 elderly patients were lost when fire swept through the Katie Jane Memorial Home, on February seventeenth, but that was nothing by comparison to Hurricane Audrey, killing an estimated 550 Gulf Coast residents in June. Three months later, in West Pakistan, a speeding passenger train met one loaded with oil, incinerating an estimated 300 victims.

One thing that worried most Americans far more than train and airplane crashes, though, light years beyond the weather or the Asian flu, was crime. To many, it appeared that the United States had gotten so wrapped up in international affairs, since 1939 or so, that leaders pledged to keep the house in order had, in fact, let the domestic front go straight to hell.

Everyone knew there had been gangsters in America, for generations, but only J. Edgar Hoover seriously questioned that regional gangs, spawned by Prohibition in the 1920s, had become increasingly well-organized, interdependent, in the previous thirty years. Even Hoover was forced to sit up and take notice in 1957, though, as events on the East Coast demanded national attention. In Washington, Senator John McClellan's Select Committee on Improper Activities in the Labor or Management Field launched a series of televised hearings that would span thirty months, driving crooked Dave Beck from the helm of the Teamsters Union, introducing Americans to his successor, Jimmy Hoffa—and to the star-crossed Kennedy brothers. Syndicate "prime minister" Frank Costello was grazed by an assassin's bullet on May second, at his apartment house on Central Park West, and scribbled notes found in his pocket documented Mafia interest in Nevada's legalized casino gambling. Five months later, Albert Anastasia, the reputed "lord high executioner of Murder, Incorporated," was riddled with bullets in a barber's chair, at the Park Sheraton Hotel. Three weeks after that, fifty-eight notorious *mafiosi* were arrested at a get-together in Apalachin, New York, while an unknown number of others escaped through the woods.

Hoover's FBI, while still officially denying the existence of a Mafia, immediately launched a new "Top Hoodlum Program," the all-powerful director commanding his agents to identify ten leading gangsters—no more, no less—in each city hosting a bureau field office. There should have been no problem filling out the roster in Los Angeles, where runty mobster Mickey Cohen had just been convicted of income tax evasion and headed off for a short stint in federal prison. He left behind a chaotic situation, racked by violence between his own cosmopolitan mob, operating on behalf of Eastern masters, and the Sicilian crowd led by Jack Dragna, the self-styled "Al Capone of Los Angeles." In fact, Dragna's bunch more closely resembled the gang that couldn't shoot straight. They had muffed no less than half a dozen attempts to liquidate Cohen, and their bumbling, small-time operations in dope and extortion led even fellow Sicilians to brand them "the Mickey Mouse Mafia." Jack Dragna died in 1957, passing the torch to even less competent successors—among them

Jimmy "The Weasel" Fratianno, who would later turn canary for the feds to save his own skin.

The mob was interesting, of course, but few grass-roots Americans saw syndicated crime as a major threat to their security. After all, had not the late Ben Siegel spoken for his fellow gangsters when he told the press, "We only kill each other"?

There were more disturbing things to think about, below the Mason-Dixon Line, where America's imperfect melting pot was on the verge of boiling over. A U.S. Supreme Court decision had turned up the heat, in 1954, demanding that the nation's Jim Crow schools be integrated "with all deliberate speed," and while Dixie's all-white leaders were pinning NEVER! buttons onto their lapels, a few daring blacks took the high court at its word. Some tried to vote, while others purchased homes in segregated neighborhoods, or moved from the back of the bus toward the front.

The reaction from members of the Ku Klux Klan, the White Citizens Council, and similar groups, was swift and predictable. On New Year's Eve of 1956, nightriders bombed a black home in Birmingham, Alabama. Five days later, a newly integrated school was bombed for the fourth time in strife-torn Clinton, Tennessee. The week after that, a desegregated bus was fire-bombed in Chattanooga. Before the month was out, bombs wrecked four churches and half a dozen homes in Montgomery, where a year-long black boycott of city buses had nearly brought the city to its knees. By year's end, another twenty-eight racist bombings had been logged from Alabama, Delaware, the Carolinas, Georgia, Tennessee, and Texas; white mobs rioted around desegregated schools in Little Rock and Nashville; blacks and white integrationists were beaten or wounded by gunfire in at least four states; in Birmingham, four Klansmen kidnapped Edward Aaron, a black pedestrian, and castrated him as part of a KKK initiation rite, afterward pouring turpentine into his wound.

Grim news, indeed, but it was all down South, and everybody knew how crude "those people" were. More frightening by far, for most Americans above what Klansmen liked to call the "Smith & Wesson Line," were the reports of mayhem among young people, advertised on television and in Congress as a crime wave of unprecedented magnitude.

Hyperbole aside, there clearly *was* a problem with America's teenagers in those years, which would be sanitized a generation later and regurgitated on the tube as *Happy Days*. Robert Lindner, a retired prison psychologist, set the tone for the Fifties in two books, *Rebel Without a Cause* and *Must You Conform?*—to which countless teens replied with a resounding "No!" Swivel-hipped Elvis Presley was bad enough, but what were Mr. and Mrs. America to make of young thugs in leather jackets, sniffing glue and setting homeless bums on fire in New York City, roaring across country on motorcycles, brawling in the streets of towns like tiny Hollister, California?

That incident, from 1947, was filmed six years later, as *The Wild One*, with teen idol Marlon Brando cast as Johnny, the leader of the pack. His gang trashed "Wrightsville" in the movie, wreaking havoc in the lives of ordinary, working-class Americans and rolling up big box office in the process.

Another Hollywood icon in those days was James Dean, a transplanted Midwesterner, bisexual and sadomasochist, described by director Elia Kazan as "a pudding of hatred." Dean idolized Brando, trailing him to cocktail parties dressed as Johnny from *The Wild One*, until Brando finally took him aside and asked if he "realized he was sick." By September 30, 1955, Dean was dead, killed in the sports car he had christened "Little Bastard," still four days from the release of his second motion picture. That film, *Rebel Without a Cause*, said it all for teen angst in the Fifties. A year after Dean's death, the studio was still receiving 2,000 letters a week from his fans, addressed to a corpse.

There were no teen idols in J. Edgar Hoover's America, though. In February 1957, the FBI director advocated publishing the names of "young thugs" so that righteous communities could give them a taste of their own medicine. They were not "bad children," he insisted, but rather "young criminals." Congress seemed to agree, but their solution was somewhat different, banning interstate transport of switchblade knives as a means of wiping out juvenile crime.

Worse even than juvenile delinquents, though, were the crazies who began to surface in America, throughout the 1950s, claiming lives at random, for no good reason at all. They maimed and killed without reason, in crimes devoid of common sense, lacking even the delinquent's lame excuse of immaturity.

George Metesky was fifty-four in January 1957, when Connecticut authorities arrested him for a series of thirty-two bombings around New York City, which had injured fifteen persons in the previous sixteen years. On January 30, Metesky was indicted in Manhattan on forty-seven counts of attempted murder, endangering lives, damaging buildings, and possession of bombs. His excuse: a grudge against Consolidated Edison, for whom he worked in 1931, because he was not compensated for tuberculosis, allegedly contracted through inhaling toxic fumes on the job.

Another New Yorker, John Francis Roche, was arrested in April 1954, for the rape and fatal beating of a fourteen-year-old girl. In custody, he confessed to five other murders, including those of a Manhattan cab driver, a sailor, and three more female victims, ranging in age from thirteen to eighty-five. Convicted and sentenced to death that November, Roche was electrocuted at Sing Sing in January 1956.

While Roche hated women, Ohio's John Wable nursed a curious grudge against long-haul truck drivers. He liked to creep up on them as they slept in their rigs and shoot them in the head at close range with a .32-caliber pistol. Two truckers were dead, with a third gravely wounded, before Wable was jailed at Uniontown, Pennsylvania, in August 1953, on unrelated charges of felonious assault. In custody, he freely confessed to the turnpike shootings, but jailers dismissed him as a "screwball" and released him on bail. By the time they recognized their mistake, two months later, Wable had gone to ground in New Mexico. Arrested there on October twelfth, he was convicted of murder in March 1954 and sentenced to die, keeping his date with Pennsylvania's electric chair six months later. To the bitter end, no one could say exactly why he killed, or how he chose his targets.

Shooting truckers was one thing, but killing helpless children was another, most particularly when the murderer was still at large. Chicago residents were horrified, in October 1955, by the savage deaths of three young boys, found in a ditch near the Des Plaines River, in the Robinson Woods Forest Preserve. The victims included two brothers, thirteen-year-old John Schuessler and eleven-year-old Anton Schuessler, together with a friend, fourteen-year-old Robert Peterson. All three had been beaten and strangled to death, following apparent sexual molestation. More than forty confessions were logged in the case, but all came from cranks with a yen for attention, and police were still seeking the killer, in vain, when teenage sisters Barbara and Patricia Grimes were beaten to death in January 1957, their naked, frozen bodies recovered from a roadside ditch in Du Page County. A Chicago dishwasher confessed in that case, but his statement later was thrown out when it was revealed as a product of police "third-degree" tactics. Eight months later, on August fifteenth, fifteen-year-old model Judith Anderson was reported missing. Her dismembered remains were subsequently fished out of Montrose Harbor where they had been dumped in two rusty oil drums. Police tried everything from backroom torture to psychics, but the string of slayings remained unsolved.

California, meanwhile, had yet to emerge as "Psycho Central," contributing some ten percent of the world's serial killers, but there was still no shortage of crazies in L.A.

One of the first had tipped his hand in 1944, while Harvey Glatman was still prowling apartments in Denver. The grim story began on November fourteenth, when an average-looking couple checked into L.A.'s Barclay Hotel, on Skid Row. They registered as Mr. and Mrs. Otto Steve Wilson, from Shelbyville, Indiana, and the Barclay's desk clerk thought nothing of it when Mr. Wilson checked out alone the next morning, assuming the wife had already gone out to their car. Four hours later, he was proved wrong, when the hotel maid ran screaming from the Wilsons' room. A woman's naked and dismembered body had been stuffed into the closet. Both breasts, both arms, and one leg had been severed, while random slashes and bite marks covered the body. Homicide investigators managed to identify her as twenty-eight-year-old Virgie Lee Griffin.

Detectives were still picking over that crime scene an hour later, when they caught their second report from another hotel, only four blocks away. This time, the killer had registered with his victim as Mr. and Mrs. O. S. Watson, checking in around midday. When he left the hotel, a few hours later, Mr. Watson made a point of asking the desk clerk to give his wife a wakeup call at 2:30 P.M. When she failed to answer the phone, the clerk went to investigate and found the battered, mutilated corpse of thirty-eight-year-old Lillian Johnson.

Police had a clear description of their man, from the two hotel clerks, and an all-points bulletin was issued. Several hours later, a beat patrolman detoured through one of the neighborhood saloons and spotted a man who matched that description, seated with a woman in a corner booth. On closer inspection, the officer noted apparent bloodstains on the suspect's hands. The capper came when Mr. X identified himself as Otto Steve Wilson, from Shelbyville, Indiana.

Within two hours of his arrest, Wilson was ready to talk. It turned out that for years, he had been harboring a morbid urge to "look inside a female to see what made her tick." His wife had left him, Wilson said, after he crept up behind her one evening and slashed her buttocks with a razor blade, lapping blood from the wounds. The U.S. Navy had discharged him on a "Section 8," for mental problems, when he was caught drinking blood on his job as a hospital orderly. Wilson blamed the two murders on "pure cussedness" and pled guilty at his arraignment, later withdrawing the plea at trial in favor of a defense claiming innocence by reason of insanity. A jury didn't buy it, and he was convicted of first-degree murder in June 1945 and was executed in San Quentin's gas chamber fifteen months later.

Almost as strange as Wilson's crimes were the "Bird of Paradise murders," a decade later in Los Angeles. The case drew its popular nickname from the first of several crimes, on February 15, 1955. Karil Graham, a thirty-eight-year-old divorcée who looked ten years younger, was found naked and beaten to death in her cliffside home, in L.A.'s Wilshire-Westlake district. The house had been ransacked, as if by a burglar, and the clumsy intruder left numerous handprints behind. Detectives and reporters alike were impressed with the painting of a colorful, exotic bird that brightened one wall of the murder room, and the sobriquet stuck.

The prints from Graham's home led nowhere, and detectives were still hoping for a break when the prowler struck again, on May twenty-seventh, clubbing and choking a twenty-five-year-old Rumanian exchange student within an inch of her life. Eight months later, almost to the day, another young woman in the Westlake district was attacked in her sleep, stripped and beaten with a blunt instrument, but her screams drove the prowler away before he could manage to rape her. On February eighth, a nineteen-year-old receptionist was clubbed senseless in her apartment, again in the same neighborhood. On May twenty-fourth, three blocks from the Graham murder scene, Laura Lindsay was beaten to death in her home where drawers and closets had been rifled by what seemed to be a very inefficient burglar.

This time, at least, detectives had a witness. One of Lindsay's neighbors reported a suspicious stranger near the scene, Caucasian, mid-twenties, five foot ten, around 150 pounds. It was better than nothing, but still little help, in a teeming city like Los Angeles. Detectives reckoned they would have to count on luck and try to catch their quarry in the act.

On June 9, 1956, they did just that. Twenty-seven-year-old Donald Bashor was surprised by a stakeout team, while breaking into a Westlake district home.

He fled on foot but was shot in the arm and captured. A background check on the Glendale native revealed that he had deserted from the U.S. Navy in 1948 and had served a year in the brig before he was dishonorably discharged. A string of burglary arrests followed, landing Bashor in the L.A. County jail by 1950. He escaped and fled to Oregon, where he was picked up on another charge and served a year before he was returned to California to complete his former sentence. Paroled in January 1954, he had been breaking into women's homes ever since—an estimated forty burglaries in all.

Bashor admitted stealing but denied a role in any murders, that is, until his prints were matched up to the Lindsay murder scene. Once he received that news, he copped to Graham's death as well. On the first day of his trial, in October 1956, he surprised the court by rising from his seat and saying, "Let's get this over with. I'm guilty." Bashor was sentenced to die and paid for his crimes with his life in October 1957.

As bad as they were, though, neither Wilson nor Bashor could hold a candle to gap-toothed Stephen Nash, a sadistic psychopath arrested at age thirty-three, in 1956, for stabbing a ten-year-old boy to death, under the Santa Monica pier. The coroner counted twenty-eight wounds in little Larry Rice's corpse. In custody, Nash proudly confessed ten more slayings, mostly "bums" and transients, billing himself as "the King of the Killers." Still, for all his hatred of homeless men, it was the slaying of a child that was his grand achievement.

"He was a kid," Nash told detectives. "It was all there in front of him, his whole life, sex, fun, all of it. Why should he have it, when I never did? I took it all away from him. Besides, I never killed a kid before. I wanted to see how it felt."

Incredulous, one homicide detective asked if Nash had ever thought about the grief he caused his victim's family. Nash replied, sneering, "If I gave a shit about the parents, I never would have killed the kid."

Convicted on the basis of his own confession, Stephen Nash was still in jail when Harvey reached L.A., but he was running out of time. The gas chamber silenced his mocking voice forever, in August 1959.

And there were unsolved crimes aplenty in L.A., dating back to the late 1940s and a string of brutal sex murders that had climaxed with the grisly mutilation of sometime prostitute and porn star Elizabeth Short, a.k.a. the "Black Dahlia." A half-dozen women had been beaten and slashed to death in the space of a year, and while authorities officially denied any link between the various crimes, reporters still tagged them "the Black Dahlia murders."

When it came to sheer craziness, though, no killer from the postwar era could hold a candle to Wisconsin's Ed Gein. A simple-minded handyman in Plainfield, Wisconsin, Gein may be America's most famous murderer, although his name is seldom heard and barely recognized today. Four decades have passed since he first made headlines, but he is still with us in spirit with his crimes inspiring such films as *Psycho* and its sequels, *The Texas Chainsaw Massacre* and *Silence of the Lambs*.

Ed Gein (rhymes with "seen") was born August 8, 1906, at LaCrosse, Wisconsin, but his family soon moved to a farm outside Plainfield. His father held jobs as a tanner and carpenter when he wasn't working the farm, and Gein's mother emerged as the dominant parent, making most of the family decisions on her own. Devoutly religious, she warned her two sons against premarital sex, but Ed later recalled that she was "not as strong" in her opposition to masturbation. Gein's father died in 1940, and his brother Henry was lost four years later, while fighting a marsh fire. Ed's mother suffered a stroke that same year, and a second one killed her in 1945, following an argument with one of her neighbors. Alone at last, Gein nailed her bedroom shut and set about redecorating the rest of the house in his own inimitable style.

From childhood, Gein had been ambiguous about his masculinity, considering amputation of his penis on several occasions. With Christine Jorgenson much in the headlines, he considered transsexual surgery, but the process was costly and frightening. There must be other ways, Gein thought, of "turning female" on a part-time basis.

Between 1950 and 1954, Gein haunted three local cemeteries, opening an estimated nine or ten graves in his nocturnal raids. He might remove whole corpses or settle for choice bits and pieces; a few bodies were later returned to their resting places, but Gein recalled that there were "not too many." At home, he used the ghoulish relics as household decorations. Skulls were mounted on the bedposts, severed skullcaps serving Gein as bowls. He fashioned hanging mobiles out of noses, lips, and labia, sometimes sporting a belt of nipples. Human skin was variously utilized for lamp shades, waste baskets, and the upholstery of chairs.

The choicer bits were specially preserved for Gein to wear at home. For ceremonial occasions, such as dancing underneath full moons, he wore a human scalp and face, a skinned-out "vest" complete with breasts, and female genitalia strapped above his own. By "putting on" another sex and personality, Gein seemed to find a measure of contentment, but his resurrection raids eventually failed to satisfy a deeper need, and he set out in search of fresher game.

No one is certain, to this day, how many living victims Gein dispatched before he was arrested. Judge Robert Gollmar thought Ed might have killed his brother, inasmuch as there was no autopsy or investigation of Henry's death. However that may be, a stronger case for murder is the disappearance of a man named Travis and his unknown male companion, last seen around the time they hired Gein as a hunting guide. One victim's jacket was recovered from the woods near Plainfield, and while Gein professed to know the whereabouts of victim Travis, blaming his death on "a neighbor," police never followed up on the lead.

On December 8, 1954, fifty-one-year-old Mary Hogan disappeared from the tavern she managed in Pine Grove, Wisconsin. Authorities found a pool of blood on the floor, an overturned chair, and one spent cartridge from a .32-caliber pistol. Foul play was the obvious answer, and while deputies recall Ed Gein as a suspect in the case, no charges were filed at the time. (Three years later, the shell casing would be matched to a pistol found in Gein's home.)

On November 15, 1957, fifty-eight-year-old Bernice Worden vanished from her Plainfield hardware store under strikingly similar circumstances. There was blood on the floor, a trail of it leading out back, where the victim's truck had last been seen. Worden's son recalled that Gein had asked his mother for a date, and on the day before she disappeared, Ed mentioned that he needed antifreeze. A sales receipt for antifreeze was found inside the store, and deputies went looking for their suspect. What they found would haunt them all for the remainder of their lives.

Inside a shed, behind Gein's house, Bernice Worden's headless body hung from the rafters, gutted like a deer, the genitals carved out. A tour of the

cluttered house left searchers stunned. Worden's
heart was found in a skillet, on the stove, while her
head had been turned into a macabre ornament, with
twine attached to nails inserted in both ears. Her
other organs occupied a box, set aside to molder in
a corner. Deputies surveyed Gein's decorations and
his "costumes," counting skins from ten heads in one
cardboard drum and taking hasty inventory of imple-
ments fashioned from human bones.

Also discovered in the search were two "fresh"
vaginas, removed from younger women, which had
never been embalmed. Judge Gollmar suggests that
one likely victim was Evelyn Hartley, abducted from
LaCrosse on a night when Gein was visiting relatives,
two blocks from her home. A pool of blood was
found in her garage after she vanished, the trail dis-
appearing at curbside. Mary Weckler was reported
missing a short time later, from Jefferson, Wisconsin,
with a white Ford seen in the area. When searchers
scoured Gein's property, they found a white Ford
sedan on the premises, though no one in Plainfield
could ever recall Ed driving such a car.

In custody, Gein readily confessed the Hogan and
Worden murders, along with a series of unreported
grave robberies. Confirmation of the latter was obtained by opening three graves: in one, the corpse
had been mutilated as described by Gein; the second
held no corpse at all; a casket in the third showed
pry marks, but the body was intact, as Ed remembered. On January 16, 1958, a judge found Gein mentally incompetent for trial and packed him off to
Central State Hospital, at Waupun, Wisconsin, where
he would live out the rest of his days.

Harvey Glatman, meanwhile, was busy settling
down to the business of life in L.A. According to the
job history included with his California rap sheet,

Glatman held "various short-term jobs" before going
to work as a TV repairman, in August 1957. British
authors Colin Wilson and Donald Seaman allege that
Harvey's mother "set him up" in the TV repair business, but the fact is that he never had a shop of
his own, but instead he worked for others—when he
worked at all—for an average of two dollars an hour.

It was enough, sometimes with help from home, to
cover the rent on a small Melrose Avenue apartment.
Landlord Irma Hurst recalled Glatman as a model
tenant, though he had a tendency to bring his work
home with him. "The place was always filled with
broken radios and TV sets when I saw it," she later
said. "He was very finicky about his car, I remember,
and he complained bitterly because a dog we kept
around the apartment house would soil the tires."

The TV repair job left him time for diversion, and
Harvey soon picked up where he had left off in high
school, with his photographic hobby. Irma Hurst
would never see a photo hanging on the walls in
Harvey's flat; afterward she told the press, "There
was nothing to indicate that Harvey cared about
photography."

But Glatman kept his hobby to himself. This time,
it was strictly a means to an end.

Los Angeles, in 1957, was the home of many
"models" who would never show up on a fashion
runway or the cover of a magazine. They posed for
money, granted, but their rates were reasonably low,
and the resemblance ended there. Most often, they
were dressed in skimpy lingerie, when they wore
anything at all. Some worked at home, while others
posed in "studios," including some with rental cameras and film on hand for shutterbugs who turned
up unprepared. We may assume that some of the
young women so engaged were also prostitutes, as

the majority of "escorts" are today, but others kept
their distance from the clients.

What you saw was what you didn't get.

Harvey could only guess what he was missing. His
experience with females, at age twenty-nine, was limited to hit-and-run encounters, hasty fumbling in the
dark. None of his victims had been raped, outside of
Glatman's fantasies. Indeed, we have no reason to
believe that he had ever seen a naked woman in the
flesh before he hit L.A.

Now, all he had to do was scan the Yellow Pages,
let his fingers do the walking through the classifieds,
to see his fantasies made flesh. A host of small-time
models, would-be starlets, advertised their services,
available to anyone with cash in hand. It was a peep-
er's paradise, a voyeur's smorgasbord.

The camera served a triple function in such enter-
prises. First, it lent legitimacy to a voyeuristic game
that may have drawn attention from police, in 1957,
if it weren't disguised as "art." Second, the photos
that resulted from a "shoot," preserved by the photographers, allowed them to relive the incident, elaborate the fantasy, while masturbating to their hearts'
content. Today, we know the game as *pictophilia*, a
kind of voyeurism, wherein sexual excitement is at-
tained by snapping photographs or viewing them,
after the fact.

And finally, at least in Harvey Glatman's case, the
camera was a shield, something for him to hide behind. In semipublic settings, he dared not produce a
weapon, tie the models up, and physically abuse
them as he would have liked to do. The camera gave
him distance, shrank the living models to a manage-
able size, and let him steal, if not their souls, at least
their sexuality.

A blessed side effect was that the camera also hid
his face from those he lusted after. Posing under

lights, blinded by flashbulbs, going through their moves mechanically, none of them could observe the jug-eared, blushing geek who focused on their breasts, thighs and buttocks while sweating through his shirt and shifting awkwardly to ease the pressure in his shorts.

Instead of realizing Glatman's dreams, though, snapping hands-off photos ultimately made things worse, reminding Glatman of the pleasures he had yet to share. The tension built inside of him, day after day.

Los Angeles was torture for a twenty-nine-year-old, unwilling virgin.

By the summer months of 1957, Harvey had his mind made up to change all that.

And soon.

7

True Detective

AS SUMMER 1957 ROLLED AROUND, HARVEY WAS SICK AND tired of waiting for Miss Right. The lethal combination of his record, looks, and personality—the painful, tongue-tied shyness that conspired to silence him with any female other than Ophelia—barred him from the kind of give-and-take relationships that others took for granted.

Naked models helped, but they were all for show. When he ran out of time and money, Glatman still went home alone. The photos helped a little, too, but they were lifeless things with no stories of their own. He needed more.

This time, at least, he had a plan.

If women didn't like him, if they would not give him what he needed—what he craved—then Harvey would take it by force. His various assaults on women through the years had all propelled him toward this moment. It was time for him to raise or fold.

He had a pistol, just in case the game got rough— and not a plastic one, this time, but an honest-to-

God .32 automatic. In 1957, California had no waiting period for firearms purchases, no background checks, no pesky licenses. You didn't even have to show I.D. It was a cash-and-carry business all the way. And if an ex-con lied about his record to obtain a gun, whose fault was that?

As for avoiding capture . . . well, Harvey decided, he would jump off that bridge when he came to it.

His target of preference was twenty-two-year-old Lynn Lykels, a pinup model he had met and photographed at one of L.A.'s many studios in early July. She lived at 1302 North Sweetzer, in West Hollywood, not far from Harvey's apartment on Melrose Avenue. Lykels knew him as commercial photographer "Johnny Glenn," an alias plucked from thin air. It was cover enough, Glatman thought, since he planned to rape Lykels at her place. So what, if she described him to police after the fact?

On the evening of Tuesday, July thirtieth, Harvey drove to Sweetzer Avenue and dropped in, unannounced. He was startled when a stranger answered the door, angry at himself for failing to consider that Lynn might have roommates. He could feel his plan beginning to unravel.

Betty Ruth Carver was another pinup model, recently arrived from Florida. At eighteen, she was still new to the game, but she could tell a loser when she saw one, and she didn't care for Johnny Glenn. Still, since a friend was visiting, she took a chance and let him in. Lynn wasn't home, she told him. It was really best to call ahead for an appointment, rather than just dropping by.

Glatman was thinking fast. He couldn't handle two young women, even with the pistol, but that didn't mean his visit had to be a total waste. He asked for Lynn's portfolio, and Betty went to fetch it. In her absence, Harvey's gaze was drawn to one of several photos on the wall. A sexy blonde, she put Lynn Lykels in the shade.

He was examining the photo, memorizing every detail, when Betty returned. His index finger lightly tapped the glass.

"Now, *she's* the type I'm really looking for," he said.

"That's Judy," Betty said. "She's not home, either."

Roommate number two. "Could I see her portfolio, as well?"

Betty returned in moments with the photographs. The more he saw, the better Harvey liked it. Paging through the album, he could feel his pulse rate quicken. He forgot about Lynn Lykels on the spot, asking more questions, trying hard to keep it casual.

The roomate's full name was Judith Ann Dull— plain Judy, to her friends. She was nineteen years old and had been modeling in L.A. "for a while," sometimes using her maiden name, Van Horn. Betty could not be sure when Judy would return. The best thing, all around, would be for Mr. Glenn to try another day and telephone for an appointment, first.

Harvey nodded and said his good-byes.

Another day or two was nothing, when he thought about it. Good things come to those who wait.

Glatman called back on Wednesday, but Judy was out on a job. Lynn Lykels took the call, pretending she remembered "Johnny Glenn." She met so many men when she was posing, pros and amateurs alike, and some of them inevitably asked for "private sessions," which might—or might not—involve film. Lynn played it straight, no tricking like some of the models she knew. But if a guy was cute, well-heeled, respectable, what was the harm in going out to dinner and having a few drinks?

Every single girl in L.A. knew you had to kiss a few frogs before you found Prince Charming.

As for Johnny Glenn, he was a blank.

"Call back tomorrow," she suggested.

Better luck, next time.

He tried again at noon, on Thursday, August first. The girls were eating lunch, but Judy took the call. Harvey ran through the spiel he had rehearsed, saying he had a "rush job" for a magazine. Would Judy pose for him that afternoon?

She hesitated, stalling him. She had a busy schedule, and the way this Johnny Glenn had been described to her by Betty Carver, she was none too anxious for a meeting. Even so, she always needed money. Maybe . . .

Harvey played his ace. His studio was occupied that day, he said, and he was hoping they could do the shoot at Judy's place. Of course, if she would rather not, could she put Lynn or Betty on the line?

The thought of shooting at her own apartment broke down Judy Dull's suspicion of the stranger. What could possibly go wrong?

"Okay," she told him. "Can we make it two o'clock?"

That would be fine, said Johnny Glenn.

Busy or not, the money had been tight of late for Judy Dull. She had been separated from her husband, Robert, since the second of June. He was a pressman at the L.A. *Times*, and while he didn't mind her modeling, per se, he drew the line at posing nude for total strangers. Judy tried to tell him how it worked—the business, breaking in—but Robert Dull was adamant. If Judy couldn't keep her clothes on, she could find another place to live.

Judy could be as stubborn as her husband. She moved out, and took Suzanne, their fourteen-month-old daughter, with her. Giving up a wife was one thing, Robert told himself, but he was not about to give his baby up and have her raised by strippers. Stopping by the Sweetzer Avenue apartment while his wife was on a shoot, he took Suzanne and left a message for Judy: See you in court.

Damned right, you will, she thought. They had a custody hearing scheduled Wednesday, the ninth of August, but lawyers cost money. If she really wanted Suzanne back, she had to come up with the cash *and* manage to persuade a judge that she was still a decent mother.

Johnny Glenn and every other man who paid her by the hour would be helping Judy get her daughter back, while simultaneously building up her reputation in the business and moving on toward something bigger, better.

Betty pegged the stranger as a creep, but that described at least one-third of Judy's clientele. Besides, he had suggested shooting in her own apartment.

How weird could he be?

"Johnny Glenn" showed up ahead of time on Thursday afternoon. Judy was waiting for him, but there was a change of plans. A friend of his had volunteered a studio, while Glenn's was occupied. Did Judy mind?

She hesitated briefly, taken by surprise, but finally shrugged it off. The price was right, twenty dollars an hour, and the time was simply wasted if she blew him off. What difference did it make?

Before they left, Judy picked out some extra clothes, including outfits for a shoot that she had scheduled after she was done with "Johnny Glenn." She wore a sleeveless, scoop-necked reddish-brown colored dress, with black patent-leather shoes. Harvey was glad to take her bag. Lynn Lykels saw them off at two o'clock and jotted down a phone number for the photographer.

If Judy was put off by Glatman's six-year-old black Dodge Coronet, she kept it to herself. He held the door for her and put her bag in back, kept up a friendly line of patter as they drove away from Sweetzer Avenue.

There was no "other studio," of course. In fifteen minutes, they were back at Harvey's place, on Melrose. He had stashed the nude pinups, cleared out the radios and TV sets, to make the flat seem more respectable, more businesslike. It was the best that he could do.

Escorting Judy from the car, he took a moment to remove his pistol from the Dodge's glove compartment, slipping it into his pocket. Judy didn't see the gun. Harvey was saving it, for later.

She was not impressed by the apartment, but she didn't need to be. Harvey was gaining confidence by the moment, drawing strength from the weapon in his pocket and the reality of a pretty woman in his living room.

At his mercy.

With the front door locked behind him, Glatman told her what he needed. He was shooting covers for the kind of "true detective" magazines that often featured women bound and gagged. Of course, to do that, he would have to tie her up.

She balked again, but twenty bucks is twenty bucks. While Harvey went to get his rope, she slipped her dress off and put on a skirt and sweater. That was better, Glatman said, when he returned. More like the girl next door. His editor would love it.

Harvey led her to an armchair, Judy leaning forward after she was seated, feeling awkward as he tied her wrists behind her back. That done, he knelt in front of her and pushed her skirt up, showing off a bit of slip and thigh, before he bound her legs together at the ankles and above the knee. The gag he slipped between her teeth and tied behind her head was yet another piece of rope. She didn't like its rough feel on her tongue, against her cheeks, but it was just a job.

His Rolleicord camera was mounted on a tripod, fitted with a Schneider Xenar f:3.5 lens. Harvey set it up a few feet from the chair and framed his shot, instructing Judy when to move and how to roll her eyes in simulated fear. For some variety, he also wanted Judy lying down. She couldn't stand, so Harvey picked her up and set her gently on the carpet, feeling powerful. She hardly seemed to weigh an ounce.

He snapped off half a roll, still working up his nerve. So far, he had done nothing wrong. He could forget about the rape, pay Judy off, and drive her home. She never had to know what he had planned for her that afternoon. If he went ahead with it, the odds were good that he would have to kill her.

No contest.

He had come too far to turn back now. The sight of Judy, with her skirt hiked up, inflamed him. Glatman had been waiting for this moment all his life. He would not let it slip away.

Judy was getting restless, lying tied up on the floor. Harvey walked over to her, knelt beside her, slipped one hand behind her neck, and helped her rise into a seated posture.

There had been a change of plans, he said. She would remain tied up, while Harvey "had some fun" with her. If she did not resist him, there would be no trouble. Harvey let her see the gun, weighing the price of chastity. For emphasis, he told her that he had done time and that he would kill to keep from going back to prison.

Judy nodded, wide-eyed, mumbling something from behind her gag. Before removing it, Harvey reminded her to keep her voice down. If she screamed for help, the next sound any of his neighbors heard would be the shot that took her life.

We only have the rapist's version of what Judy said when he removed the gag. "She said she was a nymphomaniac," Glatman recalled, "and that she was not going to cause trouble because she was estranged from her husband and that she had a custody suit pending which was due for a hearing in about a week. Any hint of her running around or engaging in unusual activities might be used against her, as her ex-husband was trying to have her declared unfit for custody of the child. She was saying this, I presume, to impress me that it was not necessary to threaten her with a gun."

Harvey bought it, putting the pistol back in his pocket. He picked Judy up and carried her into a hallway, adjoining the living room, where he placed her back on the floor. His ears were ringing, pulse hammering at his temples, keeping time with the throbbing in his groin. He went to get a drink of water in the kitchen, lingering to eat part of an apple, willing himself to be calm.

He had all night, all the time in the world. There was no need to hurry.

Judy had not moved when he returned to her, but she was bleeding from one nostril. Panic, maybe, spiking her blood pressure. Muttering disgustedly, he went to fetch a cloth and came back with an old pillow case, sat down beside her on the carpet, and held Judy's head back, pressing the cloth to her nose until it stopped bleeding. Wiping her face, he tossed the pillow case aside.

Another time, the bleeding might have put him off, but not today. He reached for Judy, tentative at first.

This much, at least, was familiar from his adolescent crimes: cupping her breast through the soft material of her sweater, running his hand along the curve of her flank, up under her skirt, to her buttocks. Trembling fingers found the buttons of her cardigan, pulling it open to expose her brassiere.

Emboldened, Harvey bent to kiss Judy's neck, lips trailing down to her cleavage. In his mind, she "seemed to be partially enjoying it." He pulled her bra down, covered a nipple with his mouth, losing track of time as he suckled, coming to himself sometime later. He could proceed no further, while Judy was bound hand and foot.

Cautiously, repeating his earlier warnings, Glatman untied her, allowing her to rise. He ordered her to strip and watched as she obeyed, shedding the sweater, skirt, slip, underwear. He felt dizzy, blood draining from his head to feed the spike of his erection.

Harvey retrieved his camera, steering Judy toward the sofa, where he ordered her to sit. He finished off the roll of film, directing her to sit with one leg raised, foot on the couch, the other dangling on the floor. When he had captured every inch of her, Glatman laid the camera aside and joined her on the couch.

He raped her twice, amazed by his own stamina, convinced that Judy loved it. Part of that was wishful thinking, Harvey's private fantasy; the rest, perhaps, persuasive acting on his victim's part, a desperate bid to save her life.

It wouldn't work, but Judy had no way of knowing that. She had to take the rapist at his word.

When he was finished with her, Judy asked to use the bathroom. Harvey showed her where it was and granted her permission to get dressed. She slipped into her dress, put on some makeup, combed her hair. When she came out, they sat together on the couch, Harvey puzzling through his next move, looking for a way to let her go alive.

"What are you going to tell your roommates?" he asked her. "Do you think they're worried? Would they call the police?"

Judy tried to reassure him, promising to come up with a cover story. She repeated her desire to avoid any scandal, "whether it was her fault or not," that might jeopardize next week's custody hearing.

Unconvinced, Harvey switched on the television, dialing through the channels in search of something to help him relax, something that would let him think.

Back on Sweetzer Avenue, the telephone was ringing off its hook. Bob Dull had called for Judy, shortly after she took off with Johnny Glenn, asking Lynn Lykels to have Judy call him at work when she returned. It was important, he said. They needed to discuss some things about Suzanne.

As afternoon wore on toward evening, there were other calls. Two more photographers rang up, complaining that Judy had missed her appointments. Lynn was frankly worried by nine o'clock, when a local contractor called to ask why Judy had not shown up for their dinner date. He had a lawyer waiting with him at the restaurant to talk about her legal problems. So, where was she?

Lykels gave him Johnny Glenn's home number, but he called back moments later, sounding anxious. The telephone number belonged to an L.A. machine shop, on Pico, and no one there had ever heard of Johnny Glenn.

The builder was concerned enough to spend that evening on the Sunset Strip, checking cafés that Judy Dull was known to frequent, all in vain. Lynn Lykels, meanwhile, placed a call to Robert Dull, who left his job and rushed to Sweetzer Avenue. They took turns calling friends and relatives, without result.

Judy was nowhere to be found.

Their last call went to L.A.P.D.'s West Hollywood station house. Adults are normally free to come and go as they please, without explaining themselves to roommates, but the circumstances of Judy Dull's disappearance were sinister enough that even jaded police were concerned. A "BOLO" call—Be On the Lookout—was issued to radio cars patrolling the Sunset Strip.

All in vain.

The rest was silence.

Back at Harvey Glatman's place, on Melrose, he sat with Judy, watching television, from approximately half-past six o'clock to 10:30 P.M. He knew that she had missed at least one other modeling appointment, by that time, and guessed that the photographer would almost certainly have called to check on her. More to the point, he noted rope burns on her wrists, deciding they would give away whatever lie she told her roommates to explain her absence—assuming, that is, that she even tried to keep her word. More to the point, she knew where Glatman lived, the color, make, and model of his car—perhaps even the Colorado license number.

If I was going to turn her loose, he thought, *I might as well go down to the police station and just walk inside with her.*

Glatman finally decided she would have to die.

He stalled through the ten o'clock news on TV, putting it off, waiting for the city's nighttime traffic to thin out. At half-past ten, Harvey announced that he had come up with a plan. He would take Judy at her word, he said, and drive her out into "the sticks," where he would drop her off with cash for bus fare back to town. If she attempted to escape in transit, Glatman said, he would not hesitate to gun her down.

As a precaution, Harvey tied her hands behind her back once more, keeping the pistol handy as he walked her to the Dodge. He drove out Santa Monica Boulevard to catch the Hollywood Freeway, south-bound, bypassing downtown L.A. to catch the San Bernardino Freeway, east of Mission Road. They drove in darkness, barely speaking, through the sub-urbs east of town. Three-quarters of an hour put them in Riverside County, rolling on through Mont-clair, Ontario, Colton, and Redlands. The desert opens out beyond Moreno Valley, but the freeway keeps on going—through Beaumont, Banning, Palm Springs, Thousand Palms.

A hundred miles from home, Glatman decided they had traveled far enough. He turned off on a lonely switchback, drove another mile or so, until he found "the point where I said it was now or never." Harvey switched the Dodge's motor off and killed the lights.

How to proceed?

He didn't want to use the gun. A bullet left ballis-tics evidence and shooting did not play into his life-long fantasies. He had rope in the car but strangling Judy where she sat involved potential difficulties, if she fought or soiled herself in death.

Glatman told Judy that he wanted sex again, before he set her free. She agreed, suggesting they use the back seat of the car, but Harvey demurred. It would be "embarrassing," he said, if someone drove by and caught them at it, parked there, on the shoulder of the road. He had a blanket in the trunk, and they could find a place off in the desert, safe from pry-ing eyes.

Reluctantly, his captive acquiesced. Harvey removed a blanket and some rope he carried in the Dodge's trunk, then he walked her off into the desert. When the car was barely visible by moonlight, Harvey spread the blanket and helped Judy seat herself. He crouched beside her and then used a foot-long piece of rope to bind her ankles tight.

Judy was startled, frightened, when he pushed her flat, facedown. The final piece of rope he carried was approximately five feet long. Before his victim could react, he jammed a knee into the small of her back, knotting one end of the rope around her pinioned ankles. Hauling on the rope, he pulled Judy's feet toward him, legs bent at the knees, ignoring her protests. His free hand cupped her chin and drew her head back, as he looped the free end of the rope around her neck, once, twice.

Releasing her chin, Glatman clutched the rope in both hands, hauling back with all his strength. Judy started thrashing as she strangled, Harvey using his knee and the weight of his body to hold her in place. It was a struggle, even so, lasting five or ten minutes before she went limp in his grasp, and he knew it was safe to let go of the rope, unwinding the makeshift noose from her neck.

Harvey would later speak of instantaneous remorse, too late to save his victim's life. "For an instant," he said, "I wanted to undo what I had just done. I lifted her head up and called out her name."

No reply.

Harvey sat beside the corpse for several minutes, "getting over the shock of it," before he noticed moonlight glinting dully on some nearby railroad tracks. It occurred to him that he should move the body to prevent it being spotted from a passing train.

Still shaking, he removed the ropes from Judy's wrists and ankles, picked her up, and lurched to his

feet, pacing off another twenty yards, until he found
a patch of loose sand. He set her down and started
scooping out a shallow grave with his bare hands,
rolling Judy's body into the depression he had made.

Before he covered her with sand, the patent-leather
shoes caught Harvey's eye. He slipped them off, then
thought of fingerprints, and used a handkerchief to
wipe them off. That done, he tossed one shoe aside
and set the other down beside him, scooping sand
over the corpse until he satisfied himself that it
would not be seen.

Retreating from the grave site, Harvey took the
shoe, picked up his blanket on the way back to his
car, replaced his ropes and blanket in the trunk. He
then made a U-turn on the narrow access road and
started on the long drive back to Hollywood.

The official missing-person bulletin on Judy Dull
went out on Friday, August second. It described elusive "Johnny Glenn" as five foot nine, approximately
twenty-nine years old, 150 pounds, brown hair, olive
complexion, big ears, with horn-rimmed glasses.
There was no such person listed in the L.A. telephone
directory and no reason to believe the name was
really his.

Sergeant David Ostroff was assigned the case and
took it seriously, touching base with every known
photographer and modeling agency in Hollywood.
No one he spoke to recognized Johnny Glenn's name
or recognized the description, and while Sergeant Ostroff heard from several women who had suffered
rape on modeling assignments, none of their assail-
ants sounded like "Glenn."

Judy's disappearance vaguely recalled the case of
model and would-be actress Jean Spangler, in October 1949. Last seen alive in Hollywood, on October
seventh, Spangler was officially reported missing two

days later, after her purse was found in Griffith Park.
A note inside the purse read: "Kirk. Can't wait any
longer. Going to see Dr. Scott. It will work best this
way while mother is away."

Over the next six days, L.A.P.D. questioned dozens
of Dr. Scotts and Kirks—including movie star Kirk
Douglas—all without result. On Sunday, October sixteenth, 200 searchers scoured Griffith Park with
tracking dogs and came up empty once again. Tabloid headlines trumpeted fears of "another Black
Dahlia type mutilation murder," but no corpse was
ever found. In August 1957, the case remained
unsolved.

Judy made the L.A. *Times* on Saturday, complete
with swimsuit photo and the apprehensive comments of her roommates. "We believe she has met
foul play," said Betty Carver. "I knew there was
something odd about the man. He told her he
wanted to shoot pinup pictures, yet he told her to
bring a selection of street clothes, which she did."

Robert Dull was initially the prime suspect in his
wife's disappearance. Eighty-odd percent of all murder victims were slain by friends or relatives in those
days, and Robert's separation from Judy had been
acrimonious, to say the least. If he would snatch their
daughter from the Sweetzer Avenue apartment while
she was at work, what might he do to guarantee
retaining custody?

A cursory investigation soon cleared Robert of suspicion, though. He was at work when "Johnny
Glenn" drove Judy off to who-knows-where and had
remained on duty through the evening, while the
anxious search for her began. There was no reason
whatsoever to believe he was involved in Judy's disappearance, and he clearly was not big-eared
Johnny Glenn.

Next, Sergeant Ostroff wondered if the missing

woman might have staged her disappearance, as a means of helping herself in the custody fight. A bid for sympathy, perhaps? It really made no sense, though, and he dumped the theory after Judy missed her court hearing, on August ninth.

By then, Ostroff agreed with Betty Carver, and he had no reason to believe that Judy would be found alive. As for the nameless suspect, he could be in Florida, New York, or Timbuctu by now. Ostroff had nothing in the way of leads to work with, and the bodies in L.A. kept piling up, meanwhile.

Unless he caught an unexpected break, the case, for all intents and purposes, was closed.

Five months after Judy Dull was first reported missing, on December twenty-ninth, a woman's skeleton was found in the desert outside Thousand Palms. James Gilmore, an employee of the sprawling Kovasevich ranch, was walking his German shepherd around ten o'clock that Sunday morning, when the barking dog called his attention to a human skull. No other remains were readily visible, but Gilmore had seen enough. He called the shepherd off and went to summon sheriff's deputies.

The search was relatively brief, once officers arrived on the scene. They paced off 120 feet from the spot where the skull had been found and were within a hundred feet of the Southern Pacific Railroad tracks, when they spied a human fibula protruding from the earth. Cautiously, they set to work with shovels and bare hands, clearing a meager six inches of soil.

The headless skeleton was a woman's, clothed in a simple reddish-brown dress. She had apparently been buried barefoot, but a single patent-leather flat was found nearby and bagged with the remains. A fountain pen, discovered near the shallow grave, was also tagged as evidence. The skeleton was driven off to the FitzHenry Funeral Home, in Indio, for examination by Dr. Robert Dexter, a pathologist employed by the Riverside County coroner's office.

Dexter's examination of the bones revealed no cause of death, no fractures of the skull nor any other evidence of physical attack, but the unnamed woman's death was still presumed to be a homicide. As Sheriff's Captain Sam Hoffman told the press, "She didn't bury herself."

That said, there was little more to be learned from the pitiful remains. In the absence of flesh or obvious skeletal wounds, such as bullet holes, no cause of death could ever be stated with certainty. Likewise, the pathologist could not determine if the woman had been raped, although her skeleton was found with underwear in place. A few strands of hair still clung to the skull, permitting Captain Dexter to describe the victim as a blond, "probably" with blue or hazel eyes, who stood about five foot three in life, tipping the scales between 110 and 120 pounds. She had been shapely, for her size: the bra—a "Sari" model, manufactured by Sarong—was a 32C. No stockings were recovered from the desert; the single patent leather shoe, a C. H. Baker brand, had the slogan "Too Smart for Words" inscribed on the insole. On the ring finger of her left hand, the woman wore a ring of ten-karat white gold, mounted with a pea-sized "pearl or pearl-like stone."

That much was fact. From there, unfortunately, Dr. Dexter went astray. He pegged the woman's age somewhere between thirty and thirty-five years, offering detectives his "best guess" that she had lain in the shallow grave for at least a year, perhaps two. It was "possible but unlikely," Dexter said, that the desert heat might have hastened decomposition "within such a short period as six months."

In fact, she had been in the ground for barely five months, and she had been murdered at the tender age of nineteen years.

As for identifying the victim, there was little to work from. Dental charts are often useful, if detectives have a known missing person for comparison, but in this case, Dr. Dexter reported that "the only indication of dental work was that one molar apparently had been extracted from the lower left jaw" at some unknown date. (It was, in fact, another error, as sworn testimony from Glatman's trial, a year later, confirmed the presence of fillings.)

Captain Hoffman, for his part, was staking his hopes on the ring, which he described as "old" and "unusual," advising newsmen that "They don't make them that way any more. We're hoping that someone will be able to help us identify the woman by recognizing the ring."

It didn't work.

Back in West Hollywood, Sergeant Ostroff heard of the discovery at Thousand Palms, but he was not about to get his hopes up. The California desert has no end of shallow graves, he knew from grim experience, and autopsy reports made the Riverside County victim eleven to sixteen years older than Judy Ann Dull. Still, it was worth checking out, and he obtained a photo of the "old, unusual" ring. Robert Dull, Lynn Lykels, and Betty Carver were unanimous in their failure to recognize the piece.

Once again, the trail went cold.

8

A Perfect Gentleman

REMORSE ASIDE, THINGS STARTED LOOKING UP FOR HARVEY Glatman after he killed Judy Dull. Within a few short days, he found a job at Universal TV, on South La Cienega, fixing television sets. The shop was four miles south of Harvey's apartment, near the Santa Monica Freeway. In L.A. time, that meant a good half-hour on the road, but it was worth it, since the job paid two dollars an hour—twice the new minimum wage that had taken effect in March 1956.

In fact, it was too good to last. Harvey lost the job three months later, the precise date and reason unknown, but it seems unlikely that he would have quit on his own after so short a time. He may have seen it coming, but it had to be a slap at Harvey's self-esteem, in any case. Within another month, authorities in Riverside County were picking over Judy Dull's bones. They didn't know who they had found—at least, not yet—but Glatman's nerves were shot.

He needed breathing room, a change of scene.

He drove the old Dodge east, across the desert,

stopping briefly in Las Vegas, on from there across Utah and into the Rockies. Ophelia welcomed him in Denver, as she always had, with no questions asked. Harvey felt at home on Kearney Street, but he had no more luck at finding work than in the years when he was on parole. As February waned, no prospects yet in sight, Glatman assessed his situation.

He enjoyed L.A., no doubt about it. He could always find a woman there, no matter if he had to hide behind a camera, paying her to shed her clothes. And if he wanted more, he knew exactly how to get it, thanks to Judy Dull.

It had been nearly seven months since Harvey killed and two months since deputies unearthed his victim's skeleton. If they had anything to hang a warrant on, they surely would have come for him by now.

No sweat.

He put his snow chains on and started driving west.

Still jobless in L.A., he seemed to get along all right. We may assume Ophelia bankrolled him, since he had never held a job for any length of time and had inherited no money when his father died. Whatever the source of his money, Glatman was able to afford a small bungalow on South Norton, close to his old Melrose Avenue pad. By that March, from all appearances, Harvey had more important matters than a paycheck on his mind.

The old, familiar hunger had returned.

Glatman was hunting.

He was smart enough to vary his technique. Police were on the lookout for a man named Johnny Glenn, presumed to be a magazine photographer, and Harvey reckoned it would take more than a change of name to keep him safe. For all he knew, some kind of bulletin might have the city's pinup models on alert, prepared to call police if anyone approaching "Glenn's" description sought them out. The dead

girl's roommates could have helped police prepare a
sketch, although it had not circulated in the press.

A clever trick, perhaps.

But he was smarter. Harvey would outfox them all.

He checked the want ads out, for old time's sake,
and found his inspiration there. The Patty Sullivan
Lonely Hearts Club was advertising for members,
and Glatman stopped by the club's office, on Vermont Avenue, to check it out. He liked the setup,
paid ten dollars to enroll, and signed on as "George
Williams," a Pasadena plumber dwelling at a spuri-
ous address.

Patty Sullivan favored the personal touch. She interviewed "Williams" and gave him some telephone
numbers. Harvey called the first one, introduced
himself, and made a date.

The plan was simple. He would meet the woman,
visit her at home, and see what happened next. If
she appealed to him, he would suggest a drive and
find himself another lonely desert road. He had the
pistol in the Dodge's glove compartment; blanket,
rope, and camera in the trunk.

Just like the Boy Scouts used to teach him: Be
prepared.

Blind dates are risky, though, and this one blew
up in his face. It wasn't that the woman hated him
on sight—Harvey had seen *that* look before—but
quite the opposite, in fact. She was a secretary,
worked in Hollywood, seemed nice enough. She
brought him tea and biscuits, smiling all the time,
but there was something *wrong*. She talked a blue
streak, bending Harvey's ear all night and hardly let
him get a word in edgewise. Maybe that was part of
it, a sense that he could not control the situation,
couldn't quite assert himself, but there was also *something else.*

The bottom line: She simply didn't turn him on.

It was ironic, but he had a certain standard to up-
hold. He could see naked women anytime he wanted
to, real lookers, so the ones he chose to rape and kill
had to be extra special. Judy Dull had set the standard, and his first contact through Patty Sullivan just
didn't measure up.

He suffered through the evening, shooting none
too subtle glances at his watch, and finally said good-
night with some crap about another date, dismissing
her from mind almost before the door closed at his
back. The number he had given her was phony. She
would never track him down.

It was a disappointment, granted, but he was not
giving up. The lonely hearts club still had good potential. If at first you don't succeed . .

Try, try again.

Shirley Ann Loy Bridgeford was twenty-four years
old in 1958, but sometimes it seemed that the best
part of life was already behind her. Divorced for
three years, with two young sons—five-year-old
Ricky Allen and three-year-old Billy Wayne—she
was tired of being on her own, without a man, struggling to make ends meet with her job as a factory
worker. She had been dating for a while, looking for
Mr. Right, but he was nowhere to be found. The last
man she had fallen for had left her flat, without a
word of explanation. Lonely and depressed at being
"on the shelf," she had been close to giving up, before a friend at work suggested that she try a new
approach with Patty Sullivan. Ten dollars wasn't
cheap, but who could put a price on love and
happiness?

Reluctantly, she visited the lonely hearts club, paid
her dues, filled out the forms, and waited for the
telephone to ring. She didn't have much faith in the
ability of strangers to arrange a perfect match . . .

but, then again, she had not done so wonderfully at that, herself.

The first call came on Friday night, March seventh, from a man who asked if Shirley would be free on Saturday. She was. And, yes, square dancing sounded like it might be fun.

"George Williams" said that he would pick her up at 7:45 P.M.

It felt strange, getting ready for a date with someone she had never even seen. You always took your chances, going out with men you met at work, in bars, whatever. But a blind date was exactly that. For all she knew, George Williams could be fat or bald, a midget or a moron. Worse, he could turn out to be a carbon copy of her ex.

In self-defense, Shirley arranged to have him greeted by a welcoming committee at her small Sun Valley home. The boys would be on hand, of course, as would her mother, Alice Jolliffe. Just in case the four of them were not enough, she also asked her sisters, Ruth and Mary, to tag along. Ruth brought her husband, Hubert Boggs, for reinforcement.

The gang of seven was waiting when George Williams pulled up to the house on Tuxford Street and rang the bell. They gave him points for punctuality and welcomed him inside. He had a pleasant manner, though he seemed somewhat reserved, and that was fine with Mother Alice. Shirley didn't need another pushy man, right now, to make demands on her then leave her in the lurch.

As far as Ruth and Hubert were concerned, the only thing about George Williams that stood out was his "enormous" ears. Throughout the fifteen minutes they sat talking to him, it was hard to keep from laughing in his face, but Ruth and Hubert managed. They could always share a joke at his expense, once he was gone.

Somehow, the big ears didn't register with Alice Jolliffe. Maybe she was busy at a mother's task, trying to see *inside* the man, but she would later be unable to describe him for police. Months later, she would fail to recognize him, even when confronted with his jailhouse booking photographs.

Harvey was glad to see the last of Tuxford Avenue. He wanted Shirley Bridgeford from the moment he laid eyes on her, despite the too-familiar look that told him he had disappointed her, and Glatman worried that her family might ruin it, somehow. Four witnesses, if he forgot about the kids, but there was no way they could trace him from a bogus name. When the detectives came around and took their statements, later—as he knew they would—the four adults might well describe him to a tee.

So what?

There had been witnesses with Judy Dull, and what good had they done? His sheet was clean in California with no mug shots for anyone to study and identify. As long as he was careful with his hands, left nothing in the way of fingerprints behind, he should be safe enough.

He had all night to play with Shirley now, aware that when he finished with her, she would have to die. He took no pleasure from the notion. He was simply looking out for Number One.

Once they were safely in the Dodge, without an audience, he sprang a change of plans on Shirley. Would she mind if, rather than square dancing, they just took a moonlight drive and got some dinner on the road? Shirley agreed, and off they went, southbound toward nowhere in particular, driving along the coast.

They stopped at a café in Oceanside, some fifty miles south of Los Angeles, for dinner. Glatman spun a web of lies to keep the conversation going, telling Shirley that he was a new arrival in L.A., but that the plumbing trade was doing well. It hardly mattered what he said. Glatman could tell her anything he wanted to, since she would never have a chance to share it with another living soul.

He could have told the truth, in fact, but what would be the fun in that? What was the point of fantasizing, if he did not come off sounding bigger, better, more successful than he was in real life?

After dinner, Glatman later said, they walked back to his car but did not leave the parking lot immediately. Rather, he maintained, they "necked and petted" for a while, Shirley enjoying it—or seeming to—before she told him it was time for her to get back home.

Glatman agreed and started driving aimlessly, first north, then east. If we believe his later statements, he had not decided yet to rape and murder Shirley Bridgeford. He "kept on thinking of her two children," Harvey said, telling himself that Shirley was a "different type" than Judy Dull. She didn't strip and show her body off to strangers. Shirley was a *nice* girl.

Still . . .

Her very presence in the car and the scent of her perfume incited Glatman. Having kissed and touched her, Harvey knew what he was missing if he did not follow through. It meant another wasted night, two hours on the road already, with nothing to show for it but an ache in his loins. He needed sex and, while he was at it, why not a few snapshots?

They were rolling eastward on Highway 78, Escondido behind them, passing through Ramona, Santa Ysabel, and Julian, into the Vallecito Mountains. If Shirley Bridgeford realized that he was taking her *away* from home, she gave no sign.

A short time later, Harvey stopped the Dodge again, along the shoulder of a dark, deserted mountain road. According to his uncontested version of events, they "necked" some more, but Shirley turned him down when he requested intercourse. No matter how he pleaded, she was adamant. She wanted to go home.

The pistol changed her mind. It gave Harvey the power to demand what no female had ever given to him willingly. It put him in control.

He ordered Shirley into the back seat, scrambling after her as she obeyed. She briefly found the nerve to push his hands away as he began caressing her, his fingers sliding underneath her skirt, slipping inside her blouse, but there was still the gun. She did not want to die.

On Glatman's order, she undressed, still pleading with him not to do this, but he may as well have been stone deaf. When she was naked, Harvey climbed on top of her and forced her legs apart. The rape was quick, all things considered. Glatman had no staying power, overwhelmed by fantasies that he had nurtured from his childhood—images that always seemed the clearest when he had a rope around his own neck.

They lay together afterward, until he noticed Shirley trembling. Mountain nights are cold in southern California, during early March, and it would be no warmer where he planned to take his victim next.

Reluctantly, he told her to get dressed and sat watching as she put her clothes back on, hiding the treasures he had managed to possess for such a fleeting time. His watch told Harvey it was well past ten o'clock. He knew he had to get a move on, finish it before he lost his nerve and ruined everything.

There was no question of releasing Shirley Bridgeford now. She must despise him, even if the pistol made her tell him otherwise, and she would summon the police at her first opportunity. Descriptions from her family were one thing, but they had not seen his car nor spent so much time in Harvey's presence.

She could send him back to prison. Worse, if they connected him to Judy Dull, she would be sending him to death.

It finally came down to him or her.

She had to die.

When both of them were dressed and back in the front seat, Harvey took out a piece of rope he carried in his pocket and secured her wrists behind her. There would be no desperate bid to save herself by leaping from the car.

He spun another lie while they were driving east, as he had done with Judy Dull, about releasing her in some remote location, buying time for him to make his getaway. Dropping out of the mountains, they entered the Anza-Borrego Desert State Park, deserted now, without another pair of headlights to be seen. Glatman was not concerned about park rangers. He could always use the pistol, if it came to that, but he did not believe it would be necessary.

Lady Luck was riding with him.

He was on a roll.

He found another place that suited him, parked the Dodge, and got out to stretch his legs. His knees were chafed, from wrestling in the back seat, but he didn't mind. He listened to the night sounds of the desert—insects, rustling wind, the flutter of a bat's wings overhead. The dead weight of the pistol in his pocket kept reminding him of what he had to do.

Get on with it.

He opened up the trunk, took out his camera, more rope, the blanket he had used with Judy Dull. It was the same rope, too. Waste not, want not. When he

had everything, he walked around the car and
opened Shirley's door.

"Come on with me."

She did not ask where they were going. Maybe she
already knew—but, then again, perhaps the camera
and blanket gave her hope. If "George" still had
more kinky games in mind, there was a chance that
she could satisfy him, yet—a chance that he would
let her live.

It was less common—*seemed* less common, anyway—for rapists to assassinate their victims in those
days. While sexual assaults were not unusual around
L.A., euphemistically described in the papers as
"criminal attacks," most of the victims managed to
survive. Some of the rapists even went to jail. As
Shirley Bridgeford stood there in the darkness, shiv-
ering, hands tied, she may have thought the odds
were on her side.

"This way."

Glatman had no idea where he was going, but the
ground was level, and the moonlight helped him
pick his way along. He liked the sense of freedom
he derived from walking in the desert, coupled with
the power of a captive woman at his side.

Shirley Bridgeford was his for the rest of her life.

They walked the better part of two miles from the
car, in silence, Harvey guiding her with one hand on
her arm. He kept the pistol in his pocket not needing
to prod her with it. There was nowhere she could
hide from him, no way she could escape.

He picked a spot at random, ordered her to stop,
and spread his blanket on the ground. She sat upon
command, well-trained.

"I want to take some pictures," Harvey said.

There was no argument from Shirley, as he knelt
beside her, looping rope around her ankles, pushing
up her skirt to tie another loop above her knees. He

gagged her with a handkerchief and sat back to admire his handiwork.

Just right.

He had a brainstorm, then. Why rush it, use the flash and risk poor quality, when he could wait until the sun came up and do it right? A few more hours would make no difference. They were all alone, nobody to disturb them.

Harvey was in charge.

He sat and talked to Shirley while he waited for the sunrise, telling her about himself. It didn't matter what he said, how much she learned, since she would never have the chance to share it with another living soul. The freedom Harvey felt with her was better than mere sex—another revelation, since he had imagined intercourse as the achievement of a lifetime. It took more than simply screwing, Harvey realized with wonder, to become a man.

It took *control*.

By half-past six A.M. the eastern sky was brightening. Away beyond the Salton Sea and Chocolate Mountains, velvet darkness lightened into shades of gray, then blushed with roseate hues of dawn. The desert sunrise is spectacular, but it takes time to warm the wasteland.

Glatman stood and stretched, joints cracking. Sunrise gave him all the light he needed to complete his task. He took the loaded Rolleicord and turned to Shirley Bridgeford, ready to begin.

She was no model, but she took direction like a pro. As stiff and miserable as she was, chilled to the bone and terrified, she offered no resistance as he told her how to sit, face toward the camera or away from it, silent behind her gag as he arranged her skirt to show a bit more thigh.

He snapped off half a roll before he satisfied himself. It was enough. The time had come to finish it.

"Lie down."

She tried, but Harvey had to help her, with her hands and legs securely bound. When she was lying facedown on the blanket, Harvey took the five-foot length of rope and tied it first around her ankles, then around her neck. It was the same technique that he had used with Judy Dull.

By that time, Shirley Bridgeford knew that she was doomed, but it was too late to resist him. She had stalled too long, and she was helpless now. No matter how she wriggled on the blanket, Harvey's foot braced on her back was all it took to pin her down.

He hauled back on the rope, grateful for leverage, while his victim shuddered, slowly strangling. Later, thinking back, he estimated that it took about five minutes for the last hint of resistance to subside.

When it was well and truly done, no sign of life remaining, Glatman stripped the gag and ropes off, laying them aside. He stooped to grab his victim by the ankles, dragged her off the blanket and across the dry, cracked earth. He rolled her body underneath a cactus, as he later said, because he "felt she should be under something."

Studying the corpse, he had a flash of inspiration, ripping off the large, flat buttons of her dress because he feared they might hold fingerprints. He took her panties as a souvenir and stuffed them in his pocket with the buttons, walked back to the murder site, picked up his blanket, ropes, and camera.

All clear.

It was well after 8:00 A.M., broad daylight, when he got back to the car and stowed his gear. The Dodge was cold, but it responded on the first try, and he made a U-turn in the middle of the narrow road. He rolled his window down and let the wind keep him awake as he began the drive back to L.A..

Along the way, he pitched her buttons from the

car, along with Shirley's purse and contents—all except for thirty cents in change, which he appropriated for himself.

It wasn't everyday that you could turn a profit on a rape.

Alice Jolliffe was frantic when her daughter failed to return on Saturday night. Of course, young women sometimes misbehaved, but sleeping over with a total stranger wasn't Shirley's style. If nothing else, she would have called to let her mother know she was all right.

Los Angeles police took Alice's report on Sunday morning, March ninth. Ordinarily, they would have put her off, but the circumstances reeked of foul play. A visit to the lonely hearts club got them George Williams's address, but it proved to be a fake. The club did not keep photos in its files.

Detectives interviewed the secretary "Williams" had visited with on March sixth, but she could tell them little of their suspect, other than the fact that he had seemed "a perfect gentleman." Her description of "Williams" matched Patty Sullivan's, but even that posed difficulties, since Alice Jolliffe could barely recall what he looked like. Hubert and Ruth Boggs remembered his "enormous" ears, but they believed he might have had a thin mustache.

The facial hair aside, Dave Ostroff thought "George Williams" sounded like a decent match for the elusive "Johnny Glenn." Big ears and glasses. Not that any of it mattered, since he had no leads on either man.

Ostroff knew Judy Dull was dead. He had no reason to believe that Shirley Bridgeford would be found alive. Pure logic told him that the man—or men—responsible, if left alone, would likely kill again.

And there was nothing he could do about it.

9

"One I Really Liked"

RECOVERING FROM HOMICIDE WAS EASIER THE SECOND time around. Glatman experienced more guilt, compounded by fear of discovery, in the wake of Shirley Bridgeford's murder, but it did not trouble him nearly as long as his reaction to the strangling of Judy Dull. By April Fool's Day, Harvey reckoned he was in the clear.

He still had not found work, but checks from Denver kept him solvent. After all this time and the disappointments that she had endured, Ophelia didn't count on Harvey making good. It was a victory of sorts that he had lasted seven years without another trip to jail, and he was still her only child, for all his little quirks.

For Harvey's part, he was intent on *staying* out of jail. One step in that direction had been the construction of a makeshift darkroom in his flat. The kind of photographs he favored could not be entrusted to the local drugstore for development. This way, he kept his secret—and the pleasure of it—strictly to himself.

The "special" photographs of Judy Dull and Shirley Bridgeford occupied a metal toolbox, sharing space with Judy's patent-leather shoe and Shirley's underpants. When he was not at home, he kept the toolbox locked and safely hidden in his closet. Only when he was alone, behind locked doors, would Harvey take his treasures out and lovingly examine them. Only then, surrendering himself to fantasy, did Harvey Glatman truly come alive.

Self-styled "experts" quarrel endlessly over the proper definition and classification of serial killers in modern society. The FBI's simplistic taxonomy, used as a launching pad for many more elaborate theories, roughly divides lust killers into "organized" and "disorganized" categories. The organized killer is one who prepares for his crime in advance, selects a particular victim, brings all the necessary tools along, and takes precautions to avoid arrest. Disorganized killers, by contrast, strike at victims of opportunity, acting on a lethal whim, often leaving clues to their identity behind. Organized killers typically have a longer run; indeed, nearly one in five of them are never caught at all.

Both types of killers frequently take keepsakes from their victims, though the FBI's psychologists perceive in the practice different motives for each group. Organized killers, they say, retain "trophies" of their kills, as a mark of achievement, while disorganized slayers take "souvenirs," with which to relive their crimes.

It is all semantic quibbling, of course, as clearly demonstrated by Harvey Glatman. An "organized" killer by FBI standards, he chose his prey deliberately, rejecting women who displeased him; he avoided capture through the use of pseudonyms, false addresses, and the concealment of his victims; he approached each killing situation with the necessary weapon, ropes, and photographic gear required to carry out the crime. By Bureau standards, Harvey's photos of the murdered women should have been mere "trophies," kept on hand as a reminder of his kills, much as a sportsman mounts deer antlers or a prize trout on the wall.

And yet, we know the photographs meant more—*much* more—to Glatman. In between the rapes and murders, he employed them daily, masturbating over them, sometimes incorporating Shirley's panties as an extra prop. Each time, he told himself the photographs would be enough to tide him over.

But they never were.

One operant model of serial murder, proposed by the late Joel Norris, describes the killer's existence as "an addiction to a specific pattern of violence that becomes the killer's way of life." Within that model, the murderer's daily existence is divided into seven more or less distinctive phases. In the *aura* phase, described by Norris as "a portal between two realities," the killer is gradually overcome by hunger—for sex, death, dominance, whatever—that progresses from an itch to a compelling need. This leads him to the *trolling* phase, in which he searches for a victim who will satisfy his needs. The *wooing* phase may be abbreviated or prolonged, involving either contact with the victim or surveillance from afar, inevitably followed by *capture* and *murder*. Once the deed is done, the killer enters a *totem* phase, reliving his crime in fantasy—often with the aid of photographs and other mementos. Finally, as the sweet rush of mayhem subsides, the hunter falls into *depression*, deepening until the vicious cycle starts anew.

It is characteristic of serial killers that the "totem" phase grows shorter over time, and the depression becomes more severe, consequently decreasing the interval between murders and increasing the violence required for a "fix." Once fantasy has been realized, masturbatory daydreams lose their potency. Why should the hunter make do with snapshots and trinkets when live flesh is there for the taking?

Colin Wilson views Glatman as the archetypal predator, his life a working model for the homicidal norm. "The first crime produces fear, revulsion, remorse," Wilson writes. "But it is also like a dose of an addictive drug. Again and again, serial killers have confessed that they were unable to stop: again and again . . . they have used the same image: that it was as if they had fallen into the power of the devil."

Seven months had elapsed between Harvey's murder of Judy Ann Dull and the slaying of Shirley Bridgeford. Now, in July 1958—barely four months after Bridgeford's death—he felt the need again. It would have been a simple thing for him to find a prostitute—they worked West Hollywood in droves—but Glatman needed more.

He thought first about the best way to fulfill his need without endangering himself. He couldn't use the lonely hearts club ruse again, so soon, but it had been almost a year since he had gone out shopping for a pinup model.

Why not?

He started browsing through the *Times* and *Herald-Examiner*. It didn't take him long to find what he was looking for.

She billed herself as Angela Rojas, but her real name was Ruth Rita Mercado. A twenty-four-year-old native of Plattsburgh, New York—upstate, on Lake Champlain—she had served in the Women's Air Force during the late Korean "police action" and received an honorable discharge. Back in civilian life, she hit the road and wound up in Los Angeles, with dreams of breaking into films. A little luck was all she needed.

But it didn't work. The lightning never struck.

Young faces are a dime a dozen on the streets of Hollywood, and Ruth Mercado wasn't even in the game. Posthumous newspaper reports would describe her as one of Glatman's "beautiful victims," but the camera doesn't lie. By Tinsel Town standards, she was no more than average—and Hispanic at that, in a town that valued blondes above all else.

Still, she was bound to try.

She found a small apartment on West Pico Boulevard, well south of where the action was, and began job-hunting. She could always waitress—several famous actresses had been discovered in cafés, according to the movie magazines—but Ruth Mercado wanted something closer to "The Business." Something with lights and cameras.

She settled on modeling for professional and amateur photographers alike. Clothing was optional, depending on the price tag, and it was a short step from the studio to stripping in the clubs on Wilshire Boulevard. It wasn't a *career*, of course—she never looked at it that way—but it would tide her over for a while, until her big break rolled around.

Meanwhile, Ruth advertised her "service" in the daily papers, paying on a weekly basis. An ad clerk who handled her business at the *Times* recalled, "She was a seemingly clean-cut, nice kid who was anything but the kind of person you'd expect in this kind of business. She was reliable, the sort who always paid her bills on time."

She dated a piano player sometimes, but it was nothing steady. Ruth saw men aplenty on her modeling gigs and when she danced for tips, but none of them impressed her much. She wasn't looking for a husband at the moment, someone who would tie her down before she even got a chance to show what she could do. No, thank you.

Every time the phone rang, Ruth was hopeful. Any time now, it could be the break she had been waiting for. And if it wasn't . . . well, a girl still had to eat.

On Tuesday afternoon, the twenty-second of July, Ruth got another call.

"I saw your ad," the stranger said.

There was no photo with the advertisement. Harvey didn't know what he was getting into, calling on a Mexican, but in the end it hardly mattered. If the woman didn't suit him, he could always take a pass and try again another day, with someone else. At worst, he calculated, he would see some skin and add some photographs to his collection.

The call was easy, once removed from human contact. Harvey introduced himself to Angela as "Frank," a magazine photographer. The same old line. They struck a deal on price and made a date for Harvey to stop by that night.

So far, so good.

He spent the rest of Tuesday afternoon preparing, double-checking his gun, loading the Rolleicord, making sure his favorite rope was in the car. Anticipation fuels arousal, but he stubbornly resisted the temptation to relieve himself. It would be better if he waited, Harvey knew. A quick peek at the photographs of Judy Dull and Shirley Bridgeford, fondling Shirley's panties as he scanned the snapshots, honed his passion to a razor's edge.

Harvey had the pistol in his pocket and camera in hand, as he left the Dodge and made his way to Angela's apartment. She was slow responding to the bell with no smile for Harvey when she finally opened up the door.

"I'm Frank," he said.

"Hi, Frank. I'm really sorry, but I didn't have your phone number . . ."

Harvey's stomach tightened. He could feel the situation slipping through his hands.

"Is something wrong?" he inquired.

"I'm sick, you know? Some kinda bug. I would've called you, but . . ."

She was a tiny thing, no more than five foot one. A solid shove, and he would be inside.

"Don't worry," Glatman told her, putting on a smile. "It's no big deal. I'll take a rain check."

"I appreciate it, really," she said, smiling now, relieved. "If you could let me have your number . . ."

"I'll call you," he said and turned away.

The anger roiled inside him as he walked back to his car. *Some kinda bug, my ass!* He knew that look, the one that told him he had been found wanting. What made this bitch so damned special that she wouldn't even take his money? She posed naked for a living, and she had the gall to put him down! How *dare* she?

Back at his apartment, Harvey took the toolbox out and carefully arranged his special photos. Anger and frustration kept him hard as he removed his clothing and began to masturbate. It only took a moment, keyed up as he was, until he brought himself to climax, gasping.

Later, maybe he would use the rope.

The more he thought about it, though, the more determined Harvey was to get back at the woman who had spurned him. She was nothing special, granted, but as Harvey brooded on the insult, Angela assumed the guise of every girl who had ever laughed at him in school, made jokes about his ears, or called him "Four-Eyes." She was every woman he had ever lusted for and knew he couldn't have because he didn't measure up.

She had a lesson coming, damn it. Harvey had a thing or two to teach her that would change her life.

*   *   *

On Wednesday evening, July twenty-third, Glatman drove back to West Pico unannounced. He knocked on Ruth's door and got no response. He tried again. Still nothing. Finally, he pressed one ear against the door but heard nothing from inside. The place was dark.

Another lousy break, but he could wait. If she was modeling, an hour or two should see her home again. If she was shopping, out with friends, whatever, she would still be coming back.

He had all night—all week, if that was what it took. No job had any claim on Harvey's time, and he was totally committed to his mission, now. Instead of picking out another model from the classifieds, he wanted *this* one, to repay her for the insult and to show her who was boss.

He found a bar nearby and killed an hour, sipping beer and smoking. Harvey wasn't much of a drinker, and he was careful not to overdo it—just enough to feel the buzz and give himself a little extra nerve to stay the course, when he already had two strikes against him.

Maybe it was fate that Angela escape him?

Bullshit.

Heading back to Pico, Harvey could not find a parking space outside of Angela's apartment. He was forced to park almost two blocks away. He considered carrying the camera with him but decided it would look too odd if he met anyone along the way. The last thing Harvey wanted was to stand out in the mind of any accidental witnesses.

He left the Rolleicord but took the pistol with him, heavy in his pocket. Coming up the walk to Angela's apartment, he could tell his luck had changed. Her lights were on, this time.

He hesitated for a moment at her door, considering what he would say if she had company—another man, perhaps. No problem, he decided. She had offered him a rain check yesterday, and here he was to cash it in. If she was not alone, he would apologize and leave, consider it an omen, scrub the mission. There could be no third attempt, if someone actually saw him on her doorstep.

Go ahead!

He knocked and waited, practicing his smile before the door eased open. Angela was visibly surprised to see him, standing in the spill of light.

"Frank, right?"

He bobbed his head. "You're feeling better."

It was not a question, but she answered anyway. "Yes, thanks. You didn't—"

"Call ahead," he interrupted her. "I know. I thought I'd take my chances. Are you free?"

"Well . . ."

This would be the sticker, Harvey knew, if she had noticed that he didn't have a camera with him. If she rejected him again, he had a choice to make: give up or rush the door.

"Okay, I guess."

She stood aside to let him in. The door clicked shut behind him as a little collie started yapping, hanging several paces back.

"Hush, now!" said Angela. "Behave yourself."

"I don't suppose there's somewhere you could put him while we're shooting?"

"Well . . ." She thought about it like it was the toughest question anyone had ever asked her. "In the bathroom?"

"Fine."

She scooped the dog up in her arms and headed for the bathroom, down a narrow hallway. Harvey used the time to lock the door and fasten the security chain. He had the pistol in his hand when Angela came back.

"Show me the bedroom," he demanded.

"Hey—"

The pistol silenced her. She led him back along the hallway to the small apartment's single bedroom. Harvey was already stiffening, anticipation stirring him, but he would have to wait a few more moments.

"Put your hands behind your back."

She did as she was told, and Harvey bound her wrists, then helped her lie down on the bed, before he tied her ankles fast. Before he left the bedroom, backtracking, he gagged her with a handkerchief and warned her not to move.

The door was locked, but he was still concerned about the possibility of someone showing up, surprising him. In that event, he needed an escape hatch. Harvey found it in the kitchen, where a back door opened on an alley. He could flee that way, if need be, and run around the block to his car.

Satisfied, he went back to the bedroom where Angela waited for him, trussed up on the bed. He sat beside her, ignoring the fear in her eyes as he began to fondle her through her clothing. It only took a moment to regain his full erection.

"I want to make love to you," Harvey said, watching Angela's face while his hand stroked her breast. "I'll untie you, if you promise not to do anything foolish."

She gave a jerky nod and said something unintelligible from behind the gag.

"All right," he said. "Remember, I still have the gun."

Untying her, he stepped back from the bed and ordered her to strip. She didn't have to see the gun, this time, before obeying. Nudity in front of strangers was her stock in trade. The main thing was to keep from getting killed, at any cost.

When she was naked, Harvey told her to lie down,

stripped off his clothes, and joined her on the bed. The gun was in his pocket, out of reach, but he was confident that Angela could not escape. She seemed so *small*.

Glatman explored her body briefly, clumsily, with hands and mouth, then mounted her. The urgency he felt permitted no delay. She did not struggle or cooperate but simply lay there. Harvey didn't notice and didn't care what she was feeling. All that mattered was the powerful sensation mounting, building, spilling over as he found release.

Harvey surprised himself that night. He was insatiable, assaulting Angela repeatedly. He lost track of the rapes over the next two hours but later estimated there had been a minimum of "four or five." When he was finally exhausted, lying sprawled across the bed, he knew he had a choice to make.

One way to go, he realized, was simply to take off and leave her there. Angela could describe him to police, but what did that mean? She had no address for him, no phone number. Detectives could waste their time chasing several thousand "Franks" around the city and never come within shouting distance of Harvey Glatman. As long as he was careful with his fingerprints . . .

The flip side of the coin would mean another trip out to the desert. Harvey had no photographs of this one, yet, and he had left his camera in the car. Unless he captured her on film, this night would ultimately lose its substance, fade in memory until he came to question whether it had ever taken place. The photographs were critical to validate Harvey's achievement and enable him to play the evening over in his mind.

"I didn't want to kill her," Harvey later told police. "She was the one I really liked."

The easy way would be for him to tie her up and go back to the car, pick up the Rolleicord, and take

the pictures here. Still, that posed problems: more
exposure to potential witnesses; a risk, however
small, that Angela might free herself and call the cops
while he was gone; the possibility that someone
might show up, despite the hour, and interrupt his
game.

He weighed the pros and cons.

The desert won.

The trick, now, was to make Angela think she had
a chance of coming out on top, surviving her ordeal.
He thought about a ruse and blurted out the first
idea that came to mind.

"I want to take you on a picnic."

Even as he spoke the words, he knew how ludi-
crous they sounded, lying naked with a stranger in
the middle of the night, short moments after raping
her repeatedly. Still, Harvey *willed* her to accept the
lie, and Angela appeared to, grasping at the flimsiest
of straws. Months later, he would tell police she
seemed enthusiastic, looking forward to their outing,
offering to bring along some brandy. Harvey wanted,
needed to believe in her believing *him*. He rolled out
of the bed and told her to get dressed.

While Angela was putting on her clothes, Glatman
demanded money, found her handbag where she
told him it would be, and helped himself to twenty
dollars. It was only fair, he thought. The picnic had
been *his* idea. Why shouldn't she defray the cost?

It was near midnight as they finally made ready
to depart. The tricky part, thought Glatman, would
be walking to the car, almost two blocks away. Suppose they met one of her neighbors, coming home
late from the movies or an all-night market.

Anything could happen.

Screw it.

They were going. Harvey was prepared to use the
pistol, as a last resort. He wasn't carrying a toy, this

time, and he had no intention of returning to the
joint. A three-time loser went away for life. He knew
that much from reading his detective magazines.

"I have to tie your hands," he said.

"All right."

When it was done, he draped a coat across her
shoulders, covering the rope that bound her wrists
behind her back. He kept the pistol in his pocket as
they left the flat, directing Angela along the sidewalk,
to his Dodge. He helped her in, the perfect gentleman, retrieved his blanket from the trunk, then ran
around and slid behind the wheel.

Glatman followed his favorite route, driving south
on the Santa Ana Freeway through Orange County,
to catch the coastal highway (now Interstate 5) south
of San Juan Capistrano. He made two stops for gas
along the way, before they got to Oceanside, each
time making sure that Angela was wrapped securely
in the blanket, cautioning her to pretend she was
asleep.

From Oceanside, he drove eastward, toward the
desert. Pale dawn was breaking as they cleared Escondido, and he kept on driving for a little while,
until he found a place that seemed secure.

Harvey and Angela spent all that Thursday in the
desert, having sex and snapping pictures. She was
bound and gagged, the way he liked it, for the photographs, but Harvey didn't need the ropes when they
were "making love." By that time, Glatman had convinced himself that Angela enjoyed what they were
doing, that it was a mutual experience. She suffered
from the heat while she was posing for him, though,
and as the day wore on, he finally relented, driving
to a cooler spot, where they could while away the
afternoon with sex and brandy, dozing now and
then, with no fear on Harvey's part that she would
try to get away.

By sundown, he was back to his original quandary: To kill, or not to kill? "I tried and tried to figure out how to keep from killing her," he said, months later, "but I couldn't come up with any answer."

Finally, despairing of a peaceable solution, he told Angela he wanted to take some more pictures, this time using a flash attachment to his camera. They drove a while on narrow, unpaved roads until they reached a point some thirty miles or less from Shirley Bridgeford's final resting place.

Taking the blanket, ropes, and camera, Harvey ordered Angela out of the Dodge. They walked some distance, Glatman scouting out locations, finally selecting one that had the backdrop he desired. He spread the blanket, smoothing it as best he could over the lumpy ground.

"Take off your dress."

Angela's white slip shimmered, almost ghostly in the pale light of a quarter-moon. She lay down on the blanket, not protesting as he bound her hands behind her back, then looped more rope around her thighs and ankles, finally gagging her, as he had done at the apartment. Satisfied with the tableau, Glatman snapped several photographs, the flashbulbs winking brightly, freezing images that he would savor through the lonely days and nights to come.

When he was finished, Harvey laid the Rolleicord aside and brought the five-foot length of rope out from his pocket, crouching next to Angela, and going through the now-familiar motions: loop around the ankles, loop around the neck, back on his feet and pinning her with one foot in the middle of her back before she could protest.

It bothered Harvey, strangling Angela. She was the one he "really liked," who meant the most to him, but he could not afford to spare her life. When she was dead at last, he stripped her corpse, except for

panties, rolled her off the blanket, and concealed her
carelessly with some loose brush from the vicinity.

There was no point in hiding her from the coyotes.
They would find her by the smell, in any case.

Back at the Dodge, he rifled through her purse and
found ten dollars he had missed the first time. Harvey pocketed the cash, her wristwatch, and her wallet. All the rest of it—her clothing, bag, the other
contents of her purse—would be discarded piecemeal
on the drive back home.

It was Sunday, July twenty-seventh, before the
manager of Ruth's apartment building missed her,
curious about the mail that overflowed her mailbox.
Rapping on the door, she got no answer but the distant, muffled whining of Ruth's collie pup. The landlord used her pass key and found the little dog and
parakeets near death from thirst and hunger. There
were no signs of a struggle, but the scene was definitely odd enough to rate investigation.

Curiously, rather than contacting the police, the
manager sat down and wrote a letter to Ruth's
mother, Francisca Mercado, in Plattsburgh, New
York. Lieutenant Marvin Jones, in L.A.P.D.'s Wilshire
Division, first learned of Ruth's disappearance when
he was informed, via telephone, by Plattsburgh authorities. Jones dispatched Sergeant Paul Light, from
the division's missing persons detail, to investigate.

A background check on Ruth Mercado told police
that she had been a nightclub stripper, when she
wasn't posing in the buff for horny shutterbugs.
Ruth's "boyfriend," the piano player, had been playing in Bermuda when she disappeared and was elim-
inated as a suspect. Light next learned that Ruth had
left her previous apartment, on South Kenmore Avenue, after being harassed with a series of obscene
phone calls. Once, shortly before she moved, some-

one had slipped a nasty note under her door. It sounded promising, at first, until the author of the note and calls was traced. A former neighbor of the missing woman, he possessed an iron-clad alibi for Wednesday night and Thursday, when she disappeared. The man had hassled Ruth, he said, because he didn't want a "cheap slut" for a neighbor.

Welcome to L.A.

Lieutenant Jones ran through the L.A.P.D. missing-persons files, noting a similarity between Mercado's disappearance and two other open cases. A year had passed since pinup model Judy Dull dropped out of sight, last seen with a jug-eared suspect who called himself "Johnny Glenn." The same description fit "George Williams," sought in the March eighth disappearance of Shirley Bridgeford, but detectives were no closer to their man—or men—than they had been twelve months ago. With Ruth Mercado, there was no description, nothing to suggest the same guy was involved. For all Jones knew, she might have skipped town on a whim, abandoning her pets the same way other runaways left children and spouses to fend for themselves.

In fact, the police had nothing to work with, no good leads to follow. Lieutenant Jones was well aware that models, would-be actresses, and strippers came and went in thousands through Los Angeles. Some made it to the silver screen, but most did not. The failures rarely left a forwarding address.

It was Monday, September twenty-second, two months after she had disappeared, before Ruth's photograph was featured in L.A.P.D.'s daily police bulletin. Her profile, numbered DR-378-293, shared space with hot-check artist Leon Payton and a list of stolen bicycles. Ruth was listed as a missing adult, with a "Special Notice: Will Not Extradite." Authorities in other jurisdictions were advised that she "May seek employment at nude modeling or as a stripper." A final notation—"Mental condition poor"—suggested the low priority of her case. Any officer who stumbled upon her by chance was urged to "Kindly Notify the Chief of Police, Los Angeles, California."

There were no calls in answer to the bulletin. Lieutenant Jones and Sergeant Light expected none. The earth had opened up and swallowed Ruth Mercado, just as it had done with Judy Dull and Shirley Bridgeford.

It would be a miracle, Jones thought, if any of the three was ever found alive.

10

"He Wasn't Very Clever"

A FEW DAYS AFTER RUTH MERCADO'S MURDER, GLATMAN found another job as a repairman, at Bruce Radio, on South Robertson Avenue. The job paid eighty-five dollars a week, and Harvey kept it for the last two months he was at liberty. This time, it would not be his attitude that got him canned, but the arrest that ultimately put him on death row.

Glatman's mental state, meanwhile, was rapidly deteriorating. Behind the bland façade, he was increasingly obsessed with dominating women and forcing them to live his bondage fantasies. Compulsive masturbation failed to satisfy him now, with three successful abductions behind him, and while the grim necessity of murdering his "dates" still nagged at Harvey, it was something he could live with. Strangling Ruth had been the worst, by Glatman's own account, but he had gotten over it in record time.

As summer faded, he was on the prowl again, hitting the studios, hunting for Number Four.

Obsession has its price, and Harvey had begun to

show the strain as autumn rolled around. His hygiene suffered, transforming the tidy nerd look into an unkempt—frequently unwashed—façade that would have made him even more repulsive to young women, if he had been forced to woo them by conventional means.

Fortunately for Glatman, he had learned to do without the amenities. All he needed was an advertisement and a phone, his blue-steel Browning .32 . . . and rope.

The Diane Studio in Hollywood, at 5353 Sunset Boulevard, provided pinup models for a price. Ostensibly, the men who hired them by the hour were professional photographers, employed by magazines or advertising agencies, but it was no surprise to anyone that few of Diane's girls showed up in print. The hourly rate was constant, either way, unless one of the models got a better price for posing in her birthday suit.

Harvey discovered the Diane Studio through the classified ads and made a call, introducing himself as "Frank Johnson." Diane herself posed for him, more than once, but Glatman's unraveling appearance—not to mention his frequently pungent aroma—increasingly put her off. When he turned up at the studio a little after eight o'clock, on Monday night, October twenty-seventh, Diane told him she was too busy to pose for him, herself. Still, it went against the grain to dump a paying customer outright. She thought about it for a moment, making up her mind.

"I have somebody you might like," she said. It would cost him $22.50 for use of the studio, she said, plus another fifteen for the model.

Harvey didn't bat an eye at the expense.

"You've got a deal," he said.

*   *   *

Lorraine Vigil came late to modeling, at age twenty-eight. An almond-eyed brunette, she had the looks for it, but she was barely getting started at an age when most successful models have been posing for a decade. Ten years out of high school, she was working as a secretary in Los Angeles and renting spartan quarters on West Sixth Street, from Harry Ellis and his wife, when she decided it was time for a change.

Like Harvey Glatman, she was browsing through the paper when she saw an advertisement for the Diane Studio, deciding that it couldn't hurt to pay a call at the office, on Sunset. Lorraine had never really dreamed of modeling, as some girls do from childhood on, but it would be a change of pace. Or, maybe, something more. "I think," she later told reporters, "I applied for it because I was lonely."

Diane interviewed the new applicant and liked what she saw, signing Lorraine on as the latest member of her team. Diane took several photos of Lorraine, as Vigil later explained to police, for display to potential customers. Curiously, the report also notes that Diane also took three shots of Lorraine in the nude but explained that "these were not to be used, only for [Lorraine's] personal use."

The best shoots went to seasoned girls, of course— or to Diane herself—but there was no shortage of would-be photographers in Los Angeles, and their money was good, regardless of their motives. If a girl knew how to watch out for herself, there shouldn't be a problem.

Lorraine had only been on the list a few days, and she had yet to draw her first assignment by October twenty-seventh. She went to bed early that Monday evening, glumly looking forward to another day of office work, but the telephone woke her around 9:00

P.M. Diane was on the line, with a possible job. Did Lorraine want to give it a try?

She did, indeed.

Diane informed her that Frank Johnson would be dropping by to pick her up within the half-hour. He was paying fifteen dollars an hour for the session, and they would be shooting at Diane's studio, on Sunset.

Lorraine scrambled to get ready, as soon as she hung up the phone. It was a rush, but the excitement brought her wide awake and gave her extra energy. She had already finished dressing, brushing out her hair, and was working on her makeup when the telephone distracted her. It was Diane again.

"Listen, Lorraine . . . about this guy . . ."

"What's wrong, Diane?"

"It may be nothing, but . . ."

"What *is* it?"

"Well," Diane went on, "he's sort of creepy. Definitely not a pro photographer, you know? Just watch yourself, all right?"

"I will."

The phone call left Lorraine uneasy, but she told herself Diane was just concerned because it was her first assignment with the agency. Perhaps the boss lady was worried she would mess things up, insult the customer somehow. Surely, Diane would not have set her up with anybody dangerous. It made no sense.

She shrugged the eerie feeling off and finished getting ready, putting on her lipstick, smoothing out her eye shadow. Frank Johnson might be "creepy," but a model had to cope with horny weirdos, now and then. Lorraine had learned that much from her initial briefing with Diane. No matter what kind of attire— or lack thereof—a girl negotiated with the customer, he didn't get to touch the merchandise.

Lorraine had butterflies in her stomach as she waited for her first client to arrive. Fifteen dollars wasn't exactly a fortune, but it would be a start. Lorraine was on her way.

She waited in the front room, making small talk with the Ellises. It was no secret that the lady of the house had strong reservations about Lorraine's choice of a second career. She never came right out and said that "model" was a synonym for "prostitute," but there was something in her eyes, the way her small mouth turned down at the corners when they talked about it. She had warned Lorraine about the kind of men who paid to look at girls, but what did that mean? Mrs. Ellis might be getting on in years, but there were certain things that she had clearly *not* experienced. Lorraine was fairly certain that no man had ever paid to take *her* photograph. It might just be a case of sour grapes.

And, yet . . .

It nagged at her, this warning from Diane, the first time out. A creepy guy? So, what?

If she was going to succeed in this new business, she would have to deal with creeps as well as normal men—assuming there were any in Los Angeles. It was the mark of a professional, she knew, to handle anything—or anyone—that came along.

It was a quarter past the hour when a rapping sounded on the door. Lorraine was startled; there had been no flash of headlights on the street outside, no sound of an approaching car. The Ellises were staring at her, neither one of them making a move to get the door. Lorraine got up and went to answer it.

The stranger on the porch had brown hair, parted on the left, but carelessly. He had a rumpled, un-washed look about him, as if he was used to sleeping in his clothes. Large ears and a prominent nose sup-ported the horn-rimmed glasses that gave him an

owlish appearance, enhanced by the way he blinked
at her.

"Diane sent me," he said, as if seeking admission
to a 1920s speakeasy.

"Frank Johnson?"

"Right."

"My name's Lorraine." She thought about the last
call from Diane and said, "You have identification?"

The stranger blinked in surprise. "Um . . . no."

"A driver's license?" asked Lorraine.

"I left it home."

Lorraine was on the verge of turning him away,
but she could not afford to blow her first job with
the agency. This *had* to be Frank Johnson. Why else
would he even be there?

Still . . .

"Diane told me to get the money first," she said.
It was a small lie, and the cash would help to put
her mind at ease.

"Well . . ." The stranger frowned and rummaged
in a pocket of his wrinkled pants and handed her
ten dollars.

"It's supposed to be fifteen," Lorraine reminded
him.

"I'm out of change, right now," the stranger said.

It was the perfect out, a way to put him off without
offending her employer. She considered it, but only
for a moment. Even if she never got the other five,
ten dollars for an hour's work was several times
what she could make behind a secretary's desk.

"All right," she said, reluctantly, and put the
money in her purse. "I'll be right back."

She closed the door halfway, not wanting to be
rude. Lorraine went back into the living room and
told the Ellises that she was leaving now. She told
them Johnson's name, informed them that she would
be posing at Diane's, on Sunset Boulevard. It felt like

cheap insurance, but she didn't know how much of it was getting through. Her landlord did not answer, and his wife was staring at Lorraine—*glaring* would be more like it—with a look of disapproval that a blind man couldn't miss.

"Well, then . . . I'm going now," she told them, giving up. "I won't be late."

She closed the door behind her, as she joined Frank Johnson on the porch. The curb was empty.

"Where's your car?" she asked him.

"Over there." He pointed to the right, nothing but darkness there, as far as she could tell. Lorraine let Johnson lead her off the porch, across the yard, along the sidewalk. Half a block down, she saw a two-door Dodge, parked on the far side of the street.

They jaywalked, Johnson moving toward the driver's side. He held the door and waited for Lorraine to sit behind the steering wheel, then scoot across. He took his place and fumbled the ignition key into its slot.

Up close, this way, she realized that Johnson smelled of cigarettes . . . and something else. She caught a pungent whiff of body odor, as if Johnson had not bathed for several days. Lorraine did her best to ignore it, concentrating on the job at hand. It was her first assignment, and they would be shooting at Diane's. As for the money he was short, Diane could deal with that.

So what, if this Frank Johnson smelled bad? All she had to do was pose for him, not cuddle with him. How bad could it be?

"We're going to Diane's, she told me," said Lorraine.

The stranger frowned again. "There's been a change of plans," he said. "She's got some other people coming over, so we have to use my studio."

A faint alarm bell sounded in her mind. "Where's that?" she asked.

"In Anaheim," he said. "It's not too far. We'll be there thirty, forty minutes, tops."

"All right," she said

But suddenly, it did not feel all right, at all.

Harvey could feel the old excitement mounting as he pulled out from the curb on Sixth Street, eastbound. He stayed on Sixth as far as Fairfax, turning south from there to pick up Wilshire Boulevard, joining the flow of nighttime traffic, heading east again.

Lorraine was quiet as they drove, and Glatman tried to keep the conversation going, telling her about the job he thought she would be perfect for. It was a magazine shoot, Harvey told her. She might even make the cover, if he got the shots he needed.

Glatman thought she seemed excited at the prospect, not that it would make a difference to the end result. He had already sized her up, deciding that she suited him. When he finished with her, once he had the photographs he needed, she would have to die.

Too bad.

The thought of murder still gave him no pleasure, but he had already proved that he could live with it.

Lorraine began to open up a little, as they drove on through what passed for darkness in Los Angeles, headlights and neon blazing as they crossed LaBrea, Highland, Rossmore, Western Avenue. She told him that he was her first assignment, and the news made Harvey smile. It would be rather like deflowering a virgin—or, at least, as close as he could come to guessing how that felt, with no experience.

Wilshire angled southeastward from Lafayette Park, through MacArthur Park, past Good Samaritan Hospital, on toward Harvey's connection with the

northbound Harbor Freeway. As he drove, he
thought about Diane, and how she would react when
Lorraine failed to show up for breakfast tomorrow.

It would mean another call to the police, of course.
So, what? Diane knew him only as Frank Johnson;
she had no address or phone number—not even fake
ones. The authorities would ask for his description,
and Diane had seen enough of him to make it
accurate.

Again he thought, *So, what?*

If he assumed the worst, detectives smart enough
to draw a link between Lorraine and his three other
victims, they would still be no closer to making an
arrest. Harvey would have to cool it for a while, back
off the modeling approach until the heat died down
again, but there were always other ways to meet
young women.

Harvey had already gotten away with murder
three times in L.A., evading what was widely touted
as the nation's most professional big-city police department. The cops weren't even close, as far as he
could tell. There were no stories in the newspapers
connecting the disappearances of two pinup models
and a factory worker in the past fifteen months.
Would reporters sit on something like that to assist
the police?

No matter.

Glatman was well ahead of the game. For the first
time in his life, he felt significant—*powerful*—not only
for the dominance he exerted over the lives of his
chosen victims, but for the skill he had displayed in
dodging homicide investigators. He had started out
an amateur at rape and murder, graduating almost
overnight to leave the cops with three—count 'em,
three!—unsolved mysteries on their hands.

It would not have occurred to Harvey that he
owed his freedom more to luck than to any great

intelligence or skill. So far, he had selected women
whose passing, while traumatic to family and friends,
barely caused a ripple in the broader fabric of L.A.
Two of them had been mothers, granted, but they
were *single* mothers, a pinup model and a human
cog on an assembly line. They were not socially or
economically *significant*. And, as for Ruth Mercado,
well . . .

More to the point, no one was really looking for
them any more. Judy Dull and Shirley Bridgeford
were presumed dead by police, but lacking bodies—
and they did not count the "two-year-old" skeleton
from Riverside County—there was nothing left for
homicide detectives to investigate. Ruth Mercado,
meanwhile, was simply a Mexican stripper who
dropped out of sight with no witnesses to place her
with a man, much less a suspect matching the description of the elusive "Johnny Glenn–George Williams." If police found Ruth alive, she faced a
misdemeanor count of cruelty to animals that no one
in his right mind would pursue to trial. If she was
dead . . . again, so what?

Dumb luck, but Glatman didn't see it that way.
Adolescent burglaries aside, he had never shown any
great aptitude for stealth. Each time he pulled a
stickup or grabbed a woman off the street, he had
been arrested within hours or days.

Until he wised up and started disposing of
witnesses.

Now, he was going on a year and a half, three
rape-murders behind him, number four in the works,
and the cops were still clueless. He had already
tested L.A.'s finest, and they didn't cut the mustard.
It was three for three, his game, and Harvey saw no
reason to believe that they would *ever* catch him, if
he kept it nice and simple, chose his targets carefully,
and cleaned up afterward.

The desert was his friend. Why should he worry,
when coyotes, rats, and insects did the dirty work?

"Excuse me?"

Number Four had asked him something. He had
missed it.

Careful.

"Where's your studio, again?"

"A little further," Harvey said. "In Anaheim. It
won't be long."

He saw the ramp he wanted coming up, his cutoff
to the Santa Ana Freeway, headed south.

He smiled to himself and switched the turn signal on.

"I did not become alarmed," Lorraine told reporters, after the fact, "until we entered the Santa Ana
Freeway, and he began driving at a tremendous
speed. He wouldn't answer my questions or even
look at me."

Frank Johnson had changed, in the wink of an eye.
He had been amiable, somewhat mousy, on the first
part of the drive. But now—

Suddenly, he frightened her with the way he was
driving and the grim look on his face. She had begun
to worry that there might be trouble at the studio . . .
until they passed the last off-ramp for Anaheim and
left it in the rearview mirror, fading fast.

"Hey, what's the deal?"

Johnson ignored her, seeming focused on the road
to the exclusion of all else. It finally hit Lorraine that
probably there was no studio at all. She thought
about Diane for just a second, angry, but she couldn't
hold the rage. Fear took priority.

The next stop after Anaheim is Santa Ana, but
Frank Johnson stayed on the freeway, flicking glances
at his mirror and watching for patrol cars, as he kept
his speed above the posted limit. Lorraine considered

jumping from the car, but Johnson kept on driving in the middle lane. A leap at that speed would mean crushing impact with the pavement, and she also ran the major risk of being flattened by another vehicle.

Lorraine decided she would stick it out and wait to see what Johnson had in mind.

Approaching Tustin, he pulled over to the right-hand lane and slowed a little, as if watching for an exit. They were still traveling too fast for Lorraine to bail out, but if they left the freeway for a surface street, she might yet have a chance.

She saw the highway sign ahead, bright green, with "Tustin Ranch Road" inscribed in white, reflective letters. Johnson did not use his turn signal. With another quick glance at the mirror, he gave the steering wheel a slight tug to the right and left the freeway, following the broad loop of the exit ramp.

"I think we've got a flat," he said, surprising her.

Lorraine could not help frowning. She would certainly have heard and felt a blowout at the speed they had been traveling, but there was nothing—not a sound or a vibration. Even now, as they were slowing down and coasting toward the shoulder of a narrow, darkened road, there was no rumble from a flat. The Dodge ran straight and true.

"I don't think—"

"Just be quiet!"

"Listen, you—"

The pistol in his hand made her forget what she had planned to say. She didn't know where it had come from, but he had it pointed at her face.

"I'm an ex-con," he told her, "and I'll kill you if you give me any trouble. I don't give a damn about the gas chamber."

"What do you want from me?" she asked him, stalling. It was obvious. He had not driven her this far and pulled a gun simply to get his money back.

"I want sex," Johnson said, confirming her worst fear. "I need to tie you up. Hang on."

The automatic wobbled as he reached into his pocket with his free hand, drawing out a length of rope.

"Now, turn around and put your hands behind your back," he said.

Lorraine half-turned away from him, doing as she was told. She felt him fumbling with the rope, knotting a loop around her right wrist, pulling her left arm further back.

"Please, don't!" she begged. Lorraine could feel the hot tears brimming in her eyes, and her face flushed with panic as she thought of what could happen if she let him bind her hands.

"I'm telling you—"

It struck her, then: If he was using both hands on the rope, it meant that he had laid the pistol down, somewhere. Impulsively, she jerked away from him. Frank Johnson grabbed her by the neck and shook her roughly.

"I'm losing my patience with you!" he snapped. "With my record, I'd just as soon kill you and go to the gas chamber, as not."

The pistol was back in his hand now and aimed at Lorraine. She grabbed for it with no idea how it worked, or whether she could keep the gun from going off. Frank Johnson cursed and threatened her but did not pull the trigger as Lorraine hung on, her fingers tightly wrapped around the automatic. With his free hand, Johnson clutched the rope that bound her right wrist, yanking on it as if it were a leash, trying to make her behave.

Grappling with him in the Dodge, Lorraine, nearly hysterical, was sickened by the body odor he exuded. Neither of them spoke coherently, the driver hissing curses through clenched teeth, Lorraine sobbing as she fought for control of the gun.

When it went off, the gunshot sounded loud as thunder in the car. The bullet pierced her skirt and scorched a track across the outside of her thigh. Frank Johnson seemed as startled as she was and recoiled from her with a dazed look on his face.

"I shot you!" Johnson said, sounding bewildered, dazed.

Lorraine knew she would never have a better chance. She twisted free of Johnson's grip and found the inside handle of the passenger's door, yanking sharply on it as she threw her weight against the door, pushing off with her feet.

The door flew open, spilling Lorraine onto the shoulder of the road. She skinned her palms and knees, scrambled to her feet in a rush, braced for another gunshot. The next one, she knew, would not be wasted. It would drill her skull or punch a hole between her shoulder blades.

She dodged to her right, away from the open door and the glare of the dome light, gasping as a hand clutched her sweater, hauling her backward. Instead of shooting her, Frank Johnson lunged out through the open door in close pursuit. He tackled her, and both of them went sprawling on the shoulder of the highway, rolling over, Lorraine kicking and scratching, trying to get a fresh grip on the pistol.

Days later, looking back, she spoke of "cars, millions of cars" passing by, headlights illuminating the combatants, but no one stopped to help her.

She was all alone and fighting for her life.

"He wasn't very clever," she told reporters, afterward. "I bit his wrist, and he cried out. Then, suddenly, I found I had the gun in my hand. I turned it around and pointed it at him. If I had known how to fire it, I believe I could have killed him."

Johnson froze in his tracks, waiting for the gun-shot. He was still standing there, hunched forward like a wrestler, arms extended, when the bright glare of approaching headlights washed across his sweaty face.

Highway patrolman Thomas Francis Mulligan had drawn the swing shift that Monday, working from 2:00 P.M. until 10:00 P.M. at night. He was off duty when he turned his motorcycle onto Tustin Ranch Road, already starting to relax and looking forward to a good night's sleep. A few more minutes and he would be on the freeway, headed for the station, and from there, toward home in Costa Mesa.

Policing California's labyrinthine highway system is a full-time job for several thousand lawmen, seven days a week. Within the limits of a given city, the municipal police are charged with tagging speeders, drunken drivers and the like, and coping with the aftermath of traffic accidents. Unincorporated areas and state (or interstate) highways fall to the Califor-nia Highway Patrol, with occasional support from the appropriate county sheriff's office. Highway Pa-trol officers are not technically restricted to traffic stops, serving also as support troops during riots and disasters, manhunts, and pursuit of fleeing fugitives from justice, but the average day for a patrolman on the highway sees more tickets written out for moving violations than arrests for major crimes.

That Monday afternoon and evening had been strictly average for Patrolman Mulligan, but now that he was off the clock, it was about to change. His end-of-watch report describes what happened next.

Driving south on Tustin Av., approx. 200 yds. So. of the Santa Ana Freeway, observed a vehicle parked on the right dirt shoulder, headed S.E.

next to an orange grove. As I passed the vehicle going S.E. I noticed the dome light was on and the right front door was open. It appeared as though two figures were struggling between the vehicle and the grove. I turned around to investigate. I pulled up approx. 25 feet to the rear of the vehicle, with my motorcycle. My headlight picked up two struggling figures alongside the vehicle, near the right rear, in the dirt. As I arrived, a female was lying on the ground struggling quite violently with a man on top of her. They both jumped up when I appeared. The female came running back toward my bike, screaming, "He's trying to kill me!! He's trying to kill me!! Help me!! He's crazy!! Here's his gun. I got it away from him!" She was quite hysterical and broke down and started crying. The subject was walking back toward the girl and myself. I ordered him to stand still and keep his hands out of his pockets. He was wild eyed and quite irrational at this time. His clothes were disarranged and dirty and his mouth was bleeding. He appeared to be emotionally unstable.

"He had a lunatic stare," Mulligan later told reporters. "I'll never forget that wild look he had in his eyes. He was sloppy-dressed, and I don't think he had had a bath in a week. It took three or four minutes for him to get hold of himself."

Mulligan denied interrogating Harvey at the scene, but after Glatman had calmed down a bit, he apparently made a statement, recorded in the arrest report as follows: "I just wanted to scare her. I just wanted to tie her up. I don't know if I would have raped her or not, but I might have. I've been out here for about three months from Colorado. I'm not working right now. I just met her tonight. I met her through Diane.

She runs a model agency in Hollywood. It's my gun. I've had it quite a long time. No, I do not have a permit for it. Back where I come from, you don't need one."

The brief report follows through Officer Mulligan's reaction to the statement. "I called the dispatcher for a sheriff's unit and a California Highway Patrol unit to roll to the scene," Mulligan wrote. "Tustin P.D. arrived approx. two minutes after my call, followed by Officer[s] Knapp and Virus, C.H.P.[,] and then a sheriff's unit rolled up. I turned the prisoner and the gun over to them. Upon arrival, Sgt. Sissel, Tustin P.D., handcuffed the subject. Subject turned over to Sheriff's Officers Mann and W. Williams."

As far as Mulligan was concerned, the case was "to be handled to conclusion by Sheriff's Department," but none of them had a clue, yet, as to what that conclusion would be.

The initial felony report filed by Deputies Mann and Williams picks up where Officer Mulligan's arrest report left off. That document provides the following account:

> When assigned arrived at scene, two CHP officers and Sgt. Sissel of Tustin Police Department were at the scene. Officer Thomas Mulligan of CHP stated that the victim and the suspect were scuffling beside the suspect's car. Officer Thomas Mulligan stopped and found the victim with the above described gun in her hand, a length of heavy 3/16 inch cotton rope tied in a slip knot around her right wrist.
>
> After assigned talked to CHP officer Thomas Mulligan, the victim was taken to the Sheriff's patrol car and Officer W. H. Williams talked with suspect. The victim was sitting in the front

seat of the suspect's car with the rope still tied
around her right wrist. . . .

The victim gave her name at first as Lorrie
Beck, but later told Deputy Mann that her name
was Lorraine Vigil.

The true name of the suspect is Harvey Murray Glatman. The suspect was not questioned by
assigned except as to his name and address. Both
victim and suspect were turned over to Investigators Coley and Pittsenbarger. The gun and
length of rope and fired shell casing were put in
the evidence locker. The shell casing had been
moved from its original position before assigned
arrived, it was on the back floor of the car. I.D.
was taking pictures of the car before it was im-
pounded by Tustin Garage.

Detectives Coley and Pittsenbarger picked up the account in their report.

Contacted both victim and suspect at the scene
on Tustin Ave. as given in the initial report by
Deputies W. Williams and Mann. There were
several officers at the scene upon assigned's
arrival.

Received information from Deputies Mann
and W. Williams that an assault to commit rape
had occurred at this location.

Suspect was placed in the assigned's vehicle
with Officer Pittsenbarger remaining in the vehicle with suspect.

Victim was moved from Deputies Mann and
Williams['s] patrol car and placed in the identification vehicle, as assigned checked the scene
and the suspect's vehicle with identification tech-
nician Steelmon.

The scene was photographed along with the vehicle and the contents of the vehicle.

It was noted that there was a bullet hole in the right hand end of the front seat of the vehicle along the outer edge. This bullet entered from the top of the seat, traveled down and outward, exiting from the end of the seat and entering the door on the vehicle. The bullet did not come out of the door.

This bullet hole was photographed and the bullet was recovered by Steelmon. Inside the passenger compartment of the vehicle was found[,] in the floor of the rear seat compartment, three brown paper bags. One on the right-hand side contained three quarts (jars) containing a clear liquid believed to be water, several green apples, shaving soap. One in the center but was nearer the left-hand side, contained cigarettes, peanut butter, apple sauce in cans, toilet tissue; one on the left-hand side of the vehicle, behind the driver's seat, contained a camera, several rolls of film, size 120, part of a box of 32 cal. automatic shells, a shell clip for a 32 caliber automatic with three shells in same, a camera light meter, several pieces of small rope. This last mentioned bag was photographed. An overall photograph was taken showing the three bags. In the rear seat there was a portable radio, a pillow, a grey in color cotton trousers, miscellaneous papers, maps, etc. In the trunk compartment was found a camera tripod, an old table type radio, three dress shirts in a paper bag (clean), a small green tool box containing miscellaneous small tools, a 2 ½ gal. can of gasoline, a cloth zipper type clothes [sic] contained a top coat and several items of clothing (men's)[,] blankets, several

large pieces of cloth such as may have been used
as bedding at one time.

All of the above mentioned, were left in the
vehicle at the scene by the undersigned in the
care of Steelmon who was still in the process of
taking photographs. Sgt. Broadbelt also remained
at the scene with the vehicle and Steelmon.

As for Harvey Glatman, he was on his way to jail,
still hoping he could make the best of what was
shaping up as a disaster.

11

"Aren't Three Enough?"

GLATMAN WAS BOOKED AT THE ORANGE COUNTY JAIL, IN Santa Ana, under case number DR-77009. There are conflicting reports of the initial charges filed against him: Deputies Mann and Williams list the charges in their report as attempted rape and assault with a deadly weapon, supported by identical charges on Officer Mulligan's C.H.P arrest report; Detectives Coley and Pittsenbarger, meanwhile, recorded the charges as assault to commit rape and suspicion of murder. If correct, the latter charge was clearly added on a hunch with nothing to back it up at first. Still, it was better to be safe than sorry.

The investigators didn't know it yet, but they were onto something. They would pick up all the evidence they needed, once their suspect started talking.

At the Tustin garage, Harvey's Dodge gave up another surprise: red rubber gloves, the standard household kind, and $200 in cash, hidden beneath the front floor mat. Another $750 was removed from Glatman's wallet, the total leading officers to suspect that he might be a robber.

They didn't know the half of it.

Back in Santa Ana, Lorraine Vigil—having discarded the "Lorrie Beck" pseudonym—was describing her wild night to Detectives Coley and Pittsenbarger. As noted in their report,

> . . . [I]t was learned that victim had a bullet hole in the right hand side of her skirt, caused by a bullet from a gun that suspect pulled on victim in the vehicle, at which time a scuffle ensued between victim and suspect over the gun and the gun was accidentally discharged, the bullet going through victim's skirt and into the vehicle as mentioned above.
>
> The bullet did contact victim's right leg, causing a small skinned place on the outer right leg. Also some powder burn. The bullet contact did not cause any bleeding.
>
> Victim was photographed of all bruises about the face, neck, arm and leg. The skirt and slip were removed from victim at Sheriff's Office and placed in the evidence locker.

Harvey Glatman, meanwhile, was spinning a tale of his own, trying to cast himself in the best possible light, all things considered. As recorded by Coley and Pittsenbarger in their report, Harvey claimed,

> That last Thursday, he thought some about getting a model for photographing and possibl[y] raping the model or at least satisfy his sexual desires whatever they may have been at the time that he committed the planned act. (general rape was the intent). And that about 8:00 P.M. 10-27-58, he put food and water in his vehicle and went to the Diane Studio, 5353 Sunset Blvd. for the purpose of h[i]ring a model.

Upon contacting a person known to him as Diane at the Diane Studio, arrangements were made by Diane for a fee $22.50 to her (Diane) and an additional fee to be paid the model, for suspect to pick up the victim at her home. Diane gave suspect victim's address and name written on a piece of paper. (This paper tagged and placed in evidence.) Suspect stated that victim believed that he was going to return her to Diane's Studio for the photographs.

Suspect stated in substance the same as victim regarding what occurred at the front door of victim's home, the conversation as they drove along the freeway and what happened at the scene on Tustin Ave. In addition to what was stated above, suspect further stated what his intent was for committing the act. Suspect stated that his intent was to satisfy his sexual desire. "I was going to screw her if I had to satisfy myself, maybe I would have satisfied by petting her, I don't know how far I would have went."

Suspect wanted to tie victim so as to have her under his control and would not have to worry about victim getting away before he had finished what he wished to do.

Suspect was asked why he put food and water in the vehicle before leaving home, and he answered, "[W]ith the record I have and if she jumped out of the car or got away from me and reported what I had attempted to do the police would be looking for me and I would have used the food and stayed away from home or any place, would have parked on some out of the way road for several days. Even if I had completed the act I desired, and let the victim out some place, she may have reported it and anything can go wrong some time. I just wanted to be prepared in case anything went wrong.["]

Suspect stated that he had given the act quite a lot of thought as to committing the sexual act with some female but did not have any particular female in mind, just anyone that could be arranged for by the Diane Studio. Did not decide upon any place to commit the act. Just any place that he may have driven to.

The conversation with suspect was tape recorded. Suspect's clothes were removed and placed in identification locker.

Harvey's record of assaulting women and his careful preparation for the bungled rape attempt belied his story of a rash, impulsive act. In Santa Ana, Sheriff's Sergeant Danny Rios had a hunch that there was something far more sinister involved. For openers, he set his deputies to work reviewing local files, searching for any case where pinup models had been raped or turned up missing. At the same time, he sent out an all-points bulletin to the Los Angeles Police Department and the L.A. County sheriff, seeking any cases from their files that seemed to fit.

Lieutenant Marvin Jones, at L.A.P.D.'s Wilshire Division, received the APB and thought at once of Ruth Mercado. There was nothing to suggest a link, beyond the fact that she had been a model, but he saw from the report that Glatman lived nearby, on Norton Avenue. It was a short drive to the bungalow, and Jones took stock of it from the outside: white paint that had begun to peel; tar paper on the roof; bars on the windows. When he made his way inside, Jones found the walls covered with pinup photos, many of them nudes, some showing women bound and gagged.

Lieutenant Jones sent two of his sergeants, Pierce

Brooks and Elmer Jackson, to help question Glatman on the Bridgeford and Mercado disappearances. By the time they arrived in Santa Ana, Captain Jim Bruton and Detective John Lawton were already on hand, representing the L.A. County sheriff's homicide division, armed with questions about Judy Dull and several other women who had turned up dead or missing during recent years.

Glatman was cagey at first, repeating his admission of the "impulsive" attack on Lorraine Vigil, denying any further knowledge of assaults on women in the area. Investigators Brooks and Jackson knew about the quick search of his bungalow on Norton, the peculiar photographs Lieutenant Jones had found, and Harvey struck them as a shaky liar who would crack with just a little pressure, properly applied.

No one had briefed the suspect on his right to silence. Seven more years would pass before the United States Supreme Court's historic *Miranda* decision, but Glatman might have waived the right, in any case. Harvey still hoped he could talk his way out of the corner, bullshit the detectives, and string them along. If they had not turned up his secret stash of photographs and other souvenirs, their case fell back on vague suspicion.

Harvey did not fret about the prospect of a lineup. Even if he was identified by Judy Dull's roommates and Shirley Bridgeford's family, what did that prove? They could place him with the missing women, but they could not prove the two were dead, much less that he had been responsible for killing them.

Unless they found the toolbox.

Glatman stalled them for the next two days, talking in circles, waiting for a glimpse of evidence that would condemn him on a murder charge. It stood to reason that detectives must have found his stash, by now, but nothing was revealed to him. The cops worked in rotation, grilling Harvey, dropping names of dead and missing women. Harvey recognized three, drew a blank on the rest, playing dumb across the board. His stomach knotted when someone suggested a polygraph examination. Glatman's nerves were on a razor's edge already, and he cherished no illusions of his own ability to beat the box.

Polygraph (or "lie detector") test results are inadmissible in California courts—and rightly so, say critics, who suggest that one in every three or four examinations gives out false results. The polygraph, those critics note, is built to measure respiration, pulse, and blood pressure, which *may* reveal a subject's tension when he lies—or which, conversely, may respond to illness, medication, guilt from unrelated issues, or the simple nervousness produced from being questioned by police. Ironically, both fans and critics of the polygraph agree that many hardcore criminals, particularly psychopaths devoid of conscience, can defeat the polygraph at will.

Glatman could have declined the test—a lawyer almost certainly would have advised him to decline—but he felt cornered now. If he refused, police would take it as a sign of guilt, the next best thing to a confession. On the other hand, if he could only put a lid on his anxiety and catch a break. . . .

Harvey agreed, and Sergeant Danny Rios made arrangements for the test on Thursday afternoon. Veteran polygrapher Joe Ogle ran the test, with half a dozen homicide detectives standing by, and Glatman seemed to handle the preliminaries well enough. The hitch came when Harvey was shown a photograph of Ruth Mercado, at which point, Sergeant Rios said, "the polygraph needle about hit the ceiling."

Still wired to the box, Harvey was grilled about Ruth until he broke down. "You can't beat the machine," he muttered. "I suppose you found my tool-box. You're just playing with me now."

Sounding almost relieved, Harvey admitted strangling Ruth, still known to him as Angela Rojas. And while he was on the subject, he added, "I killed a couple of other girls, too."

Authorities drew a blank on Glatman's reference to the toolbox, but it was clearly preying on his mind. Captain Arthur Hertel, representing L.A.P.D. Homicide, secured a search warrant and sent another team to scour the bungalow on Norton. They were luckier this time and found the toolbox stashed in the garage. Locked inside it were the damning photographs and tokens from the dead that would eventually send their murderer to join them. Captain Hertel initially played it close to the vest with the press, reporting only that the contents of the box linked Glatman to Mercado. Searchers, he proclaimed, had found some photographs of Ruth, along with her I.D., "some underclothing and other undisclosed items."

In fact, there were a total of twenty-two snapshots, including glossy black-and-whites, along with color transparencies. More than enough, with any luck at all, to seal Glatman's fate.

While detectives patted themselves on the back, Harvey was busy spilling his guts in Santa Ana. John Lawton handled the interrogation for Judy Dull's murder, eliciting a matter-of-fact confession to the crime. Harvey described the pickup and the rapes at his apartment, their drive to the desert, the way he had strangled Judy and planted her corpse in the sand.

When it came to the photos, Harvey sounded almost boastful, explaining how he had chosen fine-grain Panatonic-X film for the black-and-whites, processing the Ansochrome color transparencies all by himself. He might not be a pro, but he was good enough.

Pierce Brooks handled the grilling on Shirley Bridgeford, while Elmer Jackson did the honors for Ruth Mercado. "With each one," Harvey explained, "I did it the same way. After I attacked them, I knew I had to kill them, for they could identify me and identify my car. So I would drive into the desert, sometimes on the pretext of taking more pictures, sometimes without any reason. I would make them kneel down. With every one it was the same. With the gun on them, I would tie this five-foot piece of rope around their ankles. Then I would loop it up round their neck. Then I would stand there and keep pulling until they quit struggling."

It might have been easier to shoot the women, Harvey conceded, but that would have been "too messy." Against the evidence that he had taken pains to cover up his crimes, Glatman told police that he had often toyed with the thought of surrender. "I didn't have guts enough to give myself up," he explained. "I wanted to do it, but I just couldn't."

Confronted with the evidence from his toolbox, Glatman avoided discussion of his morbid fantasies and put a new twist on the items. As recorded in the L.A. *Times*, "he told deputies that he had kept incriminating evidence of his crime so that if he was ever caught, he would be convicted."

The reporters bought it, or pretended to—in 1958, they never would have been allowed to print the truth of how he used those photographs, regardless—but police knew better.

What they *didn't* know, so far, was whether they had seen the limit of their subject's guilt.

From the moment he confessed to murder, Glatman was an instant suspect in a string of unsolved homicides that spanned the continent. Police in St. Petersburg, Florida, were curious about Harvey. So were Mexican authorities, investigating the death of a young woman found along Highway 10, north of Ensenada, on the same night Glatman was arrested, but Harvey had an airtight alibi for both cases, the latter being his arrest in Tustin.

Another long shot was the case of Donald Norman Zellmer, a thirty-two-year-old Garden Grove resident missing since October twenty-sixth, hauled out of the ocean by commercial fishermen on Halloween morning. Zellmer had vanished from under his wife's very nose, on Sunday night, while they were drinking at a bar in Newport Beach. He was last seen, she said, with another man who bore a "remarkable" resemblance to Harvey Glatman. Mrs. Zellmer had left them alone, according to her statement, after the stranger made "amorous advances," and she feared there would be trouble. Los Angeles police declared themselves "very interested" in having Zellmer's widow take a look at Glatman, but once again, the report came to nothing. Bartenders in Newport Beach disputed the identification, declaring that the anonymous suspect bore little or no resemblance to Glatman. His polygraph test bore them out, and another case went back into the "unsolved" files.

An older homicide from Boulder, Colorado, seemed more promising at first glance. Police in Harvey's old hunting ground were still trying to identify a "Jane Doe" victim, age about twenty, whose nude, battered body was found in an outlying canyon on April 9, 1954. Glatman had been in the neighborhood, still on parole, but he staunchly denied any part in the crime, and the polygraph exonerated him.

Two other L.A. homicides of interest to investigators as they questioned Glatman were the murders of thirty-year-old Ruth Goldsmith, found on April 5,

1957, and twenty-four-year-old Marjorie Hipperson, killed on June tenth of that year. Both had been strangled with stockings in their own apartments, and while Harvey had been in Los Angeles when both crimes occurred, he denied any contact with the victims. Once again, the polygraph supported his denial.

Marjorie Hipperson had been a nurse as was another victim mentioned by police in their grilling of Glatman. Geneva Ellroy had been forty-three years old when she was strangled by persons unknown, her body discovered near Arroyo High School, in suburban El Monte, on June 22, 1958. Like Goldsmith and Hipperson, she had been strangled with a stocking, which the killer left wrapped tightly around her neck, together with a piece of cotton cord. The victim's purse and panties had been missing from the scene; her bra was found underneath the body when it was removed by ambulance attendants. El Monte Police Captain Orval Davis told the press that Ellroy had been murdered elsewhere then transported to the site where she was found.

Although the timing and method of murder made Harvey a natural suspect in Geneva Ellroy's death, there were also telling discrepancies in the case, missing panties and handbag aside. Ellroy had not been driven "to the country" for disposal, and the instrument of death was left around her neck. Of course, detectives had no basis for comparison, as yet, since they had only found one of Glatman's actual victims, Judy Dull, and her skeletal remains were still unidentified.

Harvey, for his part, tried to set them straight. He didn't know Geneva Ellroy, he insisted, and he couldn't find El Monte if his life depended on it. The polygraph supported his denials, but some authorities remained unconvinced, L.A. Sheriff's Captain

C. W. McGowan telling the press "we are by no means satisfied" with Harvey's claim of innocence. Orange County's Sergeant Rios echoed that sentiment, telling reporters that he "wouldn't be surprised if the suspect had killed two or three others," but he was willing to admit that there was no hard evidence supporting that belief.

Through all the peripheral interrogations, Glatman stood fast, proclaiming his innocence of any but the three crimes he had already confessed. "I'm in as deep as I can get," he told police. "Aren't three enough? There isn't anything worse can happen to me. I guess they can only give me one shot of gas."

With the confessions behind him, Harvey seemed to feel better. He followed detectives to his first, brief meeting with the press. It was a switch for Glatman, blinking while the flashbulbs flared in *his* face, but he kept his wits about him, answering questions from the battery of reporters.

"I really didn't like to kill," he said, in answer to one question. "I didn't have that urge. It was just that I got past the point of no return."

What did he mean by that?

"I was afraid they'd identify me," he replied. "Well, not me, because nobody had my picture out here. But the car. They'd make that."

Why were his victims strangled, another journalist asked, when Harvey had a gun?

"Ever since I was a child," he said, "I have been fascinated by rope. It seems as if I always had a piece of rope in my hands."

Or around his neck, for that matter.

All things considered, Harvey held no grudge against police for bringing his murder spree to an end. He was resigned to his fate, but Harvey was not without feeling for others.

"It's my mother I really feel sorry for," he told

the press. "This is going to be harder on her than on me."

Reporters wasted no time in pursuing that angle, telephoning Ophelia in Denver to break the news of Harvey's arrest before she heard about it from her son or the police.

"Oh, my God in heaven!" she reportedly cried, upon hearing the news. "Not my boy! Not my boy! He was always so good. He never hurt anybody."

It was the same old story, harking back to her denial from the days when Harvey was invading homes and stopping women on the street with a toy gun. There were at least four women in Los Angeles who would have disagreed with her, but only one of them was still alive to tell the tale.

12

"This Is the Place"

GLATMAN WAS BARELY FINISHED WITH HIS MARATHON confession, Thursday night, when he was hustled to a squad car waiting in the jailhouse parking lot. Surrounded by detectives from Orange County and Los Angeles, he was driven south from Santa Ana, into San Diego County. There, his escort rendezvoused with sheriff's deputies Roy Williams and James Hathaway, assigned to join the search that was about to be conducted on their turf.

The hour made no difference to these lawmen. They believed that Harvey was the three-time murderer he claimed to be—had proof enough, perhaps, to nail him with the photographs and other trophies he had kept—but they were bent on wrapping up the package with as little wasted time as possible. If that meant searching desert wasteland through the night with Glatman as their guide, so be it.

Anyway, the more humane among them thought, his victims had the extra effort coming to them. They had died alone and helpless, terrified. Their loved ones had been wondering for months, what had become of them, where they had gone. They had been lying in the desert long enough. Another stall would add insult to injury.

There was another reason, too, for taking Harvey to the desert in the middle of the night. If they delayed the trip, there was at least a fifty-fifty chance that he would change his mind, clam up, perhaps recant his statements. It was not uncommon for a murderer to blurt out some incriminating comment, help the cops along, then later change his mind and take it back. Some changed their pleas at trial and claimed confessions had been beaten out of them (a charge that was more likely to be true of L.A.P.D in the 1940s than in Harvey's day, although it still went on from time to time). More than a few had tried to rewrite history *after* their trials, while they were sitting on death row.

If Glatman had a chance to sleep on his confessions, lie there in his cell until the sun came up and think about the penalty he faced, it could make all the difference in the world. Forget about his stated wish to die: that was another claim that homicide investigators heard with nagging regularity. Sometimes it was legitimate, but more often it was an emotional reaction to the moment or a craven bid for sympathy.

And there was something else to think about, as well. If Harvey changed his mind and pled innocent at trial, there was a chance, however slim, that some do-gooder judge might play along and rule his statements inadmissible. In that case, the D.A. would have to try the case with nothing but the evidence retrieved from Harvey's pad on Norton; that meant photographs and Glatman's little stash of souvenirs. And you could never tell what it would take to make a jury see the light.

They had the photographs, some of them shocking,

but the women were alive when they were taken. A
slick defense attorney might persuade twelve level-
headed jurors that the women had enjoyed the kinky
stuff, a little bondage for variety. Mercado was a
stripper and nude model, which would likely deni-
grate her in the jury's view and make it plausible, at
least, that she might pose for bondage photos in her
birthday suit. Bridgeford had been divorced, tied
down with two kids and a full-time job. Your average juror might suspect that she had "been around"
and perhaps start wondering if infidelity or worse
had prompted her divorce.

All that aside, the fact remained that Harvey's photos, in and of themselves, did not prove that the
women were, in fact, deceased. An argument could
be advanced that all three women were alive and
well when Glatman finished with them.

So, where were they? Any lawyer worth his fee
would have no difficulty painting Ruth Mercado as
the next thing to a hooker, one of those who pull up
stakes and vanish on a whim. There had been nothing much to keep her in L.A.—no steady job, no
steady man, no movie parts.

It would be harder to dispose of Shirley Bridgeford, but it could be done. What mother in her twenties had not entertained the fantasy of packing up
and moving on, leaving the brats behind, to find herself some breathing room and a brand-new life? It
happened all the time around Los Angeles.

There were the *other* souvenirs, of course, but what
did they add up to, really? Harvey's stash included
panties and a woman's shoe, but while they might
prove he was kinky, neither item could be positively
linked to a specific victim. He had Ruth Mercado's
wristwatch and I.D., which made a match, but Harvey's mere possession of the items did not prove that
she was dead. Ruth might have left them at the photo

shoot, for instance. Even if the suspect copped to stealing them, it was a misdemeanor petty theft, and Ruth was not around to press the charge.

The prosecution needed more. It needed bodies— or enough of one, at any rate, to prove a homicide had been committed. Skulls would do, if there were dental records for comparison. Bodies would cancel any "reasonable doubt" that might dissuade the jury from convicting Glatman, if his statements wound up being disallowed as evidence.

And finding bodies meant they had to start the search *right now*, while they had Harvey in the mood to hang himself. Tomorrow might be too late.

The two-car caravan rolled south along the San Diego Freeway, turning off at Escondido, headed east from there into the desert, on Highway 78. Harvey directed them to Earthquake Valley, calling for a halt on Vallecitos Road, eight miles and change below the junction known as Scissors Crossing. They were eighty-two miles northeast of San Diego, in the middle of Anza-Borrego Desert State Park.

A brilliant desert moon was shining on them as they piled out of the car, detectives buttoning their suit jackets against the late-night chill. Only the San Diego County deputies wore boots, and the remaining officers—all city boys—knew they would have to watch their step, look out for rattlesnakes and such, while they were following their mousy point man through the scrub brush, seeking human bones.

There would be little else to find, they realized. Harvey's most recent kill had taken place some fourteen weeks ago, and by his own account, the body had been left uncovered. The victim before that—the one they were seeking first—had lain exposed to the elements and scavengers for nearly eight months.

The officers would take what they could get.

Harvey pointed out the spot where he had stopped his Dodge that night in March, raping Shirley Bridgeford in the back seat before he marched her off into the desert. The path from there led over rocky, broken ground, but Glatman knew his way. They hiked a quarter-mile beneath the moon, flashlight beams wobbling in the night, before they reached a dusty gulch. It was approaching 1:00 A.M. on Halloween.

"This is the place," Harvey announced. "It will be on the left side of a bush."

The officers fanned out, Deputies Williams and Hathaway remaining with their tour guide, for security, as he joined in the search. Glatman wasn't going anywhere, handcuffed without a car, but it was better not to take the chance.

It took the best part of an hour, closing in on 1:55 A.M., before he pointed out a tan coat, barely discernible at first glance from the desert soil where it lay, beneath a thorny Joshua tree.

"There it is," he said, softly. "That's hers."

Nearby, lay other articles of clothing and a human leg bone. More remains were scattered down the wash, they saw now, carried away from the kill site by animals or flash-flood waters. It would take some time and a larger team to photograph and gather all the bones.

Confronted with his victim one last time, it was reported to the press that Harvey blanched and turned his back, raising manacled hands to cover his eyes. The story may be true—no newsmen were on hand to witness the event—but a belated show of squeamishness would not help Harvey's case. He had already gone too far, revealed too much.

He was as good as dead.

One of the San Diego officers reported their find

by radio, and the search team remained in place until another deputy arrived to take charge of the crime scene. Shirley Bridgeford had been alone in the desert since March eighth, but she had company now, and more would be along come sunup to conduct another search and salvage what they could.

With one death scene secured, Glatman directed his keepers to the next, a half-hour further down Vallecitos Road. When they had driven twenty-five or thirty miles to the southeast, toward Carrizo Springs and the Imperial County line, Harvey spotted a large-bluff outcropping and called another halt.

"Right here," he said.

They left the cars again, Glatman leading the way overland, trudging with his head down, hands cuffed in front of him, watching his step. At 4:00 A.M., he found the spot he sought and nodded to his escort. Once again, the search began, and it was shorter this time. Harvey had come closer to the mark.

"Over here!" one of the searchers called.

They stood around another human skeleton, this one described in press reports as "virtually undisturbed," dark hair still dangling from the skull.

"Yes, this is her," Glatman confirmed. "Look at her panties."

The detectives were satisfied. Without further questions, they led Harvey back to the road. Another call was made, another officer dispatched to stand watch with the dead until sunrise.

Harvey was finished for the night. A trip to Indio, to find the grave of Judy Dull, would be postponed for three more days. The trip was longer, going back, as Glatman's escorts bypassed Santa Ana, headed for the L.A. Central Jail, downtown. Upon arrival there, he was booked for suspicion of murder, the name and number of his victims still unspecified.

After booking, Harvey was allowed to shower and shave before officers took him to the police cafeteria for his first meal of the day. Breakfast for Glatman that Halloween morning consisted of frankfurters, corn, and mashed potatoes, washed down with coffee, gelatin, and French apple pie à la mode for desert. The L.A. *Times* reported Glatman as "so hungry that at times he stuffed food into his mouth with his hands."

The meal made Glatman sleepy, recalling the fact that he had enjoyed his last nap, of sorts, some thirty-six hours earlier. A jailer led him from the cafeteria to the solitary cell that would be his home for the next five days and left him there.

Beyond those walls, in the free world that Harvey would never share again, survivors of his year-long murder spree were waking to another day of doubt and pain.

By midday on Friday, searchers had recovered all but a few minor bones from the skeletons of Shirley Bridgeford and Ruth Mercado. The remainder would never be found—carried off by scavengers, perhaps, or washed away by one of the desert's rare rain storms—but authorities had everything they needed to nail the lid on Harvey's coffin. Even if he somehow weaseled out of his confession, there were still the photographs of all three women bound and gagged (some of them nudes), the souvenirs that he had taken from each kill, and now the physical remains of two dead victims, pointed out to the police by Harvey himself.

It was, in police jargon, "a dead-bang case."

By Saturday, Dr. Jack Armstrong, a forensic odontologist on the L.A. County coroner's staff, was busy comparing sun-bleached teeth with the known dental records of Shirley Bridgeford and Ruth Mercado. His confirming I.D. of the dead, when it came, would remove any doubt that the two missing women were, in fact, Harvey's victims.

It would be grim news to the survivors of the dead, who in at least two cases clung to hope—far-fetched, at best—that they would someday find the missing, safe and sound.

Judy Dull's child custody case had gone to husband Robert by default, in her absence, although her death had yet to be legally confirmed. It was *assumed*, of course—by Robert, by Sergeant Dave Ostroff in Hollywood—but the law moves sluggishly in declarations of death where no corpse or other hard evidence exists.

And one of Judy's former roommates, meanwhile, still professed to think she was alive.

Betty Carver Bohannon, married now and living in Santa Monica, retired from the modeling game, learned of Glatman's confession when reporters showed up on her doorstep. She wistfully recalled meeting Judy in May or June of 1957 at a Hollywood photographer's studio. They were birds of a feather, instantly simpatico, and Betty had invited Judy to move in the same day, sharing digs with herself and Lynn Lykels, on North Sweetzer. Over the next few weeks, they had often discussed Judy's failed marriage and the bitter quarrel with Robert over custody of little Suzanne.

"Judy was going to get a job in a dime store," Betty told reporters, "to prove she was worthy of her child." In fact, an interview was pending, and Judy had been confident of nailing down the job. "If he [Glatman] had only come one day later," Betty added, "she would have been alive today."

Perhaps, but Betty had never *really* believed that her roommate was dead. Oh, Glatman—or Johnny Glenn, as she knew him—had been "creepy," all

right, trailing Judy around the apartment before they
left together, but it still "never entered her head that
she could have been killed."

Why not?

"Judy was not the Hollywood type at all," Betty
offered, as if that judgment granted some protection
from the world at large. "She and I were like sisters.
I can't picture her dead. She was so full of life and
everything."

It came down to wishful thinking, then, a frail tat-
ter of hope, blown away at the last by Glatman's
confession. All that remained was the task of retriev-
ing her bones—or confirming, as some lawmen already suspected, that they had already been found,
the previous December, outside Thousand Palms.

Shirley Bridgeford's mother, likewise, had never
given up on the hope that her daughter might one
day return. Residing now in San Fernando, a few
miles north of the old Sun Valley digs, Alice Jolliffe
cared for her grandsons and never stopped looking
for evidence that Shirley was alive. Shortly before
Glatman's arrest and confession, in fact, Jolliffe had
seen a newspaper photo taken at the scene of a car
crash in Burbank, noting a resemblance to Shirley in
one of the bystanders. She had telephoned Burbank
police for help, to have them check it out, and their
negative report was relayed to her on Halloween—
the same day Glatman's confession made headlines
in Los Angeles.

Now, her slender hopes dashed, Alice Jolliffe was
doubly disappointed. No matter how long she sat
staring at the photos of her daughter's murderer, she
could not seem to recognize "George Williams" from
the meeting in her home, eight months before. Shirley's sister, Ruth Boggs, and husband Hubert had no
such doubts. They both remembered those "enormous" ears, and while they were convinced that

"Williams" wore a thin mustache, the discrepancy was irrelevant.

With all the evidence they had in hand, authorities were not concerned about recruiting witnesses. Glatman would be the state's best witness, on his own. As Harvey spelled it out himself, he was already in too deep to wriggle free.

Lorraine Vigil was the hero of the hour for cutting short Glatman's run, but she was faced with unexpected problems of her own in the wake of his capture. By Halloween morning, "still badly bruised and highly nervous" when the story went public, Lorraine was fearful that the notoriety would cost her secretary's job in Los Angeles.

She was also on the verge of being homeless.

"I don't like this publicity," Mrs. Harry Ellis told reporters, explaining her decision to evict her now-famous tenant. "I warned Lorraine about the hazards of being a model, but she would not listen to me."

She was listening now, but it appeared to be too late.

The harm was done.

Glatman's case had all the makings of a jurisdictional nightmare. His four victims had all been abducted from Los Angeles County, with two murdered in San Diego County, one killed in Riverside County, and the last assaulted with a deadly weapon in Orange County. That meant four separate district attorneys were involved in the case, each one of them an elected official who recognized the vote-grabbing appeal of convicting a headline sex killer. That kind of trial made communities safe, and frightened women—not to mention their husbands, brothers, and fathers—were likely to repay the favor at election time.

Orange County clearly had the weakest claim,

where charges were concerned: attempted rape and
assault with a deadly weapon paled in comparison
to multiple murders. Los Angeles County initially
wanted the case, arguing that every major witness
lived within its jurisdiction, but L.A. could only prosecute for kidnapping, and all concerned were in
agreement that Harvey should face capital murder
charges.

It finally came down to numbers, at least as far as
San Diego County D.A. James Don Keller was concerned. His county had two corpses compared to Riverside's one. In Keller's mind, his office had a clear
priority, and L.A.P.D. Homicide Lieutenant Harold
Brown agreed, telling reporters that "the thinking
now is that San Diego will prosecute."

"We certainly plan to go ahead here within the
bounds of the jurisdiction of this county," D.A. Keller
told the press on Halloween. "After I study the facts,
I intend to confer with district attorneys of other
counties involved to determine the place of original
prosecution."

The prosecutor's conference was officially scheduled for Monday, the third. In the meantime, Glatman had one final murder to confirm.

On Monday afternoon, Harvey was formally arraigned before Municipal Judge Louis Kaufman, on
three counts of murder and one count of kidnapping.
Deputy Public Defender Floyd Davis was assigned
to the case for that hearing, reporters noting that Harvey "appeared unconcerned" as he shared the holding pen with twenty other prisoners while waiting
for his case to be called. Rumors were already abroad
that Glatman wanted to plead guilty and be on his
way to death row without unnecessary delay, but
Floyd Davis sought a three-week postponement of
his client's preliminary hearing. Judge Kaufman split
the difference, scheduling the prelim for November

nineteenth. In the meantime, he ordered Glatman held without bail.

From the courthouse, Harvey was driven to his old digs on Melrose, for a last look around. Ironically, the apartment was now occupied by a legitimate professional photographer, walls decorated with what the L.A. *Times* called "tastefully done salon prints, including a few nude studies." Those photos were a far cry from the snapshots Harvey favored, but he ventured no opinion of them as he showed police around the flat, pointing out the spot in the hallway where he had raped Judy Dull and the location of the sofa where they later sat and watched TV.

Reporters were granted brief access to Glatman this time, but he kept his mouth shut, turning blank stares on the handful of news hawks who peppered him with questions. Spurned, the press found "owl-eyed" Harvey to be "in a sulky mood."

The next leg of his journey, well beyond dark now, took Harvey and his escorts into Riverside County, rolling toward Indio with sheriff's detectives John Lawton and James Wahlke. He led them to a spot within twenty-five feet of Judy Dull's grave, four and a half miles west of Indio, but there was nothing left to find. Her skeletal remains had been recovered ten months earlier. Still, he was on the mark, a final piece of physical corroboration—which, as it turned out, the state would never actually need. Back at the Indio sheriff's substation, Harvey clinched it by identifying his fountain pen, dropped at the murder site, along with remnants of Judy's clothing.

While Harvey was in transit from the court to his old flat, then out to Riverside, Don Keller's prosecutor's meeting was in progress, at the office of L.A. County Chief Deputy District Attorney Manley Bowler. Present for San Diego County were Keller himself, Chief Deputy William T. Low, and Deputy

D.A. Claude Brown. Riverside County sent Deputy D.A.s William Mackey and Roland Wilson, with investigator Jim Lasseigne. Also on hand were Lieutenant Tom Isbell and Sergeant Robert Majors from the San Diego County sheriff's office and Captain Arthur Hertel and Sergeant Pierce Brook from the L.A.P.D. homicide division. Orange County had already bowed out, deferring to those jurisdictions which had a shot at executing Glatman for his crimes.

The meeting could have been a down-and-dirty struggle over "dibs" on Glatman, but if we believe the sketchy press reports, it went down smoothly, with few disagreements, none of them major. Los Angeles and Riverside Counties deferred to San Diego for the prosecution, for purely logical reasons: homicide cases were normally tried in the jurisdiction where the crime took place, and San Diego had two-thirds of the victims. Riverside could always file on Judy Dull, at some later date, but it would be a waste of time and taxpayer's money.

As Glatman himself had already pointed out, the state could only gas him once.

The next step, now that the most critical decision had been made, was to effect transfer of custody from Los Angeles to San Diego. There is no extradition rule within a single state, and Harvey's transfer was a fairly simple thing.

Once he was safe and sound in San Diego's jail, the D.A.'s office could begin its task of sending Harvey to his death.

And on from there, perhaps, to hell.

13

"I Was Sort of Shocked at Myself"

ON WEDNESDAY, NOVEMBER FIFTH, L.A.P.D. SURREN-
dered their prisoner to a two-man escort team from the
San Diego County sheriff's office. Lieutenant Tom Isbell
and Sergeant Robert Majors took delivery, with a warrant based on a complaint in Shirley Bridgeford's case,
and they made the two-hour drive back to San Diego
without incident, stopping for dinner along the way.

It was after 8:00 P.M. when Harvey sat down with
Isbell and Majors in one of the San Diego sheriff's
grilling rooms. A tape recorder occupied the table
between them, and Majors switched it on as he prepared to capture Glatman's story for posterity.

"The following conversation," Majors began, for
the tape's benefit, "is taking place in the San Diego
County sheriff's office in San Diego County. This is
November the fifth, 1958. The time is 8:05 P.M. State-
ments recorded here are in reference to San Diego
County sheriff's cases number 98813 and 98814.
Those present at this interview are the defendant—
is the defendant—Harvey Murray Glatman, Sergeant
R. B. Majors, Lieutenant Tom Isbell."

Majors consulted his notes, taking care to touch all the bases required by law.

"Yes, that covers everything, I guess," he said at last, then addressed himself to Glatman. "Now, Harvey, as we told you before we turned the machine on, we wanted to start at the very beginning and get the entire story regarding the four girls: Judy Dull, Shirley Bridgeford, Angela Rojas—or as she was known, as Ruth Mercado—and Lorraine Vigil. Now, if you will start right at the beginning, how you first met Judy, and your first meeting with her, and from there on through the full time you knew her and had any dealings with her. . . ."

Another pause, as Majors remembered another legal technicality.

"Harvey," he said, "before you make any statement here that will be recorded on this tape, I would like for you to know that everything you say is being recorded, the recording machine is set up here in your presence, and that everything you say here can he used against you in your prosecution for murder. Do you understand that?"

"Yes, sir," Harvey said.

"And with that understanding," Majors continued, "you are willing to tell us of your activities concerning the death of Judy Ann Dull; concerning the death of Shirley Ann Bridgeford, which is our case number 98814; concerning the death of Ruth Mercado, which is our case number 98813; and concerning your assault on Lorraine Vigil?"

"Yes," Harvey answered.

"Okay," Majors said. "Would you start with Judy Ann Dull, that being the first person that you had contact with of the four, and relate to us, from the time you met her, your activities until her death."

"Well," Harvey replied, "I had met her first through her roommate, who had shown me some

pictures of her and told me that she was a model
and she might be interested in working occasionally
for amateur photographers as well as professional.
And four or five days before I had actually met her
is when I first learned through a roommate of hers,
and on August the first, 1957, I called her about noon,
and I asked her if she was available for a modeling
job that afternoon, and she said she was free for the
afternoon, and we made an appointment for two
o'clock to meet at her apartment, and I arrived there
a few minutes before two, and—"

Majors interrupted him to ask, "Where was this
apartment?"

"1302 North Sweetzer, in Los Angeles," Harvey
told him. "And she picked out some clothes, including some extra ones that she said she needed for
another assignment after we were through, and we
left her apartment, and we went in my car over to
my apartment."

"Now, Harvey," Majors asked his prisoner, "what
was the conversation you had with her regarding
why she should go with you?"

"Well," Harvey said, "I told her that I had fixed
up my apartment more or less as a studio, that I had
my own lights and equipment over there, and it
would be more suitable than her place in any event,
and she was perfectly willing to . . . she didn't care
where she was modeling, so much, as long as she—"

Another interruption. "Was there any talk about
price at this time?" Majors asked.

"Well, I understood that she usually received
twenty dollars an hour for any modeling that she
did," Harvey replied.

"Did you give her any money?"

"Not at this time, no."

"I see," Majors said. "Go ahead, then."

"Well," Harvey said, taking the interruptions in

stride, "we got over to my apartment about a quarter after two that afternoon, and she got out of the car. Now, I had a gun in the car, in the glove compartment, which I had just usually kept in that place, and I had slipped that into my coat pocket, and we went on up to my apartment—that's at 5924 Melrose, in Los Angeles—and when inside, I told her that I wanted to take some pictures that would be suitable for illustrations for mystery stories or detective magazine stories—stories of that type—and that this would require me to tie her hands and feet and put a gag in her mouth. And she was agreeable to this, and I did tie her hands and feet and put a gag in her mouth, and I took a number of pictures. I don't remember exactly how many, of various poses, and changing the pose from picture to picture."

Sergeant Majors interrupted him again. "I'd like to ask you a question, Harvey. Did you have any intention of submitting these pictures to a mystery-story magazine?"

"No."

"One more question: What was your intention when you made your first contact with Judy?"

"Well," Harvey said, "my primary motive—I had two. I did want to take some pictures of her, but aside from that, I was interested in having sexual relations with her, and that was the main reason that I had had her come to my apartment."

"Okay, proceed," Majors said. "Now, you say you shot the pictures. That was the last part you said. You shot several?"

"Yeah," Harvey said.

"Were any of them in color?"

"Most of them were in color."

"You also shot some black and white?" Majors asked.

"Yes. I shot a few at the end of a roll that was

already in the camera, which I never developed, and I later threw the roll away. I more or less destroyed it."

"Okay," Majors said. "Well, go ahead, then, Harvey."

Glatman picked up the narrative as if Majors had never stopped the flow of words. "And the last picture that I had shot of her had her on the floor," he said. "She was on the floor, and she was still tied as I had tied her originally, and at this point I was still a little hesitant. I waited a few minutes, and she was getting kind of restless, and I finally made up my mind to go through with it, and I went over to her and I put my hand around her shoulders and just below her neck, and I sat down on the floor beside her. I propped her up in a sitting position, and I told her that I was going to keep her there a while, and that I wouldn't hurt her if she did as she was told and didn't give me any trouble, and that I was going to have some fun with her. And I also took the gun out of my pocket and showed her that to—as a sign of the seriousness of it, and also to help get her in the frame of mind where she would be more or less docile. And I also told her that I had a record, and that doing what I had done already, that I was already in serious trouble, just by the action up to that point. And this, of course, was all to impress her that . . . well . . . to scare her actually, into being submissive. And then, she indicated that she would like to say something, by moving her head."

Majors tried to interpose another question. "Why did she have to move her head to indicate that she—"

"Well," Harvey said, seizing the chance to interrupt Majors for a change, "as I told you before, she . . . when taking the pictures, I had put a gag in her mouth, and she wasn't able to speak. So, I removed the gag, but I cautioned her to talk quietly and not to make any loud noises or scream, or anything like that. She told me that . . . she said she was a nymphomaniac, and also that she was not going to cause any trouble because she had been estranged from her husband, and she had a custody suit pending, and she was—which was due to come up for a hearing in about a week—and that any hint of her running around or engaging in any unusual activities or anything, might be used against her, as her husband . . . I guess was, she thought . . . trying to have her declared unfit for custody of the child. And she couldn't afford to have anything like that going on, so that she was saying this, I presume, to impress me that it wasn't necessary to threaten her with a gun or anything like that."

"I see," Majors said. "Now, this conversation was taking place while she was on the floor?"

"Yes."

"And where . . . how was she tied at this time?"

"Well," Harvey said, "her hands were tied behind her back, and her ankles were tied."

"I see. And what clothing did she have on?" Majors asked.

"Well, she had on all her clothing, which was somewhat . . . uh . . . partially. . . ." Harvey swallowed hard and tried to control his voice. "No, I'll correct that," he said. "She had been wearing a skirt, which was not on, and she had on her sweater, which was unbuttoned down the front, and she had on her bra and a slip—half slip—and shoes and stockings, and so forth."

"I see," Majors said. "Okay."

Harvey took it as a signal to continue. "And she sounded as though she was sincere," he went on, "or that this was not just an act she was putting on, and so I pretended to believe her—on that she wouldn't raise any fuss then and there—and I slipped the gun back in my pocket. And I had picked her up, and I carried her into a little hallway adjacent to the living room there, where we had been taking the pictures, and I had put her down and left her in there by herself, in the same condition as she was on the floor in the living room, and I went back into the living room. And I put the . . . took the film out of the camera since it was all . . . roll was used up, and I put the camera away, and the tripod away, and moved the furniture back where it originally, usually belonged. And I think I went into the kitchen there and got a glass of water, and as I recall, I took something out of the icebox—a piece of apple, something like that to eat—and then I went back into that . . . where I had left her in the hallway there, and I sat down beside her. And I started to run my hands over her body and squeeze her, and I was kissing her around the neck and the breasts, and she said . . . she seemed to be getting kind of . . . seemed to me to be partially enjoying it. She was . . . her skin was kind of moist, and she seemed to be very warm, and—"

"In other words," Majors broke in, "you mean that you were arousing her passion?"

"Yes, yes!" Harvey seemed desperate to believe that Judy had desired him. "She had indicated to me that she had a somewhat difficult time controlling herself around men. I . . . I understood that's what she meant by nymphomaniac when she had mentioned that, and after—I don't recall exactly how long we kept this up—I untied her hands and her feet, and she removed . . . I told her to remove most of her remaining clothing. She took her shoes off and rolled her stockings down. I guess she had a panties and garter belt, and she removed those, and just unhooked her brassiere, and we went into the living room, and—"

This time, Harvey interrupted himself. "Well, now, wait a minute," he said. "I had said previously that I had taken the film out of the camera and put it away before this, which is not correct. I didn't. I had two shots left—I believe, two or three—and I had her sit on the couch. I wanted to use up the film then and there, and she was virtually nude. She still had . . . her stockings were rolled down, down by her ankles already, and I think she still had her bra on, although it had been unhooked and everything. And I finished the roll of film then and took pictures of her sitting on the couch with her facing the camera, virtually naked, and with one . . . I believe one foot was . . . one leg was on the couch and one dangling on the floor. And I finished up the roll of film that was in the camera. That was just one roll of color film that I had shot."

"I see," Majors said. "Now, let me ask you, Harvey, did she object to these photos?"

"No," Harvey replied. "She didn't offer any verbal objection."

"Do you think that she would have posed for those, had you not used the gun?" Majors asked.

"Well," Harvey hedged, "I have no way of knowing whether she would or not, 'cause I had already produced the gun. So, it was impossible to know for sure, but she didn't offer any verbal objections, and at this time I didn't have to resort to any reminder or anything. She just went ahead and did as I asked her, the first time I asked."

"I see," Majors said. "Okay, then. You took the pictures, and then, what?"

"Yeah," Harvey said, collecting his thoughts. "Well, then I went over, and she had now completely . . . I told her, you know, to finish taking her stockings off, and she removed the brassiere completely, and now she was completely naked. And I went over—I had taken off, now, my coat and my shirt, my trousers and my shoes, and I just had my shorts and socks on, actually—and I went over to the couch, and I sat down with her. And we both were sitting there, and I more or less pulled her over so she was sort of on my lap, you might say, and again I had run my hands over her body and squeezed her, and kissed her in various parts of her body, including her face, mouth, neck and breasts, and so forth. And again, I can't say for exactly how long this continued, but it was some time, and then I told her I wanted to have intercourse with her, and to just lay back on the couch. And I removed my shorts, and I had intercourse with her. And then, immediately after that, we both sat up, and we washed up a little, and I don't recall now . . . I might have asked her at this point, it's not too clear . . . whether she was hungry or wanted anything to eat, or a glass of water, and I know I went in and I got another glass of water. And I was a little nervous, myself, and—"

"She still wasn't tied up, again?" Majors asked.

"No, no," Harvey replied, "not at this point. But I had always kept my coat. It still had the gun in the pocket, actually in a position where I could . . . that is, where she couldn't get to it, and I could, if the necessity arose. And after a while, I came back to the couch, and we had intercourse again in the same manner, and she went into the bathroom and washed up, and cleaned up, and she wanted to know if she could fix her face a little, and everything.

"Oh!" Harvey caught himself again. "I had left something out, which I had mentioned previously in telling about this. I'll inject it here. It's not vital, but at the time when she was in the hallway, before I had untied her—"

"And when she was on the floor?" Majors asked.

"And she was on the floor," Harvey agreed. "Her hands and feet were still tied, and I had gone into the kitchen. When I came back, she had a nosebleed for some reason, or she was trying to hold her head back, and her nose was bleeding. I don't know why because she hadn't been struck or anything—unless in trying to move around slightly, she might have jarred her head against something. I had left her leaning against the wall, more or less, and I just grabbed the first piece of cloth that was laying close by because I kept some of my dirty laundry in that room. It was an old pillowcase, and I used that to hold over her nose. It was bleeding quite freely, and we held her head back until it stopped. And [the] reason I mention this, include this, is that the police did find a pillowcase in my room after I was arrested, and it was all sort of . . . quite a few blood stains on it. And one of the photographs of Judy, the ones that were taken after she was on the couch naked, if you look at it real close or magnify it a little, you'll see that one looks like a little blood . . . just dry, you know, just a speck. She . . . we had wiped it off, but there was just a little blood showing on one nostril. Just a dab . . . like a person . . . just like you'd notice on your own nose, if you'd had a nose bleed and hadn't wiped it too thoroughly. I don't know why I overlooked this in sequence, on this, because I had mentioned it several times before, but—"

"I see," Majors cut him off. "Let me ask you a question, Harvey."

"I thought I had better stick it in there," Glatman said, "before we went any further because—"

Again, the sergeant interrupted him. "This pillowcase that you say that the Los Angeles police found in your apartment with blood on it, was that the pillowcase that you used to wipe the blood off of her when she had the nose bleed?"

"Yes, yes," Harvey said. "It was a torn pillowcase, anyway, and so I had never used it again. I saved a lot of old clothes and rags and stuff there because when I moved from place to place, as I did a lot of times, I used that for packing. Actually, I used to pack stuff in boxes, cardboard boxes and things, and some of it was fragile and breakable, and I used to save a lot of any old clothes and rags and stuff like that, as a packing material."

"I see," Majors said.

"So I had quite a few old rags laying around, and I just didn't throw that out."

"Okay. Now, Harvey," Majors continued, trying to bring him back on track, "we were to the part, going back to the story, where she wanted to go in and wash up and put makeup on. Is that right?"

"Yeah," Harvey said. "She wanted to know if it would be all right if she used the mirror in the bathroom, and everything, and to wash up and freshen herself up a little. She took her purse in there, and I told her she could get dressed then, and she took her clothes in with her, too, and she put on some . . . combed her hair back a little, put on makeup, and . . . you know, like girls do all the time."

"Now, let me ask you, Harvey," Majors interjected, "did you warn her again about making any noise, or screaming, or attempting to get away?"

"No," Glatman said. "Not specifically there, because there was no way she could get out of the bathroom without jumping down two stories because this was a second-floor apartment, and she didn't seem like she was on the verge of doing any such thing. She had been, more or less, going along with everything I said, and she didn't give any indications that she was getting unusually nervous or jittery, or

anything like that, so I didn't think it was necessary
to warn her. I don't recall warning her about anything, at this point. And meanwhile, I got dressed,
too, and after she was through in the bathroom, she
came back in the living room, and I told her to sit
down in the chair and just relax for a while. And I
sat down on the couch, and I began to wonder now,
just what I was going to do next. How was I going
to resolve this thing, now that I had gone through
all this, and I sat there for quite a while. It was getting late in the afternoon, very late in the afternoon
now, and I was trying to think mainly of how to
release her, or could I release her, and what would
happen if I did. What would she do about reporting
this, what had happened? And I asked her several
times, something like, 'Judy, what are you going to
tell your roommates when you get home?' Or, 'Do
you think they're unusually worried about you? Do
you think they may have called the police by now?
That they may be very worried about you?' And she
had indicated that she would try to cover this up,
that she wouldn't . . . that when she got home, she
would just make up some story as to where she had
been, because by this time, she had already missed
her one appointment that she—the one that she was
supposed to go to after she was through with me.
And also, she mentioned again about the custody
hearing for her baby, and she said that . . . repeated
that she couldn't afford to have any kind of a scandal
or sign of improper activities, whether it was her
fault or not, whether she was forced into something,
or whether voluntarily or involuntarily. The mere
fact that she was liable to such things, as she thought
it might just about wreck her chances of getting any
custody of her baby, and she mentioned that. And,
as I say, this went on for some time. I questioned
her intermittently like that, trying to decide in my

own mind, and I had thought . . . because the thought had crossed my mind that the safest thing to do would be to kill her because she knew where I lived, and the car and the color and the make, and maybe the license number, or the state from which the license was issued. And I was trying to think of how . . . actually weighing one factor against another. As my own fear of returning to prison and the chances . . . what the chances would be of having her successfully make up a story, whether I could believe her. And whether, if she did make up a story, whether anybody else would believe, or whether they would question her to a point where she finally decided to tell them actually what happened and everything. And, as I say, I don't recall just how much time passed. Time—when you're thinking, trying to think as hard as I was, then—time goes usually pretty quickly. You don't notice it so much. But it seemed to be . . . oh . . . maybe 7:30, eight o'clock, and I guess I finally decided that I would probably not be able to take the chance, although this wasn't a final decision on my part, but that I probably would—if I could work myself up to the pitch to do it—that I would kill her to cover up the other crimes that I had already committed with her."

Harvey had taken his time, working up to the lethal decision, but now he was on a roll.

"And I decided that I would take her out in the country somewhere," he continued. "And I thought . . . I wasn't too familiar with this area, but I knew that this highway running east from Los Angeles led out to the desert, out by Indio, or in that direction, and that it was very . . . pretty deserted out that way, and I would probably head out in that direction. And we sat there, in the apartment. I wanted to wait until it was dark, and a little later in the evening, and things were pretty quiet around the

street, and the apartments and everything—less like-
lihood of running into somebody on the way out.
And we sat there, and I turned on the television set
to help pass the time. And she was still sitting in the
chair. She had been dozing for a while, and she woke
up, and she wanted to know if I would rather have
her sit over on the couch with me, rather than sitting
by myself over there, and her in the chair. And I
said, sure, that I was thinking about something. So,
she came . . . got up out of the chair and came over,
and I sat with both feet on the couch, facing the
television set, and she came over and I had . . . she
sat down on my lap, and I just put my arms around
her waist, and we sat there until about . . . well, it
was 10:15. I remember because I watched the ten
o'clock news, and I remember after that, I told her
we were going to leave pretty soon—leave the apartment. I told her I was going to drive her out, a long
way out in the sticks, and then I was going to let her
out of the car and give her money. That, I promised
her, and that it would be more than enough for bus
fare back, and she could walk to the nearest town,
or hitch a ride or something, and then catch a bus
the rest of the way. So, I told her that I was going
to tie her hands while we're on the way out, just as
a precaution, and then I again warned her not to . . .
that I would let her out when I was ready, not for
her to take it on herself to try and break away. And
I tied her hands, and gathered up some of her stuff
that she had brought along, and we got in the car.
We went downstairs and got in the car, and pulled
out of the garage, and headed out on the San Bernardino Freeway. And after we had gotten out of—well
out of Los Angeles—I stopped the car for a few minutes and untied her hands, and then I continued
along the road. And all this time was still debating
with myself whether I could actually go through with

Harvey Glatman in custody. *Los Angeles Times Photographic Archive Department of Special Collections University Research Library, UCLA*

Victim Judy Ann Dull, photographed by Glatman in the killer's apartment, moments before she was raped and murdered.
Corbis-Bettmann

Victim Shirley Bridgeford, photographed by Glatman in the San Diego County desert, shortly before her murder.
Corbis-Bettmann

Alice Jolliffe, mother of victim Shirley Bridgeford, with
Bridgeford's two sons. *Los Angeles Times Photographic Archive
Department of Special Collections University Research Library, UCLA*

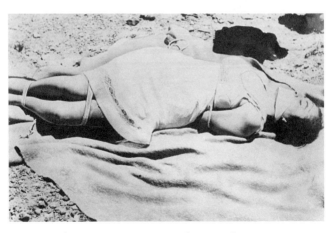

Victim Ruth Mercado, posed and photographed by
Glatman in the desert, before she was strangled to death.
Corbis-Bettmann

Lorraine Vigil describes how Glatman tried to choke her, before she disarmed him and held him at gunpoint. *Los Angeles Times Photographic Archive Department of Special Collections University Research Library, UCLA*

Harvey Glatman in custody, escorted by L.A.P.D. homicide
detective Pierce Brooks. *Los Angeles Times Photographic Archive
Department of Special Collections University Research Library, UCLA*

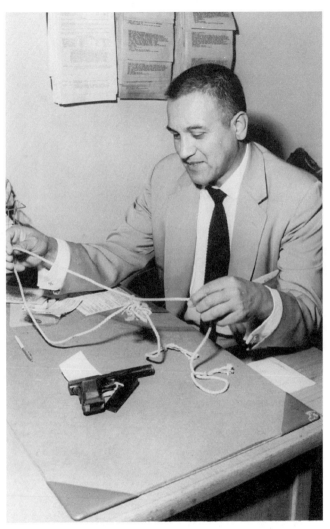

A homicide detective examines Glatman's strangling rope and pistol. *Los Angeles Times Photographic Archive Department of Special Collections University Research Library, UCLA*

Glatman (far right) with police at the desert site where
skeletal remains of one victim were recovered. *Los Angeles
Times Photographic Archive Department of Special Collections
University Research Library, UCLA*

Ophelia Glatman arrives to visit her son at the San Diego County jail in November 1958. *San Diego Historical Society, Photograph Collection*

it or not, and kept trying to justify it to myself, and try to justify it to myself by trying to assume that there wasn't any other thing I could do, except . . . unless I was ready to . . . almost a sure risk of going back to jail. As a matter of fact, I thought . . . actual thought I had . . . was that if I was going to turn her loose, I might as well just drive her back to Los Angeles and go down to the police station and just walk inside with her."

"Well," Majors interrupted, "had you, at this time, determined that if you did kill her, how you would do it?"

"Yes," Harvey said. "I had decided that while I was back in the apartment. I had, more or less, decided. First, I thought maybe a shot would be . . . from the gun . . . would be the quickest and surest way. And then, I had thought that . . . whatever way I was thinking of, though . . . I didn't want any prolonged suffering on her part, or any pain, or . . . or, where she would have any knowledge of it ahead of time, anything like that. It had to be quick, and just as quick as possible, and painless as possible, because if I had seen her suffering, or if she had been aware of just what was going to happen to her, I don't think that, even under fear of going to jail or anything like that, I could have . . . I just probably couldn't have done it. That's all there is to it."

"But now," Majors said, "you had decided then that you would strangle her?"

"I had decided, yes," Harvey said, "that I would maneuver her into a position where I could get a rope around her neck and do it as quickly as possible. I couldn't think of any other way that would be as little suffering, except, possibly, a properly placed bullet, but I just decided on that."

"Is there any other reason why you didn't shoot her?" Majors asked.

"Well, I probably had in mind that should the body be found, that the bullet itself is matchable with the gun. That is, I know for . . . from reading, not from experience, but from reading . . . that bullets can be traced back to specific guns. And, while I didn't expect at that time the . . . I knew that unless I was picked up for something else, anyway, the gun wouldn't be found, that it probably wasn't of any major importance because it probably . . . wouldn't be decisive anyway, in that—"

"By the way," Majors cut in, "did you keep the gun loaded all the time, Harvey?"

"Yes," Glatman said. "The gun was loaded all the time. That is, ever since I carried it around with me, whether I intended to have any immediate use for it or not, it was always loaded and usually in the glove compartment of the car."

"I see," Majors said. "Well, then, you headed out the freeway, and you say you stopped and took the ropes off her wrist—"

"Yes," Harvey said. "A few miles outside Los Angeles, on that road, and I continued on, and I didn't have any specific destination in mind, except to get out into, more or less, desert country which I knew was out in that area. And I kept driving, and actually to . . . more or less to give myself more time to actually . . . to back out if that's what I really wanted to do. And I still wasn't sure, even though I had decided to do it, that I could actually, at the last instant, do it. It's one thing to decide on something like that, but when you get right to it, you just might not be able to do it. And finally, I just reached the point there, where I said it's now or never, and I had pulled over . . . by this time we were out . . . which later turned out to be near Indio. I didn't know where, at the time, but it was desert country from what I could see out there. It was certainly deserted.

I didn't see any house, or any houses or lights in the immediate vicinity, or anything, and I pulled off. There was enough room on the shoulder of the road for me to pull the car off the side of the road, and I told Judy that I wanted to have intercourse, sexual intercourse, with her once more before I turned her loose. And, of course, that was a pretext to get her out of the car, and she wanted to have . . . she agreed to this, but she wanted to use the back seat of the car, and, of course I wanted to get her out of the car, so I told her that the sand . . . the ground out there looked like it was just sand, soft sandy desert there, and I told her . . . well, I had . . . it was pretty dangerous to do that in the car because we were just on the shoulder of the road, and not well off the road. And I said it could be very embarrassing if somebody stopped by here, and I told her, 'Well, I have a blanket in the back, in the trunk of the car, and we can take that and just sort of spread it out on the sand. You won't get all dirty or nothing.' And I said, 'We can do it there,' and this seemed to be reasonable enough to her, so that she didn't argue about it. And I got the blanket out of the car, and we walked away from the road, and there was a railroad track running parallel to the road, a few yards off the road, on the right side. And we crossed that tracks, and we went a few yards beyond the tracks, and I spread the blanket out, and I told her— before we'd had any intercourse or anything like that—I told her . . . I said, 'Judy, I want to tie your hands and feet for a minute.' And she asked me why, and I said, 'I just want to, that's all.' And I said, 'I don't want you to argue about it . . . just . . . just want to do it because I want to do it.' And she didn't ask again, or anything. She didn't give me any argument, asking about it. So, I had taken the same ropes that I had used in the apartment—which I had put back in my coat pocket before we left the apartment—and I tied her ankles. I had her lay face . . . well . . . I tied her wrists while she was standing up yet, and then I had her sit down on the blanket, and I tied her ankles together."

"Her wrists were tied behind her?" Majors asked.

"Yeah," Harvey said, "behind her. And I tied her ankles together while she was sitting down, and I had her roll over on her stomach. And then, I had a third length of cord, and I tied one end of that around between her ankles, and put a knot in that, so it would hold firm, and then I bent her legs back as far as they would go—that is, bent them at the knees, pulled her ankles back toward her head as far as it would go. And I put one knee in the small of her back, and I lifted her chin off the blanket with my hand, and I just very quickly—as fast as I could because at this point I knew that she . . . right about now, she was going to get very worried and fearful . . . and if she started . . . really knew, now, what was coming, or what I intended to do . . . she might have started begging, and I just wouldn't have been able to go through with it. And I felt that if I didn't do it right at that minute, I wasn't going to do it, and I might as well take her back to the police station and walk in and say, 'Here I am.' And just very quickly, I had her, held her chin up in my hand, and I just took the other end of the rope that was tied to her ankles there, and I just very quickly looped it around her neck twice and just pulled. Then, I let go of her chin and put both my hands on the end of the rope which I had in my hand, and I just pulled it as tight as I could and as hard as I could. And, of course, the other end was looped around her ankles, so that was more or less anchored there, and all. The both hands, then, were pulling on that piece of rope."

"And you kept your knee in the middle of her back, did you?" Majors asked him.

"Yes," Harvey replied. "I kept my knee in the middle . . . small of her back."

"And how long would you say you held her in that position?"

"Well," Glatman mused, "I couldn't say exactly, but it seemed like five minutes or so."

"Then what did you do, Harvey?" Majors prodded.

"Well," Harvey said, the worst of it over, "then I let loose of the end of the rope that I was holding, and I remember . . . I was sort of shocked at myself, right at that instant. Just for an instant, I wanted to undo what I had just done, and I remember lifting her head up again, and I called out—not real loudly, but I said . . . I said, 'Judy! Judy!' I remember saying it twice, even though I knew she couldn't answer me. I assumed she was already dead, but I did it anyway . . . just seemed to be just a reaction, and I thought maybe . . . well, when you're in that particular . . . just for an instant, there, you just weren't rational at all. Just for that . . . and then I sat there for a few minutes, sort of getting over the shock of it, and then I began thinking again, and I noticed that we weren't too far from the railroad tracks. And I thought, well, maybe I better move her body back away from the tracks a little further because somebody on a passing train, during the day, might notice her, you know. And I thought it would be better if the body wasn't found, and I didn't have any specific reason for thinking it would be better if it wasn't found . . . I just didn't want it found, and so I . . . first, I took the rope from around her neck, which I had just left there all this time—it had stayed in place because it had been so tight that it just cut into the flesh and just held there more or less by itself. And I unraveled that, and I took all the ropes off her wrists and ankles, and put them back in my pocket. And I picked her up, and I carried her away from the tracks . . . oh, what I guess, maybe twenty, twenty-five yards further away from the tracks. And I noticed that the sand around here was all just very soft—sort of like you'd find at the beach, almost, very soft. And I didn't have any digging instruments, but I . . . it was so soft that I could scoop it out with my hands, and I just . . . just hit me that maybe I should cover the body up, and I scooped out a little depression in the sand with my hands, and I put her in this little depression, and then I pushed the loose sand, that I had scooped out, back over the body, and I took her shoes off. I remember thinking about, possibly, fingerprints on the shoes, which were smooth leather, and it might hold a print. And I wiped them off with my handkerchief, and I walked a few yards away from where I had left her, and I tossed one shoe just as far as I could throw it. And then, I decided the other shoe . . . maybe I shouldn't throw it so close. First shoe, it was so dark, I wouldn't even have begun to go back and look for it. I just left it where I threw it, and the second shoe, I decided to throw somewhere else, a greater distance away. And then I went back and picked up my blanket, and—"

"Just a minute, Harvey," Sergeant Majors interrupted. "If I might ask at this time, in this little grave that you dug, how did you lay her in there? Facedown, or what?"

Harvey frowned. "I don't recall exactly if she was facedown, or faceup," he replied.

"I see. Okay, go ahead."

"I say I don't recall whether she was facedown or faceup. I just don't remember at all which way she was facing, up or down. It was dark. I don't even know whether I noticed."

"Did you," Majors asked him, "did you check her to make sure that she was dead?"

"Well," Harvey said, "I didn't have any exact means. I just assumed from . . . I did . . . I remember, before I had picked her up and carried her, that I did try to see whether she was . . . any breathing, or . . . and I remember, maybe I tried to feel a pulse or something, and of course, I didn't. I'm not an expert at that, anyway, at feeling a pulse. I . . . she even . . . if a person would have had a weak pulse, I might not have felt it, but I assumed from the length of time and tightness with which I pulled the cord that I just didn't believe she could be alive any more. I think it would have been virtually an impossibility for her to have been alive, at that point."

"And then," Majors said, "after you covered her over, you went back to the blanket, and then, what?"

"I picked it up," Harvey said, "and I took the blanket and the one shoe back to my car, and I started up the car, and I made a U-turn there in the road, and I started back toward Los Angeles."

"And, did you have any of her belongings with you?" Majors asked.

"Yes," Glatman said. "We had put some of her belongings—some of her clothes—in the car before we had left the apartment, and her purse was still in the car and everything. Of course, she had a lot of little items in the purse."

"What did you do with these items of hers?"

"Well, some of them, I had stopped at different places along the road," Harvey explained, "and I had thrown them away from the road at various points on the way back to Los Angeles. Not all the stuff, but some of it."

"And what did you keep?"

"Well . . . I kept some of the bigger items, some of the larger items of clothing, and the purse itself, and some of the contents that I still had with me when I got back to my apartment."

"I see," Majors said. "Did she have any money in the purse?"

"A few cents in coins," Harvey said.

"What did you do with that?"

A shrug. "I put that in my pocket."

"I see. What eventually became of these items that you had, of hers?"

"Well," Harvey said, "eventually, they were discarded by me in out-of-the-way places, woody or brushy areas, where they probably wouldn't be found."

"Over how long a period of time did you keep them, finally get rid of them?" Majors asked.

"Well, I think that . . . I think that after . . . I kept them for a couple of days. And one evening, I took them . . . I had broken some of them up, like the purse and the smaller pieces . . . and some of her clothing, I had torn into smaller pieces . . . and I took some of the . . . all of these things that I was going to get rid of, and I discarded them in various places, like I mentioned."

"Harvey," Majors asked, "do you have in your possession anything that belongs to her, now?"

"No, I do not," Glatman said. "I don't recall that I kept anything that belonged to her."

"Did you ever go back to the scene of her death?"

"Not specifically," Harvey said. "I had passed by that same road but not specifically to return to the scene or anything. It was on other travels, and I just happened to be using that road. Of course, I had . . . going past Indio, there, I just went past the road on that road, but not specifically in any way to return to the scene, or try and locate it again, or anything like that."

"Did you ever stop or ever attempt to locate it?"

"No, I didn't."

"Did you ever—"

"Not . . . that is," Harvey interrupted, "except after I was arrested, and I went out with the police, trying to establish the spot."

"Did you ever hear any more about her?" Majors asked.

"Yes, I—"

"Or read anything about her?"

"Yes," Harvey repeated. "I read an article in a magazine about her, about her disappearance. This was about seven months later, and I also read an article in the paper about a body that had been found in that area, but I . . . I couldn't, of course, be sure. There was no identification made, and I didn't know whether it was her, or whether it wasn't."

"Did you ever again see either one of her companions?" Majors asked.

"No," Harvey said. "You mean her roommates?"

"Yes."

"No, I didn't see either one of them again."

"Is there anything else that you can think of concerning the Dull girl," Majors said, "that hasn't been covered or should be mentioned?"

"No, nothing specific," Harvey replied, "or that would be of any real importance. Otherwise, I'm sure I would remember it."

"Let me ask you, Harvey," Majors said, "did, on that occasion, you take any water or food along with you, from your apartment?"

"Well, I . . . we did take just . . . no water, but I took a couple of pieces of candy, and I think a couple of apples that I had. And we had eaten that during the drive."

"I see. Did you, while she was with you, make any stops at any service stations or cafés, or anything like that?"

"No," Harvey said. "Not while she was with me."

"Okay," Majors said. "That just about covers that part of it. It's now five minutes after nine, and we'll have to change tapes here, Harvey, and get a drink of water. Okay?"

"Yes, fine."

"All right."

It had taken him exactly one hour to relate the details of Judy Dull's death, but Harvey wasn't finished, yet. In fact, he was only getting started.

14

"She Didn't Seem to Be Breathing at All"

AFTER A FIFTEEN-MINUTE BREAK, SERGEANT MAJORS AND
Lieutenant Isbell rejoined Harvey in the small interrogation room. A fresh tape rolled as Majors spoke
into the microphone.

"This is a continuation of a statement started at
8:05 P.M.," he said, "here in the San Diego County
sheriff's office, on November fifth, 1958. This portion
of the statement will concern the death of Shirley
Ann Bridgeford. Those present are Harvey Glatman,
the defendant; Sergeant R. B. Majors; and Lieutenant
Tom Isbell. Harvey, for the sake of the record, I will
again admonish you that all statements which you
make at this time are being recorded on tape, which
you are aware of, and that all statements made by you
and recorded on this tape can be used against you in
your prosecution for the murder of Shirley Ann
Bridgeford. With this warning, do you desire to make
a statement?"

"Yes," Harvey replied.

"Well," Majors said, "as you have done before,
will you now tell us everything that you can concern-

ing your meeting with Shirley Ann Bridgeford, and all that occurred up to and including her death?"

"Well," Harvey began, "I . . . I met Shirley indirectly through a club to which she had given her name. It was commonly referred to as a lonely hearts club. That's where girls usually register for blind dates, and for a fee, men usually can obtain their names and phone numbers or addresses, where they might obtain a date or something of that nature . . . companionship."

"Pardon," Majors said. "May I interrupt just a moment to state that this statement is being started at 9:20 P.M."

"And, uh, I had gone to this club," Harvey resumed, "which is located on South Vermont Street, in Los Angeles. I don't recall the street number, but it was a place called Patty Sullivan's. And I went into the club, and I told the woman—who identified herself as Patty Sullivan—that I was new in town, and that I wanted a date, and I didn't know anyone in town, and that I had decided to try and obtain a date through this club. And I paid her ten dollars, and she looked through her files, and she wrote down the names and telephone numbers of five girls who were about the same age as I was, and she gave me that list."

"May I ask," Majors interposed, "did you give her your name?"

"Well, I gave her a false name," Glatman said.

"What was that name?"

"The name I gave her was George," Harvey said. "I believe it was George Williams, and that's the name she knew me by. And there were five names and numbers that she had given me, and Shirley's name and number was one of the five."

"Harvey," Majors said, "going back to the Dull recording, did you tell her your true name?"

"No, I didn't," Harvey admitted.

"What name did you use?"

"I used another phony name," Harvey said. "Johnny Glenn."

"Johnny *Glend?*" Majors asked.

"Yes, that's the name she knew me by," Glatman said.

"Is that *Glenn* or *Glend?*" the sergeant pressed.

"Well, I didn't actually write it out," Harvey explained. "I meant it to be *Glenn*."

"I see. Okay, we'll go ahead with this," Majors said.

"Well," Harvey resumed, "I had called several of these girls on the telephone, and I talked with them, but I hadn't made any appointments or dates with them. One girl I had called, and I had gone over to her apartment and talked with her for a while— about fifteen or twenty minutes—and we had a little to eat there, but I left and didn't make any dates or appointments with her for any future time."

Majors interrupted once again. "May I ask you here, now, too, Harvey, about what date, month, day, and year was this that you got the names from the lonely hearts club?"

"I don't recall the exact date," Glatman said, "but it was in the month of March, the early part of March of this year, 1958. And, about Thursday of that week, I called Shirley through a neighbor. She didn't have her own phone, and the number I had gotten was that of a neighbor who allegedly would call her to the phone. Well, anyway, the neighbor did call her to the phone, and I talked to her on the phone, and I introduced myself as George Williams. And I told her that I had gotten her telephone number from Patty Sullivan, and I wanted to know if she would be interested in a date for Saturday night. And she said she would be, and I made an appointment with her to pick her up at her house about eight o'clock. That's Saturday of that week, and—"

"Harvey, can I interrupt you for a moment?" Majors said. "When you contacted the lonely hearts club, it was for the purpose of becoming acquainted with a girl?"

"Yes," Harvey said.

"At that time, when you made this contact to locate a girl, what was your reason for wanting to locate one? What were your intentions?"

"Well," Harvey said, "my reason for wanting to locate one was that I wanted to have female companionship, leading to sexual intercourse."

"Okay," Majors said. "Continue."

"Well, I went over to Shirley's house as per appointment," Harvey went on, "and I got there around the time I said I would, and I went into the house. I parked across the street and went into the house and introduced myself. And I guess a number of her family were in the house—some in the living room, and some in the other room—and she said she was just about ready, and for me to wait just a few minutes. So, I waited. Well, I don't recall exactly, now, the address. It was out in San Fernando Valley, quite a ways out. I think the street . . . as I recall it now . . . was named Tuxford Street, but I don't recall the number."

"And while we're on it, Harvey," Majors interjected, "looking at the calendar, I see that there's a Saturday, March the eighth, this year. Could that be the Saturday that you went to her house? If you wish to get up and look at the calendar, there, it's underneath the back page."

"I can't . . . I can't . . . even that doesn't help," Harvey said. "I can't swear whether it was the eighth or the fifteenth."

"I see," Majors said.

"It seems to me it probably was the first week," Harvey continued. "That is, it probably *was* the eighth, but I'm not absolutely sure, now. It might have been the fifteenth. I don't . . . I just don't recall."

"That's okay," Majors told him. "Well, then, you were in the house, and they told you to wait."

"Yes," Glatman agreed. "Yes, she told me to wait a few minutes, while she went inside, and I guess she was finishing putting on her makeup, or whatever she was doing, and getting her coat. And after a few minutes, she came out, and we left the house."

"Now, who was in the house?" Majors asked. "Who did you meet?"

"Well, I . . . she introduced someone," Harvey said, thinking it over. "There was a girl there she introduced as her sister, and some woman I think she introduced as her mother. And there were quite a number of people. There was a couple of children I . . . that I noticed that she didn't introduce. I don't recall her saying . . . somebody probably said something about who they were, but I don't remember it. And there were some people sitting . . . it seemed to be a kitchen. You could see from the living room, and I don't recall who they were. It seems to me they were introduced as members of the family in one way or another, relatives of some kind. Well, we left the house, and we went and got in my car. We started driving back toward downtown Los Angeles, and I asked her whether she would rather go to anything specific, like a movie, or whether she would just rather drive around, or—"

"Was this during the day or night?" Majors asked.

"No, this was in the evening," Harvey said, "a little after 8:00 P.M. And she said she didn't care too much which it was, and I said, 'Well, how about going for a drive, then?' And I didn't feel like, especially . . . wasn't in the mood for a movie . . . and she said all right. So, after I got in toward Los Angeles, I got on the freeway, and I thought I might

like to go down by Oceanside, or somewhere in that
neighborhood. It's a nice drive, down that way, and
I hadn't been down that way before. But I heard it
was a resort town, so I thought we would just head
down in that direction, and we went out on the Santa
Ana Freeway—that's U.S. 101—and started driving
toward Oceanside. And while we were driving, I
got . . . I asked her if she wouldn't mind moving . . .
object to moving over a little closer, and would she
mind if I put my arm around her, and all that. And
she didn't object. And so, we were driving down 101,
and I was driving with one hand, necking a little,
and patting her with the other hand, and she didn't
object or anything. She seemed content with it. She
was pretty shy. She didn't . . . she wasn't very talk-
ative, and even in answer to a direct question, she
didn't speak out very loudly. I tried to ask her a few
questions, you know, just a little conversation going
about herself, but she . . . she wouldn't carry the
conversation at all. She just would either answer very
briefly, or as few words as possible, but she more or
less was sitting there, sort of with her head resting
over my shoulder, and I had my arm around her . . .
the way we headed down . . . and I kissed her a few
times on the face, because she had her head right
over there, and even though I was driving, I could
take my eye off the road long enough for that. And
we just kept driving like that, until we got to
Oceanside—which I judge, I guess it took about . . .
from the time we left her house, maybe two hours,
or a little over. And we stopped in Oceanside, and
went in and got something to . . . I asked her if she
was hungry, and she said she could eat something,
and we went into a little café or something, there,
and we got something to eat—some sandwiches and
some pop. And she thought while it was getting
pretty late . . . and maybe we ought to get starting

back because it would take a couple of hours to get back to her home. And, of course, I still . . . was my intention . . . I wanted to have some sexual intercourse, and I didn't want to just drive straight on back. And I had suggested we go back a little different route. There's another highway a little to the east—runs parallel to that 101; it's 395—and there's a connecting road close to Oceanside . . . U.S. or State Highway 78."

"When you speak of Oceanside," Majors said, "you mean Oceanside here in San Diego County?"

"Well," Harvey said, "I don't know what county it's in. I . . . it's right off Highway 101, as you come by the—"

"Now, another thing," the sergeant cut him off. "You speak of these different highways and connecting highways. How do you know about these? Have you ever—"

"No," Harvey said. "I had a road map in the car with me that I usually . . . well . . . I had it ever since I came out here because I didn't know my way around too well, and any time I wanted to go anywhere, I just referred to that map, right on the spot."

"I see. Go ahead."

"And so," he continued, "I got on Highway 78 and went over to . . . I guess it's a place called Vista, or some place there, where . . . I think it connects with the other highway—or, is it Escondido? I don't know if it connects in Vista or Escondido. Well, anyway, I got on the highway, and I think it's just above Escondido that it connects, and I turned north towards Los Angeles on that 395. And I drove a few miles up the road, and I spotted a place where there was a little wide turnout place—you know, sort of flat, where a car could pull off, maybe ten or fifteen yards or so off the road, something like that. And I turned off there, and I parked the car, and I told

Shirley that I . . . that . . . well, we could spend a little time here and neck for a while, or something, and that it was Saturday night. She could sleep late Sunday, or whatever. It wouldn't hurt her to stay out a little later. And so, she . . . again, I don't know whether she approved too strongly, or maybe she still thought it was getting a little late, but she didn't raise any great objection. So, we sat there and we petted a while, and then I suggested that we have sexual intercourse, and *that* she *didn't* want to, and she wanted to go home. And I tried to talk her into it for a little while. And meanwhile . . . all the time, I was petting with her, and she seemed pretty set against it. And so, by this time I guess I was worked up pretty good, and that's what I came out there . . . why I wanted the date in the first place. So, of course, up to this point there had been nothing wrong happen, or anything like that, and . . . but I had the gun in the car with me, and I had . . . as I recall, I had it. I don't remember whether it was in my coat pocket, or whether I had it on the floorboard of the car. I just don't recall clearly. But, anyway, it was either one or the other, and I got the gun in my hand, and I showed it to her, and I told her that . . . again, I cautioned her not to be frightened, I wouldn't shoot her if she did what I told her to. And again, I told her I wanted to have sexual intercourse, and that if she did what I told her, I wouldn't shoot her. And I guess she got pretty scared, but I told her to go on in the back seat of the car, and so we both . . . after she went in, I went in the back seat, too, and I took my clothes off, and I made her take her clothes off. And we had intercourse there, and then we sat there for a while, and after a while we had intercourse again, and—"

"Let me ask you a couple of questions, here, Harvey," Majors said. "You both had all your clothes off, is that right?"

"Well," Glatman replied, "I just had my socks on, or something like that. And I don't think . . . she still had her stockings on . . . but essentially all of her clothes."

"And you were in the back seat when you had intercourse?"

"Yes."

"And previous to that time, now," Majors said, "when you produced the gun, did you just show it to her, or did you point it at her?"

"Well, I . . . well, I guess it was pointing at her, all right."

"She definitely saw the gun?"

"Oh, she saw it, yes," Harvey said. "And it was pointed in her direction, and I don't doubt it."

"Okay," Majors said. "Go ahead, then."

"And so, after that, I . . . I let her put her clothes back on, and I put mine back on, and we got . . . went around . . . and we both got back in the front of the car, and we sat there for a little while, just sort of resting. And I was thinking what I was going to do now, and I . . . again, I was thinking almost the same thing I was with Judy—that she could identify my car, now, and the plates and everything, and that I had already committed three, actually several crimes, because of the gun, rape . . . and, actually, it was kidnapping, holding her there against her will, and everything. And I . . . I just decided that for my own safety . . . wouldn't let me let her go. Then, at that point, I was . . . she could identify me. I wasn't worried, again, about facial identification because her whole family, practically, had seen me in the house. I wasn't too much worried about that, but I was afraid she could identify even the license plate on the car, even just if it was, she could recognize it was a Colorado plate because I had a record in Colorado, that any notification of a general description . . . even of me to the authorities there would probably come up with me as a suspect, anyway. And so, I took out the map . . . we were still sitting there . . . and I was looking in that area, and I saw this . . . out past Escondido, there. There's a state highway runs across the desert, there, and there's another road leads off there . . . it's . . . and there's marked state park on the map, and it seemed to me like it would be a pretty . . . more or less deserted area there, not too thickly settled or anything."

"Well, then, Harvey," Majors interrupted, "was it this time, then, while you were parked there with her, that you definitely made up your mind you were going to have to kill her? Is that right?"

"Yes," Glatman said.

"Uh huh. And so, then you got the map to pick out the best spot where you could go?"

"Yes," Harvey agreed, "just roughly. I didn't have any specific point, but just on that area, on that road along there . . . somewhere, when I got there, I would just pick out a spot, somewhere. So, I was headed, of course, toward Los Angeles, so I turned the car around, and I made a U-turn there on the highway and headed back through Escondido."

"Now, wait a minute," Majors said. "Before we get any further, was she at this time completely free, or was she tied?"

"Oh, yeah," Glatman said. "I had . . . no . . . before I started, I saw we were going to have to pass through Escondido, and it looked like a fairly good-sized town on the map. I never been there, but it looked like it was . . . they've got the . . . by the different symbols, they indicate population . . . and it looked like a fairly sizable town. So, I didn't want her raising any . . . just in case . . . ruckus, while we were passing through town, so I had tied her hands behind her back, and then I started out. I made the U-turn and started out."

"I see," Majors said. "You tied her hands, only?"

"I tied her hands, only," Glatman confirmed.

"You didn't tie her feet?"

"No," he said. "I didn't think it was necessary, then. And we went through Escondido, and I think it was Highway 78. That's the one that you follow out there—I know it is, now—and we passed through several other very small towns along the way, and then we kept going until we hit the junction where this . . . on the map, it indicated you turn right—that would be heading south, more or less— then, you go into this . . . I guess it's called Anza State Park, is what the map had indicated there. And I went a number of miles . . . again, I don't know just how far, must have been maybe from the . . . where we turned off the state highway . . . maybe ten or twelve miles, altogether . . . somewhere in there . . . and it all looked pretty deserted . . . didn't seem to be . . . looked pretty wild country. From where I could see—it was very dark, and it was very early in the morning now, just before dawn—but it was still pitch black, and we couldn't see too much of anything, except that it looked very wild and pretty deserted, all the way around. So, I just . . . after about twelve or fifteen miles or so, I just pulled over to the side and stopped the car, and I told Shirley that we were going to get out and walk a while, and that maybe I'd take some pictures of her in the morning. I had the tripod. I almost always carry it in the car with me, usually leave it in the trunk, and I had the camera, and I had some film with me in the car. And so, I got the camera and the film, and we got out of the car, and we walked across the highway and walked on . . . we were in the middle of the desert, actually. It was kind of wild, a lot of brush around and everything, and we walked . . . I guess . . . turned out looked like about a mile. It's hard to tell distance, but I guess about . . . maybe . . . almost a mile off the road."

"Now," Majors said, "let me go back and ask you again, when you got out of the car with her, did you leave her hands tied?"

"No," Harvey said. "I omitted that after we passed Escondido, I stopped the car and untied her hands."

"I see."

"I hadn't said that before," Harvey went on. "I omitted . . . I forgot to add that in, this time, but I untied her hands. She wasn't tied at this time, no."

"When you tied her hands back there at that spot," Majors asked, "where you had intercourse with her, what reason did you give her at that time for tying her hands?"

"Just the reason I told you," Glatman replied. "I told her that . . . I said, 'I'm going to . . . there's a town here, a few miles down the road, we're going to pass through, and I don't want you to get any ideas.' And I told her it would be safer for her if her hands were tied that she might not get an impulse that she might otherwise, if she thought she had a . . . she might get excited or something, and I wouldn't be able to control her. She might jump right out of the car."

"What I'm getting at, Harvey," Majors said, "is, did you give her any reason why you were tying her hands and taking her back out there? What did you tell her you were going to do?"

"Well, I didn't tell her what I was going to do. I just—"

"You didn't give her any reason?"

"No," Glatman said. "I just told her . . . well . . . I didn't want to go back, and maybe we'd just drive all night, and maybe go back the next day. I didn't give her any specific . . . tell her we were going anywhere or gonna do anything in particular. I just told her that I just wanted to keep riding a while, and maybe all night."

"Now," Majors said, "you were down at the spot where you parked the car. You said on the side of the road. The two of you got out of the car, and you hiked over, you said, probably—almost a mile?"

"Seemed like a mile, yeah," Harvey said.

"Now, what were you carrying with you, you and her?"

"Well," Harvey answered, "I think she had her purse with her, and I had the camera and some film, and some pieces of rope in my pocket, and the gun, and the tripod."

"And did you have any water or food along with you on this trip?" Majors prodded.

"I had some candy and some light food along, in the car," Harvey said, "and I think I had some water. I'm sure I did . . . had some water. I think I did, yeah."

"Did you carry any of that over to the spot?"

"No," Harvey said. "I didn't . . . carried some of the food . . . I put that in my pocket, but I don't think I took any water. I wasn't particularly thirsty, and it was—"

"Did you take a blanket?" Majors asked.

"Oh, yeah, took a blanket."

"What blanket was this?"

"I don't recall, exactly," Glatman said. "I had a couple of blankets in the trunk that I took from Denver, and I hardly ever used them here. Actually, I had about three blankets that I could have used. I had a real old one in there that I never used for anything, except just to wrap something, or to . . . as a wedge in the . . . you know, if I had stuff packed in there, sort of packing things in the trunk. But I had about three blankets, and ones . . . one I used for myself at night in the apartment, and the other two, I just left in the car, because you just don't need them out here, very often."

"You don't recall which blanket it was you took over there, then?" Majors pressed.

"No, I don't."

"Would it be . . . could it be the same one that you used—"

"It could have been," Harvey answered, trying to be helpful. "I don't recall exactly which one."

"I was going to say, could it be the same one you used with the Dull girl?"

"It could have been, yes," Harvey agreed. "And so, we got out there, and I found a spot that didn't seem to be too rough. It wasn't very big but just seemed to be a little flatter. Flat ground. I told her, 'Well, this is . . . we'll just stop here and sit down a while.' And I gave her some of the candy to eat."

"Where were you carrying the gun at this time?" Majors asked.

"In the coat pocket," Glatman replied.

"In the coat pocket? You weren't carrying it in your hand?"

"No. I didn't see any reason to carry it in my hand."

"She knew you had the gun with you?" Majors said.

"I assumed she did, yes. And it didn't seem like too long," Harvey continued with his story, "and it started to get light out, and I decided to wait out until the sun got up over the hills and take some pictures. And I decided that I would kill her the same way I did . . . I killed Judy . . . and I used the pictures as an excuse to tie her up without alarming her or getting her so she would become unduly scared as to why I wanted to way out there tie her up, and—"

"Did she fight you any when you were tying her?" Majors inquired.

"No."

"How did you tie her?"

"The same way I did Judy," Glatman replied. "I tied her hands behind her back. This was, now, after the sun had just gotten up over the hill, there . . . and I tied her ankles, and I laid her face down on the . . . well, I took some pictures. I took about five or six pictures of her that way, in different poses."

"Did you have a gag in her mouth?" Majors asked.

"I think in some of them or maybe all of them. I don't recall, offhand, whether I did. I'm sure I did for some of them, at least, and then after the last picture, I think I told her I wanted to take one more in a little different position. And I had this . . . again, this third piece of rope, and I tied that around the other ankles, around the rope that was around her ankles, in the same manner as with Judy, and I did just about the same things I did with Judy. I lifted her, I put my knee in the small of her back and pulled her legs, her ankles back, so . . . you know . . . they're bent at the knees. And I looped the rope around her neck twice and pulled as hard as I could."

"In other words," Majors said, "the identical same way as you did Judy?"

"Almost identical," Harvey agreed.

"With the knee in the back?"

"Yeah, to hold her . . . to hold her down."

"Was this on a blanket?" Majors asked.

"Yes, she was on a blanket."

"She was on a blanket?"

"Yeah."

"Now, would these be the same—" Sergeant Majors hesitated, reaching for a glass of water on the table. "This water'll taste good," he said, sipping it.

"Now, would these be the same ropes that you used for Judy?"

"They might have been," Harvey admitted. "I had a number of lengths of rope that I had used for packing my belongings when I had moved, and they were all . . . they had all been mixed together, and after this other . . . Judy . . . and those ropes had been mixed in again with the others, and I don't know for certain that that was the same pieces, actually."

"Did you tell Shirley at any time that you were going to kill her?"

"No," Glatman said, emphatically. "I never told her that I was going to kill her."

"Then, you tightened up on the rope around her neck?"

"Yes."

"You had your knee in the middle of her back," Majors said. "About how long did you hold her in that position?"

"I guess, about five minutes or so," Harvey said. "It seemed like that, I guess. It seemed like about five minutes."

"And then you—"

"Then, there didn't seem to be any sign of life," Harvey broke in. "She had gotten unconscious, and as Judy did, it seemed very quickly, and there didn't seem to be any sign visible of life. And, of course, now it was daylight, now, and her eyes were closed, and she didn't seem to be breathing at all or anything. So, I assumed she was dead, then, by that time."

"I see." Majors took a moment to collect his thoughts. "Well, then, in this particular instance, in the Bridgeford case, you killed her in the very spot where you took the last pictures?"

"Yes," Harvey said.

"Uh huh. Then, what did you do after you released

the hold around her neck, the rope around her neck?"

"Well," Harvey said, "I took all the ropes off that had been around her, and I . . . just for some reason, I thought she ought to be underneath something. Although it was way out in a very desolate place, it wasn't as though there was any danger of her being discovered or anything, I just . . . I don't know why . . . I just thought she ought to be under something. So I . . . a few feet away—a few *yards* away— there was sort of a pretty tall, funny looking plant. I guess I don't know what kind of plant. It's not a tree or bush, or maybe it's some kind of cactus or something, but it was pretty dense and tall, and it sort of leaned over at an angle. It had grown straight up, so I just picked her up, and I carried her over there. Actually, I didn't carry her all the way. She was a little heavy, and it was kind of hard ground to walk on, anyway, so I didn't carry her too far, and then, I think I dragged her part of the way over."

"About how far," Majors asked, "would that be from where you killed her?"

"Maybe fifteen or twenty yards," Glatman said.

"In an uphill direction?"

"Not especially. It was . . . it wasn't either up or down. It was on about the same level. It was a sort of a little slope, but it was on the same . . . just about the same level."

"I see. Then, you drug [sic] her to that spot. Then, what did you do?" Majors asked.

"Well," Harvey said, "I remember I took her shoes, and I put them in . . . there was a . . . this was a sort of clump of these things, and I put them in this clump."

"That was right alongside of her?" Majors pressed.

"Yeah, right alongside of her. And I remember she had a white . . . sort of a whitish-colored coat that she had been wearing, and it had big, flat, round buttons on it, and I started to wipe them off with my handkerchief. I don't recall touching them, but I just started to wipe them off, anyway, and they looked like they were just sewed on with ordinary thread, so I just pulled them off, and I put them in my pocket to throw away later. And then, I remember, I think I wrapped her in the coat, and then I went back and picked up all the things that I had brought out there—the blanket, the camera and everything, and her purse. And I think, at that point, I left."

"Why did you take the buttons off of the coat?" Majors asked.

"Well, I just thought possibly there were fingerprints on them," Harvey said, "and that's why I had started to wipe . . . but they looked like they come off so easy, I just decided to just pull them off and throw them away."

"Those items you just mentioned," Majors said, "you took all those back to your car with you, eventually?"

"Yes."

"Now, do you recall removing any of her clothing there, other than the shoes?"

"No," Glatman replied. "I don't recall removing any other of her clothing."

"Do you recall what color panties she had on?" asked Majors.

"Yeah, red," Harvey told him.

"Bright red," Majors confirmed. "The reason I ask you that, Harvey, is after we found her remains out there in the coat, when we raised the coat up, the red panties were underneath this coat. That's why I asked if you recalled taking any of her clothes off."

"No," Harvey insisted, "she was still wearing the pants when I left."

"Well . . . that you're sure of?"

"That I'm sure of," Harvey confirmed.

"Well, then," Majors continued, "are you sure that she was dead when you left her?"

"Absolutely, I'm sure," Harvey said.

"You're absolutely sure of that."

"Well—" Harvey was starting to doubt, now. "I . . . she couldn't have been alive. I'm not a doctor or anything, but it just would have been fantastic, impossible, under the . . . that she would have been alive. Just wasn't possible."

"Did you make any tests on her, such as feeling her pulse or breathing?" Majors asked.

Frowning, Glatman said, "No, at the time . . . right after . . . before I had removed the rope from her neck, for breathing . . . I tried to see any faint sign of breathing. Her face was blue. Her eyes were, of course, closed, and there wasn't any movement at all, unless I moved her."

"Do you recall the rope making a mark on her neck?" Majors asked.

"Yes," Harvey said. "It made a very severe mark."

"It did?"

"Yes."

"Uh huh." The sergeant still sounded skeptical. "Then, you couldn't give us any explanation of how these panties would be underneath the coat?"

"No, I can't," Harvey said, "unless due to natural action or animals, or something that may have . . . I understand there are coyotes that are . . . whatever some of those kind of things in that area . . . and possibly they had picked at the body, or something like that."

"Now, when you left her," Majors said, "you left her on the coat, or did you put the coat over her?"

"No," Glatman said, "I sort of just wrapped it . . . she was on the coat, and I sort of tried to wrap it around her as much as I could, and of course, it wouldn't hold because the buttons were gone then. I couldn't button her, but I did remember she was on the coat. I had spread the coat out, and then I just . . . before I got her to there . . . I laid her down on the coat, and I sort of wrapped it."

"I see," Majors said. "You recall whether she was lying facedown or faceup?"

"I believe I left her facedown," Harvey said.

"Uh huh. Now, in that clump of bushes, that day that we went out there, we found . . . along with one shoe, a sort of bluish-green portion of a dress or a woman's . . . yes, would be a dress. Do you recall putting that in there?"

"Yes," Harvey said, "I think I do. I think that tore off when I was dragging her over. I had gotten . . . I think, partially pulling her by that dress . . . and it was just a piece that ripped off as I was dragging her, and I just laid it in there with the shoes."

"I see."

"That was the . . . that bluish-green color, sort of . . . that was the color of the dress she was wearing," Glatman said.

"Then," Majors continued, "now again, my memory has slipped me. Again . . . what items did you take back to the car with you, that belonged to her?"

"Well, her purse and all its contents," Harvey said. "I believe that's all that . . . and the buttons."

"Was there any money in the purse?" asked Majors.

"Just a few cents in coin," Harvey replied, "and I . . . I believe . . . think it was about thirty cents."

"What did you do with that?"

"I kept that," Harvey said.

"You kept that for yourself?"

"Yes."

"Okay. You took your camera equipment, blanket,

and these items you just remembered, all back to your car. About what time would that be, Harvey?"

"Oh," he said, "I didn't look at my watch, but the sun had been up now for some time. It might have been 8:30 in the morning. Eight, 8:30, maybe. I don't know. It could have been a few minutes, either way."

"Could it have been 9:30 or ten o'clock?" Majors asked.

"Probably not," Glatman said. "I don't think I took that long. After all this happened, I wanted to get out of there as fast as I could."

"So, you went back to your car, then. And then, what did you do?"

"Well," Harvey said, "I turned it around, and I started back on the road that would take me back to Los Angeles, through Escondido—just about the same route that we had taken on the way down."

"And what did you do with these items of hers?" Majors asked.

"Well, I stopped at different places along the road and the motel. Any articles that . . . like lipstick thing, compact, she had in her purse . . . things like that, I'd wipe it off with my handkerchief, then I got out of the car and threw them away."

"I see. And where would that be?" Majors asked. "Would that be before you got to Escondido?"

"Just about all of it was thrown away before I got to Escondido," Glatman said.

"About how many stops did you make to throw these items away?"

"I'd say I made a half a dozen," Harvey said.

"And what was your reason for making so many stops?" the sergeant asked.

"Well," said Harvey, "I just thought it would be better not to throw everything in one spot. An occasional item like that, even if somebody just happened to cross it, it wouldn't attract any special attention . . .

if just things like that, you might see laying around, you know. Somebody in a passing car just threw it out or something like that. Nothing unusual about it."

"Now, Harvey, going back to when you made this date with her to pick her up, you . . . at that time, put water in your car, did you?"

"Yes, I had some," Harvey admitted.

"And some food?"

"Yes, I had some food in the car, too."

"Well, then, was that . . . did you at that time have in mind the fact that you might have to kill her, and if you did, you'd take her to the desert and have these items along?"

"Well," Harvey answered, warily, "I had assumed the possibility. As I told you, I had gone out with the idea of having intercourse, and I had hoped it would be sort of the [sic] voluntary, and that nothing out of the way would happen. But I also was prepared for what I did, under the circumstances. That's the way they turned out."

"In other words," Majors said, "if she would not submit willingly, and if you had to have intercourse with her by force, then you knew if that occurred, then you would have to dispose of her? Kill her?"

"Yes," Harvey admitted. "I . . . I knew that for the same reason that I explained previously about Judy, that . . . that I probably would do that."

"But if she had of submitted willingly and could have convinced you that it was something that she wanted to do, then you would have taken her back to Los Angeles?"

"Yes, sir. Then, I would have had absolutely no reason to . . . at all, to even to think of that, and I would have just driven back to Los Angeles and driven her home."

"But if you did have to use force, where there

would be a chance of her making a report to the police, and if you had to use force, you naturally assumed that she would report it to the police?"

"Yes," Harvey said, "I assumed."

"Then you had already figured ahead that if that were necessary, then you would have to kill her?"

"Yes, sir."

"Do you have in your possession, anywhere, any articles that were taken . . . that you took from Shirley Bridgeford?"

"No," Glatman replied.

"They were all disposed of along the highway?"

"Yes, sir."

"Have you ever had occasion to go back to the spot where you killed her?" Majors asked.

"Only once with the police," Harvey said, "after I had been arrested."

"That was last week?"

"Yes," Harvey said. "That was Thursday night—or, actually, when we got there, it was Friday morning."

"That's when I was along?" Majors asked.

"Yes."

"Well," Majors turned to Tom Isbell, "is there anything you wish to bring out, Lieutenant?"

"No," Isbell replied. "I think that Harvey pretty well covered it. There's nothing that you can think of?"

"No," Harvey said. "I can't think of anything of any consequence that I left out."

"Okay, then," Isbell said. "What time is it?"

"That will conclude the statement by Harvey concerning the Bridgeford girl," Majors told the tape machine, "at 10:15 P.M., on November fifth."

Glatman had earned himself another break, but he was still not finished with his grisly tale of death and suffering.

15

"She Was Getting to Look Pretty Sick"

AFTER ANOTHER SHORT BREAK, ISBELL AND MAJORS RE-
turned to the stuffy interrogation room. A fresh reel
of tape was threaded onto the recorder, and Majors
switched it on.

"The following statement," he began, almost by
rote, "is under San Diego County Sheriff's Department report number 98813, concerns the death of one
Ruth Mercado, known to the defendant as Angela
Rojas. Those present at this time are the defendant,
Harvey Murray Glatman, Sergeant R. B. Majors, Lieutenant Tom P. Isbell. The time is 10:25 P.M. The date
is November the fifth, 1958. The place is the interview room, San Diego County Sheriff's Department.
Harvey, I would like to admonish you again that
whatever you say here, concerning this case, is being
taken down on the tape recorder, which is operating
in your presence. Anything you say can be used
against you in your prosecution in regards to the
death of Ruth Mercado. With this warning, are you
willing to make a statement?"

"Yes, sir," Harvey replied.

"Whatever you say here will be said by you free and voluntarily?"

"Yes, sir."

"Well, then," Majors continued, "will you tell us the time that you first met Ruth Mercado, and everything that transpired, to the best of your knowledge, up until and including her death?"

"Well," Harvey began, "should I refer to her as Angela Rojas or Ruth Mercado? I know her now by both names."

"Well," Majors said, "just refer to her as to the way you know her. We have it on record as Ruth Mercado, alias Angela Rojas."

"Well, I knew her, when I first met her, as Angela Rojas," Harvey said, "so I'll use that name, then. Well, I first had contacted her at her home by telephone because of an ad she had had in the paper. She was advertising as a model who had her own studio, private studio, and she ran a little ad in the classified section of the paper—the Los Angeles paper—and I had called her in July of this year, about her modeling. I wanted to get some information as to how much she charged, and things like that, and what hours she worked, and so forth, and . . . I'm trying to think of the exact day it was. I think . . . I don't know whether it was the second or third week of July. I think it was the second week, but I'm not positive, absolutely positive in my mind about that. But I called her, and she gave me her address, and I went over to the address she gave me, to see her, to talk to her in person about modeling, and to see what kind of person she was."

"You recall this address?" Majors asked.

"I don't . . . as I recall now, it was 3714 Pico, West Pico Boulevard. To the best of my knowledge, that's the street address. And I went over to her address, and she let me into what I took to be her studio.

And it was in the back part of . . . well . . . it was
sort of a hotel that was not built up so much as it
was spread out, and her apartment . . . or, at least,
her studio that I knew at that time, was in the back.
There was a couple of buildings, separate buildings
with . . . they ranged into apartments, and the place
I went was in back of the main building and on the
first floor, there. And I went in and talked to her for
a while, and she showed me some of her photographs that she has in an album, and I asked her
different things about her modeling, like just what
specifically . . . how she charges, and how much experience she had, and general things like that."

"About how long were you there?" Majors asked.

"Oh, I guess about twenty minutes or so," Glatman replied. "And I told her . . . well . . . I would
probably be calling her again. I didn't want to take
any pictures that evening, but that I would contact
her again in the near future. And I did call her on
the telephone the next night, and I got no answer,
but I had been with several of these girls before, and
I knew that during the week, at least, they were almost always home in the evening to answer the
phones from their ads, and that if they usually . . .
they went out . . . they didn't stay out very long,
that maybe they just stepped out for a bite to eat, or
to buy something, or to talk to somebody around the
neighborhood, or something. So, I got in my car and
drove over there, anyway, and parked in the neighborhood. Not right in front of the place, but about a
block away. And I actually didn't go over there with
the intention of shooting pictures of her. I'd gone
over there with the idea of having her . . . having
sexual relations with her. And when I got there, I
went around to the same place that I had been before,
the same door, and it was dark. There didn't seem
to be anybody in, so I went around to the front to

see the manager. And I checked with him to make
sure that was where she lived. I asked him if Angela
lived here, and he said yes. And I said, 'Can you tell
me exactly what apartment she stays in?' And he told
me around in the back, and he gave me a number of
an apartment, but it was so dark back around there,
you couldn't see any numbers, anyway. So, I went
back around there, and then I realized that right
next . . . sort of at an angle to this . . . jutting out
just a little . . . there was another door, apparently
to another apartment. And that's the one he had been
talking about, and that must be her apartment. This
other one I remembered from the night before didn't
look like it was lived in, just used for a . . . it was
just one room . . . just looked like it was used for a
studio, and that she probably had another apartment
there that she lived in, there, and it . . . of course,
was no lights on in there, either. I knocked on the
door. I thought maybe she'd be asleep or something,
in there . . . just was sort of . . . automatically
knocked, and of course, I got no answer. So, I
thought, well . . . I still thought that probably, she
wouldn't have been out too long. I know they stay
home most of the time there, to answer the phone,
so I said to myself, 'Well, I'll just kill a little time
around the neighborhood and walk up the street a
ways, something, maybe consume a half-hour or so,
and try once more and see if she's in. If not, I'll just
go home.' And so, I went up the street a ways. There
was a bar there, so I went in and sat down and had
a . . . just to waste some time, more than anything
else . . . I bought a beer and dawdled along with it,
drinking it pretty slow and smoking a cigarette. And
when I was through, I went back to the apartment
again. Angela's apartment. This time, there was this
light on in the apartment, so I assumed she was
home. I went up, and I knocked on the door, and she

answered the door, and she remembered me from the previous night. And I told her I wanted to talk to her, if I could come in for a minute. I asked her if I could come in, and I told her I wanted to talk to her about something, and she let me in."

"Excuse me, Harvey," Sergeant Majors interrupted. "Do you recall what date this was?"

"Well," Glatman said, "I think it was a Wednesday evening, but I don't remember whether it was the second week in March or the third week in March."

"March or July?" Majors asked.

Harvey blinked in surprise. "I . . . I . . . no, I'm sorry. I'm thinking . . . we were talking about Shirley so long, I was thinking about that. I mean *July*. I don't remember whether it was the second week in July or the third week."

"And one other thing," Majors said, "I want to ask you—"

"I think it was the third week," Harvey interjected, "but I'm not . . . I know it was around the middle of July."

"And possibly the third week?"

"Possibly, yes."

"I want to ask you another thing," Majors said. "When you parked your car down around the corner from where she lived that evening, did you walk . . . did you go directly around to the apartment?"

"No," Harvey said. "Well, I didn't . . . there's an alley runs behind the apartment, and as I came by that alley, I walked down the alley, and I looked at the back, when I walked past the back of the building. I saw there was a gate, and there was a fence around the building, and some garages back there. But there was a gate leading . . . apparently, with a little walk leading up to the front . . . that I noticed. And then, I walked around the alley, out to the street, and around the front, and came in the front of the building."

"Did you have a particular idea in mind," Majors asked, "when you walked around the alley?"

"Well, as I told you," Harvey said, "I had gone over there with the idea of having sexual relations with her, and of course . . . I didn't . . . she had only met me once, and I didn't really think too much . . . that she was going to just up and be agreeable. And I thought I might have to use force or threats, and if something went wrong, or something, I might have to leave very quickly. This, I saw, gave me a way out the back rather than the front, where I wouldn't have to run out onto Pico Boulevard in case I was trying to leave very quickly."

"You definitely had plans, then, of having intercourse one way or another," Majors said, "either willingly on her part or raping her. Is that right?"

"That's right, yes."

"And I'll ask you at this time, did you . . . planning ahead, did you have anything in your car for an excursion to the desert, such as water? Food?"

"Yes," Harvey said.

"And did you have your gun in your car, or was it—"

"No," Glatman said. "It was in my pocket."

"You had it in your coat pocket?" Majors asked.

"Yes."

"Did you have the ropes in your car?"

"I had some pieces of rope in my pocket, too," Harvey replied.

"In your pocket?"

"In my coat pocket," Harvey said, "that I was wearing at the time."

"Uh huh. And did you have anything along to use as a gag?" Majors asked.

"Yes. I had a piece of cloth."

"Where was this?"

"In my pocket," Glatman said.

"This was in the pocket with the rope?"

"Yes."

"And that was in your—"

"I had a pair of these red rubber gloves, also, in my pocket," Harvey interrupted.

"And what was your intention for bringing them?"

"Well," Glatman said, "I knew I would be in her apartment, and that was in case I had to handle anything or touch anything that would carry a fingerprint, that I would put the gloves on, first. That is . . . if I had . . . was resorting to any kind of force where there was crime involved, *then* I would put the gloves on, if I had to touch anything."

"Now, before I interrupted you on the continuity of your story," Majors said, "you stated that you had gone back to her apartment, and you saw a light on in there. Is that right?"

"Yes."

"Uh huh. Go ahead from there," Majors instructed.

"Well, I asked her . . . I told her that I wanted to talk to her about something pertaining to her modeling," Harvey resumed. "And I asked her if she would let me in to talk to her, and she did. And then, I went inside, and I closed the . . . there's a screen door and a sort of glass-panel door with venetian blinds hanging down . . . and I closed the door. And there's a lock that you can work from the inside, you know, and I locked it. And then, when I turned around to face her again, I had pulled the gun out of my pocket because . . . I guess I really didn't believe that there was . . . I was going to get anywhere with just propositioning her like that. I didn't know her well enough for that to . . . even really begin to try that, and—"

Majors interrupted him again. "What was she

wearing, by the way, Harvey, when she met you at the door?"

"She was wearing leotard . . . what they call, I guess, a leotard, which is a tight-fitting piece of cloth. I guess it—"

"It's a ballet dancer's costume?" Majors asked.

"Something like that," Harvey agreed. "Yeah, like that. It goes all the way from the neck down to the hips. And I cautioned her not to make any outcries or do anything, unless I told her to, and that if she behaved herself and did what she was told, I wouldn't hurt her. And she had a little dog in the apartment with her, and he was behaving in a friendly manner, but I thought it best that he be out of the way, so I got her to lead him into a little bathroom that was on the same floor, there, and we closed the door on him, so that the dog stayed in the bathroom, there. And then, I saw there was . . . I asked her where the bedroom was, and she said it was upstairs. I saw a little stairs leading up there, and I told her we were going to go upstairs. And I turned out the lights downstairs and made her go on upstairs to the bedroom."

"Were you holding your gun in your hand, yet?" Majors asked.

"At this time," Harvey said, "I was still holding my gun, and I got upstairs . . . I told her to lay facedown on the bed. And I had tied her hands behind her back, and I tied her ankles. And I went over . . . well . . . I think, first, before I did anything else . . . I think I gagged her, too, because I wanted to go downstairs and sort of look around. I hadn't seen the whole place, yet. I wanted to make sure there was a back door to the apartment, actually, and I . . . everything . . . I just would . . . thought I'd feel safer if I knew exactly how it was all laid out, the apartment, rather than half-blind spotted, just in case

somebody unexpected called on her or came around
or anything, and I had to just leave quickly. So, then
I went downstairs and looked around, and then I
came back upstairs again, and I removed the gag,
and I let her sit up on the bed. So, I . . . and I told
her what my intentions were, and I was going to
keep her there a while, and—"

"What did you tell her your intentions were?" Majors asked.

"Well," Harvey replied, "I'd have sexual relations
with her, and I was going to have some fun with
her. And I sat on the bed with her, and I ran my
hand over her body and kissed on different places
on the body. And I kept that up for . . . I don't know
just how long . . . quite a while . . . and then I
cautioned her again to . . . I told her I was going to
untie her hands and feet, and I was going to have
intercourse. Then . . . and that I still had the gun,
and not to do anything foolish, or anything like that.
And so, I made her take off the leotard or whatever
she was wearing, and I undressed, too, and I had her
lay back on the bed, and I had intercourse with her,
there. And then, after that, I asked her if she had any
money, and she said yes, she had some money hidden in a box, over with some other little boxes . . .
small box . . . on the dresser in that same room. And
she pointed out where it was, and I went over and
I got that. It was about twenty dollars, twenty-five
dollars in bills, and I put that in my pocket, in my
coat, and I think I let her put this leotard thing back
on. And I sat there for a while, and I was trying to
make up my mind whether I should just tie her
hands back there and leave—that would give me
enough time to leave, and then she could probably
walk downstairs and go out and arouse somebody
to untie her—or whether I wanted to stay with her
a while longer, maybe have some more intercourse

with her. And I asked her whether she was expecting any company, or whether any callers or anything like that might come along, and she said no. At least, she said no *first*, and then she mentioned something . . . well, her boyfriend sometimes drops around, and it was pretty late by now. And I said, 'Do you think he'd come around this late?' And she says, 'Well, sometimes he does.' But it didn't sound too good. It sounded sort of like she just thought that up, that maybe if I heard that, I'd get scared and leave, or—"

"You said it was pretty late," Majors interrupted. "What time would that have been, about, Harvey?"

"Oh, it was about 11:30," Glatman replied. "Something . . . somewhere around there. This . . . I decided that she was just making it up. But in case she wasn't, I decided I could still get out if I had to because I could run out the back and be . . . you know . . . before anyone, say come by, would actually realize there was something wrong. That I could be a long ways off, and it wouldn't be too risky."

"While they'd be at the front door, you'd run out the back?" Majors clarified.

"Yeah," Harvey said. "And I'd go right out the gate, near . . . right out in the alley there, and if it was done quietly, you could get out, and nobody would even notice. So, I decided to stay with her a while, there, and we sat on the bed, and I was still pawing her, more or less, and then she mentioned . . . I think it was here that she mentioned something about . . . I guess she thought I wanted money primarily, now, or something. She said something about she had money in the bank. She didn't say how much, and I don't remember what I said. I said something like, 'Well, I can't get at that money, it's in the bank,' or something like that. I didn't understand why she was telling me she had money in the bank, but I didn't ask her about it any more. And I decided . . . well . . . I would keep her with me a little longer, and that I would probably take her out in the car, and probably keep her through the whole next day. So, I told her to . . . that I was going to take her out and was going to ride around in the car. And I told her to get dressed in her regular street clothes, which she did. And after she was dressed, I told her that my car was parked about a block away, and that we were going to walk down to my car, and I was going to tie her hands as a precaution, and that I was going to walk right alongside of her, and that I would have the gun in my pocket and my hand on it, and that if we were to pass anybody on the street, or meet anybody, or anything like that, she was to ignore them and not . . . you know . . . not to say anything or indicate there was anything wrong. And that I . . . she had . . . I asked her if she had any kind of a jacket or something like that she could slip over her because it was kind of cool for one thing, and for another thing, I wanted . . . her hands were tied . . .and I wanted something that would cover her, reach down to her waist, at least, to . . . so that it would cover her arms and hands up there. And she said she had sort of white fluffy jacket of some kind—some kind of synthetic material—that I threw over her shoulders. And then I told her, 'Well, we better go downstairs, now, and we'll just . . . out the back door and out and down the street to the next block, and get in my car.' And she asked me could we take some brandy along. She said she had some brandy in the refrigerator, and if it was all right with me, as long as we're going, could we take that along? And I said all right, so we . . . I took two bottles of brandy out of the refrigerator that she had in there and put them in a paper sack she had in the kitchen. So, we went out the back door and down the street, there, and turned and got in my car. And then I started driving, and I was . . . at this time, just heading down south in the general direction of San Diego. I don't know just yet, just how far we were going to go, or just where. And, again, after we got out of Los Angeles . . . out past here, where . . . just about where the freeway comes to an end, I pulled over, and I untied her hands, and we kept on going. And down here . . . I figured I better pull in for some gas. I guess it was around San Clemente or somewhere. But a little before we got there, I stopped the car again, and I tied her hands behind her back, and I told her . . . I got a blanket out of the car . . . and I told her I was going to stop for gas, and I told her not to arouse the gas station attendant . . . you know . . . indicate there was anything wrong. And I said, 'The best thing you can do' . . . I gave her a pillow that was in the car . . . and I said, 'Just rest your head on that, like, and just act like you were sleeping.' And I wrapped the blanket around her, and I said, 'When we go in there, you just pretend you're sound asleep, and you don't have to say anything, and he won't talk to you or anything. You're just sleeping, that's all.' So—''

"You had her hands tied behind her?" Majors asked.

"Yeah," Harvey confirmed. "And I just wrapped the blanket around her, and I said, 'When we go in there, you just pretend you're sound asleep, and you don't have to say anything, and he won't talk to you, or anything. You're just sleeping, that's all.' So—''

Majors broke into the monologue again. "You had her hands tied behind her?"

"Yeah, and I just wrapped the blanket . . . threw, you know, the blanket over her and fixed the pillow so she was comfortable in there. She just leaned her head back, and . . . actually, maybe she didn't. She looked like she was . . . I don't suppose she actually got to sleep, but she looked just like she was asleep."

"Did you tell her what you would do to her if she attempted to escape or to—"

"Well," Harvey said, "I told her I would shoot her."

"You told her you would shoot her?"

"Yes. And so, then after we left the gas station . . . and then, I untied her hands again, and we continued on towards San Diego. And we got down here, where I noticed the signs were . . . we were coming to a junction with 80, which runs east and west. I knew that, and I knew it crossed over to the desert out there, so I just decided I'd go ahead on that road, and I switched from Highway 101 to 80, just here in San Diego, or a little ways after. I made . . . I got on Highway 80 . . . I decided I better gas up again because there may not be so many gas stations out that way. So, we repeated the process with the pillow, and tied her hands again, and put the blanket on her. By this time, it was starting to get light, but I didn't think that made too much difference because a gas station . . . even at night, when you drive in . . . is pretty well lit up. And so, I gassed up again, and continued driving till we were pretty well out from the metropolitan area, and it was kind of hilly country. And I pulled off the road a ways, in a spot where you could pull off, and we stopped there for a while. And I . . . we had something to eat. I had some food there, and we had some bread, peanut butter, and some fruit—stuff like that, some candy, stuff like that. I asked if she felt like eating anything, and she said she did. So, we ate some stuff, and I sat in the car, and I petted her for a while, and ran my hands over her, and . . . I didn't want to stay. We must have been there a couple of hours, anyway, but I didn't want to stay all day in one spot, so we drove on a little further, and pulled off again. After a while . . . and I don't remember whether it was two or three times, different . . . maybe four spots . . . I didn't stay too long in any one of them. And then, later in the day, I decided I wanted to get some pictures of her, and I had the camera and everything in the car. And I drove out toward the . . . more toward the desert until you get out of those hills out there, and I took off on a little side road somewhere, there, and went a few miles and pulled up, there. And there was a couple of small hills . . . it wasn't a real mountain or nothing . . . the little hills were . . . maybe shoot some pictures without . . . of course, there wasn't anybody around or anything, but in case a car drove by or something like that . . . have something between us and the thing. So, I got her out of the car, and of course it was pretty hot, too, and we were both pretty uncomfortable, although we had plenty of water with us. We weren't dying of thirst or anything. It was just real hot . . . and took the blanket out, went around and found a place where we could set the blanket down, and laid the blanket out flat. And I told her I wanted to take some pictures of her tied and gagged. So, she was pretty uncomfortable, and she said something about . . . well, she hoped I wouldn't take too many, or something, as she was feeling pretty bad from the heat. And I said, 'Well, I am, too. I don't think we'll stay here too long.' And so, I went ahead and took those pictures. Those are the pictures that you got that were in the box."

"In that metal box?" Majors asked.

"Yeah," Harvey said. "I took them. I just had her remove her dress, and she had on her slip and the rest of her clothes."

"About how many pictures did you take?" asked Majors.

"I think I took five or six," Glatman replied. "And she was getting pretty . . . by that time, she was getting pretty sickly looking . . . and she said she just couldn't stand the heat any more. So, I untied her and she put her dress back on, went back to the car, and got some of the water. And I wet a rag and let her mop her . . . you know . . . wrap it around her head to help her cool off. She drank some of the water, and so did I. And then, we headed back to the main highway, and we headed back . . . actually, a little toward San Diego, I think, 'cause I figured it would be a little cooler in the hill, there, to get off that real hot desert, there. And I pulled off the road again somewhere, and we stayed there the rest of the time until after dark. And we had some more to eat, and we were both kind of tired, and she sort of went half asleep on me—or maybe she was all the way asleep because she . . . she asked if she could use the pillow, and she said she was pretty tired, and I sort of . . . I was just sitting in the . . . she was in the front seat, too, and she sort of rested her head back on the back of the seat, you know, and sort of . . . I didn't go completely asleep because she could have . . . if she woke up, she could have just walked out of the car. No, I didn't have her tied . . . or I don't believe, or did . . . no . . . yes . . . *sure* I did because I . . . I was pretty tired, and I thought I might fall asleep, and . . . that's right, I *did* tie her. I think I tied her feet and her hands. I didn't gag her. I tied her feet and her hands, and I . . . well . . . I still didn't want to go asleep completely, but I . . . sort of like that. We stayed like that quite a while, and I intended to stay there till after dark. And I already decided the same as the others, now, that it was too risky to bring her back, and—"

"You had by this time decided to kill her?" Majors asked.

"Yes," Glatman confirmed. "That's why I waited there till after dark instead of starting back for Los Angeles. Because, if I had started back, it probably would have been dark, anyway, by that time I got back. And so, we stayed there till after dark, which meant till after nine o'clock when it got real dark. It's that sort of dusky, earlier . . . then waited around for a little while after it had really gotten dark. And then, I had . . . I pulled off the road and turned, made a U-turn, and headed back toward the desert. I told her something about we were going to take a different route back, or something, across the desert—that it wasn't so bad at night, that it was kind of cool, actually, on the desert at night. Went out the . . . I didn't know exactly, now, where I was going to go. I went out . . . I was going east on 80, and I finally turned off on this road, which we later went back on—when I went with the police, excuse me, to locate the body—and it turned out, actually, to be an extension of the same road. I didn't know this at the time. This was a dirt road. The other was paved, that I had come . . . it runs through Anza Park, a state park where I had brought Shirley down. I found this out later, but that was the road we were on, and—"

"In other words, Harvey," Sergeant Majors interrupted him, "you mean it turned out that it was the same road that you had previously come on with Shirley Bridgeford when you killed her?"

"Yes," Harvey said, "on the other . . . yes . . . only not on the same part of it."

"You entered it from the other end?" Majors said.

"Was a continuous . . . yes, from the other end, and if it was a . . . if I had kept going, I would have been on the same part of the road and traveled back the same way as when I brought Shirley down, although I wasn't aware of this at the time. And although the map showed the road going down there . . . but this seemed to me to be two different roads because one was paved, and one was dirt. And I thought, maybe this was just another little road that wasn't even on the map. And I remember . . . I don't know, exactly . . . I didn't keep track of the mileage and how far in we went, but I remember passing a sign that said 'San Diego County line.' And we went a few miles past that, and there was a place there that looked like it was pretty solid, off the road, where you wouldn't get stuck or something, if you pulled off the road, and so I did. I stopped the car there, and turned in and went a little ways off the road, and parked there."

"About how far off the road, Harvey?" Majors asked.

"About twenty, twenty-five yards is as far as I went," Glatman said. "And I told Angela that I wanted to take a few more pictures of her, and I told her . . . of course, this was at night . . . but I told her I had a portable flash equipment with me, and it was no problem. I could take pictures anywhere, if I wanted, at night. And I told her I didn't take as many as I wanted in the afternoon because it was so hot, and she . . . she was getting to look pretty sick and uncomfortable. So, we got out of the car, and I took the blanket and the camera and the tripod and the flash equipment . . . actually, it was pretty compact, the flash. It's an electric flash, and all fit into one little box, and there seemed to be a hill there, where we parked. It was pretty dark. There was a little moonlight but not enough, and you could see silhouettes of things, and it seemed to be a sort of little mountain or hill, just about there, and I decided . . . I walked around . . . sort of just made a circle around it. It wasn't real big. Maybe a few hundred yards is all we walked . . . and walked around it. I could see some lights way off in the distance. Of course, in the desert, you can see lights a long way off, and I assumed that was lights from . . . maybe El Centro or some place around there. So, I knew which direction I was, there, because I knew that was pretty well south of where I was. Well, anyway, I spread the blanket out there, and I told her I wanted to take the same kind of pictures I took in the afternoon. So, I tied her hands and feet, and I didn't see any reason to put a gag on her. Actually, I didn't take any pictures there. And again, I did it almost identical with the other two. And I put the third piece of rope around the ropes around her ankles, and pulled her knee, leg, or ankles back, and put my knee in the small of her back. And, I guess before she realized actually what was happening, I looped the thing around her neck twice and pulled it as tight as I could."

"This was on the blanket?" Majors asked.

"Yes," Harvey said. "She was laying on the blanket facedown."

"You didn't take any pictures?"

"No. Not there, I didn't. I just brought the thing along because I had used that as . . . to tell her why we were going out and stopping the car there and getting out there."

"Would this be the same rope that you used on any of the other girls?" Majors asked.

"It could be."

"But you're not sure?"

"No," Harvey said, "or it could have been a different piece. As I said, I had mixed the pieces. There were different pieces that I had used for other purposes, and they had been not kept separate but mixed together."

"I see. Now, this blanket that you had her lay on,"

Majors said, "was that the same blanket that you took the pictures of her on, earlier in the day?"

"Yes. That happened to be that red . . . red blanket."

"With the sort of satin binding?"

"Yeah," Harvey agreed.

"On the two ends?" Major clarified.

"Yes."

"Is that the same blanket that we showed you in Los Angeles today?"

"Yes," Harvey agreed.

"When we were in the garage there?" Majors pressed him.

"Yes."

"Lieutenant Isbell, here, showed it to you, and I believe you marked it at that time?"

Harvey nodded. "Yes."

"That would be the same blanket, then?"

"Yes."

"Now, how long did you hold the rope on her neck?" Majors asked, switching tacks.

"Oh," Harvey mused, "I guess about the same as the others. Seemed to be about five minutes. It might have been longer, but it just seems like about five minutes."

"And then, what did you do after you held the rope," Majors said, "and you finally decided that she was dead, is that right?"

"Well, yeah," Glatman said, "or just about. I just let go of it, and like in the other . . . when it's pulled that tight around there, it doesn't just unravel itself or come loose. It actually stays almost as tight, whether you're actually pulling on it or not. And what I did . . . I think, with her . . . I picked up all the stuff except the blanket and clothes, this other stuff, and I took it back to the car. And then, I came back to where she was, and then I took the ropes . . .

all of them off her . . . and I took all her clothes off, except for her pants. And I removed the blanket from under her, and I just left her that way."

"I see," Majors said. "Do you recall what color the panties were that she was wearing?"

"Pink," Harvey said.

"They were pink. And those pictures that you took of her during the day . . . were those color photos or black and white?"

"No, those were black and white," Harvey said.

"Those were black and white," Majors repeated, making sure.

"Yes," Harvey said. "I didn't take any color photos of her."

"And did you . . . did you check her to make sure she was dead, or could you have left her alive?"

"Well, I didn't make exactly a check," Harvey admitted. "There was no sign of movement in her, at all. Of course, it was dark. I couldn't see her face, but again, I just assumed that it would have been impossible for her to have lived through that."

"Did you have a flashlight with you that night or any type of light?" Majors asked.

"I had . . . I always carry a light in my toolbox," Harvey said. "In the toolbox . . . the small toolbox, not the big one that you found, there. This was my regular tools that I use in my work, and I had that in the car, but I don't recall taking the flashlight out there with me."

"In other words," Majors said, "it was moonlight enough—"

"To see where you were going," Harvey finished for him.

"To see where you were going, and to tie her up, and to—"

"Yes," Glatman said, "there was enough to see silhouettes, and just barely make out outlines of things, but not enough to see . . . it wasn't a very brightly . . . it was a waning moon, and there was enough just for visibility but not like a real bright full moon."

"When you took her from the car," Majors said, "out to the spot to where you killed her, was she tied in any manner at that time?"

"No," Harvey said. "She just walked out there with me."

"And have you ever been back to that spot since?" Majors asked.

"Once," Glatman replied.

"And that was, when?"

"With the police, to locate the body, after I had been arrested."

"I see. Did you carry the gun out there with you that night?"

"Yes," Harvey said.

"Did you carry it in your hand or in your pocket?"

"No, it was in my pocket."

"Now, when you left there," Majors said, "you took all her items of clothing with you except her panties?"

"Yes," Glatman said.

"You took her purse and—"

"Its contents," Harvey said.

"Now, what did you do with those items?"

"Most of them, I disposed of," Harvey said. "Some . . . some of her personal items I kept."

"And how did you dispose of the ones you *did* dispose of?" Majors asked.

"I threw them away as I stopped the car and got out, on the way back," Harvey said, "and just threw them away."

"In one place?" Majors queried.

"No," Glatman said. "Maybe two or three small pieces in one place, and then I'd go a few miles and stop again and throw some more away."

"Along Highway 80 as you came back?"

"Yes, along Highway 80."

"As you came back toward San Diego?"

"Yes," Harvey said.

"And what did you keep of hers?" Majors asked.

"I kept . . . I . . . she had brought along . . . I told her to bring along an extra slip and some stockings, and what she brought was a half-slip, actually. And I kept . . . that is one of the items of her clothing I kept. And I kept the stockings, two pairs—the ones she was wearing and the odd . . . the other pair."

"You kept both pair?" Majors asked.

"Yeah," Glatman said. "And I kept her wristwatch, and I kept some of her identification papers."

"And did she have any money in her purse?"

"Yes," Harvey said. "She had about ten dollars in there."

"What did you do with that?" Majors asked.

"I kept that."

"You kept that?"

"Yes, sir."

"Okay," the sergeant moved on. "Is there anything else you want to tell us now about . . . that we might have overlooked?"

"Well, I can't think of anything of . . . that seems of importance to me that I—"

"Okay," Majors interrupted him. "Lieutenant?"

"The wristwatch that you kept," Isbell said, "where did you get that from?"

"That I kept?'

"Uh huh. That's the wristwatch that belonged to Angela, I mean," Isbell went on. "Was it in her purse, or did you take it off her arm?"

"No," Glatman said, "I had taken it off her wrist."

"You took it off her wrist *after* you had choked her?" Isbell asked.

"No. I took that off before we ever left the apartment," Harvey said, "when I had first started to tie her hands. It was in the way, and I had slipped it off her wrist and just slipped it in my pocket."

"Do you know," Isbell asked, "if that wristwatch was taken by the officers from you?"

"Well, when I . . . the night I was arrested, I believe it was in the car. I left it in the glove compartment of the car, and I believe they obtained it then."

"You mentioned having intercourse with Angela in the apartment," Lieutenant Isbell said. "Did you have intercourse with her more than one time?"

"Yes," Harvey said. "I had it in the car. Did I mention that, on this tape?"

"No," Isbell said.

"Well, I should have because I know that I did," Harvey said. "I did, at one of these times that we stopped, that I mentioned. If I seem to forget some of this, it's probably . . . maybe because I've been talking so long at one time that . . . no, I did have intercourse once more during the time that we were petting, at one of these stops that we made, along after daylight. After we had passed San Diego, I did have intercourse with her once more."

"Somewhere off Highway 80?"

"Yes," Harvey said.

"Now, was that in the back seat?" Isbell asked.

"That was in the back seat of the car."

"You had her disrobe?"

"Disrobe," Glatman agreed.

"Now, you mentioned also that . . . pointedly . . . that just prior to putting the rope around her neck that you did not gag her?"

Well," Harvey said, "I don't know if that was *pointed*. Didn't you ask a specific . . . didn't you ask me specifically if I did it?"

"I don't recall whether I asked you or not," Majors

said, "but I believe you said you didn't gag her out there."

"I think that was in response to a question. I'm not . . . I don't recall . . . but anyway, I . . . I don't think I did."

"Did she make any outcry at all, or—"

"No," Harvey said. "She made . . . when the rope first tightened around her, some . . . it was cut off, actually. I guess she started to make an outcry, and probably it was just cut off. It didn't come out as a scream. It came out as a . . . just noise, which didn't last."

"Did she protest being tied?" Isbell asked. "Or did she plead with you or anything when you were tying her?"

"No," Harvey said, "not about being tied, she didn't. What she had done—earlier in the day when we were taking those other pictures—was, she complained because it was so hot, and she was feeling . . . she said she was getting a little sick from the heat. And that's why we took the five or six pictures. I didn't finish the roll."

"Do you think," Isbell asked, "that you possibly convinced her that you were going to make some flash pictures, or—"

"I believe I did," Harvey said, "because I carried all the equipment. I took the tripod, and the camera, and the box with the flash in it, all out there with me."

"About what time did you arrive back in Los Angeles?" Majors asked.

"Well, I arrived back . . . let's see, now . . . this was the . . . this was Wednesday night that we had started, and we were out all day Thursday, so it would be . . . I guess, be Friday morning. It was just getting light when I finally got back to Los Angeles."

"Six, seven o'clock, maybe, in the morning?" Majors prodded.

"Well, no," Harvey said. "It must have been a little earlier than that because this was in August."

"I see. Well . . . this was in August, now? I thought you said that this was—"

"I mean, I'm sorry. *July*," Harvey said, correcting himself.

"Did you make any attempt to conceal her body or move it from the point where you killed her?" Majors asked.

"No," Glatman replied. "I left it just exactly where I had . . . I didn't make any attempt to cover it or move it at all."

"How far would you say that she was away from your car or from the road?"

"A couple hundred yards," Harvey said. "Maybe a quarter of a mile. As much as a quarter of a mile, maybe."

"Well, I guess that's it," Majors said. "Do you recall, Harvey, how you left her laying: facedown, faceup, or what?"

"I think, facedown," he replied.

"Well, I guess that's it. Okay," Majors said. "The time now is about 11:20 P.M."

And, once again, he switched the tape recorder off.

16

"What Do You Think I Am?"

WITH THREE MURDERS BEHIND HIM, IT REMAINED ONLY FOR Harvey to describe his abortive attack on Lorraine Vigil. To that end, Sergeant Majors and Lieutenant Isbell rejoined him in the small interrogation room, with twenty minutes left to go on that long Wednesday night.

"The following statement is in regards to an assault on the person of Lorraine Virgil—or Vigil—occurring in Orange County, October twenty-seventh, 1958," Majors told the tape recorder. "The time now is 11:40 P.M., November fifth, 1958. The place is the San Diego County Sheriff's Department interrogation room. Those present are the defendant, Harvey Murray Glatman, Sergeant R. B. Majors, Lieutenant Tom P. Isbell. Harvey, I'll again admonish you that whatever you have to say here is being recorded on a tape recorder, which you are aware of, and that you don't have to make a statement; that whatever you say will be said by you free and voluntarily; and whatever you do say can be used against you in a prosecution."

"Yes," Harvey said. "I understand that."

"And with that understanding, you are willing to make a statement concerning your actions with this Lorraine Virgil or Vigil?"

"Yes."

"Will you please tell us when you first met her, the conditions under which you met her, and lead right up to the time of your apprehension." Majors caught himself, then, interrupting before Glatman could speak. "Before we get into that, Harvey, we've been talking here now for over three hours. You don't feel that you're being mistreated or anything, do you?"

"No," Harvey said. "No, I don't."

"Do you want to go with this now, or would you rather continue it tomorrow?"

"No, I would just as soon go on with it right now."

"I see," Majors said. "Okay."

"Well," Harvey picked up his narrative, "I met this Lorraine on a Monday night—that was the twenty-seventh of October of this year—and I met her through another model who had given me her name and address. And I went over to her house—that is, Lorraine's residence—which I don't recall offhand, the address, and I had—"

"That was in Los Angeles, though?" Majors asked.

"It's in Los Angeles," Glatman confirmed.

"Her . . . her address?"

"Yes."

"And about what time was that?" asked Majors.

"It was about 8:30 in the evening, and I had persuaded her to do some modeling for me, and I had paid her ten dollars in advance. And she had come with me and gotten in my car, and I had driven her onto the freeway and out on the Santa Ana Freeway."

"Did you tell her where you were taking her?" Majors asked.

"Well," Harvey replied, "I had told her that I had lived down in that direction, out past Anaheim, and around in there. And I was taking her there to . . . presumably . . . or, at least, where she thought I lived . . . and after driving for some ways on the Santa Ana Freeway, I took one of the off-ramps onto a road leading away from the freeway. And I went a few hundred yards down the road, and I pulled over to the side of the road and stopped the car. And I had a gun with me, and I . . . it was on the . . . under the seat of the car . . . and I pointed it at her, and I told her to . . . that I was going to keep her there a while, and for her not to do anything or cause any trouble, as I might probably would shoot her if she did. And she asked me if I was going to . . . if I wanted to rape her, and I said, well, maybe I would, maybe not. And she said, 'You can rape me, if you want, but don't shoot me.' And I had a piece of rope in my pocket, and I wanted to get more assured of my control over her. I wasn't too sure of her at this point. She seemed kind of edgy, and I had told her to turn a little sideways in the car, that if I was going . . . and to put her hands behind her back. And I took the piece of rope out of my pocket, and I had started to . . . I made a little loop, and I put it over one wrist, and while doing this, I had laid the gun down on the seat next to me because I needed both hands for this. And she seemed to be very balky, that she wanted to know why I wanted to tie her hands, and I told her that . . . I didn't give her any specific reason . . . I just told her that I wanted to tie them, and that she wasn't to ask questions. And she seemed, again, very upset, specifically by this. And I had pulled her back over to me. I got sort of a grip around her neck with my right arm,

and pulled her down toward me like this, and told
her not to give me any more trouble, and that she
might get hurt pretty badly if she did, but if she
cooperated, she wouldn't get hurt. And she nodded
that she would, and I released my grip on her, and
again I told her to put her hands behind her back,
and she still . . . again she seemed pretty balky about
it. So, I thought I had . . . probably had better use
the gun, to possibly scare her down a little more, till
she was more cooperative. So, I picked it up and had
it . . . started to point it at her, and . . . meanwhile,
she had turned halfway around, now, facing me in
the seat. And I guess she got hysterical at just about
that point, and she made a grab for the gun, and at
the same time started screaming and trying to reach
over me and bang on the window on the side of the
car that was toward the road. Because we were only
a few feet off the road . . . not far, very far . . . and
there was occasional cars passing, and I tried, with
my right hand, to get her back around, to . . . to get
her head down, and also to try and get her back
around, so she was facing away from me, rather than
towards me, so that I could loop my arm around her
neck again, and apply enough pressure to . . . to
force her to quiet down. Because she was . . . well,
actually, she was hysterical. She was just screaming
and was sort of kicking and . . . all at once and
everything . . . and I don't think she heard me at all
when I told her to . . . to quiet down. And I think I
threatened to shoot because at this time I still had
the gun in the position where I could, but I still
wanted to get her under control without shooting her
or anything. And shortly after this, she had got her
hand on the gun—on the barrel—and I was still trying to get her down with my right hand . . . or . . .
and to turn her around . . . but she was just jumping
around too much. I couldn't get a good grip on her,

and . . . actually, the steering wheel . . . I was behind
the steering wheel, and it was sort of interfering with
my movement a little. I couldn't turn full around,
the way I wanted to, and anyway, we . . . I was
trying to wrest the gun out of her . . . her grip, too,
so that I had full control of it again. And meanwhile,
the door on the right side opened, and the dome light
came on, too, which illuminated the whole interior of
the car. And then, I was really . . . right then, I . . .
really got nervous, then. Up to that point, I'd . . .
still was . . . felt that I could control her. After a few
minutes of that, I'd get the right . . . just . . . just
right . . . and I'd have her under control again. But
this time, with being where we weren't really
isolated . . . we were pretty close to the road, and
there was traffic going by, and somebody could see
what was . . . with the light in the car, could see
what was going on, and maybe go down the road
and call the police or something. And just about the
time that the door opened, too, the gun went off, and
I saw the bullet hole in the dress—in her skirt. And
for a minute, I thought she was shot in the leg,
and . . . although that was just for an instant because
she didn't make any cry . . . she didn't cry out or
anything. She didn't seem to be hurt, and so . . .
then, I assumed . . . well . . . it must have just went
through her skirt and missed her completely—although I found out later that it just singed her . . .
just grazed . . . they told me it just grazed her leg a
little . . . didn't hurt her too badly but just grazed
her leg. And I remember trying to reach across her.
I let loose of her with my right hand, and I tried to
just shove her enough . . . she was half out of the
car and half in . . . I tried to get her in enough, so I
could reach over and pull the door shut to get the . . .
make the dome light go off again. And I just couldn't
reach the handle. The door swung way wide open. I

just couldn't reach the thing, and as I was reaching
over . . . actually, I helped knock her right out of the
car, and she still had her right hand on the barrel,
partly over my hand and partly on the barrel of the
gun. And now, she was out of the car, and . . . of
course, I went right out after her, and she had tried
to . . . she took a step or two . . . tried to run toward
the . . . around the car, toward the road. In the meanwhile, she was still yelling at the top of her lungs,
and I had grabbed her, the, with my right hand and
spun her down to the ground. And I went down on
top of her, and how she managed to hang onto
the . . . keep her grip that . . . on the gun at that
point, I don't know, because I had spun her around
to the ground, and gone right down on top of her,
so she couldn't get up and start running."

"Now," Majors interrupted the flow, "her grip on
the gun, Harvey, was on the barrel. You had your
hand on the—"

"I had my hand on the grips," Glatman said, "and
my finger was on the . . . inside the trigger guard
where it had been all along . . . and then, the dome
light . . . the door was still open on the car, and
we . . . and we were still behind the car. The car was
between us and the road, but we were pretty well
toward the back. Our feet might have been showing
to someone coming down the road, and I remember
trying to inch her up a little forward, and . . . so I
could get close enough to the door and slam it shut,
at least to . . . to get the light out. And I couldn't . . .
I didn't know what to do, first. She was still screaming, and then . . . I know I was still looking around
to see what was coming down the road, as to . . . if
there was nothing coming, I didn't care so much if
she was hollering. I was more . . . to get the door
shut . . . and yet, if there was something coming, I
didn't . . . I thought the priority went back to keeping

her quiet till they passed . . . and let the door stay open. And I saw a motorcycle coming down the road, and . . . of course, I didn't know if it was the police, or just a private citizen, or what, on a motorcycle. And he was coming down the road, and so I had stuck my hand in her mouth, like . . . well . . . something like that . . . well, of course, they can't see that on the tape . . . but as I stuck it in there, just before the motorcycle got close to the car, she got hold of my . . . small finger on my right hand . . . that's the one that was in her mouth . . . and took a good bite on it. And, of course, while she was doing that, she had stopped making any noises because she couldn't make a scream and bite on my finger at the same time. And I was hoping . . . I was just trying to hold her like that until this motorcycle had gone past. And he did start to pass the car, but he only went a few yards past, and then I saw him . . . I could see that there was enough light there that I could see he was wearing a uniform. And I just figured, pretty quick, then, that he was the police, and he . . . I saw him go a few yards past, and then I saw him turn around, and he came right . . . he was just a few yards . . . and he came right around behind the car, there, where we were struggling. And he pulled up right behind, there, and I just gave up the ghost right then and there. And I just got up and let loose of everything . . . let loose of her . . . and I let loose of the gun, and I just stood up, and so I guess the police . . . he was . . . still didn't know just exactly what was going on. He was just getting off his cycle, and he hadn't pulled his gun out, or anything. I guess he just wasn't sure what it was that was going on. There was nobody in the car. The light was on, and he said later, he saw something moving around on the ground, and he just came back to take a look. So, when I let loose of her and let loose of the gun and everything, why, she jumped up, and she was waving . . . I remember seeing her waving the gun by the barrel. She ran up to the . . . the policeman that had stopped, there, and showed him the gun. And then, of course, he got his own gun out, and that's where I was arrested. And then, of course, pretty soon, the whole bunch of them showed up, and I was taken into custody and taken over to the Orange County Jail and questioned and then booked into the city . . . county jail, there."

"Now, Harvey," Majors asked, "on this occasion, when you dated her, and you went there to get her, you . . . as you . . . you had food and water in the car, did you?"

"Yes," Harvey answered. "I did."

"Planning that you might have to go to the desert again?"

"Well, possibly," Harvey admitted. "But, I was . . . it . . . on this particular one, I had thought ahead of time what I could do to . . . if I could get her without resorting to that. And I had decided that the car itself . . . I would take it . . . I might take a chance on the car itself, just a black car, even a Dodge . . . if she knew that was all . . . and I had been extremely careful when I picked her up not to let her see the plates at all, on the car. I had parked it a little ways from her house because it was a very dark spot in the street. I parked it across the street from where she lived and down a few doors, and when I was walking out there, I even looked at . . . I looked back, and I just couldn't tell what color the plates were at all or see any design or anything on the plates. And when I walked out of her house with her, I told her that I hadn't seen the . . . I had stopped a few doors down because I thought that's where her number was, and . . . and when I found out it wasn't, I didn't want to move the car. I just walked up, so I said the

car was down the block a few doors, and we walked
on the opposite side of the street. And I got right
opposite the door of my car and walked perpendicu-
lar, right on over, so that I was sure, in my own
mind, that she hadn't seen the plates or couldn't possibly have seen the plates on the car at all. And—"

"What name did you use?" Majors asked.

"That was the . . . if . . . now, that was . . . I didn't
know, of course, in advance, that it would work . . .
that I would be able to do this or park it in such a
way that there was no possibility of it . . . but it just
turned out, on that particular street, that it was a real
dark spot, and that she didn't walk around the car
or anything. I didn't let her walk around to the passenger side. I let her in on the side . . . on the street
so she wouldn't walk around the car or anything,
and it wasn't possible for her to have seen the
plates."

Majors tried again. "I was going to ask you—"

"There was a possibility," Glatman forged ahead,
still fixated on the Dodge's license plate. "But I . . .
there was a very good chance that on this one . . .
that I wouldn't have resorted to that. I would take a
chance on the car itself and not on the . . . as long
as it was safe on the plates."

"But if you had to," Majors said, "or you felt that
you had to—"

"Yes, I felt—"

"You would have killed her in the same manner
that you did the other?"

"I . . . probably," Harvey agreed.

"I ask you, Harvey, what name did you give her?
Did you use an alias?"

"I think I used the name Frank Johnson."

"Frank Johnson?"

"Yes, sir."

"And what other items did you have in the car?" Majors asked. "Did you have ropes in the car?"

"Yes," Harvey said. "I had some ropes in the car and some—"

"Where were they in the car?"

"They were in a sack . . . a bag in the car . . . paper bag, along with some other things."

"Did you have a gag in the car?" Majors asked.

"Yes. I had a strip of cloth that could be used for that, and some food in another sack, and some water, and—"

"And you had rubber gloves along?"

"Yes," Harvey said. "I had the rubber gloves, although—"

"Where were these items in the car?"

"They were in the back of the car," Glatman said. "Not in the trunk . . . in the back by the . . . on the floor by the back seat."

"I see," Majors said. "And where were you carrying the gun?"

"I was carrying the gun in my pocket," Harvey said, contradicting his earlier statement. "In my coat pocket."

"Well," Majors said, half-turning to Isbell, "I think that covers it pretty well, as far as I'm concerned. Lieutenant?"

"When you contacted this Lorraine Virgil, or Vigil," Isbell said, "and told her you wanted to have her services as a model, what were your intentions? What did you want her for?"

"I wanted her for sexual relations, actually," Glatman said, "although I had . . . I had an alternative that I possibly would have just used her as a model. I hadn't decided, and maybe . . . either way . . . and I didn't decide on that particular thing until the last second . . . until I passed where I would have turned off to my place, if I decided to just have her do some modeling."

"But was your intention to have sexual intercourse with her," Isbell pressed, "either voluntary or involuntary on her part?"

"Yeah," Harvey said, contradicting himself once again.

"And as you stated," the lieutenant said, "if you felt that you had to use force to have intercourse with her, and if you felt that you could get her to the car without her having . . . finding too much evidence or going hack with too much evidence . . . you would have possibly let her go?"

"Yes," Harvey said.

"But if, in your mind, after having intercourse with her . . . if it was forcible, if you felt that you or your car could be identified, then you believe that you would have had to treat her the same as you did the other three?"

"Yes," Harvey told the lieutenant. "Not me, but the car. Because I wasn't particularly . . . as I said . . . mentioned with the others . . . I wasn't too much afraid of myself, personally, being identified."

"Is there anything else you want to add, Harvey?" Sergeant Majors asked.

"No," Glatman said. "I can't think of anything."

"See," Majors told the microphone, "the time is about five minutes after midnight. It's now November the sixth."

And Harvey was ushered away to his cage.

San Diego's jailers had placed Glatman under suicide watch in a one-man cell. He had spoken vaguely, in L.A., of prior attempts to kill himself, and local authorities were determined to prevent him cheating justice. The procedure called for him to be "eyeballed" at frequent interval, to make sure he was still alive and well inside his cage.

It was routine, but still, it chafed on Glatman's nerves. At one point, turning on his watcher of the moment, Harvey bawled, "What do you think I am, a freak?"

The subject of exactly what he was had been on many minds, since Harvey was arrested on the twenty-seventh. Rape was nothing new in southern California, nor in any other part of the United States. Likewise, there had been men (and a few women, too) who killed repeatedly, almost compulsively, as long as human beings had associated in the heady mix they called society. Los Angeles had seen its share—the Nash and Bashor cases came to mind and Otto Wilson from the 1940s—but no one dreamed that there was so much worse in store a few years down the road.

"Serial killers" did not have a name of their own in 1958. Typically, if they claimed enough victims, they were lumped with the larger class of "mass murderers" and dismissed as mindless aberrations. Another four years would pass before criminologist James Reinhardt distinguished them from other multicides with the label "chain killers," and four years more until author John Brophy first used the "serial" tag for those who claim victims *in series*.

By that time, in the mid-1960s, American crime would be in the midst of a dramatic and terrifying face-lift. Before the sixties, police across America dealt with an average of two "chain killers" per year, nationwide, coast-to-coast. By the end of that tumultuous decade, the rate would rise to one case a month, minimum, and *that* rate would nearly quadruple by the early 1980s. By 1984, law enforcement spokesmen would describe serial killing—also dubbed "recreational murder"—as presenting America with an unprecedented "epidemic of homicidal mania."

Harvey Glatman, then, was ahead of his time—a point man for the new vanguard of psychopaths that would double America's murder rate in a few short years while dropping the homicide-solution rate from ninety-odd percent to the low sixties.

He was the wave of the future, in fact, but no one saw it coming. They had trouble looking past the man himself to see what lay inside.

And San Diego's prosecutors, frankly, did not care. They had Glatman cold on two counts of first-degree murder—the confessions and the desert tour, the skeletons he pointed out, the list of photographs and other souvenirs collected from his home. These murders had been sex crimes, that was obvious, but no one on the prosecution team was really interested in what made Harvey tick.

They were more concerned, at the moment, with stopping his clock.

It shouldn't be difficult, the prosecutors reasoned. Executions were still routine in California, despite the Caryl Chessman furor and rising protests from bleeding-heart types, and killers of multiple women or children ranked high on the hit list. Best of all, Harvey was making noise about his wish to die and "get it over with."

Still, Don Keller knew that he would have to watch himself, dot all the *i*'s and cross his *t*'s. One error, anywhere along the way, and Glatman might end up with life in prison, feeding off the state forever like some kind of leech.

Worse yet, he might be found insane and beat the rap entirely, win himself a ticket to Atascadero, the state hospital, where a committee of psychiatrists could one day stamp him "cured" and set him free to kill again.

Keller and William Low were not about to let that happen on their watch.

Glatman was arraigned on Thursday, the sixth of November, before Municipal Judge Harry Bowman. Two counts of murder were lodged against him, one each for victims Bridgeford and Mercado, but no plea was required at that time. Judge Bowman scheduled a preliminary hearing for 9:45 on the morning of November twenty-fifth, but Don Keller had other plans. Before the brief proceedings were adjourned, Keller announced his plan to seek grand-jury action on the case, a move that would eliminate the preliminary hearing and take Harvey straight to Superior Court.

There was nothing Harvey's new, private attorney, Willard Whittinghill, could do to block that move, but he still had a few tricks up his sleeve. There was no thought of winning Harvey's freedom, but it might be possible to save him from the gas chamber. For that, though, Whittinghill would have to get inside his client's head and find out what was lurking there.

For starters, he went to the source. Ophelia Glatman, now sixty-nine, reached San Diego on November twelfth and was allowed to visit with her son in jail. She emerged from that meeting apparently shaken, tearfully informing reporters that Harvey "is not a vicious man."

"Talk to any of the people in the jail," she challenged. "He is not vicious—he is sick."

Will Whittinghill, for his part, was quick to agree. "Glatman is rational now," the lawyer told newsmen, "but he apparently has periods of violence. He is a Dr. Jekyll and Mr. Hyde." Even now, in their jailhouse conversations, Whittinghill explained that Harvey "seems to have a fire burning inside him."

On the plus side, though, Whittinghill allowed that

"Harvey Glatman knows he has done wrong, and he wants to be punished. He told me he wants to die in the gas chamber."

It would be Whittinghill's job—and society's challenge—to save the poor, sick man from himself. A psychiatric exam was scheduled for later that week, and Whittinghill had considered trips to Colorado and New York, where he would meet with doctors who had treated Harvey in the past.

Meanwhile, the story he heard from Ophelia seemed to help. She claimed (falsely) that Harvey tried to plead insanity at his first trial in Denver, but he had been pronounced sane after thirty days of observation at the Colorado General Psychiatric Ward. (In fact, he had pled guilty on advice from his attorney.) That finding aside, he had received counseling at Colorado State Prison and again at Sing Sing. His 1951 parole to Denver was conditional upon continued psychiatric treatment, but Harvey had not followed through.

There seemed to be a general consensus, then, that Harvey was not "right," upstairs, but Whittinghill faced huge obstacles, yet, in his effort to save Glatman's life. For starters, "insanity" is itself a purely legal term. There is no such disease, per se. At law, under the time-honored M'Naughton Rule, a suspect is insane if he or she cannot tell right from wrong, or if some mental illness makes it physically impossible to act within the rule of law. A man, therefore, who thinks his next-door neighbor is a hostile alien from outer space and kills that neighbor in defense of Mother Earth may still be "sane" for purposes of trial, provided that he knew and understood his action was a criminal offense.

And that would be the rub in Harvey's case. He was on record telling the police about premeditated rapes, with his victims murdered afterward to keep them from reporting him to the authorities. Whatever strange compulsion drove him to pursue sex as a hunter stalks wild game, Glatman was clearly conscious of the legal risks involved, had taken deadly steps to hide his tracks, and by his own admission was convinced that he would kill again if freed from custody. That made him sane, within the law, and Whittinghill would have a grueling uphill climb if he intended to prove otherwise in court.

More to the point, though, Harvey didn't *want* to plead himself insane. From all appearances, he had his heart set on San Quentin and the gas chamber.

Don Keller and Bill Low were working overtime to make his wish come true.

Will Whittinghill would have to do his best to pluck a rabbit from what seemed to be a small and empty hat.

On Monday, November eighteenth, Don Keller presented seven witnesses before the San Diego County grand jury. Some of the testimony was technical, Dr. Jack Armstrong describing his identification of Shirley Bridgeford and Ruth Mercado from their dental records. Sergeant Bob Majors described Harvey's trek through the desert in handcuffs, directing searchers to the remains of his victims. Alice Jolliffe lent emotion to the proceedings, describing the night she last saw her daughter alive, leaving their home with "George Williams." Bridgeford's sister, seventeen-year-old Mary Louise Loy, was on hand to identify her late sibling in Harvey's desert snapshots, thereby sparing her mother the pain.

On Tuesday, the grand jury returned a "true bill" against Glatman, slapping him with two counts of violating California Penal Code 187: murder in the first degree. As stated in the document's dry legalese,

HARVEY MURRAY GLATMAN is accused by
the Grand Jury of the County of San Diego, by
this Indictment of the crime of Murder (PC
187) committed as follows: The said HARVEY
MURRAY GLATMAN on or about the 9th day
of March, 1958, in the County of San Diego,
State of California, and before the finding of
this Indictment, did murder SHIRLEY ANN
BRIDGEFORD.

SECOND COUNT: HARVEY MURRAY GLAT-
MAN is further accused by the Grand Jury of
the County of San Diego, by this Indictment of
the crime of Murder (PC 187) committed as follows: The said defendant HARVEY MURRAY
GLATMAN on or about the 24th day of July
1958, in the County of San Diego, State of California, and before the finding of this Indictment,
did murder RUTH MERCADO.

That Thursday, the twenty-first, Harvey appeared
before Judge John Hewicker, in Department 4 of Superior Court, and pled guilty on both murder counts.
Will Whittinghill filed an automatic motion for probation, knowing in advance that it was hopeless, but
Judge Hewicker went through the motions and ordered a review of Glatman's case by the county probation department. Sentencing on the guilty plea was
deferred to an unspecified later date.

Harvey refused to complete a probation questionnaire, but he could not escape a visit from assistant
probation officer William Lavelle. At their first jailhouse meeting, on November twenty-eighth, Glatman complained that he had already described each
of his crimes in minute detail and saw no value in
repeating his earlier statements. Finally, however, La-

velle persuaded him to go ahead, with the proviso
that their interviews should be conducted "in a more
private place." Accommodating Harvey's modesty,
Lavelle arranged for them to meet, next time, in the
county jail's library.

Before that happened, though, Lavelle wanted to
speak with Ophelia. Their meeting took place on
Thursday, December fourth, and while no transcript
of the interview has survived, Lavelle summarized it
as follows:

> Mrs. Glatman, the defendant's mother, and her
> sister were interviewed by this probation officer
> on December 4, 1958. She [Ophelia] was very
> firm in the belief that her son "must be insane."
> In speaking of his early life she was very explicit
> and candid. She termed his earlier offenses, be-
> ginning in 1945, as sudden outbursts. Up to that
> time he had been exceedingly girl-shy and
> would even "walk across the street to avoid fe-
> males." She mentioned one offense, occurring in
> Boulder, Colorado, when he forced a girl at pis-
> tol point to accompany him to the outskirts of
> that city. There they laid [sic] down together all
> night. Mrs. Glatman said her son did not molest
> the victim and eventually gave her carfare to re-
> turn home.

Unlike Lavelle, we recognize that Ophelia's statement was neither explicit nor entirely candid. For
one thing, Harvey's crimes began in 1944, six months
before his first arrest, and the later assaults on
women were clearly premeditated—Glatman armed
himself and carried rope to bind his prey—rather
than any spontaneous "sudden outbursts." In fact, if
we count the early incidents of bondage and auto-

erotic asphyxia, we may fairly say that Harvey had been building up to the attacks since he was three or four years old.

Likewise, while Ophelia continued with her insistence that Harvey "did not molest" his victims—kidnapping at gunpoint aside—we know from his Colorado confession that he sometimes partially disrobed the girls and women he accosted, fondling them before he ran away.

Ophelia's voice comes through in more detail on two questionnaires she filled out for Lavelle with her handwriting cramped and fierce. Twice, the forms asked how family members felt about Harvey being in prison. Her first answer—"understanding and sympathetic"—was offset by another that read, "We feel that he is mentally ill." "Will they try to get him out?" the form asked. "Not in his present condition," Ophelia replied. Twice, she was asked to describe Harvey's "chief weakness." The first time, she wrote, "His condition caused him to become antisocial. He did not care to mix in society, therefore keeping to himself mostly." And again: "Since first trouble was very antisocial. Would not cooperate in family living or take responsibility." Overall, she felt that "Harvey always acted as Dr. Jackel [sic] and Mr. Hyde. Very often he took a dislike to his father and just hated him, and then again he hated me for no apparent reason. Just his condition caused those actions."

Or, maybe not.

Ophelia reserved special venom for Albert, now that he could not defend himself. Twice asked if Albert had been a good provider, she first replied, "Was moderate," then changed her mind to a stern "No." "If not, why?" the questionnaire asked. "No profession or trade skill," Ophelia replied. "Needed wife's help to provide for family." And again, "Father did not set a good example in regard to home life responsibility." And yet, somehow, she told La-velle, "We led a normal, quiet life." Their time was mostly passed, she said, in "normal living."

It was Ophelia's take on Harvey's character that rang the truest in the end. As recorded by Lavelle,

> The defendant's mother terms Glatman as being "stern in character and unyielding in his deci-sion." She does not hold any hope that he will voluntarily change his plea or that he will volun-tarily request anything less than his own execution.

In that respect, at least, she truly understood her son.

While Bill Lavelle was talking to Ophelia in San Diego, Dr. J. P. Hilton was busy dictating a letter in Denver, addressed to the probation officer on Decem-ber fourth. It read:

Re: GLATMAN, Harvey Murray
    Court # CR 30.

Dear Mr. Lavelle:

Harvey Glatman first came to me in August 1945 at the age of seventeen.

At that time he had a history of having bruised his neck by tying a rope around it. He was sul-len, morose and very disrespectful and for sev-eral years had felt that everyone was against him including his parents. He had been shy with girls prior to the past year when his attitude changed completely and he became aggressive with women and would not even excuse himself after he had stepped on a woman's foot.

His past physical history was negative except for a tonsillectomy. The family history was negative except that a cousin of his father had been institutionalized.

It was my opinion at that time that this boy had schizophrenia and I understand from his mother that he has had treatment at various times since I last saw him.

If there is any further information you wish, please do not hesitate to call on me.

Sincerely
/s/ J. P. Hilton, M.D.

That same afternoon, Lavelle had his second meeting with Glatman, followed by more interviews on December fifth and eighth. As promised, once they had their privacy, Glatman restated the details of his murders, saying much the same thing he had told detectives in Los Angeles and San Diego.

Premeditation was the key, Lavelle noting that "Glatman indicates that he had planned to commit the crime of rape for some time. He desired to use the victim's apartment for this act, if possible. As a last resort he planned to use his own apartment, even though he knew he would then face the necessity of silencing his victim."

As for Judy Dull, Lavelle wrote "In discussing this case, Glatman says that immediately after the murder he was sick and could hardly believe what he had done."

It would not stop him in the future, though.

With Shirley Bridgeford, notes Lavelle, "Glatman admits that he was prepared for his trip to the desert before he met the victim at her home."

When they were finished talking, Lavelle prepared his summary for the court.

> In various interviews with this probation officer the defendant termed himself a "cold-blooded murderer." He indicates there was no compulsion driving him to murder, though he does admit he derives some satisfaction from tying women up and forcing them to submit to rape. Glatman points out that these murders were only committed out of a desire for self-preservation. In other words, he murdered only to remove potential witnesses. He logically and rationally presents his reasons for each killing. Further, these murders made him "sick" though this "sickness" did not manifest itself in a physical fashion. He claims that while actually killing these girls he had to "blank out" his mind as to what he was doing. He concentrated only on pulling the strangling rope tighter and tighter.

> In speaking of the victims, the defendant says that he suffers from remorse, even though he may not show it. He particularly is remorseful over the murder of Shirley Ann Bridgeford. This girl was not as pretty as the other two victims, who[m] he felt were too beautiful to associate willingly with him. These feelings are deeper in the Bridgeford case because she had two children.

> As to choice of weapons, the defendant indicated he preferred not to shoot the victims because it was "too messy" and there was a possibility

they might have suffered if he had shot them. Instead, he conceived his chosen method after the rape of Judy Ann Dull, because of its convenience and its seeming mercifullness [sic]. This method worked so well that he continued its use in the other cases.

Regarding his reasons for first approaching the victims, the defendant denied he only wanted to commit rape. He says he also wanted "companionship." He states that he understood murder would be a necessary conclusion of each of these offenses. However, his "needs" tended to obscure this fact until rape and kidnapping made it necessary. Among his "needs" was the "psychological satisfaction" he derived from tying his victims up. He concretely expresses this satisfaction by saying, "[T]his put them under my control."

When asked whether he would repeat these offenses if he were somehow released, the defendant replied, after some thought, "[Y]es, under the right circumstances." When questioned as to the "right circumstances" he indicated the availability of young ladies (through such agencies as model bureaus and lonely hearts clubs) at the time his "psychological needs" and desires became too great for him to control. He feels that it would have been possible for him to gain a normal sexual adjustment, if he had been fortunate enough to achieve the love and affection normally afforded individuals through a marital relationship.

He also stated Lorraine Vigil was very lucky. When asked about this, the defendant replied to

the effect that he had planned to kill her as soon
as the highway patrol officer had driven past
his automobile. He, at that time, realized he had
picked a well-frequented place and he could not
control his victim, who was hysterical. The only
course then open to him was her elimination.

In conclusion, the defendant said he could not
face the thought of a lifetime in prison. On these
grounds he earnestly requested that he be
executed.

As Ophelia had predicted, there would be no com-
promise on that score. Later in the same report, Lavelle notes:

In his various talks with the undersigned the defendant reiterated that he more than deserved
the death sentence. As a more personal reason,
he says he cannot stand the thought of spending
a lifetime in prison. Such a fate, he says, "causes
everything inside of me to collapse."

When discussing these various offenses the defendant stated he received "mental satisfaction"
from tying his victims up. He says that normal
men achieve this satisfaction through marriage.
He seems to believe marriage legally places the
female in the power of her husband. He, in turn,
achieves this satisfaction through tying up his
victims. He went on to say these offenses would
not have been committed if he had been able
to achieve what he called a "normal marriage
relationship."

Harvey would never be married, of course. At this
point, it was clear to Willard Whittinghill that he

would be very lucky indeed just to save his client from the gas chamber. That meant an insanity defense despite Harvey's objections.

And Whittinghill would need a world of help to pull it off.

Dr. Franklin Ebaugh was first to contribute, mailing off a copy of his 1951 evaluation on November twenty-sixth. Dr. Hilton had already summarized his findings for William Lavelle, but he was happy to provide another brief report for the defense, posted two days after Ebaugh's mailing.

Re: Harvey M. Glatman

Dear Mr. Whittinghill:

Harvey Glatman was under my care in 1945 at the age of seventeen and at that time it was my opinion that he had schizophrenia.

At that time a plea of "not guilty by reason of insanity" was not entered at his trial due to the fact that he pled guilty on the advice of his attorney and was sent to the State Penitentiary.

I have arranged with his mother, Mrs. Glatman, that I will if necessary, fly to San Diego and can testify if you need me and if you are certain that it would be for one day only.

Please let me know as soon as possible so that I can arrange my work accordingly.

/s/ J. P. Hilton, M.D.

On Tuesday, December ninth, Whittinghill appeared once more before Judge Hewicker, requesting a full psychiatric examination of his client. Assistant D.A. William Low, opposing the move as a waste of time, submitted affidavits from two of Glatman's keepers to suggest that he was wholly rational.

ROBERT B. MAJORS, being first duly sworn, deposes and says:

That he is employed as a Deputy Sheriff by the Sheriff of San Diego County, California, that he has been a member of the Sheriff's Department of this county for the past 17 years and that for the past two years he has been a sergeant in said department, attached to the division investigating crimes of violence;

That affiant has been assigned to the investigation regarding the murders of Shirley Ann Bridgeford and Ruth Mercado, for which the defendant has been indicted by the Grand Jury of this County; that affiant's first contact with the defendant was on the evening of October 30, 1958 when the defendant, in the custody of officers from the Los Angeles Police Department, was brought to Escondido, California; that at said time affiant observed the defendant, spoke with the defendant and defendant directed affiant and the other officers to an area in the desert where the remains of Shirley Ann Bridgeford were found, then directed affiant and the other officers to a different area where the remains of Ruth Mercado were found; that during said trip the defendant appeared to be rational, was responsive to questions asked of him by the officers, and appeared to be in full possession of his faculties; that the locations were unknown to the affiant and were found only after the details surrounding their location were provided by the defendant.

That affiant next observed the defendant on
November 5, 1958 in Los Angeles where the defendant was taken into custody by the affiant
and returned to San Diego to await trial for the
above-named murders. That enroute [*sic*] to San
Diego from Los Angeles the defendant appeared
to be calm, appeared to be rational, and when
affiant and the defendant stopped for dinner, the
defendant appeared to be hungry and ate a full
meal; that affiant discussed with defendant such
subjects as his interest in photography and his
family, and that the defendant appeared to be
rational and well oriented.

That on November 5, 1958 in the San Diego
County Jail affiant was present when the defendant was questioned regarding the murders of
Shirley Ann Bridgeford, Ruth Mercado and Judy
Ann Dull, and that throughout said interviews
the defendant appeared to be rational, was responsive to the questions, made no complaints
about his physical or mental condition, and that
he appeared sane at all times. That since November 5, 1958 affiant has seen the defendant on
numerous occasions and the defendant has appeared to be rational and sane. That affiant has
made inquiry as to how well the defendant is
behaving and getting along while in custody,
and affiant has not had called to his attention
any reports or any indication of abnormal conduct on the part of the defendant or any conduct
such as to indicate that the sanity of the defendant is to be questioned.

Low's second affidavit followed through on Glatman's general demeanor in the county jail.

LESLIE P. McKINZIE, being first duly sworn, deposes and says:

That he is employed as a Deputy Sheriff by the Sheriff of San Diego County, California; that he has been a member of the Sheriff's Department of this County for the past ten years and that for the past five years he has been a sergeant in said department.

Affiant states that he is assigned to the Jail Division of the Sheriff's Office and that for the past one year he has been assigned to supervise the upstairs cells of the San Diego County Jail during the day shift.

Affiant further states that during the time the defendant has been in the custody of the Sheriff of San Diego County, to wit: November 5, 1958 to the present time, affiant has had numerous opportunities to see, observe and speak to the defendant; that affiant's contact with and observations of the defendant have been daily except for the two days each week when affiant is not on duty;

That since November 5, 1958 the defendant has followed the jail routine and complied with the jail regulations, that he eats well, is responsive to the questions asked of him by the affiant, that the defendant appears to be normal and well oriented[;]

That defendant has made no complaints about his physical or mental condition and to the knowledge of affiant has only been seen by the jail physician once, and that was for a cold.

Affiant further states that the defendant appears to get along satisfactorily with his fellow inmates and the only complaint the defendant has made is that the radio outside the cell is constantly playing music, to which he objected.

However, when the defendant was informed that the other prisoners in the area desired to listen to the music, the defendant made no further complaints.

Affiant has spoken with the special guard whose duty it is to observe the defendant at night with the other prisoners in that area, and the special guard reports to the affiant that the defendant "sleeps like a baby".

Affiant's most recent observation of the defendant was when the defendant came out of court on December 8, 1958 at approximately 10:00 A.M., at which time the affiant spoke with the defendant, who was responsive to the questions asked by the affiant.

Affiant further states that as a result of his observation of the defendant during the period of time the defendant has been in the custody of the Sheriff, up to and including December 8, 1958, the defendant appears to be rational and sane.

It was within the court's power to deny Glatman a psychiatric evaluation, but Judge Hewicker overruled the defendant's objection and ordered the test, to be performed by county psychiatrist Dr. C. E. Lengyel no later than Friday, the twelfth. Dr. Lengyel beat the deadline by a day and sent his report to Judge Hewicker on December thirteenth.

Re: Psychiatric evaluation of
    Harvey Murray Glatman
    Superior Court No. CR-346

This thirty-one-year-old Caucasian single male was given psychiatric examination at the San Diego County Jail on December 11, 1958. Summary, results and findings of that examination are as follows:

This man is an alert individual of better than average intellectual endowment who, throughout the interview, was polite and attempted to please. He answered questions readily in a coherent and relevant manner. He displayed no press or retardation in his stream of speech. He expressed no delusional ideas and denied all hallucinatory experiences. His emotional tone was in keeping with the situation.

With particular reference to his sexual activities, this man presents findings of the sadomasochistic. Specifically, this means that this man has always felt inferior to the opposite sex. He has felt inadequate and could get real pleasure only in feeling dominant. He could only do so in situations where the partner in his sexual activity was helpless.

A very important finding is that this individual did not experience any sexual gratification or pleasure through murdering his victims but had to do this in order that he would not be detected, apprehended or otherwise identified. In other words, this individual was destroying the evidence. This is important for consideration because most of the crimes in this area are of this type.

To further summarize and differentiate: This individual shows no evidence of a psychosis. He knows right from wrong, the nature and quality of his acts, and he can keep from doing wrong

if he so desires. He can also fully cooperate with
his attorney in the presentation of his case.

/s/ C.E. Lengyel, M.D

Dr. Lengyel's report was the end of any hope Willard Whittinghill may have cherished for an insanity
defense. Coupled with Glatman's continued nonco-
operation, the document effectively sealed Harvey's
fate.

Two days later, on Tuesday the fifteenth, William
Low hammered another nail into the coffin, filing an
amended indictment that would tip the scales against
any hope for leniency in sentencing.

> HARVEY MURRAY GLATMAN is accused by
> the District Attorney of the County of San Diego,
> State of California, by this Supplemental Indict-
> ment of Having Been Previously Convicted of a
> Felony committed as follows: The said HARVEY
> MURRAY GLATMAN was, in the Criminal Divi-
> sion of the District Court of the State of Colo-
> rado, in and for the City and County of Denver,
> and before the filing of this Supplement to In-
> dictment, convicted of the offense of Aggravated
> Robbery, a felony, and the judgment of said
> court against said defendant in said connection
> was, on or about the last day of December 1945,
> pronounced and rendered, and said defendant
> served a term of imprisonment therefor in the
> State Prison at Canon City, Colorado, as No.
> 23863.
>
> SECOND PRIOR: And the said District Attorney
> of the County of San Diego further charges that
> before the commission of the offense charged in
> the Indictment, the said HARVEY MURRAY

GLATMAN was, in the Albany County Court of the State of New York, in and for the County of Albany, and before the filing of this Supplement to Indictment, convicted of the offense of Robbery second degree, a felony, and the judgment of said court against said defendant in said connection was, on or about the 10th day of October 1946, pronounced and rendered, and said defendant served a term of imprisonment therefor in the Elmira Reformatory at Elmira[,] New York.

THIRD PRIOR: And the said District Attorney of the County of San Diego further charges that before the commission of the offense charged in the Indictment, the said HARVEY MURRAY GLATMAN was, in the Albany County Court of the State of New York, in and for the County of Albany, and before the filing of this Supplement to Indictment, convicted of the offense of grand larceny, first degree, a felony, and the judgment of said court against said defendant in said connection was, on or about the 10th day of October 1946, pronounced and rendered, and said defendant served a term of imprisonment therefor in the Elmira Reformatory at Elmira[,] New York, and was later transferred to Sing Sing Prison, at Ossining[,] New York.

A purist might argue that the last two counts were actually the same, a needless repetition, since both counts referred to a single victim (Florence Hayden) but it makes no difference now. In the eyes of the law, Harvey was a three-time loser going into his latest fix, and he would have to take his medicine.
Even if it killed him.

17

Death Wish

HARVEY GLATMAN'S FINAL DAY IN COURT BEGAN BRIGHT
and early on Monday, December 15, 1958, in Department 4 of Superior Court. The proceeding was not a
trial, per se. He had already filed a guilty plea on
two counts of first-degree murder, but California law
requires a separate penalty phase in such cases before
sentence is passed. The options, simply stated, were
death or life imprisonment, and no one was betting
on leniency.

Defense attorney Willard Whittinghill's first move
that Monday morning was a waiver of his client's
right to have a jury fix his sentence. Harvey, in his
rush to die, had been insisting that there be no jury,
no protraction of the case beyond the legal minimum,
but Whittinghill was not a blind slave to his client's
death wish. Bypassing the jury was a tactical decision, based—at least in part—on the belief of many
lawyers that a sitting judge is both more knowledgeable and, perhaps, more sympathetic than a panel of
"civilians" picked at random off the street. There was
a possibility, however slim, that Whittinghill might

lead Judge Hewicker to see his client as a sick and troubled man who, if he did not rate a free trip to Atascadero, still deserved to live.

It was a long shot, granted. But it was the *only* shot.

It was Harvey's bad luck that his case had been assigned to William Low for trial. A dogged researcher and meticulous planner, Low would leave no stone unturned in covering all the bases and nailing down the evidence. Where Glatman was concerned, no quarter would be asked or granted.

William T. Low was a native of Mason City, Iowa—a town perhaps most famous for one afternoon in March 1934 when John Dillinger's gang robbed the First National Bank. Dillinger and sidekick Red Hamilton were wounded in the wild exchange of gunfire that resulted, while gang member "Baby Face" Nelson hosed the street with his Tommy gun, critically wounding the secretary of Mason City's school board. Even with their problems, though, it was a fair day for the gang: they made off with $52,000 and change.

Bill Low had missed the action by a year. Born in 1921, he moved with his family to Long Beach, California, in 1933—just in time for that city's great earthquake. The Lows later moved to Orange County where Bill attended high school and Santa Ana Junior College. He graduated from UC Berkeley in 1943 then joined the navy as a commissioned "ninety-day wonder" to serve for the duration of World War II. Back in civilian life after V-J Day, he earned his law degree in 1949 and was admitted to the California bar a year later. Hired immediately by the San Diego D.A.'s office, he rose swiftly through the ranks by virtue of his industry and dedication to the job.

On the occasion of his marriage, in 1954, Low per-

suaded his bride Myra to spend part of their honey-
moon in court observing other lawyers at work
before various juries. It was part of Low's makeup,
to do the job right, or not do it at all.

Harvey Glatman's case would be Low's first death-
penalty trial—in fact, the only one he ever tried in
his career.

And he was not about to let the killer pay less
than the maximum required by law.

The prosecutor speaks first in American courts,
presenting his case before defense witnesses are
called. In Glatman's case, Assistant D. A. William
Low was holding an unbeatable hand. There was no
question of acquittal, here, with Harvey's guilty plea
on record, but Low was still determined to seek the
ultimate penalty, to grant Harvey's wish.

Low's opening statement touched all the bases—
Harvey's guilty plea; the issue of premeditation, to
be demonstrated by Glatman's "transactions" with
Judy Dull and Lorraine Vigil; the details of specific
crimes, as outlined in Harvey's confessions. When he
was done, Judge Hewicker adjourned the court until
2:00 P.M., thereby permitting Low to gather witnesses
who had anticipated a half-day or more to be used
up in jury selection.

The state's first witness following the recess was
Deputy Edward Fisher of the Riverside County sheriff's department. He had responded to the call when
Judy Dull's skull were found near Indio, back in December 1957, observed her skeletal remains protruding from their shallow grave, and radioed for an
investigator from the county coroner's office. Five
photographs of the crime scene were introduced into
evidence and identified by Deputy Fisher in short
order. Willard Whittinghill had no questions for the
witness before he stepped down.

Next up, for a quick ten questions, was Robert Drake, deputy coroner for Riverside County, stationed at Indio. He had rolled out on Fisher's call, and now he seconded Fisher's identification of the five crime-scene photos. Again, Whittinghill had no questions on cross-examination.

Arvid Depew, retired five months earlier as the assistant coroner of Riverside County, followed Drake to the witness stand for an even shorter appearance. He had received a "Jane Doe" skull from pathologist Robert Dexter, Depew testified, and passed it on to a Riverside dentist for X-rays of the jaw and teeth. From the defense, no questions.

Dr. Jerome Wineberg took a bit longer on the stand, but not much. As Judy Dull's dentist, he recalled taking X-rays of her teeth, in February 1956. Those X-rays were entered into evidence, along with the set prepared in Riverside, for the "Jane Doe" skull. Dr. Wineberg had earlier compared the X-rays and now explained his findings to the court.

"There are two main areas for identification on the X-rays," Wineberg said. "One of them is the position of the bicuspid teeth in the lower right mandible. There is a separation of the first and second bicuspid, which appears again in the post-mortem X-rays, here. Secondly, the outline and the position of the fillings in the teeth compare identically, and . . . as a matter of fact, in the office, we superimposed some of these films, and they just fit right together."

The skull from Indio belonged to Judy Dull.

Willard Whittinghill had no questions, and the witness was excused.

Betty Carver Bohannon was next on the stand. She described her brief acquaintance with Judy Ann Dull before Low brought her to the night of Judy's disappearance.

"Now, calling your attention to the month of July,"

Low said, "specifically to Monday, July 29, 1957 . . . did a man have occasion to come to your apartment?"

"Yes, he did," Betty replied.

"About what time of the day or night?"

"It was around seven, seven-thirty at night."

"Do you see the man in the courtroom, that came to your apartment?"

"Yes," Betty answered, "I do."

"And where is he in the courtroom?"

"That is him, there," she said, pointing toward Harvey at the defense table.

She described Harvey asking after Lynn Lykels before he was distracted by photos of Judy. He had called back later, she recalled, and came to the Sweetzer Avenue apartment a second time, on August first.

"And what happened on that day?" Low asked her.

"Well, he came to . . . Judy had said that he had called her for a modeling job, and that it was to be in the apartment—the modeling was to take place there. And when he came up, he changed his story and said that he was going to shoot at his studio, instead. He asked Judy to bring along some street clothes and things, for modeling, and Judy asked him to leave a phone number, in case she got any calls, so they could call there for her. And he gave this fake number to a machine shop."

"Was Judy in good health when you saw her that day?" asked Low.

"As far as I know, she was."

"Did you ever see her alive again, after that?"

"No," Betty almost whispered. "I didn't."

After Betty had described her missing person report on Judy, Willard Whittinghill spoke up for the first time. "Your Honor," he interjected, "for the purpose of the record, I wish to state that throughout this proceedings, I do not intend to object, to cross-examine, or to put on any evidence. I am doing this in the desire of my client, to facilitate these proceedings as much as I could—his desire to get it over as quick as possible—and also based on Dr. Lengyel's report that my client knows the difference between right and wrong."

"You are representing him," Judge Hewicker replied from the bench, "and you do as you see fit to protect his interests."

Before she was excused, Betty Bohannon identified a photo of Judy Dull and her daughter, which was then admitted into evidence. She left the stand without another glance at Harvey, eyes downcast.

Sergeant John Lawton was next up for the state, describing the afternoon of November third, when he had escorted Harvey back to his former apartment, on Melrose.

"Would you tell us what occurred," Low asked, "at the time you arrived at the apartment, pertinent to this case?"

"We asked the defendant to take us to his apartment," Lawton testified, "and show us, as best he could remember, what he had done on the night or afternoon he had taken Judy Ann Dull to this apartment, which he agreed to do. At the apartment, he pointed out the various portions of furniture, which were the same as they had been when he was living there, with the exception of one chair. The room had been rearranged, but basically it was the same as it was the afternoon and evening he had Judy there. While we were there, we took pictures of the room, of him pointing out these different places in the room, in which he had her sit and lay down, including the floor, the chair, and the davenport."

Following the Melrose stop, Lawton continued,

Harvey had been driven back to Riverside County, directing his escorts to the approximate site where Judy's skeletal remains were found.

"And from there," Lawton said, "we proceeded to the [sheriff's] substation at Indio, where he partially identified what he believed to be one of the victim's shoes—a black patent leather low-type shoe—a dress, which he said could possibly have been . . . at least, it was one like that . . . and he identified a tan fountain pen which belonged to him, that he had lost. This pen had been found near the scene where Judy's body was found."

Robert Majors was next for the state, briefly describing the circumstances of his November fifth interview with Glatman at the San Diego County sheriff's office. It was all preliminary for the main event, though, as a tape recorder was delivered to the court.

"Go ahead and play it, your Honor?" asked Low.

Judge Hewicker frowned and nodded from the bench. "Go ahead."

For the next hour, interrupted for a fifteen-minute breather at 3:20 P.M., the court heart Glatman describe Judy Dull's abduction, rape, and murder in the dispassionate tone of a seasoned executioner. It was a strange experience watching silent Harvey at the defense table while his disembodied voice filled the room, recounting one atrocity after another, pronouncing a young woman's death sentence.

When the tape was finished, Majors identified a series of twelve color photographs, which Harvey had admitted snapping of his victim. Also introduced was the April 1958 issue of *Master Detective*, wherein page 35 carried an article titled "What Happened to Judy Ann?" The magazine had been recovered from Harvey's special toolbox along with the next bit of evidence: a small news clipping from December 1957, relating the discovery of an unknown woman's skeleton from the desert near Indio.

There was no quitting early in Judge Hewicker's court. Robert Dull was next on the witness stand, appearing under subpoena to describe his separation from Judy and their last telephone conversation, sometime on the day before she died. They had an appointment, Robert said, on August first, but Judy never showed.

"Did you have occasion to report her missing, with Mrs. Bohannon?" Low asked.

"Yes, I did."

"Approximately when was that?"

"It was the early morning hours of the second of August, 1957," Dull replied.

In closing, he identified the same photo of Judy that had been introduced during Betty Bohannon's testimony. That done, the witness was excused.

Low called Shirley Bridgeford's mother, Alice Jolliffe, as his next witness, to describe the last night she saw her daughter alive. Despite her previously stated inability to recognize Harvey Glatman, she now had no difficulty picking him out as Shirley's last date.

"When the defendant came there," Low said, "what name did he use, Mrs. Jolliffe?"

"He said his name was George. We later found out it was George Williams."

Daughter Mary had answered the door that fateful night, Alice testified, and Shirley soon emerged from the kitchen to greet him. "He acted like he wasn't interested in her, too much," the witness recalled. "He kept looking at Mary all the time." That aside, there had been nothing extraordinary about George Williams. "He was real polite when he was introduced," Alice said, "and I saw that like any ordinary fellow, you know . . . no different than a lot of them are . . . he acted real mannerly and everything."

Before leaving with "Williams," Alice testified, Shirley had beckoned her into the kitchen. "She said, 'I don't know,' or something like that, and I said, 'You don't have to go out with him if you don't want to.' She said, 'I will go out with him and see what kind of guy he is.' Her being the age she was, I didn't figure I could argue with her, and I thought she knew just what she was doing. And as they started to leave, he said, 'I am glad I met you.' I said, 'Thank you. I am glad I met you.' And that is the last time I saw Shirley, was that night."

Alice recounted a November third visit to the San Diego coroner's office where she had identified her daughter's coat, one shoe, the remains of her dress. Now, after identifying a photo of Shirley, Alice was excused, and daughter Mary Loy was summoned to the stand.

Mary's recollection of March 8, 1958, was essentially the same as her mother's. She had opened the door to "George Williams," now seated before her at the defense table, and sat with him briefly, in the living room, while Shirley got ready to go. Eight months later, on November third, she had accompanied her mother to the coroner's office, in San Diego, to identify Shirley's clothes. The red panties Shirley had worn, the night she died, belonged to Mary; they were borrowed for the evening, for her date. Five photographs of Shirley, drawn from Harvey's toolbox stash, were introduced as evidence. Mary identified them all.

It was enough for one day, but Low had accomplished much in two hours and twenty-five minutes. Judge Hewicker adjourned the court at 4:25 P.M. with orders to resume promptly at ten o'clock the next morning, and Harvey went back to his cell.

* * *

Robert Majors led off for the prosecution on Tuesday, recalling the overnight death tour conducted on Halloween eve. Majors described how Glatman had directed them through tiny desert towns, until he reached the spot where he had parked with Shirley Bridgeford, then led them on foot to the spot where clothes and scattered bones were found. A series of photographs were introduced and identified, depicting the scene as Majors had found it in the pre-dawn darkness. One snap showed Harvey standing with Pierce Brooks, pointing down at the matted scraps of Shirley's coat.

From there, Majors testified, Harvey led them further down the same road, through Anza-Borrego Desert State Park, forced to double-back once, before they found Ruth Mercado's death site. More photographs. In one of these, Harvey stood with an Officer Erbson from L.A.P.D., his index finger aimed at Ruth's skull lying on the ground nearby. Majors was also present on November third, when Alice Jolliffe and her daughter came to the coroner's office and identified Shirley's clothes.

The tape recorder was waiting this time, and Majors stepped down from the stand to thread the tape of Glatman's interview concerning Shirley Bridgeford. Once again, Harvey's bland voice filled the courtroom, recounting details of his second rape and kill. The tape was interrupted for a fifteen-minute break at eleven o'clock, then resumed before its stunned audience, winding down to the sign-off.

When it finished, Low presented Sergeant Majors with more photographs, the snaps of captive Shirley taken in the desert and retrieved from Glatman's toolbox. Majors identified each one before yielding his seat to the second prosecution witness of the day.

Myron Ellis had been a friend of Ruth Mercado's, meeting her six or seven months before she disappeared. On the twenty-second or twenty-third of July, Ellis recalled, he had driven Ruth to pick up a license for her collie pup, then he took her to lunch. It was between three and four o'clock when he dropped Ruth back at her apartment, the last time he saw her alive. Five photographs of Ruth were introduced, and Ellis identified each in turn before he was excused.

Robert Majors came back to the stand to introduce yet another tape recording. This time, Harvey was describing Ruth Mercado's kidnaping and death. The tape was interrupted at noon for a two-hour lunch break, but Glatman's words stayed with the listeners as they scattered, robbing some of their appetites. Most were numb by the time the tape finished, details of one murder running together with the next, and the next after that. It was a case of anesthesia by exposure, nearly robbing the individual crimes of their horror.

When the tape was finished, Low produced another envelope of photographs—these snapped by Harvey, showing Ruth Mercado in the desert, bound and gagged. Majors identified each in turn, along with Ruth's wristwatch and wallet, her half-slip and stockings, removed from Glatman's toolbox by the L.A.P.D. Glatman had recognized the several items on November fifth, and had admitted taking them as trophies of his kill.

Lorraine Vigil was the state's next witness—Harvey's sole surviving victim—and she seemed flustered, confused, from the start of Low's direct examination.

"Would you state your name again, please," the prosecutor said.

"Lorraine Vigil."

"And in what area do you live, now?"

"My parents live at 1211 Park Avenue, in San Jose, California."

"Calling your attention to the month of October, 1958," Low said, "in what community were you living?"

"Wait a minute," Lorraine said. "State that again, please."

"In October of this year, where were you living?"

"October?" she asked.

"Specifically, October twenty-seventh," Low replied.

"I was living in Los Angeles at the time."

"And what address?"

"Let's see . . . I lived at 642 Orange Drive, in Los Angeles."

It wasn't true, but Low missed the mistake. "And did you have occasion," he forged ahead, "around . . . specifically, on October 27, 1958, to receive a telephone call from Diane, or Diane's Studio?"

"Oh!" Lorraine seemed almost startled. "You are referring . . . wait a minute."

"Weren't you living on Sixth Street at that time?" Low asked.

"Oh, no," she said. "I was living with Mr. and Mrs. Ellis, at 6360 West Sixth, Los Angeles."

It got a little easier from that point on after Lorraine identified Harvey as the same "Frank Johnson" who had picked her up on the night of her near-death experience.

"What happened, and what was said, after the defendant arrived at your home?" Low inquired.

"Well," Lorraine said, "we asked him to come in because everybody that calls for me . . . they come in, and . . . in the living room, like a gentleman should . . . and he refused. But I wasn't aware . . . because it wasn't no date . . . it was . . . I was on assignment, and he was just doing me a favor to drive me there. But then, after that, when I got in his car, he said that we wasn't going there, and I asked him, 'How come?' And he said that Diane was going to use her studio. We was going to his studio. I asked him where it was, and he said downtown, and it wouldn't take long. And from downtown, it became somewhere else. I was in his car, and what could I do? I had to keep going. I didn't let him suspect, but I tried to inform myself on him."

She began asking questions, Lorraine said, and received only vague answers before she noticed that "Johnson" was speeding. "I noticed he was driving fast," she testified. "He wouldn't look at me. He wouldn't look at me, and I kept on asking where his studio was, and I asked him where he was from. And I kept worrying because I knew something was wrong, and he must have suspected that, too, but he kept driving." Finally, she said, "Johnson" had pulled off the freeway, onto a dark surface road, where he stopped the car and pulled a gun.

"What did he say?" Low asked.

"He threatened me with a very commanding voice," Lorraine replied, "just to do as he said, and he said he wouldn't hurt me. And . . . I mean . . . I took it very calmly, and I asked him what he wanted. And I realized I was going to be killed. I mean, nobody with a gun and . . . well . . . he asked me to do what he said, and he asked me to take my hand out and put my hands behind my back . . . and just to do as he said, and I wouldn't get hurt. I gave him my hand, but I knew I mustn't let him tie me."

"Did you see a rope?" asked Low.

"Yes, sir. He took the rope immediately. He was all prepared."

"Did you notice anything unusual about the rope?"

"No," she said. "I mean, it was just a little tiny rope, like that. It was already looped, to just put around your hand."

"Then what happened?" Low asked.

"Well, he asked me to put my hands back and don't give him any trouble, but . . . I did as he said, but I kept thinking I mustn't let him tie me. And again, I brought my hands . . . and I knew that . . . you know, I was going to give him trouble. So, he scoot over to me and he said, 'Now, don't give me any trouble.' He said, 'I will. . . .' And he put his arm over me, and he said, 'I will. . . .' You know . . . I could see cars going by, and he could, too. And he said, 'I want people to pretend we are necking, so don't give me any trouble. I could choke you very easily.' And he put his arm over my head, and he bruised me. I could see, if I didn't agree, he would strangle me. But again, I knew I must agree, and again, I gave him a feeling I was going to do as he said."

"Go on and tell us what happened next," Low said.

"Well," Lorraine continued, "he threatened me. He meant what he said; I know he did. I knew I was going . . . I knew he was going to kill me anyhow, and then . . . so, I agreed to do as he said, again. But the minute he wanted to tie my hands, I had to keep thinking I mustn't let him tie me. So, again, I gave him a bad time, and I started to plead. I knew pleading wouldn't do any good. So, again, he took out his gun and pointed it at me, to my body. This time, he wasn't very clever, just putting it away like that. Somehow or other, he went where I could grab the gun very fast because I knew that was my last chance, and in the car we struggled. I mentioned [sic] to get my hand and tap for help. I imagined the cars must have seen because I was tapping for all I could."

"You were tapping with your hand?" Low said.

"Yes, sir. The hand I had the rope on was tapping on the window, so people could see my attention for help . . . that it was . . . you know . . . that it was something urgent in the car, and . . . you know . . . not something else. And I was tapping with all I could, and I screamed with all I could, but he tried to get me and put me down so people wouldn't see me. And at the same time, with my right hand . . . since I grabbed the gun, it was never pointed at me, except the time he let that bullet go, and it was at my leg. He couldn't tell where my leg was because of the wide skirt I was wearing."

"Were you able to grab the gun, then?" Low asked.

"No," said Lorraine. "I grabbed the gun the second time he pointed it at me. But I was . . . at the same time I was yelling for help, I was very strong with my right hand. I mean, I had the gun to him, and away from me."

"Was the gun fired?"

"Yes."

"Tell us about that," Low said. "What happened at that time?"

"At that time, I thought . . . I think . . . the way he thought that he had injured me . . . but I knew it, and he gave me freedom then, and I immediately put my hand on the trigger. I thought to myself, empty it, but it didn't work. The trigger didn't work."

"You tried to operate the gun?" asked Low.

"Yes, sir," Lorraine replied. "He gave me freedom, and I grabbed the gun, and I tried to empty it, and it didn't work. And I knew that he had to do something to the gun, and I know I mustn't let him. And I also . . . at the same time, I knew I must get out of the car because I had battled him in the car, and nobody would see, so I must get out. So, at the same time . . . I mean, after I did that, I didn't let him suspect . . . I got my hand over and opened the door real quick, and we got out because he was battling for the gun, too, but I had most of the gun."

"Did the bullet that went off strike you, at all?" Low asked.

"Yes, it did. It strike me . . . it burn me on my leg."

"Did it go through your clothes?"

"They have proof of that," Lorraine said. "They took pictures of me, of my skirt and my leg, partial. They took pictures of my throat that same night, the way he left it."

"What happened when you got outside the car?" Low asked.

"We struggled bitterly outside the car," she said.

"And for what?"

"For the gun, sir."

"Where was the gun at this time?"

"I had the gun. Most of the gun, I had it, but he was still trying to get it. That skinny thing—"

Low interrupted her before she could explain what "skinny thing" she meant. "Tell us what happened during that struggle outside the car," he instructed.

"There we struggled, outside, bitterly," Lorraine replied. "He pulled me over to the dark, in the bushes. He overpowered me that way, and I overpowered him to the road. I wanted people to see that I was battling."

Judge Hewicker chose that point to call a fifteen-minute break. When court resumed, Low picked up with his questions where he had left off.

"Now, Lorraine," he said, "at the time of the recess, you described what happened outside the car, and the fact that you were struggling to get out from the darkened areas of the area you were in. Would you describe briefly what happened from then on?"

"Well," Lorraine said, "I overpowered him to the road, and then he tried to pull me within the body of the car. I knew he was trying to hide me, but by that time the patrolman . . . you could hear his cycle coming, and we still fought, and I fell on my knees and huddled the gun like that, and he got on top of me."

"You are referring to Mr. Glatman?" Low asked.

"Yes. He got on top of me, but I threw him over because he stood from my back. I mean, I threw him over my head. The patrolman said, 'What is going on?' And he got up. But I had the gun. I didn't know how to operate it. I ran to the officer and told him, 'Here is the gun, here is the gun.' I wanted the officer to use it."

Lorraine's testimony was the first to draw a spark of interest from the doomed defendant, reporters noting that he scowled as she described their brief struggle on Tustin Ranch Road. Perhaps it was the insult she delivered, once again repeating her earlier statement to the press, that Harvey "wasn't very clever."

Or, perhaps it simply angered him to see the one who got away.

Lorraine was excused without further questions, and Low called Orange County deputy sheriff Mark Steelemon to the witness stand. One of those who had responded to Officer Mulligan's call for assistance on October twenty-seventh, he briefly described the crime scene then identified photographs of Glatman's Dodge and its contents. Steelemon also identified the wristwatch removed from the car's glove compartment, previously entered into evidence as Ruth Mercado's. The watch, he recalled, had later been turned over to Pierce Brooks at L.A.P.D.

L.A. homicide detective Paul LePage followed

Steelemon to the witness chair, reciting details of the
Halloween search conducted at Glatman's apartment,
on South Norton. It was LePage who had found Harvey's toolbox and delivered it to Sergeant Brooks.
Ten questions were enough to take him through the
search and get him off the stand.

Pierce Brooks came next, maintaining the strict
chain of evidence. He confirmed LePage's delivery of
the toolbox to L.A.P.D. headquarters and identified
the objects found therein: Ruth Mercado's wallet and
I.D.; a half-slip; women's stockings, sundry photographs and negatives, depicting Harvey's victims in
the final moments of their lives. Brooks had conveyed the toolbox and its contents to Lieutenant Isbell and Sergeant Majors of the San Diego Sheriff's
office.

Elmer Jackson, from L.A.P.D.'s Wilshire Division,
followed Brooks to the stand. He had participated in
the search of Harvey's South Norton apartment,
which turned up varied lengths of rope. Each piece
had been tagged with Jackson's initials. Once again,
a sparse ten questions saw the witness finished and
excused.

Sergeant Robert Majors made his fourth and last
appearance as the state's final witness. Once again,
he sketched the circumstances of his interview with
Glatman, on November fifth, then booted up the tape
of Harvey discussing the Vigil assault. Mercifully, it
was shorter than the others and ended without another death. When it was done, at 4:20 P.M., Judge
Hewicker adjourned court for the day.

There was little left to say when court resumed
at 10:30 A.M. on Wednesday, December seventeenth.
Prosecutor Low began the session by resting his case,
whereupon Judge Hewicker turned to the defense.
Will Whittinghill had already informed the court that

he would call no witnesses, present no evidence, on the instruction of his client. Harvey was determined not to fight the case, intent on going to death row, and Whittinghill had given up on trying to persuade him otherwise. Still, Judge Hewicker had to ask, for the record.

"Mr. Whittinghill, have you any witnesses?"

"We rest, your Honor," Whittinghill replied. "The defense rests."

"Do you wish to argue, Mr. Low?"

"Yes," the prosecutor replied. "I have just a couple of brief remarks, your Honor." In a matter of moments, Low spelled out his case for a judgment of first-degree murder that warranted death. Glatman had carefully planned and premeditated each killing, Low reminded the court, while murder during the commission of another felony—in this case, rape—also qualified the crimes as first-degree. Judy Dull's slaying and the attempted murder of Lorraine Vigil further established motive and intent. Harvey had killed deliberately, coldbloodedly, to keep himself from being traced, identified, and sent to prison as a sex offender. "We feel," he told the court in closing, "that the evidence is overwhelming and conclusive that the murders in both count one and count two are of the first degree, and request a verdict in that degree."

It was Judge Hewicker's turn, and he wasted no time in delivering his judgment on Glatman.

"The defendant in this case was charged with two counts of murder," Hewicker said, "one involving the murder of Shirley Ann Bridgeford and the other one Ruth Mercado. In both these cases, the victims were picked up in Los Angeles County on the pretext that he was going to . . . picked up by the defendant on the pretext he was going to use them as models. And the defendant has admitted, in his recordings to

the sheriff, that his real purpose was to have intercourse with the two victims voluntarily, if they
would submit, and by force, if they would not submit. And the recordings which were played in court
show that both crimes were well-planned. Considerable time elapsed between the picking up of the two
women and their ultimate murder, and in each case,
there was premeditation, and the women were killed
because of the rape which the defendant had committed upon them, and he didn't want to be caught."

Judge Hewicker paused briefly, surveying the
court, then resumed. "Of course," he said, "the only
actual witness that appeared against the defendant
here, to give his modus operandi, outside of what
the defendant told us, was Lorraine Vigil, the little
five-foot girl that took the stand here. And I don't
imagine she weighed over 110 pounds. I couldn't
help but admire the spunk and courage and the te-
nacity of that little girl in warding off the advances
of the defendant. If she had not been as brave and
courageous and alert as she was, these things might
have gone on indefinitely."

The recordings of Glatman's confessions, Judge
Hewicker said, were the the clearest he had ever
heard presented in a courtroom—better, in fact, than
if Harvey had taken the stand to testify. "Words
were not put in the defendant's mouth," Hewicker
noted. "He was asked to relate what occurred, as to
each of the victims or intended victims, and he did
so without any coaching or leading questions, or anything like that." Each tape, in turn, revealed premeditation "and show without question murder in the
first-degree." Accordingly, on each of the two murder counts, Judge Hewicker declared, "I will find the
defendant guilty of first-degree murder."

He faced the prosecution table. "You may proceed
now, Mr. Low, with the penalty."

Low offered the bulk of trial evidence, en masse, as his first item of proof; Judge Hewicker accepted it. Next, Low introduced a certified copy of Glatman's prison record from Colorado, followed by a similar sheet from New York, identified as People's items 31 and 32.

"The people rest," said Low.

"Do you have anything, Mr. Whittinghill?" the judge asked.

"No, your Honor."

"Just one remark, your Honor." Low reminded Judge Hewicker of the court's sole discretion in fixing Glatman's penalty. "The crimes were brutal, they were carried out in a deliberate manner, and I think that it is one of the most aggravated and brutal crimes that was ever committed in San Diego County, that has come to the attention of the law enforcement officers."

"Mr. Whittinghill?"

"Nothing to say," Glatman's counsel replied.

Judge Hewicker cleared his throat. "Well, I wish to say this: The record in this case will show that the defendant has been represented by Mr. Whittinghill, his attorney whom he hired himself, and apparently Mr. Whittinghill has complied with the request of the defendant that the matter be terminated at the earliest possible time." Glatman had pled guilty on all counts, Hewicker noted, and then waived his right to trial by jury. Dr. Lengyel had confirmed that he was competent for trial and to assist in his defense.

"I was sitting here during this trial," Judge Hewicker went on, "and I was wondering if Mr. Whittinghill had asked any questions, what questions he could have asked to mitigate this case or to assist the defendant." It was hopeless, Hewicker concluded. "When you think it all over, you realize that there wasn't very much that Mr. Whittinghill could ask in this case."

As far as the penalty went, Judge Hewicker said, "I know there are a lot of people, people in high places, that don't believe in capital punishment." Thus far, however, legislative efforts to ban execution had fallen short of success. "Now," Hewicker told the court, "if life imprisonment in California meant life imprisonment, that would be one thing. Life imprisonment in this state means confinement for seven years or more—and when I say more, it depends upon the past record of the defendant. If the defendant has no past record and goes to the penitentiary for life and behaves himself up there, he may be out in a period of shortly over seven years."

And that, Hewicker said, was the problem.

"If a law could be passed and placed in the constitution, so that each legislature couldn't come along and modify it . . . if they made life imprisonment life imprisonment without possibility of pardon or parole, that would be one thing. But we don't have that; we will never have it. And there are some crimes that are so revolting that, in my opinion, there is only one penalty that can be imposed. And that is the death penalty.

"I sat here and listened to those recordings, the manner in which these women were killed, and it was really shocking," Judge Hewicker continued. "I never heard anything like it, and I hope I never hear anything like it again. The torment, the suffering these women must have suffered during the night and on the desert, being choked to death . . . it must have been horrible. And at this time, I, having found the defendant guilty of first-degree murder, I will impose the death penalty on him. I think that is the only proper judgment that should be pronounced in this particular case. Now, if counsel wishes to post-

pone the pronouncement of judgment," Hewicker
told the defense, "I will be glad to do so."

"No, your Honor," Whittinghill replied.

"You waive the time for pronouncing judgment?"

"Waive the time," Whittinghill said. "Yes, your
Honor."

"Very well," said Hewicker. "Bring your client
up."

It was the clerk's turn. "Harvey Murray Glatman,"
he intoned, "you have heretofore been charged in an
indictment found by the grand jury of this county
charging you with two counts of murder, to which
you have heretofore entered a plea of guilty as to
both counts and were, by the court this date, found
guilty of first degree murder, and it is ordered that
the death sentence be imposed. This being the time
of arraignment for judgment, have you any legal
cause to show why judgment should not be pronounced?"

Harvey's reply was a muffled "No."

Judge Hewicker spoke again. "Any legal cause
why judgment should not be pronounced, Mr.
Whittinghill?"

"No, your Honor," the lawyer replied.

"Have you any legal cause, Mr. Glatman?"

"No."

Judge Hewicker forged ahead without hesitation.
"Mr. Glatman, no legal cause having been shown
why judgment should not be pronounced, and this
is the time for pronouncing judgment upon you, it
is the judgment of this court on count one and on
count two of the indictment, upon which you have
been found guilty of first-degree murder, that you
shall suffer the penalty of death in the manner prescribed by law, by the administration of lethal gas
within the walls of the California State Prison at San
Quentin, California, until your soul has departed

your body and this earth, and that execution of this sentence is stayed until final determination of your appeal by the Supreme Court of this state. It is further ordered by this court that the sheriff of this county is hereby commanded and directed to safely convey and deliver you forthwith into the custody of the warden of the California State Prison at San Quentin, California, and that you be confined therein until final decision of your appeal to the Supreme Court of this state has been determined. And it is the further order of the court, Mr. Glatman, that the sentences and the execution of the sentences on these two counts run consecutive and not concurrent. May God have mercy on your soul."

The clerk was losing track. "Do you want that San Quentin, or Chino?" he asked Judge Hewicker.

"San Quentin," the judge repeated.

Turning back to Harvey, the clerk asked, "What is your address, Mr. Glatman?"

Harvey hesitated. "The last address I had?"

"Yes."

"Eleven-oh-one, South Norton."

"Eleven-oh-one, South Norton?"

"Yes."

"Is that street or avenue?" the clerk asked.

"That is street," Harvey told him.

"Los Angeles?"

"Yes."

"And what state were you born in?" asked the clerk.

"New York," said Harvey.

"Thank you."

It was over, at least for the moment. Judge Hewicker's imposition of *consecutive* death sentences did not, of course, mean that Harvey would be gassed twice at San Quentin. Rather, it was a legal move designed to prevent both sentences from being overturned on

a single appeal and to insure that at least one was
finally carried through.

Hewicker made his judgment formal before the
day was out.

JUDGMENT FIXING THE DEATH PENALTY
FOR FIRST DEGREE MURDER

On the 17th day of December, 1958, comes the
Plaintiff by James Don Keller, District Attorney
of the County of San Diego, by William T. Low,
Deputy District Attorney, and comes the defendant, HARVEY MURRAY GLATMAN, in person
and by his attorney, Willard Whittinghill, and
the defendant is placed at the bar of this Court
for judgment upon the verdict of the Court returned this 17th day of December, 1958, the verdict being that the Court fixed the penalty as
death for the defendant's conviction of first degree murder in Count One and Count Two of
the Indictment;

The defendant was then duly arraigned for
judgment and asked if he had any legal cause to
show why judgment should not be pronounced
against him, and no legal cause being shown by
the defendant or his attorney and no sufficient
cause being alleged or appearing to the Court,
the Court thereupon rendered its judgment as
follows:

WHEREAS, the said HARVEY MURRAY
GLATMAN having on November 21, 1958, entered a plea of guilty to the crime of murder as
charged in Count One and Count Two of the
Indictment, alleged to have been committed on
March 9, 1958, and July 24, 1958, in that he did in
the manner and form alleged in the Indictment
murder one Shirley Ann Bridgeford and one

Ruth Mercado, and that thereafter said cause came on regularly for trial in this Court before a jury on December 15, 1958, for the purpose of determining the degree of the murders; and that on December 15, 1958, the defendant and his counsel each waived a trial by jury and the District Attorney having consented to said waiver and the waiver of a trial by jury having been accepted by the Court, and the defendant and his counsel having requested that the matter of degree be determined by the Court, said cause was submitted to the Court for its verdict on the 17th day of December, 1958, and the Court, after due deliberation, found the degree of the murders to which the defendant pleaded guilty in Count One and Count Two of the Indictment to be in each case murder of the first degree.

WHEREAS, the issue of the penalty to be imposed for the defendant's conviction of first degree murder having been submitted to the Court on December 17, 1958, and a jury on this issue having been waived by the defendant and his counsel, and consented to by the District Attorney, and said waiver of trial by jury having been accepted by the Court, the Court after due consideration fixed the penalty for the defendant's conviction of first degree murder as death in each count, the sentences to run consecutively.

The defendant personally and his counsel having waived time for pronouncement of judgment and having requested immediate sentence, it is the order of the Court as follows:

Now, therefore, IT IS ORDERED, ADJUDGED AND DECREED by this Court that the defendant, HARVEY MURRAY GLATMAN, suffer the penalty of death in the manner prescribed by law by the administration of lethal gas until he is dead, within the walls of San Quentin State Prison, and that execution of this sentence be stayed until the final determination of the defendant's automatic appeal to the Supreme Court of the State of California.

IT IS FURTHER ORDERED, ADJUDGED AND DECREED by the Court that the Sheriff of the County of San Diego, State of California, IS HEREBY COMMANDED AND DIRECTED to convey and deliver the said HARVEY MURRAY GLATMAN within 10 days from the 17th day of December, 1958, to the custody of the warden of San Quentin State Prison at San Quentin, California, and that said defendant be therein confined pending the decision of the defendant's automatic appeal to the Supreme Court of the State of California.

And there Harvey would wait, while his appeal was carried out, whether he liked it or not. At least, he told the press, he was relieved that his mother was spared the ordeal of his trial. "It would have been too hard on her," he said.

The perfect son.

As for his death sentence, Harvey was philosophical, telling reporters, "It was about what I wanted."

As modern serial killers go, Harvey Glatman was a piker. While there is widespread disagreement over definition of the term itself, FBI spokesmen demand a minimum of three victims for a "genuine" serial killer, and Glatman barely made the cut. His meager body count pales to insignificance beside the more industrious efforts of Theodore Bundy, John Gacy, Dean Corll, Juan Corona, Patrick Kearney, Randy Kraft, Jeffrey Dahmer, Gerald Stano, and a host of others who have followed in his footsteps.

Still, there was something about his case. . . .

Timing was clearly part of it. Los Angelenos, never truly innocent by any stretch of the imagination, were still relatively unsophisticated when it came to savage murder in the 1950s. For that matter, policemen themselves had little experience with Harvey's brand of killing, and the FBI's Behavioral Science Unit at Quantico, the "mindhunters" who profile unknown criminals à la *Silence of the Lambs*, would not open shop for another twenty years. In that respect, at least, Harvey was something of a trail blazer.

Geography helped out, of course. All of America—indeed, the world at large—kept one eye fixed on Hollywood for entertainment, fashion tips, and steamy scandals in the tabloid press. Harvey had never preyed on movie stars, per se, but three of his four victims had been "wannabes," soiled innocents, while Shirley Bridgeford could have doubled for the girl next door. If brutal death could find such women through the want ads or a lonely hearts club, who in all of the United States was truly safe?

And, then, there were the photographs.

Harvey had gone one step beyond the usual where sex crimes were concerned. It was almost routine for rapists and lust killers to retain small tokens of their crimes—an earring, panties, now and then a severed body part—but Harvey had recorded his on film. He elevated voyeurism to a grisly art form, and the publication of his snapshots—those deemed fit to print, at any rate—allowed all of America to see what he had seen, to share the guilty tingle of excitement and revulsion.

Back in Denver, where the press had nothing good to say about a hometown boy gone bad, the death sentence was front-page news. The *Denver Post* ran excerpts from Judge Hewicker's remarks and offered no dissent from his conclusion, vis-à-vis their less-than-favorite son.

The ink was barely dry on Harvey's death sentence when reporters came sniffing after his photos. William Low had rejected various media requests for the snapshots since their initial discovery was publicized, in early November, but now, with the case officially behind him, he experienced a change of heart. Low was disturbed by vocal opposition to capital punishment, in Glatman's case or for premeditated murder in general. The release of certain carefully selected photographs, he reasoned, might help swing the tide toward common sense, protection of a civilized society against the savages it spawned from time to time.

To that end, Low selected three of Harvey's snapshots for release to the press. There was one of each victim, still living, no nudes in the batch. Judy Dull was pictured in a chair, in Harvey's Melrose Avenue apartment, bound and gagged, her sweater unbuttoned, eyes rolling toward some point above her head and to her right. Shirley Bridgeford was shown sitting upright, on Harvey's blanket, with a pinched expression on her face and cactus in the background. Ruth Mercado lay recumbent on the blanket in another desert scene, eyes closed and face averted from the camera, dressed in a slip. Aside from wrists and ankles, each woman was also bound with rope an inch or two above the knees, as if to keep her legs together and prevent Harvey, at last, from reaching what he craved above all else.

The *Denver Post* ran Harvey's snapshots on page one, to illustrate the December eighteenth report of his death sentence. Eleven days later, *Time* magazine published the photos along with a brief recap of Glatman's case. Focused primarily on Harvey's photographic hobby, *Time*'s anonymous reporter described his twenty-two crime-scene snapshots as having "technical polish, slight originality of composition, and almost no precedent in the grim annals of criminal evidence." Harvey came off sounding pleased with his death sentence: "I think my actions justify that," he reportedly said. "I knew this is the way it would be."

But not just yet.

Executions were relatively swift in the "Happy Days" of the 1950s, especially for killers who pled guilty and resisted all appeals, but California had a built-in fail-safe system (today duplicated in nearly all death-penalty states) designed to keep the wheels of justice from turning so quickly that innocent men may fall prey to the system.

It still isn't foolproof, of course, but there could be no reasonable doubt of Harvey's guilt or his compelling wish to die. Yet, he would have to wait at least six months, perhaps longer, until the state supreme court had reviewed his case.

And in the meantime, he was headed for death row. A special cage was waiting for him in the prison California inmates simply knew as "Q."

18

"No Paradise for Scoundrels"

SAN QUENTIN MAY NOT BE THE TOUGHEST PRISON IN THE state of California—some would say that Soledad or Folsom rate that dubious distinction—but it's tough enough. Almost as old as Sing Sing, it has history and attitude, a reputation to defend. When hard-core California inmates get sent to "the Big House," they are on their way to "Q."

In the early days of California's history, convicted felons were confined in former Mexican jails or tethered off the coast in prison barges that had all the charm of slave ships. In 1851, a short year after California was admitted to the Union, one General Vallejo and his business partner, Major James Estell, obtained a contract from the state to house convicted prisoners. Estell promptly leased the *Waban*, a 268-ton bark, for use as a prison ship, but the vessel had clear limitations. A new approach was needed, and without delay.

In July 1852, land was purchased for a new prison at San Quentin Point, kissing-close to San Francisco, and the first three-tiered cell block was completed in

1854. As with Sing Sing and most other prisons of
the era, the plant was erected with free convict labor.
A state investigating committee examined the new
prison and declared it "no paradise for scoundrels,"
pronouncing San Quentin "a very real penitentiary—
a place for suffering and expiation."

Such comments were construed as praise in the
mid-nineteenth century, and San Quentin's civilian
managers got right down to business, utilizing their
charges as a primary source of both labor and profit.
As at Sing Sing and elsewhere, inmate work crews
were leased out to private businessmen or to local
governments for completion of public works projects.
Many of the roads in northern California were laid
by convicts in that fashion, and there is substantial
evidence that San Quentin, under the stewardship of
Vallejo and Estell, began its career as a haven for
corrupt profiteering.

Four years later, in 1858, state legislators reacted
to public criticism of San Quentin's private management with new legislation, finally placing the prison
under state control. That same year, another inspection revealed that "of now over 500 convicts, 120
were barefoot, most were in rags, sick and infirm
inmates neglected, food inadequate, and the cells
filthy." Reforms were in order—but only to a point.

State control of San Quentin, for instance, would
not mark the end of convict labor on public or private works. Early labor unions in the Golden State,
together with small businessmen, complained about
the unfair competition presented by cheap convict
labor. It took thirteen years, but the state finally
responded, and by 1871, most inmate labor was
applied in the prison's own factories, cranking out
such diverse items as bricks, jute sacks, shoes, and
furniture.

Although San Quentin houses only men today,

women were also held there for some three-quarters of a century, until the early days of 1933. Problems predictably arose, and public hearings held in 1856 accused some guards at "Q" of "cohabiting and drinking with female inmates." Even so, another sixty-seven years would pass before the women were dispersed to other prisons. None remain at San Quentin these days, although condemned female inmates are transported there for execution—a circumstance that has not taken place in nearly half a century.

Male or female, life was hard for inmates at San Quentin in those early days. The workday was long and grueling, corporal punishment was widely applied, and assessments of the prison kitchen's output ranged from poor to "inedible." Despite the looming walls and gun towers, escapes were also a persistent problem, drawing fire from San Francisco residents over the seeming lack of security.

By 1904, with progressive reforms slowly filtering down from Washington to the several states, San Quentin initiated its first system of prisoner classification which separated inmates on the basis of offenses leading to conviction, their criminal histories, and other variable factors. Educational and vocational programs began under Warden Clinton Duffy, in the 1930s, and continue to the present day. The 1950s witnessed institution of a rehabilitation program based on indeterminate sentencing and individualized treatment of convicts, but the new approach would mean nothing to Glatman, tagged as inmate number A-50239.

Harvey was bound for death row, where rehabilitation had no meaning.

He was booked to the end of the line.

A memo to the warden, from Captain V. J. O'Malley, chronicled Harvey's arrival at "Q."

Inmate Glatman arrived at this institution at approximately 2:30 P.M. and was interviewed by the undersigned at 3:15 P.M. on December 18, 1958.

The interview lasted approximately 40 minutes. I instructed Glatman on the following topics and answered such questions as he asked.

1. He was instructed as to the position of the institution regarding his instant case and his cooperation was asked in his conduct and demeanor while confined on Death Row.
2. He was instructed that men on Death Row have certain privileges, none of which are considered rights, with the exception of the basic rights of humans, and that such privileges that are given may be revoked for misconduct.
3. The attitude of the institution toward his press interviews was explained to him and he was informed that he was at liberty to be interviewed by, or photographed by the press upon his written consent.
4. He was instructed that he would not be permitted to write for publication, and that any manuscripts found would be confiscated and destroyed.
5. He was instructed as to his writing and visiting privileges, and general instruction was given as to his canteen privileges.
6. He was instructed that his legal fight to modify or reverse his conviction would be done by either he or his attorney of record, and that

legal help in the preparing of petitions or writs by other inmates was not permissible.

O'Malley noted that "Glatman was quiet and respectful throughout the entire interview." Harvey recounted his experience in other prisons and explained how it had prompted his decision to confess. "He stated that during his time at Sing Sing he had seen prisoners who had served long periods of time," O'Malley wrote, "and that he did not wish to ever become like them." Harvey expressed remorse for his crimes to O'Malley, "but did not attempt to excuse himself." In summary, Captain O'Malley noted, "It is not anticipated that Glatman will cause us any trouble while on Death Row."

Harvey's personal property, logged on arrival at "Q," included a Heathkit radio, a toolbox and tools, a camera tripod, and a suitcase of clothes, along with $635.25 in cash. He signed a property receipt permitting the state department of corrections to keep any interest earned on his money, depositing same in the Inmate Welfare Fund. As if he had a choice, Harvey also agreed to the inspection and censorship of his mail, including destruction of any item, "should it not comply with the rules of the institution."

San Quentin's medical examiner looked Harvey over on arrival and gave him a clean bill of health. The only problem found was in his mouth, where the report described "some cavity—dirty teeth." He needed dental work, but it was not considered an emergency. If necessary, Harvey's teeth would see him through his final days without repair.

Death row is special. Inmates who have been condemned are separated from the prison's general population for security reasons, and it cuts both ways. They are presumed to be the worst inmates at "Q," and some of them rank high among the most notorious, which makes them attractive targets for any shank-happy convict in search of a "rep." Death-row inmates have no work assignments at San Quentin, and their exercise periods are limited, scheduled for times and places where they will have no contact with "mainline" prisoners. In the late 1950s, TV had barely reached death row, but there were the disembodied voices from the radio to distract or entertain.

The men confined there are literally killing time.

If Harvey had been spared the death sentence, he likely would have made himself at home in "Q." He had survived without apparent incident in Colorado, at Elmira, and at Sing Sing. Of course, his crimes were more notorious this time, at least around Los Angeles and San Diego, but he was not famous in the same sense as Charles Manson, a decade later, or "Night Stalker" Richard Ramirez in the 1980s. It is doubtful whether any fellow inmate at San Quentin would have thought him "big" enough or infamous enough to kill.

It is a point of "common knowledge" that rapists have a hard time in prison, facing continual assaults from other cons. One explanation has it that since all inmates have mothers and many of them have sisters, wives, or girlfriends, they despise all men who prey on women in the free world and exact grim retribution when a rapist comes within their reach. In fact, except where "short eyes"—child molesters—are involved, there seems to be no special animosity toward sex offenders in most prisons. There are many rapists and rape-slayers presently incarcerated in America with nothing to suggest that they are special targets of assault in prison. If they were, some of the first to go would surely be the very prison "wolves" who rape so many other inmates.

At a glance, Harvey was perfect for such preda-

tors—still relatively young, no more than average
height, of slender build. He wasn't handsome, but a
"punk" or "bitch" in prison doesn't need to be. If he
had ever suffered such indignity, however, there was
nothing in his file to document the fact, no mention
of such incidents in Harvey's long list of complaints
about his life.

Death row would keep him safe at "Q," in any
case. His greatest enemy was tedium, plus whatever
anxiety he felt while waiting for the death he claimed
to crave.

William Lavelle tried to resume his interviews with
Harvey, following the "trial," but he was out of luck.
He notes in his report that

> This investigation was originally assigned to the
> undersigned as a normal probation investigation.
> It was felt at the time that the major investigative
> effort should first be directed towards outlining
> the various offenses as completely as possible,
> and then towards the defendant's family and
> personal history. These feelings were based on
> the belief that Glatman might cooperate for a
> short time and then "freeze up," and assume a
> negative attitude. It must be stated that this did
> not happen. Further, it was felt that a full state-
> ment from the defendant would best outline
> the reasoning that led to these three murders.
> After his trial was completed the subject was
> transferred from local custody and was thus
> unavailable for further interviews. These rea-
> sons account for the somewhat sketchy per-
> sonal history.

Signing off on his report, two days before Christ-
mas, Lavelle felt there was nothing to be gained from
further interviews with Glatman.

This probation officer [he wrote] feels there is little more to add. The defendant states he feels remorse for his offenses, however, this seems to be more a reflection of what he thinks the auditor wants to hear. In substance, it is felt that the murders, the defendant's version of them, and the accompanying psychiatric reports speak plainly enough without any added interpretations.

Lavelle was writing Harvey off, small loss, but California was not ready to dispose of Glatman yet. There were procedures to be followed, rules to live by, and it made no difference to the players that the object of their rapt attention was opposed to the delay.

Harvey would die, all right, but in the state's good time.

While Glatman languished on death row at "Q," another nightmare was unfolding on the far side of the country with another killer who required submissive prey. The case had actually begun a month before Harvey killed Judy Dull, but it took authorities some time to pull the facts together—and their quarry almost got away, at that.

On June 26, 1957, Margaret Harold was parked with her date—a young army sergeant—on a lonely lover's lane near Annapolis, Maryland, when a green Chrysler pulled up in front of their car. A tall, thin-faced man approached, identified himself as the property's caretaker, then produced a gun, and climbed into the back seat. He demanded money from the couple, shooting Margaret in the head when she indignantly refused. Her date escaped on foot and called police, returning with an escort to discover that her killer had paused long enough to rape the corpse.

Nearby, a search team found a building made of cinder blocks with a basement window broken, and they crept inside. The inner walls were covered with a mix of pornographic photos and morgue shots of dead women; the only "normal" photo was a college yearbook picture that depicted Wanda Tipton, a 1955 graduate from the University of Maryland, who denied knowing anyone matching the killer's description.

Eighteen months would pass before the killer struck again. On January 11, 1959, a family of four disappeared while out for a drive near Apple Grove, Virginia. A relative found their abandoned car later that day, but no trace remained of Carroll Jackson, his wife Mildred, or their two daughters, five-year-old Susan and eighteen-month-old Janet. While police were beating the bushes in vain, a young couple reported that they had been forced off the road by an old blue Chevy that morning. The strange driver had climbed out and approached their car, at which time they made good their escape.

Two months later, on March fourth, Carroll Jackson's body was discovered by two men whose car had bogged down in the mud near Fredericksburg, Virginia. Homicide detectives found the victim's hands bound with a necktie, a single bullet in his head. When they removed his body from the roadside ditch, another corpse was found beneath it. Tiny Janet Jackson had been thrown into the ditch alive and literally suffocated by her father's weight.

On March twenty-first, hunters stumbled across a grave site in Maryland, not far from the spot where Margaret Harold was murdered in 1957. The bodies of Mildred and Susan Jackson were unearthed by investigators, both bearing signs of sexual assault and

savage beatings with a blunt instrument. A stocking
was found knotted around Mildred's neck, but she
had not been strangled, police speculating that the
tourniquet had been applied to coerce her participa-
tion in oral sex. A quarter-mile away, manhunters
found a rundown shack with "fresh" tire tracks outside, a button from Mildred Jackson's dress lying on
the floor within.

The case was still unsolved in May 1959, when
homicide detectives received an anonymous letter
from Norfolk, naming one Melvin Rees as the killer.
A Maryland native, born in 1933, Rees had attended
the state university briefly before dropping out to
pursue a career in music. On March 12, 1955, he had
been arrested on charges of assaulting a thirty-six-
year-old woman, dragging her into his car when she
refused to enter voluntarily, but the case was
dropped when his victim refused to press charges.
Melvin's friends ignored the incident, if they were
even conscious of it, viewing Rees as mild-mannered
and intelligent, a talented artist who played the
piano, guitar, clarinet, and saxophone with equal
skill. He had a taste for modern jazz, and his employment often took him on the road.

Accusations aside, there was no solid evidence
connecting Rees to any homicides before 1960, and
no one seemed to know his whereabouts until the
anonymous informant came forward with a letter
from Melvin describing his latest job at a music store
in West Memphis, Arkansas. FBI agents were dispatched to pick him up on suspicion, and a search
of Melvin's home in Hyattsville, Maryland, turned
up an instrument case with a pistol inside, plus handwritten notes describing assorted sadistic acts. One
such was clipped to a newspaper photo of Mildred
Jackson. It read, in part: "Caught on a lonely
road. . . . Drove to a select area and killed husband

and baby. Now the mother and daughter were all mine. . . ."

Nicknamed the "Sex Beast" by Maryland newsmen, Rees was soon linked to four other murders. Schoolgirls Mary Shomette, sixteen, and Ann Ryan, fourteen, had each been raped and killed in College Park, near the University of Maryland, while eighteen-year-old Mary Fellers and sixteen-year-old Shelby Venable had been fished out of nearby rivers. Rees was not indicted in their deaths, but prosecutors felt they had enough to keep him off the streets, regardless. Convicted of Margaret Harold's murder, in Baltimore, Rees was sentenced to life imprisonment, then handed over to Virginia authorities for trial. Upon conviction of multiple murder in that state, he was sentenced to death and executed in 1961.

Willard Whittinghill continued, under court appointment, as the attorney of record for Harvey's appeal. Official transcripts of the penalty trial were filed with the clerk of California's Supreme Court on January 21, 1959, which started the clock on a thirty-day deadline for delivery of Whittinghill's opening brief. By that time, however, Glatman had already written to the high court himself in a letter dated January twentieth.

To: Chief Justice Phil S. Gibson

Sir:

I am writing this letter in hopes of having my automatic appeal on a death sentence dismissed. I will state briefly the facts and my reasons for asking the court to dismiss the appeal according to rule 38 of the Rules of Appeal.

My name is Harvey Glatman. I was convicted in San Diego County of two counts of Murder 1st Degree in Superior Court of Judge John Hewicker in December 1958, and am currently in San Quentin prison awaiting execution.

I pleaded guilty to two counts of murder and in a subsequent hearing before Judge Hewicker (I waived a jury hearing and all interested parties agreed to this) the degree was judged to be the first and the penalty set was death.

I wish the appeal to be dismissed for the following reasons.

There is no doubt as to my guilt of the charges. I was adequately represented by counsel. There was no coercion used at any time, and I feel that I had a fair hearing. I do not believe that any appeal in my case would alter the outcome and that it would merely reaffirm the lower court's judgement. Therefore I do not feel that it is in my best interest or that of the State of California to be confined for an indefinite period even though that be customary. I respectfully request, therefore, that you use the power of the Supreme Court of California to dismiss the automatic appeal (or any other) which is pending before you in my behalf.

I feel this action would be in the best interests of justice, humaneness and the State of California.

Respectfully,
HARVEY GLATMAN

The reply was dated January twenty-sixth, with copies to Whittinghill and San Diego's county clerk.

Re. People v. Glatman, Crim. 6420

Dear Sir:

Your letter of January 20, 1959, addressed to
Chief Justice Gibson, has been referred to me for
answer. The court has requested me to inform
you that the record on the automatic appeal in
your case will be reviewed as in all other cases.
In the meantime the County Clerk of San
Diego County has delivered or will deliver the
copy of the trial transcript in your case to Mr.
Willard Whittinghill, 525 C Street, San Diego,
California, who represented you at your trial.

Very truly yours,
/s/ William I. Sullivan
Clerk of Supreme Court

Will Whittinghill was well aware of Harvey's
steadfast opposition to appeals, and while he had no
realistic hope of seeing the death sentence overturned, he had to give the court something. His
choice, and probably the best one available in a no-
win situation, was an appeal for reversal based on
Judge Hewicker's admission of evidence related to
Judy Dull's murder in Riverside County and the Orange County assault on Lorraine Vigil. It was admit-
tedly a long shot, but it also seemed to be the only
game in town.

Ten days after writing his letter to Chief Justice
Gibson, Harvey hit his first snag on death row. A
memo from Lieutenant B. G. Pool to Associate Warden W. D. Achuff, dated January 30, 1959, explains
the nature of the trouble.

You were informed by the writer at 11:35 P.M. this date and was [sic] informed that inmate Glatman A-50239 (Condemned) had destroyed his stool and earphones which were assigned to him in cell DR#5.

After this destruction the inmate apparently went to bed and went to sleep.

At 11:37 P.M. you were again contacted by the writer and informed that subject was again destroying articles in his cell. On advise [sic] of the writer, you agreed that subject inmate should be placed in an isolation cell on quiet status[;] this movement was accomplished without incident by Sergeant L. R. Rue, Sergeant R. E. Descombe, Officer L. J. Smith and the writer.

The subject's only reason for destroying property in his cell was that he wanted peace and quiet and this was the only way he could get it.

Pictures were taken of the damage on Saturday January 31, by the Second Watch.

Bright and early next morning, Harvey was charged with destruction of state property and a disciplinary hearing was scheduled for Tuesday, February third. Harvey pled guilty to the charge and was sentenced to seven days in solitary. The disciplinary committee's report notes that: "Subject states he became disturbed because of the noise made by other inmates who were playing checkers. Apparently pressure had been building up." Since Harvey had been isolated from the time of the disturbance, formal sentencing left him with only four days to serve, and he returned to death row cell #5 on Saturday, February seventh.

Six days later, Catholic prison chaplain Edward Dingberg filed a brief report on Harvey, pronouncing him "a pleasant and quiet person" who "gives the

impression of being somewhat withdrawn and seems
to be quite preoccupied in reading." That same day,
his first neuropsychiatric report was logged over the
signatures of chief psychiatrist David Schmidt, "psychiatrist II" A. D. Kopac, and medical officer G. G.
Kenny. The report notes that

> The subject entered the Examining Room in a
> quite cooperative, modestly tense manner, and
> replied to all queries, after initial hesitance, with
> what appeared to be complete candor; but at the
> same time, requiring some degree of assurance
> of the examiners' interest in the material before
> he answered in detail to many queries. . . .

> When questioned as to his motivation, he states
> that getting "even" with society was a big ele-
> ment in that he felt when he was first in trouble,
> he should have been placed in a hospital instead
> of prison. He further stated that he was not
> angry with the victims *nor did he kill to cover up
> the rape offenses*, and that if he had not been ap-
> prehended, he would have continued in similar
> offenses until he had been caught.

> Mental examination at this time reveals him to
> be of superior intelligence with thinking patterns
> that appear to [be] relevant and coherent. Judg-
> ment and mood appear to be within normal lim-
> its although his affect appears to be somewhat
> bland and inappropriate at times. He is oriented
> in all three spheres, and no abnormal thought
> content such as delusions or hallucinations can
> be elicited at this time.

> We are agreed that his personality patterning is
> consistent with that found in a Schizoid Person-

ality with Obsessive-Compulsive, Paranoid Features but that he is not insane. [Emphasis added]

A third report was filed on February thirteenth by Captain O'Malley, offering this assessment of Harvey:

He is a very nervous individual and becomes upset at any continued noise. He is cooperative with the officers, but likes to stay to himself. He is resigned to his fate and desires that nothing be done on his behalf. He wants his sentence carried out as quickly as possible. His eating is sporadic and sometimes he will eat nothing for two or three days. He attends the weekly movie and watches TV. He has very few visits and corresponds very little, but is cooperative on staff interviews. It is anticipated that he will probably become more nervous and upset as time goes on.

On St. Valentine's Day, Protestant chaplain Byron Eshelman reported to Warden Fred Dickson that Harvey "seems to be quite alert and intelligent." Furthermore, Eshelman noted (presumably straight-faced) that: "He reports that he has never been inclined toward violence and a recent episode on the row when he stepped out of this role was somewhat of a surprise to himself."

Two days later, another physical examination found Harvey in good health, with no complaints, making "a good adjustment to his present situation." On February seventeenth, psychologist W. A. Drummond, Jr., submitted Harvey's second mental evaluation at "Q."

When interviewed on 2/5/59, subject was still confined to Isolation, where he had been placed following an episode in which he "threw a temper tantrum" and destroyed several items of property in his Condemned Row cell. Being quite lonely, he was quite anxious to talk and was very pleasant and cooperative throughout the interview. He was quite mild mannered, pleasant and appeared to be fairly relaxed. Most of his conversation was quite rational and his affect seemed to be fairly appropriate. However, he reiterated his desire to submit to execution as early as possible, and he states that he has petitioned the Courts to suspend his automatic appeal and has also requested that his lawyer honor his wishes also.

Subject's performance on the intelligence test administered at this time substantiates earlier school reports and classifies him in the Very Superior intellectual group. His scores on the Full Verbal Scale of the Wechsler-Bellevue Intelligence Scale, Form I, indicated that he has an I.Q. of 140. His scores on all the sub-tests, which show very little scatter, were above average. He "topped" the Arithmetic and Digit Memory Span tests and received the highest possible scores on these two scales. His weakest score, although still quite good, was obtained on the Similarities Test where he experienced some difficulty differentiating between essential and superficial likenesses. None of his responses to this test indicated any perceptual or ideational distortion which might suggest evidence of gross psychopathology.

On the Bender Visual-Motor Gestalt Test, subject arranged his drawings in a rather methodical order and displayed considerable intellectual control and adaptation to reality. His perception was quite accurate but he resorted to compulsive mechanisms quite freely in order to control or conceal his anxiety, and he also gave indication of some emotional conflict in the psychosexual areas. All gestalts were very accurately reproduced and, here again, there was no evidence of any distortions suggestive of psychosis or possible organicity.

Subject's MMPI profile suggests that he is a very anxious, depressed and socially introverted individual who has extreme difficulty in the area of interpersonal relationships and marked antisocial or sociopathic tendencies. The profile reveals an extremely passive-dependent individual, with an unsociable, pre-illness personality, characterized by inability to concentrate, confusion, restlessness and extreme insecurity. Paranoid tendencies are indicated along with marked schizoid symptomatology, but appear to be well defined rather than diffuse. He is extremely sensitive and suspicious, and he seems to rely quite heavily upon compulsive mechanisms and autistic thinking. While the MMPI profile presents no conclusive evidence that the subject is suffering from a psychosis, it does indicate that he had a pronounced schizoid personality with obsessive-compulsive features and paranoid trends.

Reports from family members, friends and former employers corroborate the fact that subject has been a very moody individual who has been subject to impulsive behavior, temper tantrums[,] and has frequently experienced difficulty taking orders and getting along with fellow workers. Subject admits that he has been very restless and has never remained on one job very long, and has frequently changed residences. He states that during the time he was living in Los Angeles, he was never able to make "one friend[.]" His interpersonal difficulties seem to stem from the fact that he "can't stand stupid people," and most of the people with whom he has come in contact (including his parents) fall within this category. While it is true that subject has very superior general intelligence, it is felt that this reasoning only serves to reflect his paranoid thinking. While most of his conversation was quite rational throughout the interview, at one point he disclosed a line of reasoning which is almost as bizarre as the nature of his offense, and which also seems to fit in with his paranoid thinking by reflecting his desire to control his surroundings. He states that just prior to his becoming involved in his present series of offenses, he entertained the idea of visiting an ear specialist because he felt that his hearing was too acute and a source of great annoyance to him. He was hoping to find a doctor who would be able to perform an operation which would reduce his hearing by "about 90%," and equip him with a hearing aid so that he would only have to listen to things in which he was personally interested. Further questioning, at this time, obtained no admissions from subject that these annoying noises were hallucinatory in origin. He states that they were merely the usual sounds that are always in existence, but which other people are able to ignore because their hearing is not as acute as his.

Subject appears to have no insight into why his hostility has repeatedly been expressed towards women, but does admit that his relationship

with his mother has always been rather poor, as
it has also been with his father. He states that
ever since his first arrest and conviction, when
he felt that he needed psychiatric treatment but
was committed to prison, he has felt the need
for revenge but he never knew how it would be
expressed. "At that time, I felt as those [sic] they
had taken my life so I must have one in return."
He states that the killing of the first victim was
not planned but was prompted by "self-defense"
because she was able to identify him. He states
that this killing was a difficult one for him, but
that they became easier after this period. He is
at a loss to explain the second killing because,
as he states, the victim said, and he believed her,
that she would not report the incident. *He adds
that she appeared to be a nymphomaniac who seemed
to enjoy the whole affair and might even appreciate
a repeat performance.* It would appear that his behavior seemed to follow a rather ritualistic,
obsessive-compulsive nature, over which he claims
to have had little, if any, control. *In attempting to
explain why he tied his victims, he states that he feels
he can trace this to an incident which occurred between him and his father at the age of three. He states
that he has been obsessed with tying up ever since,
but would not elucidate any further.* It was about
this time that he felt the guards might be listening to our conversation and expressed a desire not to go into more explicit detail, in spite
of the interviewer's assurance that his suspicions
were unfounded.

In summary, while this man did not impress the
interviewer as being overtly psychotic at the
time of the interview, there seems to be no doubt
about his having a markedly schizoid personal-

ity with paranoid and obsessive-compulsive features. [Emphasis added.]

Having overlooked William Lavelle's probation report from San Diego, filed seven weeks before his interview with Glatman, Drummond knew nothing of the incident from age three or four when Harvey supposedly tied his own penis to a dresser drawer . . . and so, the mystery of Glatman's obsession with bondage remained unresolved.

While Harvey was talking about his past, more or less, some people he had never heard of were thinking and talking about him. Public reaction to his case varied widely. One anonymous "Christian friend" sent twenty dollars to San Quentin with a list of religious radio programs in the hope that Harvey might buy a small set and tune in for "much comfort and peace." Others, like the nameless "citizen" who listed his return address as general delivery, Hollywood, California, had a different prescription in mind.

The "*Sex*" Criminal Glatman wants the Death Penalty, but should he have *what* he wants? I do not think he should be rubbed out, but put into a position where no one knows "*who*" he really is: He should be placed at "hard" work, relieved of his gender[,] and reminded ever [sic] so often that "God is the one who gives life and *God* is the one who takes life." Capital punishment is archaic. Those who kill should be placed at *hard* labor, deprived of benefits, and given time to restitution [sic] *though* they should never be paroled.
    It is assumed that he is adult normal, not insane. How can psychoanalysts say a machocist [sic] is a *sane* person? To me this is sentamental-

ity [*sic*] and twisting the law to serve mass hysteria. *Do not execute this man.*

There is a sex institution [*sic*] at Atascadero, California. This man should be placed there as Mr. "X," his *sex* removed. He should be placed at hard labor for the rest of his life. This is dealing with the man in the "law of cause and effect" where it hurts the most.

Capital punishment should be abolished. The people who do wrong should meet their punishments *in life*: It is uncertain what becomes of them when they are dead. Many people think it is the end. But there is a cult of thought which called [*sic*] "spiritualists," which places juvenile delinquency and insanity in a place where people, weak in their minds, become "obsessed" & carry out crimes which they cannot afterward explain. Make the criminal pay with hard work till natural death overtakes him. Let him learn the lessons of life by cause and effect. We do not hate people, we hate the things they *do*.

Needless to say, the unnamed citizen's suggestion was ignored.

Soon after Drummond's interview was filed, Harvey addressed a letter to San Quentin's warden.

Dear Sir;

I am writing this as a request to be moved from my present cell #5 to another one somewhere on the back bar. My reasons are as follows.

There are on either side of me two fellow "dead men," with whom I have no quarrel but are prone to noises which to put it bluntly are slowly driving me nuts. (One thinks he's a singer and the other just has a variety of weird noises.) This is something that has plagued me for a long time (on the outside too) and I am not able to control it.

My reason for asking to move to the back bar is that because of the acoustics in this block sounds travel a long way and merely shifting a few cells away is useless. Also being acquainted with those on the back bar I don't think this problem would be present there.

I hope you will act favorably on this request as it is very important to me.

Respectfully
Harvey Glatman
A50239

This time, by going through channels, Harvey got his wish. A note scrawled in the upper left-hand corner of his letter indicates that he was moved, as per his request, on March second.

Appeals of criminal convictions, barring allegations of new evidence, do not address issues of guilt or innocence. Rather, appellate courts examine trial records for procedural errors or constitutional issues, seeking any evidence that the defendant has been denied a fair trial. Depending on the case and the appellate judge, such evidence may range from flagrant violations of due process (a coerced confession, for example) to the seemingly trivial (typographical errors in a search warrant or even the direction a witness was facing during courtroom testimony).

Whittinghill's brief to the court, offered without any real hope of success, alleged that admission of evidence relative to Judy Dull's murder and the Vigil

assault had been improper and prejudicial, effectively
stacking the deck against Glatman and insuring that
he would receive the death sentence. No one expected it to fly, least of all Whittinghill, but he had
to do *something*.

It was Friday, June fifth, before California's Supreme Court announced its decision on Glatman's
appeal. Five pages of the seven-page document were
devoted to recapping the facts of Harvey's case, from
his October arrest through his confessions and the
nocturnal trek that uncovered remains of two victims. Finally, on the penultimate page, Chief Justice
C. J. Gibson addressed the substance of Whittinghill's appeal.

Evidence was also received regarding the circumstances surrounding the killing of Judy Dull
and the Lorraine Vigil incident. No objection was
made to the introduction of this evidence, and
defendant cannot now question the propriety of
its admission. (People v. Feldkamp, 51 A.C. 234,
238.) Moreover, the evidence was properly admitted with respect to both the degree of the
crimes and the penalty. The facts of the Dull case
were similar and in many respects identical with
those relating to Shirley and Ruth, and it was
shown that defendant was following substan-
tially the same procedure with Lorraine Vigil
when his attempt to have intercourse was interrupted by the arrival of a police officer. The evidence of other similar offenses would have been
admissible on the issue of guilt to show defendant's motive and intent (People v. Coefield, 37
Cal. 2d 865, 869-870; People v. Peete, 28 Cal. 2d
306, 314-317; cf. People v. McCaughan, 49 Cal.
2d 409, 421-422), and it was likewise admissible
on the issue of the degree of the crime to which

he pleaded guilty. The evidence of the other crimes was admissible in the proceeding to determine the penalty under section 190.1 of the Penal Code, which provides that any evidence concerning the commission of the crime is admissible in the trial determining the guilt of the defendant may be admitted on the issue of penalty.

We find no error in the record, and the judgment is affirmed.

The court's decision was unanimous, officially filed one month later, on Monday, the sixth of July. Bright and early Thursday morning, Judge Hewicker issued a new order pronouncing judgment of death against Glatman, containing identical wording from his original order of December seventeenth. That same day, an identically worded death warrant was dispatched to Warden Dickson at San Quentin. Warden Dickson penned a curt acknowledgment to the San Diego Superior Court on Monday, July thirteenth.

The wheels were in motion, now. Barring a federal appeal (which Harvey refused) or clemency from the governor (an impossible dream), only procedural red tape stood between Glatman and death.

In the meantime, on July fourth, Ophelia Glatman signed an eye-donor's form for the University of California eye bank. She signed as donor, the form witnessed by her brother and his wife, but a letter from Warden Dickson at San Quentin, dated six days later, clearly indicates that Harvey was to provide the actual "gift."

Dear Mrs. Glatman:

Thank you for mailing the University of California Medical School forms regarding the disposition of your son's body when execution of judgment is carried out. We shall endeavor to keep Harvey from knowing about this until your wish is fulfilled. Your cooperation in this matter is very much appreciated.

Very truly yours,
F. R. DICKSON, Warden

While Harvey's life was winding down, the state went through its necessary motions, touching all the bases. On July twenty-eighth, Agent Raymond Stonehouse, with the state Department of Justice, reported to Sacramento that "[I]nterviews with the judge, prosecutor, and investigating officers indicate that GLATMAN received a fair trial and that there is no reason for clemency consideration. GLATMAN himself states that he is ready and willing to be executed for his crimes."

By that time, a second psychiatric report had already been filed on Glatman by Doctors Schmidt, Kopac, and Gross, dated July 20, 1959.

This subject refused to enter the examining room but was quite cooperative when interviewed in his cell. He required some degree of mild persuasion but was then reasonably candid and cooperative, answering any and all queries.

He declined to review his present case and also stated he did not feel he should comment on the present legal aspects of it.

Mental examination at this time continues to reveal him to be of superior intelligence and with overall thinking patterns well within normal lim-

its. Content of speech appears to be relevant and
coherent and with no evidence of delusional or
unusual thinking. Judgment and mood are
within normal limits and affect appears to be
generally appropriate. He is oriented in all three
spheres, temporal, spacial and personal, and no
abnormal thought content such as delusions or
hallucinations can be elicited at this time.

We are agreed that his personality patterning
continues to be consistent with that found in a
Schizoid Personality with Obsessive-Compulsive
and Paranoid Features but that he is not insane.

Chaplain Eshelman, two days later, reported that
Harvey "appears quite willing to discuss most any
subject, but has not spoken of any particular remorse
or amazement over his own self-confessed offenses.
He does seem to imply that he failed to receive the
kind of help or treatment that could have deflected
him from his bizarre behavior if he had been dealt
with in a different way during his youth."
On July twenty-third, Associate Warden Louis Nelson wrote of Harvey as follows:

When he first came on the Row, he was very
nervous and easily upset, but since his case was
decided and a date set, he seems very happy
about the whole thing. He eats and s[l]eeps well
and of late, he has been playing cards during the
exercise periods. He usually attends the weekly
movie but seldom watches TV. He is very cooperative with the officers in the unit and has never
presented a disciplinary problem. As noted
above, he seems very happy about having his
date set, and is very eager to get it over with,

saying, "That's what I have been looking forward to!"

Judge Hewicker, meanwhile, was less than pleased
with progress on the case. Harry Towne, a spokes-
man for the state department of corrections, wrote to
Hewicker on July tenth, soliciting comments as part
of Glatman's *pro forma* clemency review, but that letter and a subsequent personal visit were ignored.
When Towne wrote again, on July twenty-ninth, he
received a stinging reply.

Dear Sir:

I have your letter of July 10th in the above entitled matter and also your letter of July 29th.
After receiving your letter of July 10th a repre-
sentative of your office, whose name I do not
now remember, called on me and asked me
whether or not I was going to answer your letter
of July 10th, and I told him "No." That I had
tried Glatman without a jury and everything I
had to say about the case was contained in the
transcript, and if the Governor and the Adult
Authority were interested in what I had said,
they could look at the transcript.

I feel that since Governor Brown had seen fit to
commute the death sentence of Wein, the rapist
from Los Angeles, he having raped only eleven
women in that community, on the ground that
the women although having been raped, had not
been transported a sufficient distance to consti-
tute kidnapping in the Governor's opinion, I had
no desire to contact the Governor in any capital
case in the future. That the Legislature had laid
down the law on kidnapping and the Supreme

Court had interpreted the statute, the United
States Supreme Court had denied Mr. Wein a
hearing, and since Governor Brown was the Attorney General during all of these proceedings
and contended that the distance that the women
had been transported constituted kidnapping
under the statute, I thought he was forclosed
[sic] in taking a different attitude as Governor.
After all, we have three authorities in this state,
the Legislature, the courts, and the Governor. I
think, and thought, that when the court, the Legislature and the Attorney General had spoken, it
was not up to the Governor who had been the
Attorney General, to about-face and say that
rape of eleven women did not warrant execution
when the highest court of the land had stated
that the Legislature had so decreed in its legislation, and the case came within the legislative
intent.

Rapists seem to have a special consideration in
this state. Chessman after raping all the women
he did is still alive after eleven years. Governor
Knight commuted the life sentence of Felix
Friend because he only raped and murdered a
woman. Croaker—life sentence commuted because he only murdered a woman. Glatman only
raped three women and murdered all three.

I am not going to urge the Governor to take any
action one way or another in the Glatman case.
I told the world what I thought about the case
at the time and that's it. If the Governor wishes
to show special consideration to someone who
is not entitled to it, that is his privilege, but I
feel that it is a waste of time for me to write
letters urging certain things when I know, and

the Governor has publicly stated, that he is opposed to the death penalty.

What I did in the Glatman case I think was justified and I have no difficulty in sleeping at night. I hope what the Governor did in the Wein case and what he does in future capital cases where he commutes the sentences permits him to sleep at night too.

With kindest personal regards, I remain

Sincerely,
/s/ John A. Hewicker.

That salvo brought a response one week later from Governor Edmund Brown's secretary, Cecil Poole. Courteous to a fault, Poole's note reminded Hewicker that "[A]s you may not be aware Section 4803 of the Penal Code imposes upon trial judges, including yourself, a duty to furnish the Governor with such recommendation upon request. The language of the statute does not appear to justify non-compliance simply because a trial judge finds himself in disagreement with other actions of the Governor in which he has no involvement."

Judge Hewicker, unchastened, replied to Poole on August tenth. His letter read, in part:

I was fully aware of Section 4803 of the Penal Code prior to the receipt of your letter. What bearing or relevancy that section has to Mr. Glatman's situation I am at a loss to comprehend, as I know of no request that Mr. Glatman has made to receive either a pardon or commutation of sentence. If such application has been filed by

him I would appreciate your sending me a copy
of the same by return mail. . . .

I might state, Mr. Poole, that I may not be "Involved" in other cases such as the Wein case, in
which I wholeheartedly disagree in the action
taken by the Governor, and although I did not
try the Wein case I wish to assure you that I
have the right to advise the Governor at any
time when I disagree with any of his actions,
especially in an action such as the Wein case,
and I care not whether the Governor appreciates
my remarks or not. In fact I would be surprised
and amazed if he did approve of my remarks
in the Wein case in view of the action which
he took.

From the comments I have heard from law-abiding citizens of this State relative to the Wein matter, I assure you the Governor's action was very
distasteful to law-abiding citizens.

In conclusion, I feel I have done my duty as a
citizen and as a judge in the Glatman case and
I have complied with all pertinent and relevant
sections of the Penal Code whether it meets either with your or the Governor's approval.

I trust this letter is received in the cooperative
spirit in which it is written.

Secretary Poole fired back on August nineteenth,
advising Hewicker that "[N]o constructive purpose
would be served by conducting a running discussion
concerning the manner in which the Governor's Constitutional powers are exercised or engaging in any
controversy with you on the subject." It was Gover-

nor Brown's policy, Poole wrote, to conduct "a thorough investigation and review" of all capital cases, and "[I]t is solely for this purpose that inquiries were made in the Glatman case."

Smelling surrender, Judge Hewicker managed to have the last word, in a letter dated August twenty-fourth.

I, also, see no constructive purpose for a running discussion in our correspondence relative to the above-named defendant, but from your last letter I gleaned that Mr. Glatman had not actually filed an application with the Governor for a pardon or commutation of sentence. I was pretty certain in the first instance that he had not done so because he wishes to get it over with. Since he filed no such application I know there was no duty on my part to furnish the Governor or anyone else with any recommendation or statement under Section 4803 or the Penal Code or Section 4801 of the Penal Code.

I am pleased to learn that the Governor is trying to discharge his duties under Article VII of the Constitution of the State of California.

As Harvey had long been interested in television, now TV was interested in him. Harold Keen, of KFMB Channel 8 in San Diego, wrote to Warden Dickson on July thirtieth, requesting permission to film interviews with Glatman and inmate Raymond Cartier, also sentenced to death in San Diego's Superior Court. The interviews, if permitted, would be broadcast as part of Keen's regular *People in the News* program. Both inmates declined the request, and

Dickson advised Keene that "This is pretty much the feeling of all the men on Condemned Row: they do not care to be put on exhibition."

On Tuesday, August eighteenth, with one month left to live, Harvey penned a letter to the district attorney's office in San Diego County.

To whom it may concern;

I have been informed that you want notification from me concerning the disposition of the camera which was used as evidence at my trial.

This is to notify you that the Rolleicord camera which is fully paid for and which legally belonged to me at the time of my arrest and which was taken from my car and later used at my trial now belongs to Norman Berman of 2901 Monaco St., Denver, Colo.

I have given the above mentioned camera and its carrying case along with any other photographic accessories (specifically a light meter) that were taken from my car on the night of my arrest.

I therefore expect that the above mentioned items will be turned over to Mr. Berman at the earliest possible date in any convenient manner.

/s/ Harvey Glatman

Ten days later, Doctors Schmidt, Kenny, and A. L. Larson logged their third psychiatric evaluation of Glatman. It reported that

This inmate on Condemned Row first refused to come to the examining room on Condemned

Row after leaving a cluster of inmates with whom he was talking, waving a denial at the doctors and returning to the group who seemed to take this as quite a joke. After the Committee discussed his case at some length between themselves, for about fifteen minutes, he agreed to talk to the doctors, after having talked privately to Dr. Larson for a short period.

He entered the room smiling and guardedly started talking about the weather and what a nice day it was, stating that he would have to be careful not to get into any arguments, or to answer any direct questions we had, because we were all pretty capable people and he was afraid that by answering any direct statements, he would indirectly expose his attitudes and feelings, which he preferred not to do. He again declined to comment on the crime for which he has been convicted and sentenced to execution; but he did talk at some length about his attitude towards other people, other inmates on Condemned Row, towards the officers there, lawyers, medical men and psychiatrists. He went into considerable detail in discussing legal and medical insanity and his feelings that many psychiatrists who work for the State, county and institutions are hypocritical, untruthful and are not fair either to the patients they examine or to themselves, because they really are political or "prison political psychiatrists who have no personal interest in an individual and have no interest in medical truth and science." He feels that such political psychiatrists make politically convenient diagnoses, sending all mentally disturbed and mentally ill inmates of Condemned Row to execution.

He showed he had a good stream of mental activity and speech which is fair quality and good quantity, and he was in a rather agitated mood, showing some anxiety and tension. His mental trend showed considerable resentment and hostility, even though at times this was very superficially controlled. He discussed the adjustment of other inmates on Condemned Row and further amplified his feelings of hopelessness about his impending execution. He showed that he has no hope and wants no hopes raised. He reminds us that he has requested to be executed, and he thinks that he, himself, is mentally ill; but not legally insane. He shows good memory and orientation of time, place and person, and shows no delusions or hallucinations.

We are all agreed that he has a Passive-Aggressive Personality with Neurotic elements and Overcompensatory Psychosexual Aggression and that he is not legally insane, and knows the crime of which he has been convicted and for which he has been sentenced to execution.

On Friday, September fourth, Associate Warden Nelson wrote to Judge Hewicker from San Quentin, updating him on Harvey's case. The letter read:

Friday, September 18, 1959, at ten o'clock a.m., is the date set for the execution of Harvey Murray Glatman, A-50239, condemned inmate of this institution.

I am sending you this notice for your informa-

tion. In the event of any change in the scheduled
date, this notification will be void.

/s/ L.S. Nelson
Associate Warden in Charge

Harvey had two weeks left to live, and death could
not come soon enough to suit him. On that point, at
least, his prosecutors and the loved ones of his victims heartily agreed.

19

The Green Room

CALIFORNIANS, BY AND LARGE, HAVE ALWAYS FAVORED capital punishment. There are dissenters, of course, some of them highly vocal, but when given a choice, the resounding majority always votes for death. So it was in the early days of statehood, and so it remains today, despite a brief interim in the 1970s when death penalty statutes were dismissed across the board by a United States Supreme Court ruling, and the states were told to start from scratch.

Hanging was the normal mode of execution in 1851, when capital punishment was first established under the California Criminal Practices Act. Twenty-one years later, it was still the means of choice under the new California Penal Code. County sheriffs handled executions on their own until the state took over, in 1893, removing all condemned prisoners to San Quentin. It was merely a change of scene, however, and the gallows remained busy until 1938, when construction began on the new gas chamber.

It was a notion spawned on the European killing fields of World War I and refined through studies of wartime deaths conducted in the 1920s by Major D. A. Turner of the U.S. Army Medical Corps. Theoretically, at least, Major Turner was concerned with antidotes, but his study included the gassing of cats. Although toxic gas would be banned from military use by the Geneva Convention of 1929, it seemed just the ticket for disposal of condemned inmates at home.

Nevada pioneered the technique at Carson City, on February 8, 1924, with a Chinese killer named Gee Jon. It took him six minutes to die, but the assembled witnesses agreed his death seemed "peaceable" and "painless."

No one had a chance to ask Gee Jon.

Eight other states followed Nevada's example over the next fifteen years, typically citing the adoption of lethal gas as an effort to make executions more humane. Warden James Holohan ordered the changeover at San Quentin, although he would retire before his innovation went to work. A supporter of capital punishment, Holohan still regarded hanging as a form of torture, and he rejected the electric chair on identical grounds. Lethal gas, he decreed, was the best way to go: "One breath, and you're unconscious."

San Quentin's gas chamber—dubbed the "green room" for the warden's choice of paint and described by one observer as "an ugly green wart"—was easily the most famous (or infamous) in America, thanks to such high-profile inmates as "Red-Light Bandit" Caryl Chessman and Barbara Graham (portrayed by Susan Hayward in a posthumous film titled *I Want to Live*). Another case that sparked debate was that of Burton Abbott, executed in March 1957, four months before Judy Dull's murder at the far end of the state. Governor Goodwin Knight telephoned San Quentin with a last-minute reprieve for Abbott, but his call came too late: the green room was already filling with gas, and there could be no turning back.

Construction began on San Quentin's gas chamber in March 1938, with the early test runs conducted on pigs—regarded, physiologically speaking, as the animals most similar to man. Reporters had a field day with those trials, unable to resist jokes about "smoked ham" and convicts unable to "save their bacon," but the gas chamber worked.

How well it worked, though, was another question. Prison authorities continued to tout the green room as a quick and painless means of execution, but eyewitness accounts told a rather different story. San Quentin's first execution of humans was a doubleheader, in December 1938. Inmate Robert Lee Cannon fought the gas for twelve minutes, while Albert Kessell lasted fifteen. A proper hanging, by contrast, is virtually instantaneous, with death resulting from a broken neck.

Still, hanging had the feel of lynch mobs, raucous mining towns with unpaved, muddy streets—the kind of history that modern California meant to leave behind. Lethal gas was the wave of the future, challenging electrocution as the mode of death *du jour*.

Like every other act of government, executions proceed according to "The Book." At "Q," on the last day of his life, a condemned inmate is removed from death row and lodged in a special holding cell that measures four-feet, six-inches wide by ten-feet, six-inches deep. Thirteen vertical steel bars comprise the fourth wall, welded and bolted through six horizontal slats of steel. Each "overnight" cell contains a mattress and commode. Outside, two guards are stationed to observe the inmate day and night to ensure that he does not cheat the state by means of suicide.

But, even so, Oscar Brust, a letter carrier condemned for killing his wife and stepson, managed to cut his own throat with a sliver of glass. He was dead half an hour before sentries noticed anything amiss. Twenty-four-year-old Robert Pierce had tried the same stunt a year earlier, but grandiosity got the better of him, and he slashed himself in front of the prison chaplain, who swiftly summoned help. It took four guards to subdue him, but they couldn't stop the bleeding, so they rushed Pierce to the green room, desperate to gas him before he bled to death. As they strapped him into the chair, blood spurting from his throat, he cried out, "God, you son of a bitch, don't let me go like this!"

But go, he did, in something close to record time.

In the normal course of events, a condemned inmate receives his last meal of choice, within limits: no steak knives, no bones he might choke on. Visits from the warden and the prison chaplain follow that repast, allowing the inmate to make his peace with God, if he is so inclined. With fifteen minutes left to live, the inmate dons a new white shirt and blue jeans, neither having pockets because deadly gas may linger there and endanger the handlers of his corpse. A physician examines the inmate to confirm that he is lucid, in compliance with state law. (One convict, gassed in 1954, was so delusional that emergency electroshock therapy was ordered on the spot; after taking his jolt, he was rushed to the chamber before it wore off.)

The green room lies a few yards distant from the last-night cells, an airtight octagonal chamber with an oval door, like that of a diving bell, and five thick windows. Inside, securely bolted to the floor, are two chairs with perforated seats. A special vacuum pump ensures that any accidental leak will draw air *in* from the outside instead of venting gas into the antechamber where the witnesses line up against a metal rail.

Signs order them to "Keep Outside Railing at All Times."

The green room, when in use, is heated to a temperature of 80° Fahrenheit to prevent gas from condensing on the windows, walls, and floor. Beneath one chair—or both, in the event of double executions—sits a bowl. Above each bowl, suspended from hooks at the end of long rods, dangle bags of cheesecloth or similar gauzelike material, each containing one pound of sodium cyanide crystals or pellets. Next door, in the mixing room, executioners prepare two one-gallon containers filled with a mixture of hydrochloric acid and distilled water. That done, they stand ready for the "guest of honor" to arrive.

The condemned man is barefoot, protected from unwelcome chills by a thin strip of faded carpet. Inside the chamber, he is buckled to a chair with leather straps around his ankles, arms, chest, and waist. The long tube of a stethoscope extends through the wall of the chamber, its diaphragm taped to the inmate's chest, while a physician listens at the other end, outside. The inmate has been told that it is best if he counts to ten and then breathes deeply when he smells something like rotten eggs.

After the guards clear out and lock the chamber's door, the executioner feeds his solution of acid and water through a tube and into the bowl beneath the inmate's chair. That done, he waits until the warden signals for him to proceed. When the signal is given, he pulls a red-painted lever which rotates one of the long metal rods, thus lowering the cheesecloth bag of pellets into the diluted acid. Their chemical reaction produces pale fumes of hydrocyanic-acid gas, which proceeds to fill the chamber, rising from the floor like fog.

Some inmates hold their breath, but it is hopeless. The assembled witnesses will wait all day, if necessary, to report a job well-done. The length of time required to kill with lethal gas is never constant, varying from case to case, dependent on the inmate's health and other factors. Some lose consciousness almost immediately; others cling to life for minutes, gasping, grimacing, and thrashing in the grip of their restraints. Inmate Leandress Riley freed both hands before the pellets dropped, undid his chest strap, and was working on the one around his waist before the gas kicked in. Still fighting for his life, he covered his face with both hands as the fumes rose around him. Two hours later, when the gas cleared, guards found him sitting with his neck arched, eyes wide open, staring at the green room's ceiling "as if looking for help from above."

Once the attending physician confirms death, the chamber is vented to expel gas, a fan sucking fumes through a chimney. Normally, the clearance takes fifteen or twenty minutes, but the gas remains lethal for an hour, so ammonia is sprayed in the chamber to neutralize any remnants. The guards return, wearing gas masks, and remove the inmate's corpse. His clothes are burned, and the body is scrubbed with ammonia or chlorine bleach before it is released to handlers from a funeral home. In the event a body goes unclaimed by relatives or friends, it will be cremated at state expense.

Ashes to ashes.

The soul, if it exists, is someone else's problem.

Beginning on September fifth, two weeks before his scheduled execution, Harvey was the object of a special scrutiny. Each shift of death-row guards submitted a daily "pre-execution report," including comments on the inmate's conduct, attitude, sleep patterns, and the ways in which he passed his waking hours. His attitude and conduct ranged from "fair" to "good"; he slept soundly, for the most part, and spent the rest of his time watching television, reading, playing cards or dominoes—the usual.

On September fourteenth, Cecil Poole spoke with Willard Whittinghill and reported back to Governor Brown that Glatman's attorney had no plans for a last-minute clemency plea. Whittinghill did register an objection to Dr. Lengyel's "fifteen minute interview" with Glatman, voicing a belief that "the Criminal Procedure should be changed so as to permit a lawyer to enter a plea of not guilty by reason of insanity even though over the objection of his client."

On Tuesday, the fifteenth, Doctors Schmidt, Gross, and Kopac filed yet another neuropsychiatric evaluation of Glatman. It read:

The subject entered the interview room in a quite cooperative but slightly more tense fashion; but he replied to all queries without hesitation even though he chose not to discuss certain subjects such as his offenses or what might have been done at an earlier date to avoid his committing these offenses. He did state that as far as he was concerned, he had no legal action pending in his case and preferred execution rather than commutation to a life sentence. He is aware that his execution date has been set for September 18, 1959, and is in accord with this procedure.

Mental examination at this time reveals an adequate stream of mental activity and speech pattern of good quality and quantity which demonstrated to a moderate degree, his somewhat increased tension over his approaching execution date. Thought processes appear to be relevant and coherent and integrated well within normal limits at this time. Affect is appropriate to the matter under discussion and his mood appears to be moderately depressed with a superficial hyper-active, smiling facade. He is oriented in all three spheres—temporal, spatial and personal, and no abnormal thought content such as delusions or hallucinations can be elicited at this time.

We are agreed that his personality patterning is consistent with a Passive-Aggressive Personality with Schizoid, Obsessive-Compulsive Neurotic and Overcompensatory Psychosexual Aggressive Elements; but that he is not legally insane and is aware of the crime for which he has been sentenced to execution.

That same morning, in Kenner, Colorado, Ophelia Glatman penned a note to Associate Warden W. D. Achuff authorizing the state "to dispose of the remains of my son Harvey Glatman in accordance with the procedures in such cases." Harvey had requested cremation, and so it was ordered. No further mention was made of donating his eyes.

The following day, Cecil Poole submitted a five-page report on Glatman's case to Governor Brown. After presenting bare-bones details of Harvey's early life and brutal crimes, Poole concluded that "[H]ere again the failure of criminal procedures in this country to afford adequate protection to the public is manifest." Poole noted the warnings contained in Harvey's psychiatric evaluations, dating back to Elmira Reformatory in New York, and Ophelia's spoken wish that Harvey might die rather than becoming "involved in notorious crime."

Yet Glatman [Poole wrote], uncured and unchanged was released on parole and allowed to go free. It is obvious now that the public was thereby exposed to a cruel danger. The mother's dreadful premonition has come true.

"There must be something better than this," Poole went on, "that we can devise for our State." And yet, he acknowledged, it was too late for Harvey, reminding Governor Brown that "Glatman may not be commuted without approval of a majority of the Justices of the [California] Supreme Court."

In response to Poole's report, Governor Brown asked Dr. Bernard Diamond, a psychiatrist from San Francisco, to visit Harvey on death row. Dr. Diamond arrived at the prison around three o'clock on Thursday, the seventeenth, spending an hour and a quarter with Glatman in his cell. No record of the interview remains, but Dr. Diamond stopped by the warden's office on his way out, to call Cecil Poole in Sacramento. As a result of that call, Governor Brown issued a press release declaring that he would not interfere with Harvey's execution.

By the time Dr. Diamond signed out of the prison at five o'clock, Glatman had already been moved to an "overnight" cell. Lieutenant F. V. Bartlett, Sergeant J. L. Moore, and Officer J. T. Snead were his escorts, delivering Harvey to his last earthly home at 4:42 P.M.

He had less than eighteen hours to live.

From the moment of his transfer, Harvey was under a microscope, his every move observed and noted. His first order of business was writing a note to Warden Dickson. It read:

I have a subscription to "Time" magazine and since I will expire before the subscription I would like to transfer said subscription in order that the magazine will continue to be available on the "row" until it stops coming.

I would like you to authorize the magazine to be delivered to [Caryl] Chessman #66565 who after reading it can circulate it around the "row."

Thank you
Harvey Glatman A50239

Next, Harvey wrote out the preferred menu for his last supper, facetiously heading it "Gas Chamber Special." He requested a shrimp cocktail, a rare T-bone steak with French fries, and a banana split, all to be washed down with a "bottle of beer (any major brand)." When the meal arrived at 6:00 P.M., the beer had been vetoed, replaced by asparagus and a salad. Harvey made up the difference that night, downing another banana split and a Coke at 11:45.

Between meals, it was recorded that he "smoked a lot" but seemed to be in "good spirits." The prison would later announce that Harvey "rejected spiritual counsel," but the D.W. (death watch) Log for that night records that Chaplain Dingberg spent two hours with Glatman, from 7:35 to 9:35 P.M.; Chaplain Eshelman arrived five minutes later and remained until eleven o'clock. Sleep was elusive, but Glatman finally dozed off around 5:45 A.M., only to wake again at ten minutes past six.

His last day on earth.

Harvey's breakfast arrived at 7:30: eggs, bacon, and potatoes; buttered toast with jelly; orange juice and coffee. Dr. Gross stopped in for a quick checkup at 8:15 A.M., with Chaplains Dingberg and Eshelman close on his heels. Eshelman left after forty minutes, but Father Dingberg would remain until the bitter end.

Down the hall, officers were getting ready for the

send-off. First, they checked the telephone in the death chamber, confirming it was functional, just in case Governor Brown had an unexpected change of heart. The fourteen scheduled witnesses, all male, assembled well ahead of time. Their number included physicians Gross and Kopac from the prison staff, Willard Whittinghill, and Pierce Brooks for L.A.P.D. The other witnesses included four from San Quentin, two from San Francisco, two from nearby Irvington, one from Sacramento, and one from Los Angeles. No relatives of the condemned or his victims were present.

Some states conduct their executions in the dead of night, as if it were a chore best done while decent people are asleep, like taking out the trash. In California, though, the job is done by daylight, but you couldn't swear to it inside the minifortress of death row. In Harvey's case, the execution was scheduled for 10:00 A.M., with Lieutenant Bartlett in charge. Executioners W. W. Metzler and M. W. Pickett went to work at ten on the dot, mixing acid and water beneath one of the gas chamber's chairs.

It is tempting to speculate on Harvey's thoughts as he shuffled from the death cell to the green room, surrounded by uniformed guards. Condemned inmates are handcuffed and shackled as they walk that "last mile" to prevent any last-minute outburst of violence. There is nowhere to run on death row, no hope of escape, but each man reacts differently at the hour of his death. Some kick and scream, fighting all the way, while others go limp and have to be carried.

Sedatives are available upon request, a small nod to mercy at the finish line, but we will never know if Harvey was sedated on his short walk to the chamber. We can only guess what he was thinking, feeling, as the leather straps were buckled tight around his arms and legs, across his chest, around his waist.

Bondage had been a favorite kinky game of his since childhood. Was there any thrill remaining in it now?

Three decades earlier, serial killer Peter Kurten, the "Dusseldorf Vampire," had been guillotined for his crimes in Germany. On the eve of his death, Kurten confided to a prison psychiatrist that he was looking forward to decapitation as the greatest rush of his life. If only he could hear the fresh blood spurting from his own severed neck before he slipped into oblivion. . . .

Since adolescence, Harvey had achieved release by strangling himself to the point of semiconsciousness. Was there a final tremor of excitement, now, as he anticipated suffocating with an audience? Was he afraid as he sat waiting for the smell of bitter almonds? Or was he, in fact, relieved that it would soon be done?

No one can say.

Doctors Gross and Kopac recorded Harvey's final moments in detail, a dry and clinical recital. He "walks in calmly" at thirty seconds past the hour and is quickly buckled into the chair, reported "sitting upright, calm" at 10:01. The chamber's door is shut and locked some thirty seconds later, Harvey's pulse recorded at a rapid 160 beats per minute. The sodium cyanide pellets drop at 10:03 A.M., Harvey "gasping, head back" even before the gas unfurls around him. The fumes reach his face one minute later, and his pulse spikes to 200, respiration cut in half, as he "slumps forward, head back." By 10:04 and thirty seconds, Harvey's pulse has plummeted to sixty; he is "gasping, head on chest." For the next two minutes, he slouches with chin on chest, emitting an "occasional gasp." By 10:07, he is "drooling saliva." Three minutes later, the physicians record his last breath and last visible movement. His heart stops beating sixty seconds later, and Glatman is officially pronounced dead at 10:12 A.M.

It was done.

Associate Warden Louis Nelson reported Harvey's execution to Judge Hewicker, in San Diego.

The People of the State of California
vs
HARVEY MURRAY GLATMAN

To the Honorable Superior Court of the State of California, in and for the County of San Diego:

I, Louis S. Nelson, Acting Warden of the California State Prison at San Quentin, do hereby certify that the accompanying Warrant of Execution was received at this institution on July 13, 1959, and I do certify that the body of Harvey Murray Glatman was delivered to this prison by the Sheriff of San Diego County on December 18, 1958.

I further certify that in accordance with the provision of Section 3605 of the Penal Code, I invited two physicians of good standing, the Attorney General of the State of California, and twelve reputable citizens to be present and witness the execution, and a Minister of the Gospel and such friends of the defendant, not to exceed five, as designated by him, together with such peace officers as I deemed expedient.

I further certify that on the 18th day of September, One Thousand Nine Hundred and Fifty-Nine, at 10:12 A.M. the annexed Warrant was executed within the walls of the State Prison at San Quentin, California, as designated by the court in which judgment was rendered, administering

lethal gas to Harvey Murray Glatman until he
was dead.

The names of the two physicians and the twelve
reputable citizens are hereunto attached and made
a part of this return as witnesses of the execution,
and I further certify that no other persons than
those mentioned in Section 3605 of the Penal Code
of the State of California were present at the execution. Dated: September 18, 1959.

/s/ L.S. Nelson
Associate Warden in Charge

Ironically, while Harvey's execution was reported
that Friday in Denver, on page ten of the *Rocky
Mountain News*, he failed to make the cut in Los
Angeles. Soviet Premier Nikita Khrushchev was in
town on the eighteenth, anxious to visit a decadent
Hollywood movie studio, and Mayor Norris Poulson
met him at L.A. International Airport, whisking the
Russian entourage off to 20th Century-Fox for a com-
missary brunch with Frank Sinatra and Bob Hope.

Harvey was history in Tinseltown.

Besides, he had played to some lousy reviews.

Ophelia Glatman had wished her son dead, back
in 1946, but she missed his execution and displayed
no interest in claiming his corpse, which was transported to the Napa State Hospital for cremation at
12:45 P.M., on September eighteenth.

But she wanted his camera.

Harvey's letter of August eighteenth notwithstand-
ing, William Low reviewed Ophelia's affidavit, certified by a Denver notary public, and ordered the
camera—logged as People's Exhibit #28—released to
her on Wednesday, October 7, 1959. That same afternoon, various photographs of Harvey's victims were

released to the San Diego County D.A.'s office for destruction.

On Wednesday, November eighteenth, Low was back in court, requesting custody of People's Exhibits #10, 21, 23, and 30—various tape recordings of Harvey's confessions. The request was swiftly granted on the basis of Low's affidavit that he was "the owner and lawfully entitled to the possession of" said exhibits.

The only other piece of evidence worth anything to anyone was Ruth Mercado's wristwatch, and Ruth's mother sought to retrieve it with an affidavit sworn in Plattsburgh, on November thirteenth.

STATE OF NEW YORK
COUNTY OF CLINTON

FRANCISCA PATRICIA MERCADO, being duly sworn, deposes and says:

That she resides at 27 McKinley Avenue, City of Plattsburgh, Clinton County, New York, and is the mother of the late RUTH RITA MERCADO. That except for the brother of the decedent, Michael Mercado, age 16, who resides with the deponent, the deponent is the only living relative and heir of Ruth Rita Mercado, as further attested by an affidavit of heirship filed in the Superior Court of the State of California, County of Los Angeles in the Estate of Ruth Rita Mercado, No. 410380.

That the purpose of this affidavit is to request the Office of the San Diego County District Attorney to return People's Exhibit No. 24, a wrist watch, belonging to the decedent, and used as evidence in the prosecution of Harvey Murray Glatman, DA 35559.

/s/ Francisca Patricia Mercado

Seventeen days later, on December first, William Low obtained a court order releasing the watch to Ruth's mother. By that time, Harvey Glatman was long since forgotten in Los Angeles, except by those whose lives had intersected his and therein were irrevocably changed.

It was December twenty-eighth before Ophelia was heard from again, reaching out to Associate Warden Achuff with a curious question.

Dear Mr. Achoff [sic],

I have tried to write this letter for the past three months but I could not get myself to do it. I would like a favor from you. I was told by some people here that Harvey's execution did not take place at the scheduled time for some reason, but instead it was postponed till the following morning, and that the chaplain stayed with him that night in his cell. Not knowing which chaplain of the prison was with him at that time, I can not write to him direct.

I would very much like to know if Harvey during that interval revealed anything to the chaplain that was not known before and how he spent those tortures [sic] hours of waiting. I am going around in a trance trying to satisfy my mind whether he remained to the last the same as when I visited him in June and my sister saw him in August. When I was there last time he prevailed on me not to come at the last days. He wanted to lessen the grief and pain it would have inflicted on both of us. I am fighting very hard to keep up. It is only through the good people of Denver whom I know—and some that I don't know— that have helped me through so far. I hope you

will grant me this wish if possible and soon.
Thanking you in advance. [Emphasis added]

I remain yours,
/s/ Mrs. Ophelia Glatman

There is no record of an answer from the prison,
but Ophelia had nothing to fear. Harvey had taken
his secrets to the grave, leaving nothing but questions behind.

Betty Bohannon and Lynn Lykels would still pause
from time to time and think, "What if . . . ?" Suppose
the stranger known to them as Johnny Glenn had not
been drawn to Judy's picture? Which of them might
have wound up at Thousand Palms?

Bob Dull may never have been reconciled with
Judy; he could only brood about it now, while young
Suzanne grew up without her mother.

Likewise, Rick and Billy Bridgeford would be
forced to make their way alone, though Grandma
Jolliffe and Aunt Mary tried their best to make up
for the loss.

Lorraine Vigil would start from scratch—new job,
new flat—and she would do her best to leave the
notoriety behind. L.A. helped out in that regard,
well-versed in losing track of those who let the lime-
light slip away.

But Harvey died as he had lived, observed by
strangers who were hopelessly beyond his reach.
And in the end, he did not even have his favorite
piece of rope for company.

Epilogue: "It's Better This Way"

BACK IN 1947, AT ELMIRA, DR. RYANCALE HAD SPOKEN briefly of Harvey Glatman's desire to become a famous criminal. On balance, though, it would appear that the last thing Harvey ever truly craved was notoriety. He would have been content to rape and kill anonymously, had the choice been his, but luck or Fate had done him in. Once caught, the prospect of impending death was a relief. The gas chamber would spare his mother and himself a lifetime of embarrassment.

It is unlikely that the local blackout on his execution would have troubled Harvey, either. Death was personal, and most of those who shared his world had managed to ignore him for three decades. In his childhood, when they *weren't* ignoring him, they laughed at him and called him names. Years later, as an adult, Harvey knew they were still laughing, but they sneaked it then, behind his back.

All things considered, it would probably have been a treat for Harvey to be truly, finally forgotten . . . but it simply was not in the cards.

A short year after Harvey's death, distinguished
British film director Michael Powell (best known for
The Red Shoes) released his movie *Peeping Tom* about
a sadistic voyeur who photographs his victims while
stabbing them to death with a blade concealed in his
camera tripod. Critics and viewers were outraged at
the film's release, in 1960, but it was soon eclipsed
by Alfred Hitchcock's *Psycho* (loosely based on the
life of Ed Gein). Ironically, time yields perspective,
and *Peeping Tom* is today considered a classic piece
of psychocinema.

A few months later, in April 1961, Ruth Beck—an
editor for the Sterling Group, publisher of various
"detective" magazines—wrote to California's director of corrections, announcing plans for stories on
Glatman and Erma Mae Broadhurst, convicted of killing her husband in Los Angeles six years earlier.
Clearly, Ms. Beck had not done her homework because she wrote: "Although we are anxious to publish these stories, we would first like to know the
current status of the above criminals, since we would
not want the appearance of such a story to interfere
with efforts to rehabilitate them, if they have been
paroled, or if parole is imminent."

In Harvey's case, at least, they had nothing to fear.

Nearly six years after Harvey's execution, Ophelia
was still trying to cash in her son's life insurance
policy but meeting resistance from John Hancock
Company Mutual. On March 19, 1965, she addressed
another letter to Associate Warden Achuff, at San
Quentin.

Dear Sir:

   You will see from the enclosed form which is
a standard one, what the insurance co. requests

in order to release the money coming to me from Harvey's insurance policy. They want proof of death. None of these questions in the enclosed form are applicable to Harvey's case. The Dr. will surely know how to produce proof of Harvey's death that is all they must have. Hope you will give this your early attention.

Thanking you in advance.

Sincerely yours,
/s/ Mrs. Ophelia Glatman

Dr. P. J. McNamara wrote to John Hancock eleven days later, confirming Harvey's execution and remarking that the insurance company's claim form "was not entirely pertinent to this case." Apparently, the information was not satisfactory, since a letter of May twenty-fifth, written by Ophelia to a "Mr. O. Shriver" at San Quentin, enclosed yet another claim form from the Hancock company. "I hope," she wrote, "that the information you will reveal in regard to Harvey Glatman's death will be satisfactory to them." No further correspondence is on file, and no record remains as to whether the money was finally paid.

Glatman had been in the ground ten years when Jack Webb dusted off his case and made it the centerpiece of his latest made-for-television *Dragnet* movie. *Dragnet* had already been around for twenty years by then, starting as a summer replacement on NBC radio and later making the leap to the tube. From day one, it was a shameless L.A.P.D. propaganda vehicle, and if names were altered "to protect the innocent," facts took a beating, too, in the interest of promoting L.A.'s "thin blue line" between civilization and savagery.

Webb's 1969 production was a perfect case in point. Vic Perrin played the lethal shutterbug who claimed his victims from the ranks of lonely hearts clubs, and there were some chilling scenes of late-night photo sessions in the desert, but beyond that point, Webb's "truth" veered into fantasy. For starters, Webb's detectives—Jack himself as Sergeant Joe Friday and Harry Morgan as Detective Bill Gannon—were hot on the killer's trail with a full-blown homicide investigation, collecting leads around L.A. as they raced the clock to save his next victim. In truth, as we have seen, Glatman's crimes were investigated as missing persons cases, not homicides, and one of those was handled by the L.A. County sheriff's office.

It is while depicting Harvey's capture, though, that Webb outdoes himself. Instead of being disarmed by a gutsy victim and arrested almost accidentally by a California Highway Patrol officer, Webb's killer is surrounded by prowl cars on a barren hilltop with his latest victim locked inside a trailer hitched to his car. Cornered in a brutal downpour, the soggy strangler threatens to push the trailer—and his victim—off a cliff if the police do not retreat and let him go in peace. Joe Friday saves the day by crawling up the muddy slope behind his man and tackling him bare-handed. It is all in vain, though, as they check the trailer out and find the latest victim is already dead.

More than two decades later, in 1991, best-selling mystery author Mary Higgins Clark thought enough of Harvey's case to use it as the basis for her novel entitled *Loves Music, Loves to Dance*. The villain of the piece is Michael Nash, a.k.a. "Charles North," a New York psychiatrist with an upscale clientele, busily at work on a book about dating through personal ads. Nash/North is fairly knowledgeable on the subject, since he uses personals to lure his female victims, strangling them and dancing with their corpses, after which he leaves them with a dancing slipper on one foot. The product of a tragic childhood (his father was executed for killing Michael's mother), Nash is also responsible for killing his adoptive parents in a rigged boat explosion. He is also a foot fetishist, whose strangling of women began fifteen years before the story's opening: a female classmate, whom he loved in secret, spurned the dancing shoes he bought her as a birthday gift. His goal is to eliminate ten women, one for each toe in the game of "This Little Piggy."

FBI agent Robert Ressler, a pioneer in the field of criminal profiling, consulted with Clark on the novel and appears in the story, more or less, as rugged G-man "Vincent D'Ambrosio." Even with such expert guidance, though, Clark goes astray on the simple facts of Harvey Glatman's case. In an interview appended to the paperback edition, she credits Harvey with seven victims, going on to describe him as "the first serial killer to be recognized in criminology to use the technique of personal ads to lure his victims."

In point of fact, Harvey was not the first. He wasn't even close.

Indiana's Belle Gunness, a classic "black widow," advertised for prospective husbands on a national scale, around the turn of the century, killing at least twenty victims—some reports claim thirty-two and upward—at her farm near La Porte. A decade later, French "Bluebeard" Henri Landru played the lonely-hearts game with women, robbing and murdering at least ten before his arrest, in April 1919. Confident to the bitter end, Landru was convicted of multiple murder despite the fact that no bodies were ever found, and he went to the guillotine in February 1922. Back in the United States, in 1918, "American Bluebeard" Helmuth Schmidt killed himself in a

Michigan jail cell, following his arrest for the murder
of one Augusta Steinbach. As police pieced together
his history, it appeared that Schmidt had robbed and
murdered several other women through the years,
luring his victims with newspaper ads that sought
"a suitable lady to marry soon." Cannibal child-killer
Albert Fish met his last confirmed victim in 1928 after
answering a "Situation Wanted" ad in White Plains,
New York. The boy who placed the ad, young Edward Budd, was looking for a summer job and Fish
considered killing him, but settled on Budd's
younger sister instead. It took six years to solve the
case, but Fish was finally convicted of Grace Budd's
murder in 1935 and executed in Sing Sing's electric
chair on January 16, 1936. Three years before Fish
was arrested, serial killer Harry Powers went to the
gallows in West Virginia, convicted of murdering five
victims whom he seduced via "lonely hearts" newspaper ads. Suspected of ten times that many slayings,
Powers merely smiled and told his jailers, "You've
got me on five. What good would fifty more do?"

If Glatman had not been the first to do his hunting
through the want ads, neither would he be the last.
Another Harvey, surname Carignan, was sentenced
to hang in Alaska for murdering a woman back in
1949. A clumsy sheriff's procedural errors led to commutation of the death sentence in 1951, and Carignan
was paroled nine years later. He moved to Washington, checked in and out of prison there on various
felony convictions, and was on the street again by
May 1973, when young Kathy Miller answered a
newspaper ad for sales clerks at Harvey's filling station. A month later, her naked body was found in
the woods, wrapped in plastic, skull crushed with a
hammer. Carignan was questioned but remained at
large for over a year before he was finally arrested
for another beating death, this time in Minnesota.

Maps found in his possession were marked with 181 red-ink circles, some of them identifying points where women had been killed or brutally assaulted in the northern states and Canada. Convicted of two murders and two assaults in March 1975, Carignan was sentenced to 150 years in prison, but Minnesota statutes mandate his release no later than the year 2005.

Earl Daughtrey favored Dixie for his crimes, but he appreciated want ads, too. Born in Georgia, the same year Harvey Carignan was sentenced to hang in Alaska, Daughtrey first displayed his violent tendencies in high school with the botched strangulation of a female classmate. Other attempted murders followed, but Earl seemed to lead a charmed life. His victims either couldn't manage to identify him, or the state agreed to counseling in lieu of jail. His luck ran out in 1973 with convictions in Florida and Georgia, but he was released ten years later by a parole board that "honestly believed he had gotten his act together." Police and FBI agents have publicly described him as the probable killer of three women between 1985 and 1987, alleging he targeted victims who advertised items for sale in local newspapers, but no homicide charges have ever been filed. The husband of one victim, twice convicted of killing his wife and twice released on appeal, has filed a wrongful death suit against Daughtrey in that case, seeking $32.5 million in damages.

If Daughtrey's case remains clouded by doubt, there are no questions in the case of Robert Hansen, a baker and sportsman in Anchorage, Alaska, blamed for the death of seventeen women in the decade between 1973 and 1983. A big-game hunter who had tired of stalking four-legged game, Hansen alternated between killing prostitutes and women who answered his personal ads in a local singles' paper, seeking female companions to "join me in finding what's around the next bend, over the next hill." For Hansen's prey, the grim end was a one-way airplane trip to the Alaskan wilds, where they were stripped and raped, then given a running head start, before Hansen stalked and killed them with a rifle or his trusty bow and arrow. Arrested in June 1983, after a teenage captive escaped his clutches and summoned police, Hansen emulated Harvey Glatman by confessing his crimes and leading police on a tour of rural grave sites. In February 1984, Hansen pled guilty on four murder counts, receiving a sentence of life plus 461 years in prison.

If his use of the want ads to locate victims was less than original, Harvey *did* rank as one of the first serial killers known to keep photographs of his prey. He had been gone five years before British "Moors Murderers" Ian Brady and Myra Hindley emulated his technique, in 1964, compelling a ten-year-old girl to pose for pornographic snapshots then tape-recording her screams as she was tortured to death. The photographs and tape were used as evidence against them at their murder trial, in 1966, and helped put them away for life.

Los Angeles team killers Lawrence Bittaker and Roy Norris also kept a grim library of audiotapes and snapshots to commemorate their work. They met in prison and conceived a plan to collaborate, once they got out, in killing at least one girl from each "teen" age—thirteen through nineteen—for the sheer delight of it. For most of 1979, they prowled L.A. in Bittaker's van, dubbed "Murder Mack," abducting, raping, torturing, and killing at least five girls. At their arrest, a tape recording of one torture session was seized by police along with some 500 photographs of young women, many still unidentified. Roy Norris pled guilty on five counts of murder in March

1980, receiving a forty-five-year prison sentence in return for his testimony against Bittaker. Loony Lawrence, nicknamed "Pliers" for his favorite instrument of torture, was convicted on all counts and sentenced to death in March 1981. (The judge also imposed an "alternate" sentence of 199 years and four months in prison to take effect if Bittaker's death sentence was ever commuted.)

Oregon foot fetishist Jerome Brudos was another ghoulish shutterbug, though he preferred to photograph his victims after they were dead, dressed up in frilly underwear he kept around the house for special shoots. One snapshot, taken of a corpse suspended by the wrists, shows Brudos in the background, his reflection captured in a full-length mirror as he snapped the picture. Arrested in May 1969, he pled guilty on three murder counts a month later and remains in prison to this day, consoling himself with mail-order shoe catalogs.

Christopher Wilder cut a bloody swath across America in 1984, killing at least eight women and abducting two others who managed to survive. A sometime race driver, Australian born, who lately made his home in Florida, Wilder went on the road after he fell under suspicion for two Miami-area slayings. Despite a posting to the FBI's "Ten Most Wanted" list, he still haunted shopping malls and fashion shows, introducing himself to prospective victims as a professional photographer and arranging "shoots" that turned into nightmares of torture, rape, and murder for his chosen models. Spotted by police at a New Hampshire gas station, on April thirteenth, Wilder drew a pistol and grappled with the officer who sought to disarm him. Two shots were fired in the scuffle, gravely wounding the policeman and killing Wilder instantly.

California photographer Charles Rathbun is the latest to follow Glatman's example, convicted in the slaying of one pinup model and named as the prime suspect in a second murder. Twenty-seven-year-old Linda Sobek, a model and ex-NFL cheerleader, vanished on November 16, 1995, after telling her mother that she had an appointment to meet a photographer named "Chuck." Eight days later, photos of Sobek and a crumpled page from her appointment book were found in a roadside dumpster, in the Angeles National Forest, and tips soon led police to photographer Rathbun. He, in turn, led them to Sobek's grave, explaining that her death had been an "accident," occurring when he tried to demonstrate a driving technique for their photo shoot and clumsily struck her with the car. Evidence of sexual assault gave the lie to his statement, and Rathbun was convicted of murder in November 1996 and sentenced to life imprisonment without parole. No charges have been filed against him in the 1992 murder of twenty-year-old model Kimberly Pandelios, found buried not far from Sobek's final resting place in March 1993, but authorities call Rathbun the prime suspect—indeed, their *only* suspect—in that case.

Pros like Rathbun—and some amateurs like Harvey Glatman—maintain their own darkrooms, but the invention of Polaroid self-developing cameras and compact minicams has made life infinitely easier for killers with a taste for recording their achievements on film or videotape. Milwaukee's Jeffrey Dahmer liked to photograph his victims before they went into the acid bath, and Kansas City's Robert Berdella went a step farther, snapping shots while he tortured male captives with caustic injections and electric shocks. In northern California, homicidal soulmates Leonard Lake and Charles Ng kept a video library of rape-and-torture sessions, depicting the grim fate of victims slaughtered in their rural bunker, near Wilseyville. Farther to the north, in Oregon, Satanists John Jones and Jason Rose were convicted in 1989 of killing a nineteen-year-old woman "while deliberately effecting a human sacrifice." The chief evidence against them: a videotape of the slaying in progress.

It should not be supposed that Glatman's legacy is all one-sided, though, a thing of unrelenting evil. L.A. homicide detective Pierce Brooks came away from the case with a vision for investigating "unrelated" homicides and disappearances, a system that would somehow let police from coast to coast touch base with one another and compare notes on their worst, most puzzling cases. Over time, Brooks was convinced that a computer—or a *network* of computers—was the key to keeping track of murderers who drifted aimlessly around the country, here today and gone tomorrow, leaving death and shattered lives behind.

It would require some twenty-seven years for Brooks to see his dream come true, but he did not give up. In 1982, he testified before the U.S. Senate, pleading for appropriations to establish VICAP—the FBI's embryonic Violent Criminal Apprehension Program—which would solicit information on unsolved murders and other serious crimes around he country, collate the material, and look for patterns that suggested transient serial killers at large. With any luck, thought Brooks and his associates in the FBI's Behavioral Science Unit, such information could be used to "profile" unknown subjects—UNSUBs in bureauspeak—and interrupt their vicious killing sprees.

"Profiling" remains controversial today, hailed by some investigators as a boon to their profession, derided by others as useless "voodoo" or "wizardry," stealing time away from good old-fashioned detec-

tive work. The most spectacular case on record—
some say the *only* successful case—involved New
York's "Mad Bomber" in the early 1950s. Police had
no leads to their UNSUB, and forensic psychiatrist
Dr. James Brussel was given a crack at the case out
of sheer desperation. Brussel described the UNSUB
as a middle-aged man of foreign descent, unmarried,
and residing with a relative. At his arrest, Brussel
predicted, the bomber would be wearing a double-
breasted suit with the jacket buttoned. He further advised police on techniques for baiting the bomber,
dropping comments to the press that would provoke
a letter in response.

It all sounded foolish to certain old hands with the
N.Y.P.D., but the brass took Brussel's advice, and the
bomber responded to their taunts with an angry letter, blaming Consolidated Edison for his affliction
with tuberculosis. A review of Con Ed's personnel
files led detectives to one George Metesky, a middle-
aged immigrant who lived with his two maiden sisters, and he swiftly confessed to the bombings. On
the day of his arrest, he wore a double-breasted suit,
the jacket buttoned up.

Dr. Brussel was the man of the hour in 1955, but
sadly, no one has been able to replicate his success
in the forty-odd years since Metesky's arrest. Modern
profiles are frequently accurate, but their precision is
only apparent with a suspect in custody, and few (if
any) profilers since Brussel can legitimately claim
that their assessment of an UNSUB led to his or
her arrest.

On the flip side of profiling, we have cases where
the unknown subject's sketch is worse than useless.
The manhunt for L.A.'s "Skid Row Slasher" is a case
in point from the mid-1970s. A panel of psychologists
examined evidence from the Slasher's crimes, deciding that their UNSUB was a tall, emaciated white

man with shoulder-length stringy blond hair and latent homosexual tendencies, perhaps—but not positively—the victim of some unspecified congenital deformity. So confident were the assembled "mindhunters" that they had sketches prepared of their man, revealing a long-faced "hippie" type with drooping eyelids and a dour expression. Police could tempt him out of hiding, they suggested, with insults attacking his manhood and courage.

Ironically, one day after the sketches were published in Los Angeles, the *real* Skid Row Slasher dropped his I.D. near a crime scene and was picked up by police on charges unrelated to the murder spree. Sufficient evidence was found to indict, try, and convict him on multiple homicide charges. There was only one problem: defendant Vaughn Greenwood was husky, average height, short-haired, with no deformities . . . and he was *black*. In short, the profilers had missed on every count—except, perhaps, for his sexual taste, which remains in dispute to this day.

Problems aside, the time was ripe for VICAP in the 1980s, with a rash of grisly, headline-grabbing murders terrifying citizens from coast to coast. Congress voted funding for the project, and President Ronald Reagan announced creation of the FBI's National Center for the Analysis of Violent Crime (NCAVC) in June 1984. Eleven months later, Pierce Brooks was at Quantico to see the VICAP computers receive their first case from the sticks, after which he returned to his retirement home in Oregon.

What role did Harvey Glatman play in all of this? G-man Robert Ressler, in his memoir *Whoever Fights Monsters*, contends that Brooks conceived the germ of VICAP in the late 1950s after he was "put in charge of the investigation of two seemingly unrelated murders of young women." Brooks had been frustrated, Ressler informs us, since he believed one man "might be responsible for both murders, and possibly some others in the area," but with no method of widespread communication, Brooks was reduced to paging through old newspapers in the library. His goal: to determine "whether other murders had been committed that matched the MO of the killer he believed he was chasing." Finally, Ressler writes, "To make a long story short, this spadework eventually led to the conviction of Glatman, who when confronted with the evidence confessed to the murders." (Ressler also notes that Brooks was a witness to Harvey's execution "in 1957.")

But, wait. The dogged Sherlock Holmes scenario described by Ressler is not merely flawed; upon examination, point by point, it is revealed to be a work of total fiction.

First off, L.A.P.D. was not investigating *murders* in the Glatman case before Harvey's arrest. It had two missing persons cases, Bridgeford and Mercado, which Pierce Brooks—as a detective with the homicide division—would not have been assigned to investigate. The only one of Harvey's victims who had been recovered prior to his arrest was Judy Dull, and her remains were not identified until *after* Harvey's confession. In any case, Judy's disappearance was investigated by the county sheriff's department and did not involve Pierce Brooks.

A second problem with the Ressler story is that Brooks and his newspaper search for unsolved homicides, assuming it occurred, did not in any sense "lead to" Glatman's arrest and subsequent conviction. Harvey was caught red-handed with Lorraine Vigil, after she disarmed him, and even then, there is a chance he would have overpowered her, except for the chance arrival of a California Highway Patrol officer. No investigation led to his capture, and L.A.P.D. had no part in the arrest.

Finally, it is not true, as Ressler states, that Glatman confessed his crimes "when confronted with the evidence" collected by Brooks. In point of fact, the very opposite was true: Harvey confessed to homicide investigators and directed them to his toolbox, containing photos and other souvenirs of his crimes. Brooks could hardly have presented any evidence to Glatman, in the Santa Ana jail, because there *was* no evidence, no murder case at all, before Harvey confessed.

What, then, is the truth of Pierce Brooks and his VICAP vision? It is very possible that Glatman's case inspired Brooks to devise a new communications system *after* he reviewed the evidence, while Harvey's trial was pending, or while Glatman was awaiting execution at San Quentin. Over time, with the proliferation of computers in America, Brooks would revise and modify his plan, keeping pace with new technology, until the dream came true, almost three decades later.

On the other hand, it may have been a different string of murders altogether that produced the VICAP brainstorm. Authors Colin Wilson and Donald Seaman, in their book *The Serial Killers*, confirm that Brooks hatched his original idea while working on two "unusual" murders in 1958, but they draw no link to Glatman, whose case is detailed elsewhere in the book. Considering the state of random violence in Los Angeles, together with the fact that California has produced some ten percent of all known serial killers in the twentieth century, it is entirely possible that Brooks derived his notion from another, unrelated case.

We'll never know, since Brooks was tight-lipped on the subject, and he took the secret to his grave.

*   *   *

Pierce Brooks was not the only one involved in Glatman's case who would go on to bigger, better things. Assistant D.A. William Low was appointed as a Municipal Court judge in 1964 and moved up to Superior Court four years later. Don Keller, toasting his aide's promotion to the bench, was still unhappy with the loss. It was, he said, like "celebrating a broken leg or having your house burned down."

Bill Low had earned a reputation as one of California's best prosecutors, and he soon won kudos from his colleagues on the bench, as well. "He is as good a judge as he was a prosecutor," declared Judge Gilbert Harelson, "and he was an outstanding prosecutor." Judge Earl Maas added, "A friend of mine on the appellate court once said of Bill that he was deadly. That was because he was always a perfect gentleman, always polite, and he could really put the scare to you if he wanted to, and there was no way the appellate court could do anything about it."

Attorneys for both sides also held Low in the highest regard. District Attorney Edwin Miller once opined, "He's the most experienced, knowledgeable and respected judge in the area of criminal law here. He's fair, objective, and as cool a judge as we have on the bench." Alex Landon, Executive Director of the Defenders Program of San Diego, agreed: "I enjoyed trying a case before him, because he was always extremely fair and impartial. I've always been impressed by the fairness and concern he's shown my clients. I think he's always looking to make sure his sentences were punishment, but also meaningful."

On October 27, 1985, after twenty-one years on the bench—and twenty-seven years to the day after Harvey Glatman's arrest—Low's retirement was announced in San Diego. Announcing plans to travel with his wife, Low told reporters, "The courthouse has been my office for twenty-one years. I'll miss it."

But not for long, as it turned out. Low remained on call as a visiting judge and was still hearing cases in 1997, a full dozen years after his retirement. Opinions of his work, by all accounts, remain enthusiastic. As one San Diego P.D. detective said, "He was a helluva prosecutor, and he's a helluva judge."

As for Harvey Glatman, Low's one and only capital case, there are no regrets. Harvey was one of a kind, in Low's experience, a grim aberration, undeserving of mercy.

"I investigated the case myself," he recalled. "I talked to the witnesses and I tried to bring in the best case I could, feeling that if I tried the case to the best of my ability, I'll be satisfied."

Ultimately, there was little satisfaction to be gleaned from Harvey's case by anyone whose life he touched and tainted. Grief and misery were Glatman's legacy, along with nagging questions.

How did Harvey get to be the way he was?

Did something in his early childhood—the kind of abuse hinted at in his February 1959 psychiatric interview, perhaps—trigger the bondage fetish that would lead him first to choke himself, then others?

How did he attain his view of "normal marriage" as a relationship in which the husband wholly dominates his wife, both physically and mentally?

Can the rejection of one's peers in adolescence, mixed with unrequited lust, drive one to such extremes of violence? Or, was Harvey Glatman simply a "bad seed," somehow genetically ordained to rape and kill?

There are no answers to those questions.

Harvey took them with him to the green room and the brooding silence of the grave.

Notes

2. "A Healthy, Normal Child"

p. 14: Statistically, Jewish serial killers are scarcer than the proverbial hen's teeth. Of some 1,400 repeat killers in my personal files, only one other comes readily to mind: David ("Son of Sam") Berkowitz, who was, in fact, adopted by a childless Jewish couple, also in New York. It is, perhaps, significant that neither Berkowitz nor Glatman were *practicing* Jews. Throughout adulthood, to the end of his days in San Quentin, Harvey Glatman listed his religion as "none."

p. 15ff.: Historical background on Jewish immigration to America, and specifically to the Bronx, is drawn from several sources. They include Irving Howe's *World of Our Fathers* (New York: Simon and Schuster, 1976), Max Dimont's *Jews, God and History* (New York: Signet Books, 1962), and Leonard Dinnerstein's *Antisemitism in America* (New York: Oxford University Press, 1994).

p. 16: Dimont makes his peculiar claim on page

365 of *Jews, God and History*. It is clearly refuted by
Leonard Dinnerstein's *Antisemitism in America* and
Gustavus Myers's *History of Bigotry in the United
States* (New York: Capricorn Books, 1960).

pp. 23–24: Material on the 1920s Ku Klux Klan
comes from *Hooded Americanism*, by David Chalmers
(New York: Random House, 1965) and from my own
encyclopedia of the KKK (New York: Garland Publishing, 1991).

pp. 24–25: Henry Ford's anti-Semitic activities are
described by Dinnerstein and Meyers in their respec-
tive surveys of bigotry, including the quotations
used here.

p. 25: Curiously, the New York Municipal Archives
have no record of Albert's marriage to Ophelia, and
next to nothing is known about their early married
life. The circumstance of their meeting is here sur-
mised from the 1925 New York City Directory, listing
Albert's employment with Instructo Millinery Supply, and from the fact that Ophelia, as late as December 1958, still listed her occupation as "millinery."
Their operation of a stationery shop is noted from
interviews conducted by California probation officers, in preparation of Glatman's after-sentence report, dated December 23, 1958. A "social history" of
Glatman, filed by San Quentin corrections counselor
Frank Ornellas in February 1959, notes that "[u]nfor-
tunately, there is at best only a paucity of information
concerning subject's early family history[,] which is
complicated by subject's refusal to discuss his
background."

pp. 25–26: Ophelia Glatman alluded vaguely to
Harvey's first bondage experiments in an interview
with the *San Diego Union*, on November 13, 1958 and
described them more fully in the after-sentence report, dated December 23, 1958. The first suggestion
that his "experiment" may in fact have been deliber-

ate child abuse—never previously published—is found in a psychological report from San Quentin Prison, filed in February 1959. (See Chapter 18.) Glatman's description of his parents is taken from an undated summary report prepared at Colorado State Penitentiary. Statistics on the childhood activities of serial killers are drawn from my own *Serial Slaughter* (Port Townsend, WA: Loompanics Unlimited, 1992).

p. 27: Harvey's meager medical record from early childhood has been reconstructed from a medical history taken on January 14, 1947, shortly after his admission to Elmira Reformatory, in New York, and from the recollections of his mother, recorded in a social history prepared at San Quentin Prison, dated February 18, 1959.

pp. 28–29: Information on Depression-era Nazi groups is taken from Myers's *History of Bigotry in the United States* and Dinnerstein's *Antisemitism in America*, together with John Roy Carlson's *Under Cover* (New York: E. P. Dutton, 1942), and my own *Racial and Religious Violence in America* (New York: Garland Publishing, 1991).

p. 31: No record has survived to pinpoint the date when Glatman's parents left the Bronx for Colorado. Glatman's after-sentence report from San Diego, dated December 23, 1958, puts the move sometime in 1930 when Harvey would have been two years old. The "social history" of Glatman, prepared at San Quentin in February 1959, agrees that the family left New York in 1930, but then injects a hopeless contradiction by stating that Harvey made his first appearance in a Denver schoolroom in September 1938, when he was nearly eleven years old. (The same report claims that Harvey received "all his formal education" in Denver.) Glatman himself, in interviews from 1945 and 1958, described the move as taking place when he was ten or eleven years old, that is to say, sometime between December 1937 and December 1939. I have accepted Glatman's version of events in this case, since it corresponds with his enrollment at Denver's Sherman Elementary School, as a sixth-grader, in September 1938.

3. "Girl-Shy"

pp. 32–35: Background material on Depression-era Colorado, and Denver specifically, was drawn from two sources: *Colorado* by Carl Abbott, Stephen Leonard, and David McComb (Boulder: Colorado University Press, 1982); and *Denver* by Stephen Leonard and Thomas Noel (Niwat, CO: University Press of Colorado, 1990). Information on the 1920s Colorado Klan comes from Chalmers's *Hooded Americanism* and my own KKK encyclopedia.

p. 35: Albert Glatman's occupation as a Denver cabby is described in California court papers, prepared after Harvey's October 1958 arrest, but notations from Harvey's school records disagree. At Gove Junior High School, Albert's occupation is listed as "untying machines"; East Denver High, meanwhile, logged him as a "collector" for a Denver jewelry store, but the name of the shop is illegible, and no further information on the subject is available.

pp. 35–36: Glatman's memories of adolescence are compiled from an undated evaluation performed at Colorado State Prison and from the California probation department's after-sentence report, dated December 23, 1958. A telling paragraph from his social history, prepared at San Quentin in February 1959 and apparently based on remarks from Ophelia, notes that "There is little information about the family interpersonal relationships. There is some indication that the father was irresponsible and inadequate[,] while the mother was ineffectual. The

mother reports that subject hated his father and
sometimes hated her, much to her distress."

p. 36: Ophelia Glatman's description of the early
bondage incident comes from an interview published
in the *San Diego Union*, on November 13, 1958.

p. 36: Professor Beitenecker is quoted by William
Ecker, Steve Katchis, and William Donovan, in "The
pathology and medicolegal aspects of sexual activity." *The American Journal of Forensic Medicine and Pathology* 12(1):3–15.

p. 37: The drowning fantasy is quoted by John
Money in *Lovemaps, Clinical Concepts of Sexual Erotic
Health and Pathology, Paraphilia, and Gender Transposi-
tion in Childhood, Adolescence, and Maturity* (New
York: Irvington Publishers, 1986), p. 246.

pp. 37–38: The occasional link between autoerotic
asphyxia and transvestism is described by Ray
Blanchard and Stephen Hucker in "Age, transvestism, bondage, and concurrent paraphilic activities in
117 fatal cases of autoerotic asphyxia." *The British
Journal of Psychiatry* 159 (September 1991): 371–77.

p. 38: The anonymous physician's treatment of
Harvey was described by Ophelia Glatman in her
November 13, 1958, interview with the *San Diego
Union*.

pp. 38–40, 44: I owe my knowledge of Glatman's
school years to Kay Logan at East Denver High
School, who thoughtfully provided me with a copy
of his records. The documents include a handwritten
notation of transmission to the California state prison
at San Quentin on January 12, 1959. Glatman's social
history, prepared at San Quentin in February 1959,
states that he entered Gove Junior High on March 4,
1939; no explanation is offered for his brief tenure at
Byers. The same social history states that "in grade
9A his Otis I.Q. was 118," and while this may be
accurate, Glatman's surviving school records bear no

indication of it. Sketchy details of the bike accident in 1939 were obtained from Glatman's medical history, taken at Elmira Reformatory in January 1947, and from the social history completed at San Quentin twenty-two years later.

p. 39: There is a minor controversy regarding the date of Glatman's enrollment in high school. A letter dated January 27, 1959 from George Wagner, Jr., supervisor of Denver Public Schools Department of Pupil Personnel, informed San Quentin's chief psychiatrist, Dr. David Schmidt, that Harvey entered East Denver High on February 2, 1943. I have opted for the date used in this chapter, since it came directly from Glatman's permanent record. The date presented in Wagner's letter is apparently a simple typographical error. (Wagner also wrote that Harvey "enjoyed the band while at Smiley," a notation which remains unexplained to this day, since none of his schools bore that name.)

pp. 41–42: Glatman's early, undiscovered crimes are summarized in the undated Colorado prison report and in the California probation report dated December 23, 1958. His sudden change of attitude toward women is noted in a letter from Dr. J. P. Hilton in Denver to probation officer William Lavelle, dated December 4, 1958. In the absence of ancient police records, his May 1945 arrest is described from coverage in the *Denver Post*.

p. 41: Fetish burglary, conducted either for the simple thrill of breaking in or for the theft of certain sex objects, is not unusual. A short year after Glatman's first arrest, in 1946, another teenager, William Heirens, was arrested and charged with three murders in Chicago. Like Glatman, Heirens admitted obtaining a sexual thrill from invading women's homes, sometimes stealing their underwear. Two women who interrupted his forays were brutally killed; the third victim was a six-year-old girl, abducted from her bedroom in the dead of night and dismembered. Continued burglaries led police to arrest Heirens a short time later, and he confessed his crimes, attempting to blame an alter ego he called "George Murman" (short for "Murder Man"). Heirens was sentenced to life and remains in prison today, having changed his story in the meantime to assert that he was framed by corrupt Chicago police.

p. 44: The press missed Glatman's July 1945 foray into kidnapping, but minimal documentation survives. The Boulder P.D. arrest card and appended notations from the police blotter were generously supplied by Robert Gillice, director of public information for the Boulder Police Department.

pp. 45–46: Dr. Hilton's diagnosis is contained in two letters from November 28 and December 4, 1958, respectively addressed to probation officer William Lavelle and to Glatman's defense attorney, Willard Whittinghill.

p. 46: No court records of Glatman's first criminal trial have survived, and spokesmen for the Colorado Department of Corrections reportedly could find no record of his incarceration, even when I provided Glatman's inmate number. The dates and other material presented here are drawn from brief newspaper accounts and details of Glatman's rap sheet provided by the California Superior Court in San Diego.

pp. 47–48: The anonymous, undated evaluation of Glatman prepared at Colorado State Prison was supplied, along with other records, by the Superior Court clerk in San Diego, California.

p. 48: The unnamed psychiatrist's recommendation was described by Ophelia Glatman in her November 13, 1958, interview with the *San Diego Union*. Whoever the doctor was, he cannot have "treated" Harvey very long: paroled on July 27, 1946, Harvey pulled his first known robbery in New York City exactly three weeks later.

4. Better Off Dead

pp. 49–54: Police records from 1946 have not survived in Yonkers or Albany. Glatman's bungled Yonkers holdups and his brief career as the Albany "Phantom Bandit" are reconstructed from coverage in the *New York Times* and the *Albany Times-Union*, coupled with statements he made in California, following his last arrest.

p. 51: Ophelia Glatman's version of the Yonkers robbery is quoted from her interview with the *San Diego Union*, November 13, 1958.

p. 51: Florence Hayden's account of the August twenty-second incident is taken from the *Albany Times-Union* of August 26, 1946.

pp. 52–54: Details of the Goldstein-Berger incident and the official reaction, culminating in Glatman's arrest and plea bargain, are drawn from coverage in the *Albany Times-Union*.

pp. 54–55: No court record has survived of Glatman's case in Albany. The description of his plea bargain is drawn from brief coverage in the *Albany Times-Union*.

pp. 55–57: Historical background on Elmira Reformatory is drawn from *The Encyclopedia of American Prisons*, by Marilyn McShane and Frank Williams III (New York: Garland Publishing, 1996).

pp. 57–61: Glatman's New York prison records were destroyed, with many others, by a fire, sometime in 1984. The items that survive, and which are quoted here, were obtained from the California State Archives in 1997. They include two medical histories taken at Elmira Reformatory (dated October 25, 1946, and January 14, 1947), plus Dr. Ryancale's psychiatric report, No. 1167, dated January 3, 1947. (The verba-

tim transcripts of Harvey's interrogation under sodium amytal, sadly, have not survived.) Excerpts
from another, lost report are found in Glatman's California after-sentence report, dated December 23, 1958.

pp. 61–67: Background material on Sing Sing
Prison is taken from McShane and Williams, *The En-
cyclopedia of American Prisons*, and from Carl Sifakis's
Encyclopedia of American Crime (New York: Facts on
File, 1982).

pp. 63–66: Reverend Dwight is quoted by Carl Sifakis in *The Encyclopedia of American Crime*, p. 450;
Alexis de Tocqueville and Colonel Barr are quoted
in the same source, p. 451.

p. 66: The descriptions of torture at Sing Sing after
Warden Lynds are drawn from *New York Times* reports, published on November 13, 1869, and July 26,
1913, respectively.

pp. 67–70: Despite the 1984 blaze which destroyed
Sing Sing's records from the period of Glatman's incarceration, I was fortunate enough to find some
New York files preserved in the California State
Archives, where copies were sent prior to his 1959
execution. The surviving documents include a psychologist's report, dated September 8, 1948, and Harvey's Educational Accomplishment and General
Adjustment Record, filed on August 10, 1949. Other
details are included in copies of two letters: the first
dated December 30, 1958, from Sing Sing Warden
Wilfred Denno to authorities at San Quentin; the second dated April 2, 1959, from senior parole officer
Harold Canavan, also addressed to San Quentin authorities. Ophelia Glatman is quoted from her interview with the *San Diego Union*, November 13, 1958.
Colin Wilson is quoted from *The Killers Among Us*,
Book II: Sex, Madness & Mass Murder, coauthored with
Damon Wilson (New York: Warner Books, 1997), p.
285.

5. A Frightening Environment

p. 71: Detective William Rehm, of the Westchester County (N.Y.) Sheriff's Department, first suggested an explanation for the disposition of Glatman's Yonkers case in a March 1997 telephone interview. His theory was later confirmed via clippings from the *Yonkers Herald Statesman*, supplied by Barbara Petruska, at the Yonkers Public Library, and in correspondence from L. Stanley Clevenger, executive adminstrator of the New York parole board, addressed to Warden Fred Dickson at San Quentin on April 2, 1959. The latter item was obtained from California's State Archives in June 1997.

p. 72: Dr. Ebaugh, in a November 1958 letter to Glatman's defense attorney, claimed to have treated Harvey "in 1950," but this is clearly a mistake, since Glatman spent that whole year in Sing Sing.

pp. 72–78: Dr. Ebaugh's observations on Glatman are quoted from an undated report which he furnished to defense attorney Willard Whittinghill in November 1958. I obtained a copy, with other pertinent documents, from the San Diego Superior Court in January 1997.

p. 78: Dr. Ebaugh's 1958 comments are taken from his November twenty-sixth letter to Willard Whittinghill and from a California probation report dated December 23, 1958.

p. 78: Glatman's "home address" in Denver was listed on his San Diego booking sheet, in November 1958. By that time, he had lived in Los Angeles for twenty-two months (minus the brief retreat to Denver). His difficulty finding work is explained in an after-sentence report, dated December 23, 1958.

pp. 78–79: Glatman's undated suicide attempts are described in the California after-sentence report, dated December 23, 1958.

p. 79: Glatman's post–Sing Sing employment record is included on his San Diego booking sheet, supplied as part of the file I received from the San Diego Superior Court in January 1997. Glatman's parole date was provided by the New York State Parole and Pardons Board.

p. 80: Glatman's performance on parole is summarized on the second page of a letter dated April 2, 1959, written by New York senior parole officer Harold Canavan to administrators at San Quentin Prison.

6. Psycho Paths

pp. 82–83: Background material on L.A. in the 1950s is derived from John Weaver's *Los Angeles: The Enormous Village* (Santa Barbara: Capra Press, 1980).

p. 83: Mack Edwards claimed his first victim, eight-year-old Stella Nolan, in June 1953. Two more children, eleven-year-old Brenda Howell and thirteen-year-old Don Baker, were killed on the same day, in August 1956. If we believe the killer's subsequent confession, he then took a twelve-year break before murdering sixteen-year-old Gary Rochet, in November 1968, and another sixteen-year-old, Roger Madison, the following month. The last to die was thirteen-year-old Donald Todd, reported missing by his family in May 1969. Eleven months later, a guilt-ridden Edwards finally presented himself to police and led them to Stella Nolan's grave. His other victims could not be recovered, since it would have required massive freeway demolition, and Edwards was uncertain as to the precise location of their graves. Sentenced to die for his crimes, Edwards grew impatient at the sluggish pace of California executions and hanged himself in prison, on October 30, 1971.

p. 83: The uncertain reference to Glatman's study

of TV repair in Sing Sing is included in his California
after-sentence report, dated December 23, 1958. No
record of that study is available from Sing Sing, although records from that prison, preserved in the
California State Archives, confirm his study of *radio*
repair.

pp. 83–84: Highlights from the history of television
are taken from *The People's Almanac* by David Wal-
lechinsky and Irving Wallace (New York: Doubleday, 1975).

pp. 84–85: The summary of grim events from 1956
and 1957 is taken from a morbidly delightful tome,
The Pessimist's Guide to History, by Stuart and Doris
Flexner (New York: Avon, 1992).

pp. 85–87: Events from the realm of organized
crime in this period are derived from two excellent
books by Carl Sifakis: *The Encyclopedia of American
Crime* and *The Mafia Encyclopedia* (New York: Facts
on File, 1987).

pp. 87–88: Incidents of Southern hate crimes during
1956–57 are taken from my own *Racial and Religious
Violence in America* (New York: Garland Publishing,
1991).

pp. 88–89: The 1950s juvenile-crime scene is sur-
veyed more completely in my own *Waste Land* (New
York: Pocket Books, 1997), a study of the Charles
Starkweather case.

p. 90: The Chicago triple murder was solved, by
pure dumb luck, some thirty-nine years after the fact.
Federal agent Joe Delorto was investigating the 1977
disappearance of candy heiress Helen Brach, following leads into the world of corrupt horse racing,
when, in November 1991, an informant told Delorto
that he could identify the killer of Robert Peterson
and the Schuessler brothers. The suspect he fingered
was sixty-one-year-old Kenneth Hansen, a bisexual
with a reputed taste for young boys. Background in-

vestigation showed that Hansen had lived on Chicago's North Side at the time of the triple slaying and had worked at a stable close by where the bodies were found. Hansen had moved across town shortly after the murders, opening his own stable, and Delorto's informant had gone to work for him there, recalling conversations in which Hansen spoke of killing three boys in 1955. A second friend of Hansen's, located by police in July 1994, reported similar conversations; several other men described incidents wherein Hansen had picked up young boys and driven them back to the stable for sex. Police believe that the 1955 triple murder resulted from a similar transaction, Hansen flying into a homicidal rage when Peterson and the Schuesslers rejected his advances. Detectives further state that at least three other men had knowledge of the crime: eyewitnesses (perhaps active participants) included Hansen's late brother Curtis and an unnamed man who left the country soon after the slayings; Hansen's employer, mob-connected Silas Jayne, had learned of the slaughter committed at his stable, helping Hansen cover his tracks in lieu of facing any heat. (Convicted of ordering his own brother's murder in 1971, Jayne died in prison sixteen years later, taking many secrets to his grave.) The sole survivor of that gruesome afternoon, Ken Hansen was indicted on three counts of murder in August 1994. Thirteen months later, following an eight-day trial, jurors deliberated for one hour and forty minutes before returning guilty verdicts on all counts. On October twentieth, Hansen was sentenced to "not less than 200 years, nor more than 300 years" in prison.

p. 95: For a full treatment of Elizabeth Short's murder and related crimes in 1940s Los Angeles, see *Daddy Was the Black Dahlia Killer* by Janice Knowlton and Michael Newton (New York: Pocket Books, 1995).

pp. 95–98: Ed Gein was certified competent for trial eleven years after his arrest, in 1968, resulting in a verdict of not guilty by reason of insanity. He was returned to the Wisconsin state hospital, where he lived quietly until his death, in July 1984. The best account of Gein's bizarre life is found in Harold Schechter's *Deviant* (New York: Pocket Books, 1989). Another useful volume, written by the trial judge in Gein's case, is Robert Gollmar's *Edward Gein* (New York: Charles Hallberg, 1981). Paul Anthony Woods examines Gein as a social phenomenon, including his role as the inspiration for various horror films, in *Ed Gein—Psycho!* (New York: St. Martin's Press, 1995).

p. 99: Irma Hurst is quoted from the *Los Angeles Times*, October 31, 1958.

pp. 99–100: Nude "modeling" continues today as a form of adult entertainment in many parts of the country and abroad. Pictophilia is described in Brenda Love's *Encyclopedia of Unusual Sex Practices* (New York: Barricade Books, 1992).

pp. 100–01: Concerning Harvey's virginity, the social history prepared by counselor Frank Ornellas at San Quentin, in February 1959, notes that "Although subject refused to discuss his sexual development, the police reports show subject as admitting that his first heterosexual act was with the first victim he killed."

7. True Detective

p. 103: Glatman's alias is also spelled phonetically as "Glen," "Glynn," and "Glinn" in various published accounts. In fact, there is no evidence that he ever wrote the name down. I have used the spelling indicated in his statements to police and the subsequent trial transcript.

p. 103: Lynn Lykels's surname is spelled "Lykles" in several press reports. I have preferred the spelling found in Glatman's trial transcript, since no more official source is available.

p. 104: Contrary to the oft-repeated claims of various "authorities," Glatman did not select his first two victims from the want ads, nor was he the first serial killer to use the technique. See the epilogue for details.

pp. 106–15: Judy Dull's murder is described primarily from Glatman's statement to police in San Diego, recorded on November 5, 1958, and reproduced verbatim in his December 1958 trial transcript.

pp. 115–16: Jean Spangler's case is still officially unsolved. One L.A.P.D. homicide investigator suggested, in October 1949, that Spangler was "recovering from an illness she wishes kept secret"—i.e., an abortion—but the theory remains untested, since no trace of her was ever found.

pp. 117–19: The discovery of Judy Dull's remains is described in front-page articles from the Riverside County *Daily Enterprise* (December 30, 1957) and the Indio *News* (December 31). I am indebted to Timothy Summerlee, at the Indio Branch Library, for supplying those clips when the newspapers themselves were hopelessly beyond my reach. Captain Hoffman and Dr. Dexter are quoted from those press reports.

pp. 118–19: We should not judge Dr. Dexter too harshly for his errors in estimating Judy Dull's age and date of death. Precision in such matters, most particularly when no flesh remains, is largely a Hollywood fable, absorbed by the public from movies and television shows where "dramatic license" often springs light years beyond the bounds of modern pathology. The estimated time of death for fresh bodies is only that—an estimate—and detectives count themselves lucky if the time can be roughly pinned down to a twelve-hour spread. Complete decomposition, to the point where only bones remain, renders the guesswork doubly difficult, if not impossible. As for the estimate of Judy's age, Dr. Dexter may have been misled by his examination of her pelvis, which would clearly demonstrate that she had borne at least one child. That finding would, of course, lead him to err on the side of caution and probability for his era, placing his "best guess" well beyond the teenage years. At the same time, his public statements, which appear to say that "Jane Doe" had no dental fillings, are less easily explained and may have retarded efforts at identification.

8. A Perfect Gentleman

p. 120: A report from San Quentin corrections counselor Frank Ornellas, dated February 18, 1959, records Glatman's employment at Universal TV, then adds: "Following this, he stated that he worked at numerous other T.V. shops for various periods of time but declined to identify them. Part of the time he was unemployed and was receiving money from his mother. It appears that subject's employment since completion of his parole in 1956 has been rather sporadic, scattered and of a highly unsettled nature." The employers listed in the text are those identified on Glatman's rap sheet, following his arrest in Orange County.

p. 122: Glatman described his experience with the Patty Sullivan Lonely Hearts Club, long since defunct, in his various statements to police and California state probation officers. A summary, including reference to his first unsuccessful date, is included in the after-sentence report, dated December 23, 1958.

Colin and Damon Wilson elaborate slightly, while reporting Glatman's case in *The Killers Among Us, Book II: Sex, Madness & Mass Murder*.

pp. 123–24: Shirley Bridgeford's background is reconstructed here from sources including the *Los Angeles Times* and the *San Diego Union*, as well as two books by British author Colin Wilson: *The Serial Killers* (coauthored with Donald Seaman) and *The Killers Among Us, Book II: Sex, Madness & Mass Murder* (coauthored with Damon Wilson).

pp. 124–32: Shirley Bridgeford's murder is reconstructed primarily from Glatman's confession, recorded in San Diego on November 5, 1958, and reproduced verbatim in his trial transcript, obtained from the California State Archives in June 1997.

p. 132: Alice Jolliffe's report to the police and Sergeant Ostroff's reaction are described in *The Killers Among Us, Book II: Sex, Madness & Mass Murder*, by Colin and Damon Wilson. Conflicting descriptions of "George Williams" were also reported in the *Los Angeles Times*.

9. "One I Really Liked"

p. 134: The most telling criticism of the FBI's classification system comes from fictional madman Hannibal ("The Cannibal") Lecter in Tom Harris's novel *The Silence of the Lambs* (New York: St. Martin's Press, 1988). Lecter describes the organized-disorganized breakdown as the brainchild of "a real bottom-feeder," and while his sarcasm stings, he has a point. Indeed, the ink was barely dry on documents outlining the FBI system when analysts at Quantico announced a new "mixed" category for killers combining traits of both the "organized" and "disorganized" types.

p. 134: The actual statistic for unsolved serial murders, based on a review of 1,405 cases from my personal files, is eighteen percent, or slightly less than one in five. Of those cases, 1,290 have been recorded in this century, with the great majority since 1960. For reasons unknown—and endlessly debated—the United States, with roughly five percent of the world's population, has produced about 75 per cent of the planet's known serial killers in the twentieth century—and 84 per cent since 1980, when the most dramatic increase was recorded.

p. 135: Norris described the "phases" of serial murder in *Serial Killers: The Growing Menace* (New York: Doubleday, 1988), pp. 22–34.

p. 136: Wilson is quoted from *The Serial Killers*, co-authored with Donald Seaman, p. 154.

p. 136–38: One newspaper reports Mercado's middle name as "Ann," presumably borrowed from Judy Ann Dull or Shirley Ann Bridgeford in the process of listing victims. Mercado's background is described from information reported in the *Los Angeles Times*.

pp. 138–47: As with the first two murders, Ruth Mercado's slaying is reconstructed primarily from Harvey's confession, recorded in San Diego on November 5, 1958 and reproduced verbatim in the transcript of his trial.

p. 146: Author James Ellroy, treating Glatman's case in *My Dark Places* (New York: Alfred A. Knopf, 1996), reports that Ruth Mercado "strangled herself" while hog-tied and straining against her bonds, but that description of events contradicts Glatman's confession, as recorded in court documents and various newspapers of the day. In those statements, Glatman made it clear that he killed Mercado in the same way—and possibly using the same rope—as he had his two previous victims.

pp. 147–49: The abortive investigation of Ruth Mercado's disappearance is described by Colin and

Damon Wilson in *The Killers Among Us, Book II: Sex, Madness & Mass Murder*. I obtained a copy of the September twenty-second L.A.P.D. bulletin from Judge William Low (formerly assistant district attorney and Harvey Glatman's prosecutor), in San Diego.

10. "He Wasn't Very Clever"

p. 150: Glatman's employment at Bruce Radio is documented on his arrest report, from October 1958.

p. 151: No record has survived of Diane's last name. Prolific crime writer Jay Robert Nash, in his *Bloodletters and Badmen* (New York: M. Evans, 1973), *Encyclopedia of World Crime* (Chicago: Crime Books, Inc., 1990), and *Encyclopedia of 20th Century Murder* (New York: Paragon House, 1992), describes another one who got away as twenty-year-old French model Joanne Arena, but I have been unable to confirm the story from an independent source, and Nash's account of Glatman's case is so riddled with errors that we must question whether the incident ever occurred. All three books present erroneous dates for Glatman's birth and execution, while *Bloodletters* incorrectly states that Lorraine Vigil telephoned Glatman, in response to *his* newspaper advertisement for models. The *Encyclopedia of World Crime* (from which the *Encyclopedia of 20th Century Murder* was later condensed, without corrections) further complicates matters with a prefatory note, warning would-be plagiarists that the massive six-volume text has been deliberately "seeded" with errors to assist in future litigation! Regardless of the author's intent, this bizarre approach to scholarship renders the Nash encyclopedias essentially worthless for serious research.

p. 151: In *The Serial Killers*, authors Colin Wilson and Donald Seaman refer to Glatman's near-miss with an anonymous model "in September" 1958, but that account seems to be a garbled version of actual events. Indeed, Wilson corrected the error when he described Glatman's case at greater length in *The Killers Among Us, Book II: Sex, Madness & Mass Murder* (coauthored with Damon Wilson).

p. 152: Contemporary reports disagree on Lorraine Vigil's age. The *Los Angeles Times* described her as twenty-eight years old, on October 31, 1958, while the *Santa Ana Register* listed her as both twenty-seven *and* twenty-eight, on October thirty-first and November first, respectively. She was twenty-eight again in the *Register* account of November second and in *Facts on File* for the week of October twenty-seventh. In the absence of a birth certificate or other official document, I have adopted the majority consensus on her age. Nothing is known of Lorraine Vigil's background, and while contemporary reports are mum on the subject, her performance on the witness stand at Glatman's trial (see Chapter 17) makes it seem that she spoke broken English, almost in the manner of a European immigrant. The mystery, along with her use of the name "Lorrie Beck" in her first statement to police, remains unsolved. The unexplained nude photos of Vigil are described in a report filed by Orange County Sheriff's investigators Coley and Pittsenbarger, dated October 28, 1958. If they were ever found, no record of them has survived.

p. 152ff.: All quotes from Lorraine Vigil in this chapter are taken from an interview published in the *Los Angeles Times* on October 31, 1958.

pp. 152–53: Controversy continues over the exact timing of Diane's call. The nine o'clock estimate is drawn from Lorraine's statement to Detectives Coley and Pittsenbarger, given on the night of the attack. Two months later, at Glatman's trial, she testified that Diane telephoned "between 8:00 and 8:30 P.M." I have preferred the first account, as being fresher in her mind, and therefore probably more accurate.

pp. 154–64: The attack on Lorraine Vigil is described from various sources, including her own statements to authorities and the press, as well as Glatman's recorded confession of November 5, 1958, reproduced verbatim in his trial transcript.

p. 163: Vigil's report of passing cars is curious and uncorroborated, her reference to "millions" clearly an exaggeration fueled by panic. Without exception, every published account of the attack describes it taking place along a "dark and lonely" road, without witnesses. Contemporary press reports make no mention of other motorists at the scene, and no reports were phoned in about the incident by civilians—although such apathy would not be surprising in metropolitan California, then or today.

p. 163: One report, in the Santa Ana *Register* of October 31, 1958, disputes Lorraine's story of disarming Glatman in the struggle. Arresting officer Thomas Mulligan is paraphrased in the story as saying that Glatman "purposely gave the gun to her" after Mulligan arrived on the scene, "so the officer would not shoot him."

p. 163: In fact, simple mechanics may have saved Glatman's life. Authors Colin and Damon Wilson report that the pistol "misfired" when Lorraine tried to shoot him. Barring faulty ammunition—and we know the cartridges in Harvey's gun were fine—a loaded semiautomatic pistol only fails to fire if (a) the safety is on, or (b) the action is jammed. Again, we may assume that the safety was not engaged on Harvey's gun, since it had already fired once, and it is doubtful Glatman would have put the safety on while he was grappling with Lorraine. A jam is much more likely, normally occasioned when the weapon fails to eject a spent cartridge. This could easily have

happened in the present case, where Lorraine was
apparently clutching the gun as it fired. Her grip may
well have prevented the pistol's slide from moving
as it should have, thus leaving an empty round in
the chamber.

pp. 164–66: Officer Mulligan is quoted from his
C.H.P Report of Arrest and/or Investigation, File No.
40-2132-58, dated October 27, 1958. Additional comments are quoted from the Santa Ana *Register*, October 31, 1958.

pp. 166–67: Deputies Mann and Williams are
quoted from their Initial Felony Report, Case No. DR-
77009, dated October 28, 1958.

pp. 167–69: Detectives Coley and Pittsenbarger are
quoted from their report on Case No. DR-77009,
dated October 28, 1958. The spelling of Officer
Steelmon's name is presented here, as found in the
original report, although his name is spelled as
"Steelemon" in the transcript of Harvey's trial.

11. "Aren't Three Enough?"

pp. 171–73: Statements provided by Lorraine Vigil
and Harvey Glatman are quoted in the report of Orange County Sheriff's detectives Coley and Pittsenbarger, Case No. DR-77009, dated October 28, 1958.

p. 173: The role of Sergeant Rios in Glatman's case
is described in the Santa Ana *Register*, October 31,
1958. Lieutenant Jones's response to the APB is discussed by authors Colin and Damon Wilson, in *The
Killers Among Us, Book II: Sex, Madness & Mass
Murder*.

pp. 175–76: Judge William Low, formerly assistant
district attorney for San Diego County and Glatman's
prosecutor in 1958, described Ogle in a telephone interview as "one of the best" when he came to poly-
graphy. Be that as it may, Glatman's polygraph test

appears to have deviated greatly from standard procedure. In a normal "lie detector" test, the subject is interviewed thoroughly before he or she is ever attached to the machine. That preliminary interview covers any and all matters to be dealt with in the final test, including formulation of specific questions which the subject, while "wired," is expected to answer with a simple "yes" or "no." Surprises, like the trick with Ruth Mercado's photo, are deliberately avoided, and subjects are discouraged from speaking at length, since rambling anecdotes make errors in evaluation much more likely. Glatman's polygraph test, as described by observers, apparently broke all the rules.

p. 179: The Santa Ana *Register* (November 1, 1958) mistakenly dates the discovery of Geneva Ellroy's body from July fifteenth. The actual date is included on her autopsy report, which I obtained in 1993, while writing *Daddy Was the Black Dahlia Killer* with Janice Knowlton. Despite mystery author James Ellroy's self-described obsession with his mother's unsolved slaying, many of the details contained in his numerous media interviews are erroneous and directly contradict the autopsy report. For a more complete treatment of the case, see *Daddy*, pp. 277–9 and 360.

p. 180: Sergeant Rios is quoted from the *Los Angeles Times*, November 1, 1958.

pp. 180–81: Glatman's comments to the press, and his mother's reaction to the news of his arrest, are quoted from the Santa Ana *Register*, November 1, 1958.

12. "This Is the Place"

pp. 185–87: Glatman's death tour is described primarily from media reports in the *Los Angeles Times* and *Herald-Examiner*, the San Diego *Union*, and the Santa Ana *Register*. Reports in the *Union* and the *Times* disagree on whether Mercado's remains were separated from Bridgeford's by a distance of twenty-six or thirty-two miles, respectively.

p. 188: Once again, as far as we know, there were no reporters present to watch Glatman eat. The description of his table manners may have come from jailers, or it may be pure invention. Certainly, the papers of the day were not averse to dramatizing news reports with manufactured details. (For more detailed treatment of the L.A. media's reaction to a sensational crime, see *Daddy Was the Black Dahlia Killer*.) By that Friday morning in 1958, the *Times* had already weighed in with descriptions of "mousy, jug-eared Harvey M. Glatman," while the San Diego *Union* misprinted his middle name as "Morris." Both papers would consistently describe his victims as "three beautiful Los Angeles women," presumably making the murders that much more atrocious.

pp. 189–91: The reactions of Betty Carver Bohannon and Alice Jolliffe are quoted from the *Los Angeles Times*, November 1, 1958. Lorraine Vigil's landlady is also quoted from the *Times*, October 31, 1958.

13. "I Was Sort of Shocked at Myself"

pp. 195–218: Glatman's San Diego interrogation for the murder of Judy Dull is reconstructed from the tape recording made on November 5, 1958 and later played in open court at his trial. The dialogue is found in Glatman's trial transcript, pp. 50–78. This transcript was originally described as "lost" by the clerk of San Diego's Superior Court, but a copy was retrieved from the California State Archives. No changes or deletions have been made, except to correct obvious typographical errors from the original court transcript. Ellipses (. . .) used in this and in the next three chapters, where presented in Harvey's confessions, indicate a pause or hesitation in speaking rather than deletion of text.

14. "She Didn't Seem to Be Breathing at All"

pp. 219–41: As in the previous chapter, Glatman's interrogation on Shirley Bridgeford's slaying has been reconstructed from court transcripts of the original recording. Again, as with the Dull interrogation, nothing has been changed, with the exception of obvious misspellings in the record, and occasional insertion of punctuation marks, to create coherent sentences from a record which is, otherwise, essentially one long, run-on sentence spanning transcript pages 103–32.

15. "She Was Getting to Look Pretty Sick"

pp. 242–66: Glatman's interrogation regarding Ruth Mercado was reconstructed here in the same manner, and from the same source, as dialogue in the preceding two chapters. Discussion of Mercado's death is found on pp. 139–69 of the original court transcript.

16. "What Do You Think I Am?"

pp. 267–77: Glatman's statement on the Vigil assault, as in the previous three chapters, is quoted from the transcript of his trial, pp. 198–211.

pp. 280–81: Whittinghill and Ophelia Glatman are quoted from the *San Diego Union*, November 13, 1958.

p. 283: A copy of Glatman's indictment was obtained from the San Diego Superior Court.

p. 283: It is a point of curiosity that on the same day as Glatman's guilty plea, another accused serial killer—fifteen-year-old Caril Ann Fugate—received a life sentence for her role in one of eleven murders committed by her psychopathic boyfriend, Charles Starkweather, in a bloody crime spree spanning Nebraska and Wyoming. For a full treatment of that case, see my book *Waste Land* (Pocket Books, 1998).

p. 294: William Lavelle's observations are quoted here from his after-sentence report on Glatman's case, dated December 23, 1958.

pp. 285–86: Ophelia's questionnaires, in partial form, were retrieved from the California State Archives. Curiously, the documents are both redundant and incomplete: the first two pages are entirely missing, while *three* pages are labeled "Page Three," including two duplicates from one form (filled out with different answers), and one from an entirely different questionnaire; likewise, there are three "Page Fours"—two from one form (again completed with different, sometimes contradictory answers), and one from another, unidentified questionnaire. While curious, the duplication is finally more telling than a single take on Ophelia's view might have been.

p. 290: There are at least two ways of analyzing Harvey's take on "normal" marriage. It is possible that he was simply ignorant of any give and take between the sexes, having grown up dateless and without a single girlfriend. On the other hand, there is a possibility—however slim—that Harvey may have witnessed something in his home, between his parents, which determined his outlook on marriage. Assuming such events occurred—and I am obviously guessing, here—they also may have had some impact on his taste for bondage, starting at an age far younger than the "average" S&M enthusiast.

pp. 290–91: Lavelle is quoted, once again, from his after-sentence report of December 23, 1958.

pp. 292–95: The Majors and McKinzie affidavits are

a part of Glatman's file, released by the clerk of San Diego's Superior Court in 1997.

pp. 295–97: Dr. Lengyel's brief psychiatric report on Glatman was sealed in Superior Court records, in San Diego, released to me in 1997 via court order from Judge William Low, Harvey's former prosecutor.

pp. 297–98: The supplemental indictment is also part of Harvey's file, obtained from San Diego Superior Court.

17. Death Wish

p. 301ff.: All dialogue from Glatman's trial is drawn verbatim, with occasional corrections in punctuation or spelling, from a transcript obtained from the California State Archives, in June 1997.

p. 310: The court recorder erroneously identified Lorraine's landlords as "Mr. and Mrs. Salas." The surname is corrected here.

p. 312: Glatman had made the same mistake with Lorraine Vigil that he had with Florence Hayden, twelve years earlier, putting down his weapon to free both hands for his rope.

p. 320: Judge Hewicker was incorrect, at least, in his prediction that California would "never have" life imprisonment without parole. Following a 1972 declaration that the state's death penalty statute was unconstitutional, new legislation was passed providing for execution only in certain cases that include particular "special circumstances." In such cases, juries may now recommend—and judges may impose—a sentence of death or life imprisonment without the possibility of parole.

pp. 323–25: Judge Hewicker's formal order of judgment was obtained as part of Glatman's file from the San Diego Superior Court.

pp. 327–28: *Time* magazine profiled Glatman's case and published his photos in its issue of December 29, 1958. William Low described his motives and decision on release of the photographs in a personal interview.

18. "No Paradise for Scoundrels"

pp. 329–31: Historical background on San Quentin Prison is drawn from *The Encyclopedia of American Prisons* by Marilyn McShane and Frank Williams III.

pp. 332–33: Captain O'Malley's memo of December 18, 1958, was retrieved as part of Glatman's file from the California State Archives, in June 1997. His property receipts and medical test results come from the same source. Unless otherwise noted below, all documents and correspondence quoted in this chapter were also found in the archives.

pp. 335–36: Lavelle's observations are quoted from his after-sentence report, dated December 23, 1958.

pp. 339–41: Glatman's letter to the state supreme court was found in his file at the California State Archives; Sullivan's reply was obtained from Harvey's Superior Court file, in San Diego.

pp. 344–49: Drummond's report was obtained from the California State Archives, in June 1997.

p. 348: Harvey initially used the "nymphomaniac" claim to describe Judy Dull. This application of the label to Shirley Bridgeford, apparently for the first time, may indicate simple confusion on Glatman's part, or perhaps a need to believe that each of his victims "enjoyed" being raped.

p. 348: It seems clear, from a comparison of the Drummond and Lavelle reports, that Glatman was referring to the incident from early childhood, which his mother had described as an apparent voluntary act. In light of his statement to Drummond, vague as it may be, the possibility—even probability—of deliberate abuse (whether inflicted as a punishment or otherwise) cannot be lightly dismissed.

p. 351: In one Massachusetts case, the felony convictions of two alleged child molesters were overturned, with a new trial ordered, because the young victims, while subject to full cross-examination in open court, were allowed to testify with their backs turned to the defense table. An appellate court ruled that the seating arrangement effectively deprived the defendants of their Sixth Amendment right to "face" their accusers in court. Jurisdiction clearly makes a difference in such findings, though, since a New York appellate court upheld the conviction of a molester whose nearsighted victim was permitted to testify without wearing her glasses. The decision held, in effect, that while the rapist had an absolute right to see his accuser, *she* was not required to see *him*.

pp. 352–53: Chief Justice Gibson is quoted from the California State Supreme Court's decision affirming Glatman's death sentence, issued on June 5, 1959, and formally filed on July seventh.

p. 361: Glatman's letter to the San Diego D.A.'s office was obtained as part of his file from the Superior Court in San Diego. Additional research has failed to trace Norman Berman or shed any light on his relationship to Glatman.

pp. 363–64: Nelson's letter to Judge Hewicker was obtained as part of Glatman's file from the San Diego Superior Court.

19. The Green Room

pp. 365–70: Historical information on lethal-gas executions and the San Quentin chamber in particular is taken from three sources: *The Encyclopedia of American Crime* by Carl Sifakis; *Murderers Die* by Denis

Bryan (New York: St. Martin's Press, 1986); and Geoffrey Abbott's *The Book of Execution* (London: Headline Book Publishing, 1994).

p. 369: One objection to lethal gas as a mode of execution was its reliance on the condemned inmate as a passive accomplice in his own destruction, forced, in effect, to "commit suicide" by the simple and unavoidable act of breathing.

p. 370: Serial killer David E. Mason was the last man to die in San Quentin's gas chamber, on August 24, 1993, condemned for the murders of four elderly victims in 1980 and the slaying of a fellow inmate in May 1982. Since Mason's departure, California legislators have included lethal injection as an optional form of execution for condemned inmates. Under guidelines established by the U.S. Supreme Court in the 1970s, California's abbreviated list of capital crimes today includes treason, train wrecking, perjury causing execution of an innocent defendant, homicide by an inmate serving life, and first-degree murder with "special circumstances"—a list of aggravating factors including torture, multiple murders, and murder for hire.

p. 370: The pre-execution reports on Glatman, spanning the two weeks from September fifth to the seventeenth, are preserved in the California State Archives. Cecil Poole's memo to Governor Brown was obtained from the same source.

pp. 371–72: Harvey's final psych evaluation was part of the voluminous file obtained from California's State Archives in June 1997.

p. 372: Correspondence relating to the proposed donation of Harvey's eyes include a note from Ophelia to Associate Warden Achuff, dated September 15, 1959, and a memo from Achuff written the following day.

pp. 372–73: Poole's final report to Governor Brown is preserved in the California State Archives.

p. 373: Dr. Diamond's visit to death row is documented in a memo from Associate Warden Nelson, dated September 17, 1959. Governor Brown's press release of the same date was obtained from California's State Archives.

pp. 373–74: Harvey's note to Warden Dickson and the menu for his last supper are preserved in the California State Archives. His alleged rejection of clergy was reported in the *Rocky Mountain News*, September 18, 1959.

pp. 374–75: Glatman's final hours are documented from various sources, including the San Quentin "D.W. [death watch] Log," various memoranda, the official Execution Record, his death certificate, and the signed receipt for his corpse. All were obtained from the California State Archives in June 1997.

pp. 377–78: Warden Nelson's affidavit was obtained as part of Glatman's file from the San Diego Superior Court.

p. 378: Khrushchev's Hollywood visit is described in various daily papers from September 1959 and in John Weaver's *Los Angeles: The Enormous Village*.

p. 379: Various affidavits and court orders concerning disposition of Harvey's camera and photographs, along with Ruth Mercado's wristwatch, were obtained from the clerk of the San Diego Superior Court.

pp. 380–81: Ophelia's letter to Associate Warden Achuff is preserved in the California State Archives. No response is included in that file.

Epilogue: "It's Better This Way"

p. 383: Ruth Beck's correspondence is preserved in the California State Archives.

pp. 383–89: Many life insurance policies refuse payment if the insured is killed during commission of a felony or executed on conviction of a crime. Ophelia's correspondence on this matter was obtained from the California State Archives in June 1997.

p. 386: Gunness's homicidal activities were exposed in April 1908 after fire razed her La Porte, Indiana, farmhouse. Remains of multiple victims were found on the property, and a headless female corpse was initially identified as Belle's, but most students of her case now believe she escaped, faking her own death by substitution of a "Jane Doe" alternate whose head was never found. The case is covered in detail by Janet Langlois in *Belle Gunness: The Lady Bluebeard* (Bloomington: Indiana University Press, 1985).

p. 386: Henri Landru's crimes are examined by Dennis Bardens in *The Ladykiller* (London: Peter Davies, 1972).

p. 387: An extreme sadomasochist (among other things), Albert Fish liked to torture himself by inserting needles into his groin. A prison X-ray, taken after his arrest for Grace Budd's murder, revealed at least twenty-nine needles in his lower body, some eroded with time to mere fragments. Those needles have been credited by several sources as causing the malfunction of Sing Sing's electric chair when Fish was executed on January 16, 1936. Whatever the cause, it is known that the chair "blew a fuse" on the first attempt to kill him, and the executioner was forced to throw the switch a second time. The best book on Fish is Harold Schechter's *Deranged* (New York: Simon & Schuster, 1983). Other worthwhile treatments are found in Michael Angelella's *Trail of Blood* (New York: New American Library, 1979), and

The Cannibal by Mel Heimer (New York: Lyle Stuart, 1971).

p. 387: Carignan, nicknamed "Harve the Hammer" after his weapon of choice, is amply treated by Ann Rule in *The Want-Ad Killer* (New York: Signet Books, 1983).

pp. 388–89: Robert Hansen's case is described in two books: *Fair Game* by Bernard DuClos (New York: St. Martin's Press, 1993), and *Butcher, Baker* by Walter Gilmour and Leland Hale (New York: Onyx Books, 1991).

p. 389: Many books have been written about the Moors Murders, with most available only in Britain. The best overall treatment of the case is probably Emlyn Williams's *Beyond Belief* (New York: Random House, 1967).

pp. 389–90: Curiously, Bittaker and Norris have yet to rate a book of their own, but the case is reported in various anthologies including my own *Hunting Humans* (Port Townsend, WA: Loompanics Unlimited, 1990) and Robert Markman's *Alone with the Devil* (New York: Doubleday, 1989).

p. 390: Ann Rule details the Brudos case in *Lust Killer* (New York: New American Library, 1983). A subsequent, shorter treatment of the case by Robert Ressler in *Whoever Fights Monsters* (New York: St. Martin's Press, 1992) includes serious flaws, including the false statement that Brudos was on parole from a prior murder conviction when he killed five women in Oregon. It appears that Ressler (or coauthor Tom Shachtman) confused Brudos with Harvey Carignan, discussed above.

p. 390: Bruce Gibney treats the case of Christopher Wilder in *The Beauty Queen Killer* (New York: Pinnacle Books, 1984).

pp. 390–91: Charles Rathbun's case is detailed by

Clifford Linedecker in *Death of a Model* (New York: St. Martin's Press, 1997).

pp. 391–92: At least five books were published about Jeffrey Dahmer before his case went to trial, and others have since been released. Most are hasty accounts, culled from news clippings or swiftly written by reporters covering the case, and none are truly complete. Robert Berdella's case is amply covered, complete with grisly photographs, in *Rites of Burial* by Tom Jackman and Troy Cole (New York: Pinnacle Books, 1992). Joseph Harrington and Robert Burger describe the case of Leonard Lake and Charles Ng in *Eye of Evil* (New York: St. Martin's Press, 1993). The case of homicidal Satanists Jones and Rose is reported in my own *Raising Hell* (New York: Avon, 1993).

pp. 397–98: William Low and his admirers are quoted from an article in the San Diego *Union-Tribune*, October 27, 1985. Additional information was obtained from Low when I interviewed him in January 1997.